General ~~Editor~~ *Stanley Wells*

Supervisory Editors: Paul Edmondson, Stanley Wells

T. J. B. SPENCER, sometime Director of the Shakespeare Institute of the University of Birmingham, was the founding editor of the New Penguin Shakespeare, for which he edited both *Romeo and Juliet* and *Hamlet*.

STANLEY WELLS is Emeritus Professor of the University of Birmingham and Chairman of the Shakespeare Birthplace Trust. He is general editor of the Oxford Shakespeare and his books include *Shakespeare: The Poet and His Plays*, *Shakespeare: For All Time*, *Looking for Sex in Shakespeare* and (with Paul Edmondson) *Shakespeare's Sonnets*.

JOHN PITCHER is a Fellow of St John's College, Oxford. His publications include an edition of Francis Bacon's *Essays* for Penguin Classics and *The Winter's Tale* for the Arden Shakespeare.

William Shakespeare

CYMBELINE

Edited by John Pitcher

PENGUIN BOOKS

PENGUIN BOOKS

Published by the Penguin Group
Penguin Books Ltd, 80 Strand, London WC2R 0RL, England
Penguin Group (USA) Inc., 375 Hudson Street, New York, New York 10014, USA
(a division of Pearson Penguin Canada Inc.)
Penguin Group (Canada), 10 Alcorn Avenue, Toronto, Ontario, Canada M4V 3B2
(a division of Pearson Penguin Canada Inc.)
Penguin Ireland, 25 St Stephen's Green, Dublin 2, Ireland (a division of Penguin Books Ltd)
Penguin Group (Australia), 250 Camberwell Road, Camberwell, Victoria 3124, Australia
(a division of Pearson Australia Group Pty Ltd)
Penguin Books India Pvt Ltd, 11 Community Centre, Panchsheel Park, New Delhi – 110 017, India
Penguin Group (NZ), cnr Airborne and Rosedale Roads, Albany, Auckland 1310, New Zealand
(a division of Pearson New Zealand Ltd)
Penguin Books (South Africa) (Pty) Ltd, 24 Sturdee Avenue, Rosebank 2196, South Africa

Penguin Books Ltd, Registered Offices: 80 Strand, London WC2R 0RL, England

www.penguin.com

First published in the Penguin Shakespeare series 2005
1

General Introduction and Chronology copyright © Stanley Wells, 2005
Introduction, The Play in Performance, Further Reading, Account of the Text and Commentary
copyright © John Pitcher, 2005

All rights reserved

The moral right of the editors has been asserted

Set in 11.5/12.5 PostScript Monotype Fournier
Typeset by Palimpsest Book Production Limited, Polmont, Stirlingshire
Printed in England by Clays Ltd, St Ives plc

Contents

General Introduction

Every play by Shakespeare is unique. This is part of his greatness. A restless and indefatigable experimenter, he moved with a rare amalgamation of artistic integrity and dedicated professionalism from one kind of drama to another. Never shackled by convention, he offered his actors the alternation between serious and comic modes from play to play, and often also within the plays themselves, that the repertory system within which he worked demanded, and which provided an invaluable stimulus to his imagination. Introductions to individual works in this series attempt to define their individuality. But there are common factors that underpin Shakespeare's career.

Nothing in his heredity offers clues to the origins of his genius. His upbringing in Stratford-upon-Avon, where he was born in 1564, was unexceptional. His mother, born Mary Arden, came from a prosperous farming family. Her father chose her as his executor over her eight sisters and his four stepchildren when she was only in her late teens, which suggests that she was of more than average practical ability. Her husband John, a glover, apparently unable to write, was nevertheless a capable businessman and loyal townsfellow, who seems to have fallen on relatively hard times in later life. He would have been brought up as a Catholic, and may have retained

Catholic sympathies, but his son subscribed publicly to Anglicanism throughout his life.

The most important formative influence on Shakespeare was his school. As the son of an alderman who became bailiff (or mayor) in 1568, he had the right to attend the town's grammar school. Here he would have received an education grounded in classical rhetoric and oratory, studying authors such as Ovid, Cicero and Quintilian, and would have been required to read, speak, write and even think in Latin from his early years. This classical education permeates Shakespeare's work from the beginning to the end of his career. It is apparent in the self-conscious classicism of plays of the early 1590s such as the tragedy of *Titus Andronicus*, *The Comedy of Errors*, and the narrative poems *Venus and Adonis* (1592–3) and *The Rape of Lucrece* (1593–4), and is still evident in his latest plays, informing the dream visions of *Pericles* and *Cymbeline* and the masque in *The Tempest*, written between 1607 and 1611. It inflects his literary style throughout his career. In his earliest writings the verse, based on the ten-syllabled, five-beat iambic pentameter, is highly patterned. Rhetorical devices deriving from classical literature, such as alliteration and antithesis, extended similes and elaborate wordplay, abound. Often, as in *Love's Labour's Lost* and *A Midsummer Night's Dream*, he uses rhyming patterns associated with lyric poetry, each line self-contained in sense, the prose as well as the verse employing elaborate figures of speech. Writing at a time of linguistic ferment, Shakespeare frequently imports Latinisms into English, coining words such as abstemious, addiction, incarnadine and adjunct. He was also heavily influenced by the eloquent translations of the Bible in both the Bishops' and the Geneva versions. As his experience grows, his verse and prose become more supple, the patterning less apparent, more ready to accommodate the rhythms of ordinary speech, more colloquial in diction, as in the speeches of the Nurse in *Romeo and Juliet*, the characterful prose of Falstaff and Hamlet's soliloquies. The effect is of increasing psychological realism, reaching its greatest heights in *Hamlet*, *Othello*, *King Lear*, *Macbeth* and *Antony and Cleopatra*. Gradually he discovered ways of adapting the regular beat of the pentameter to make it an infinitely flexible instrument for matching thought with feeling. Towards the end of his career, in plays such as *The Winter's Tale*, *Cymbeline* and *The Tempest*, he adopts a more highly mannered style, in keeping with the more overtly symbolical and emblematical mode in which he is writing.

So far as we know, Shakespeare lived in Stratford till after his marriage to Anne Hathaway, eight years his senior, in 1582. They had three children: a daughter, Susanna, born in 1583 within six months of their marriage, and twins, Hamnet and Judith, born in 1585. The next seven years of Shakespeare's life are virtually a blank. Theories that he may have been, for instance, a schoolmaster, or a lawyer, or a soldier, or a sailor, lack evidence to support them. The first reference to him in print, in Robert Greene's pamphlet *Greene's Groatsworth of Wit* of 1592, parodies a line from *Henry VI, Part III*, implying that Shakespeare was already an established playwright. It seems likely that at some unknown point after the birth of his twins he joined a theatre company and gained experience as both actor and writer in the provinces and London. The London theatres closed because of plague in 1593 and 1594; and during these years, perhaps recognizing the need for an alternative career, he wrote and published the narrative poems *Venus and Adonis* and *The Rape of Lucrece*. These are the only works we can be certain that Shakespeare himself was responsible for putting into print. Each bears the author's dedication to Henry Wriothesley, Earl of Southampton (1573–1624), the second in warmer terms than the first. Southampton, younger than Shakespeare by ten years, is the only person to whom he personally dedicated works. The Earl may have been a close friend, perhaps even the beautiful and adored young man whom Shakespeare celebrates in his *Sonnets*.

The resumption of playing after the plague years saw the founding of the Lord Chamberlain's Men, a company to which Shakespeare was to belong for the rest of his career, as actor, shareholder and playwright. No other dramatist of the period had so stable a relationship with a single company. Shakespeare knew the actors for whom he was writing and the conditions in which they performed. The permanent company was made up of around twelve to fourteen players, but one actor often played more than one role in a play and additional actors were hired as needed. Led by the tragedian Richard Burbage (1568–1619) and, initially, the comic actor Will Kemp (d. 1603), they rapidly achieved a high reputation, and when King James I succeeded Queen Elizabeth I in 1603 they were renamed as the King's Men. All the women's parts were played by boys; there is no evidence that any female role was ever played by a male actor over the age of about eighteen. Shakespeare had enough confidence in his boys to write for them long and demanding roles such as Rosalind (who, like other heroines of the romantic comedies, is disguised as a boy for much of the action) in *As You Like It*, Lady Macbeth and Cleopatra. But there are far more fathers than mothers, sons than daughters, in his plays, few if any of which require more than the company's normal complement of three or four boys.

The company played primarily in London's public playhouses – there were almost none that we know of in the rest of the country – initially in the Theatre, built in Shoreditch in 1576, and from 1599 in the Globe, on Bankside. These were wooden, more or less circular structures, open to the air, with a thrust stage surmounted by a canopy and jutting into the area where spectators who paid one penny stood, and surrounded by galleries where it was possible to be seated on payment of an additional penny. Though properties such as cauldrons, stocks, artificial trees or beds could indicate locality, there was no representational scenery. Sound effects such as flourishes of trumpets, music both martial and amorous, and accompaniments to songs were provided by the company's musicians. Actors entered through doors in the back wall of the stage. Above it was a balconied area that could represent the walls of a town (as in *King John*), or a castle (as in *Richard II*), and indeed a balcony (as in *Romeo and Juliet*). In 1609 the company also acquired the use of the Blackfriars, a smaller, indoor theatre to which admission was more expensive, and which permitted the use of more spectacular stage effects such as the descent of Jupiter on an eagle in *Cymbeline* and of goddesses in *The Tempest*. And they would frequently perform before the court in royal residences and, on their regular tours into the provinces, in non-theatrical spaces such as inns, guildhalls and the great halls of country houses.

Early in his career Shakespeare may have worked in collaboration, perhaps with Thomas Nashe (1567–c. 1601) in *Henry VI, Part I* and with George Peele (1556–96) in *Titus Andronicus*. And towards the end he collaborated with George Wilkins (*fl.* 1604–8) in *Pericles*, and with his younger colleagues Thomas Middleton (1580–1627), in *Timon of Athens*, and John Fletcher (1579–1625), in *Henry*

VIII, *The Two Noble Kinsmen* and the lost play *Cardenio*.
Shakespeare's output dwindled in his last years, and he
died in 1616 in Stratford, where he owned a fine house,
New Place, and much land. His only son had died at the
age of eleven, in 1596, and his last descendant died in
1670. New Place was destroyed in the eighteenth century
but the other Stratford houses associated with his life are
maintained and displayed to the public by the Shakespeare
Birthplace Trust.

One of the most remarkable features of Shakespeare's
plays is their intellectual and emotional scope. They span
a great range from the lightest of comedies, such as *The
Two Gentlemen of Verona* and *The Comedy of Errors*, to
the profoundest of tragedies, such as *King Lear* and
Macbeth. He maintained an output of around two plays
a year, ringing the changes between comic and serious.
All his comedies have serious elements: Shylock, in *The
Merchant of Venice*, almost reaches tragic dimensions, and
Measure for Measure is profoundly serious in its examin-
ation of moral problems. Equally, none of his tragedies
is without humour: Hamlet is as witty as any of his comic
heroes, *Macbeth* has its Porter, and *King Lear* its Fool.
His greatest comic character, Falstaff, inhabits the history
plays and *Henry V* ends with a marriage, while *Henry
VI, Part III*, *Richard II* and *Richard III* culminate in the
tragic deaths of their protagonists.

Although in performance Shakespeare's characters can
give the impression of a superabundant reality, he is not
a naturalistic dramatist. None of his plays is explicitly
set in his own time. The action of few of them (except
for the English histories) is set even partly in England
(exceptions are *The Merry Wives of Windsor* and the
Induction to *The Taming of the Shrew*). Italy is his
favoured location. Most of his principal story-lines derive

from printed writings; but the structuring and translation of these narratives into dramatic terms is Shakespeare's own, and he invents much additional material. Most of the plays contain elements of myth and legend, and many derive from ancient or more recent history or from romantic tales of ancient times and faraway places. All reflect his reading, often in close detail. Holinshed's *Chronicles* (1577, revised 1587), a great compendium of English, Scottish and Irish history, provided material for his English history plays. The *Lives of the Noble Grecians and Romans* by the Greek writer Plutarch, finely translated into English from the French by Sir Thomas North in 1579, provided much of the narrative material, and also a mass of verbal detail, for his plays about Roman history. Some plays are closely based on shorter individual works: *As You Like It*, for instance, on the novel *Rosalynde* (1590) by his near-contemporary Thomas Lodge (1558–1625), *The Winter's Tale* on *Pandosto* (1588) by his old rival Robert Greene (1558–92) and *Othello* on a story by the Italian Giraldi Cinthio (1504–73). And the language of his plays is permeated by the Bible, the Book of Common Prayer and the proverbial sayings of his day.

Shakespeare was popular with his contemporaries, but his commitment to the theatre and to the plays in performance is demonstrated by the fact that only about half of his plays appeared in print in his lifetime, in slim paperback volumes known as quartos, so called because they were made from printers' sheets folded twice to form four leaves (eight pages). None of them shows any sign that he was involved in their publication. For him, performance was the primary means of publication. The most frequently reprinted of his works were the non-dramatic poems – the erotic *Venus and Adonis* and the more moralistic *The Rape of Lucrece*. The *Sonnets*, which appeared in 1609, under his name but possibly without his consent, were less successful, perhaps because the vogue for sonnet sequences, which peaked in the 1590s, had passed by then. They were not reprinted until 1640, and then only in garbled form along with poems by other writers. Happily, in 1623, seven years after he died, his colleagues John Heminges (1556–1630) and Henry Condell (d. 1627) published his collected plays, including eighteen that had not previously appeared in print, in the first Folio, whose name derives from the fact that the printers' sheets were folded only once to produce two leaves (four pages). Some of the quarto editions are badly printed, and the fact that some plays exist in two, or even three, early versions creates problems for editors. These are discussed in the Account of the Text in each volume of this series.

Shakespeare's plays continued in the repertoire until the Puritans closed the theatres in 1642. When performances resumed after the Restoration of the monarchy in 1660 many of the plays were not to the taste of the times, especially because their mingling of genres and failure to meet the requirements of poetic justice offended against the dictates of neoclassicism. Some, such as *The Tempest* (changed by John Dryden and William Davenant in 1667 to suit contemporary taste), *King Lear* (to which Nahum Tate gave a happy ending in 1681) and *Richard III* (heavily adapted by Colley Cibber in 1700 as a vehicle for his own talents), were extensively rewritten; others fell into neglect. Slowly they regained their place in the repertoire, and they continued to be reprinted, but it was not until the great actor David Garrick (1717–79) organized a spectacular jubilee in Stratford in 1769 that Shakespeare began to be regarded as a transcendental genius. Garrick's idolatry prefigured the enthusiasm of critics such as Samuel Taylor Coleridge (1772–1834) and William Hazlitt (1778–1830). Gradually Shakespeare's reputation spread abroad, to Germany, America, France and to other European countries.

During the nineteenth century, though the plays were generally still performed in heavily adapted or abbreviated versions, a large body of scholarship and criticism began to amass. Partly as a result of a general swing in education away from the teaching of Greek and Roman texts and towards literature written in English, Shakespeare became the object of intensive study in schools and universities. In the theatre, important turning points were the work in England of two theatre directors, William Poel (1852–1934) and his disciple Harley Granville-Barker (1877–1946), who showed that the application of knowledge, some of it newly acquired, of early staging conditions to performance of the plays could render the original texts viable in terms of the modern theatre. During the twentieth century appreciation of Shakespeare's work, encouraged by the availability of audio, film and video versions of the plays, spread around the world to such an extent that he can now be claimed as a global author.

The influence of Shakespeare's works permeates the English language. Phrases from his plays and poems – 'a tower of strength', 'green-eyed jealousy', 'a foregone conclusion' – are on the lips of people who may never have read him. They have inspired composers of songs, orchestral music and operas; painters and sculptors; poets, novelists and film-makers. Allusions to him appear in pop songs, in advertisements and in television shows. Some of his characters – Romeo and Juliet, Falstaff, Shylock and Hamlet – have acquired mythic status. He is valued for his humanity, his psychological insight, his wit and humour, his lyricism, his mastery of language, his ability to excite, surprise, move and, in the widest sense of the word, entertain audiences. He is the greatest of poets, but he is essentially a dramatic poet. Though his plays have much to offer to readers, they exist fully only in performance. In these volumes we offer individual introductions, notes on language and on specific points of the text, suggestions for further reading and information about how each work has been edited. In addition we include accounts of the ways in which successive generations of interpreters and audiences have responded to challenges and rewards offered by the plays. The Penguin Shakespeare series aspires to remove obstacles to understanding and to make pleasurable the reading of the work of the man who has done more than most to make us understand what it is to be human.

Stanley Wells

The Chronology of Shakespeare's Works

A few of Shakespeare's writings can be fairly precisely dated. An allusion to the Earl of Essex in the chorus to Act V of *Henry V*, for instance, could only have been written in 1599. But for many of the plays we have only vague information, such as the date of publication, which may have occurred long after composition, the date of a performance, which may not have been the first, or a list in Francis Meres's book *Palladis Tamia*, published in 1598, which tells us only that the plays listed there must have been written by that year. The chronology of the early plays is particularly difficult to establish. Not everyone would agree that the first part of *Henry VI* was written after the third, for instance, or *Romeo and Juliet* before *A Midsummer Night's Dream*. The following table is based on the 'Canon and Chronology' section in *William Shakespeare: A Textual Companion*, by Stanley Wells and Gary Taylor, with John Jowett and William Montgomery (1987), where more detailed information and discussion may be found.

The Two Gentlemen of Verona	1590–91
The Taming of the Shrew	1590–91
Henry VI, Part II	1591
Henry VI, Part III	1591

Introduction

Cymbeline, one of Shakespeare's last plays, is an unusual and perplexing work of art. Some of the difficulty we experience with it is due to its form and structure. There are frequent changes of texture and mood, and the plot, while not all that complicated, certainly needs close attention from readers and audiences to appreciate its subtleties of contrast and convergence. But in *Cymbeline* Shakespeare also does something which, for centuries, has baffled, disappointed and outraged his critics, and even his admirers: he deliberately combines and mixes up things, making what should be (to some minds) distinct and separate look indivisible, or at least pretty much the same. The first person to get annoyed with Shakespeare about this was his contemporary and rival, the dramatist Ben Jonson. He plainly saw what Shakespeare was attempting in *Cymbeline* and in the other plays written around the same time, *The Winter's Tale* and *The Tempest*, and he found it deplorable. His own plays, Jonson claimed, were true to nature and to the nature of men. The ancients (classical philosophers, poets and critics) had discovered for all time what this nature was, and so any significant divergence from their understanding must be avoided, otherwise an artist would create something inauthentic or possibly even aberrant and horrible.

Shakespeare, according to Jonson, had ignored these fundamental rules, and his plays had suffered because of it. Worse still, he thought, audiences in the public theatres had been misled by Shakespeare and they had come to cherish rather than to shun what he was doing wrongly. They actually liked the comedies and tragedies Shakespeare wrote for them that showed protagonists during the course of months or even years (against the view urged by the ancients that the action of a play should be confined to a single day), and they tolerated palpable sillinesses such as an army being represented onstage by three actors carrying between them a drum, a flag and a couple of rusty swords.

By 1610 Shakespeare had written more than thirty plays, about half of them comedies of love and marriage, and the remainder histories and tragedies. At this point, when he began to draw on the plots and marvellous happenings in romance stories, his travestying of nature became worse still from Jonson's perspective. In 1614, about three years after the first performance of _Cymbeline_, Jonson blurted out that what bothered him most about Shakespeare's mistakes was that they blurred the lines of separation between high and low art and between upper- and lower-class people. In the Induction (or preface) to his play _Bartholomew Fair_ (first performed 1614) Jonson, speaking about himself as the author, in the third person, tells the audience that if 'there be never a servant-monster' nor 'a nest of antiques' in the Fair, 'who can help it?' The audience can be sure that it won't find freakishness in this play, since the author 'is loath to make nature afraid in his plays, like those that beget _Tales_, _Tempests_, and such like drolleries, to mix his head with other men's heels'. Shakespeare's monstrous creations, in other words, _The Winter's Tale_ and _The Tempest_, appal nature, because they turn everything upside down, including the social order. By 'drolleries' Jonson means farces and crude entertainment for the plebs, and the 'servant-monster' he refers to is Caliban, Prospero's deformed slave in _The Tempest_. Caliban is so grotesque that in one comic routine, when he is hidden under a tarpaulin, his head and heels are literally mistaken for each other. With a touch of true spite, Jonson implies that it is Shakespeare who is really the monster because he has misused his brains to please lower-class tastes (and in that sense he, unlike Jonson, has mixed 'his head with other men's heels'). _Cymbeline_ was apparently so much of a drollery that Jonson couldn't even be bothered to name it, but the 'nest of antiques' is probably a jibe at the scene in Act V when Jupiter hovers on his eagle over a group of ancient British ghosts (there is a pun in 'antiques' on 'antics', or low-grade actors whose grimaces and odd behaviour on stage made them look like gargoyles).

The hard things that writers say about each other don't always contribute much to our understanding of their work, and many times we can safely leave their professional and personal disputes to gather dust in libraries. With _Cymbeline_ and the other late plays, though, the situation is different. In recent years scholars have realized that Shakespeare didn't take Jonson's criticisms lying down, or treat them with lofty disdain. Indeed it appears that he relished tackling criticism head on, especially in the late plays, and that he didn't do this just to settle a score with one of his contemporaries. Aristotle, the most senior of ancient authorities, had declared that dramatists should avoid using a deus ex machina to resolve complications in the plot. What was Shakespeare's response in _Cymbeline_? To have Jupiter (his deus) winched down on a stage machine (a chair on a pulley) thundering that he, the god, was about to resolve everything that had gone wrong for the hero Posthumus. Another of the ancient authorities, the Roman poet Horace, when he wanted to show how little he thought of popular drama, wrote that on occasions, right in the middle of a play, irrespective of the story and just to please the crowd, a couple of boxers would be sent on stage, or maybe even a bear. Shakespeare's response in the middle of *The Winter's Tale* was, of course, to send on a bear, one who could resolve a complication in the plot by eating a character who mustn't be allowed to get home and reveal where he had abandoned a baby princess. It shouldn't really surprise us that Shakespeare might care just as much as Jonson and the classical critics about what drama ought and ought not to do, even if he chose to say what he thought, not in prologues and notebooks, as Jonson did, but through his plays themselves. The mixing up of things in *Cymbeline*, so that emotions and conduct are in flux and not always congruous, is his contribution, purposeful and serious, to the biggest aesthetic debate of his day: how the primary genres of tragedy and comedy could be reconciled within a single play, and connected through the phenomenon of wonder. Perhaps, as is argued later, the mimesis needed for this – a more expansive way of representing on stage how people feel and think – was what Shakespeare was seeking in *Cymbeline*.

The neoclassical line Jonson took on Shakespeare's plays – that human nature doesn't change, and dramatic art shouldn't change away from it – survived for a century or so among scholars and critics, even as Shakespeare came to be fêted as England's national poet. *Cymbeline* was left largely in peace by its early editors, but then in 1765 the old critical regime showed its teeth one final time when Samuel Johnson turned on the play, snarling that it was nothing but incoherent bits and pieces. 'To remark the folly of the fiction', he wrote, and

the absurdity of the conduct, the confusion of the names and manners of different times and the impossibility of the events in any system of life, were to waste criticism on unresisting imbecility, upon faults too evident for detection and too gross for aggravation. (Woudhuysen, *Johnson on Shakespeare*, p. 235)

Not many people have been as harsh about *Cymbeline* as this, although George Bernard Shaw said some very damaging things about it. Dr Johnson's remarks are unfair – anachronisms and mingling occur in Shakespeare plays he admired – but they are still valuable because they demand that we explain what is holding the play together, that we give an account of the 'system of life' in *Cymbeline* in which such impossible manners, conduct and events can make sense. To do this we need to look at the play from the angle of stories and storytelling, and to consider first how a playgoer in 1611 might have responded to the plot.

STORIES

Cymbeline was probably written in the middle or second half of 1610 (the reasons we can be so exact are set out on pp. 156–7). The earliest known performance of *Cymbeline* was the one seen by the astrologer Simon Forman the following spring, most likely at the Globe. Forman's synopsis of what he saw is much more detailed than the descriptions we get from other eyewitnesses of stage plays at this date. His account is not at all polished – he probably assembled it from notes he took while watching the performance – but the way he retells the stories is revealing. 'Remember,' he writes, 'the story of Cymbeline, King of England in Lucius' time,' and how Lucius, the Roman ambassador,

came from Octavius Caesar for tribute; and, being denied, after sent Lucius with a great army of soldiers who landed at Milford Haven, and after were vanquished by Cymbeline, and Lucius taken prisoner; and all by means of three outlaws of the which two of them were the sons of Cymbeline stolen from him when they were but two years old by an old man whom Cymbeline banished, and he kept them as his own sons twenty years with him in a cave. And how one of them slew Cloten that was the Queen's son going to Milford Haven to seek the love of Innogen the King's daughter, whom he banished also for loving his daughter. And how the Italian that came from her love conveyed himself into a chest, and said it was a chest of plate sent from her love and others to be presented to the King; and in the deepest of the night she being asleep, he opened the chest and came forth of it, and viewed her in her bed and the marks of her body, and took away her bracelet and after accused her of adultery to her love etc. And in the end how he came with the Romans into England and was taken prisoner and after revealed to Innogen, who had turned herself into man's apparel and fled to meet her love at Milford Haven, and chanced to fall on the cave in the woods where her two brothers were; and how by eating a sleeping dram they thought she had been dead, and laid her in the woods and the body of Cloten by her in her love's apparel that he left behind him; and how she was found by Lucius etc. (quoted from E. K. Chambers, *William Shakespeare*, 2 vols. (1930), vol. 2, pp. 338–9)

Forman recalls almost all of the play from seeing it just once, although he does make mistakes and he leaves out things. He calls Cymbeline King of England rather than King of Britain – a mistake Englishmen still make – and he does not mention important scenes and characters (notable omissions are Pisanio and the Queen). He also misremembers details (the 'chest of plate' left with Imogen is supposed to be a gift for the Emperor, not for Cymbeline), and when he recalls how Cloten went 'to seek the love of Innogen the King's daughter, whom he banished also for loving his daughter' he appears to confuse Cloten, who was planning to rape the Princess, with Posthumus, her husband.

The most significant aspect of Forman's account, though, is his rearrangement of the three stories that make up the plot. He identifies them all, but puts them in a different order. In the play the love story – known as the wager plot because of the bet on Imogen – is presented on stage first, with the abduction of the princes only mentioned, almost in passing, to intrigue us. The princes and Belarius, the old man who stole them from their nursery, don't actually appear until Act III, after the story of Rome demanding tribute from Britain has been introduced. Forman retells the play, not in the sequence of events on stage but in terms of social and political hierarchy. Rome comes first (Lucius is Rome's envoy, superior even to Cymbeline and his heirs), then the defeat of the Roman army by the Britons, and finally, via the killing of Cloten, there is the story of what happens to Imogen while Posthumus is away. Forman's chief interest is obviously in Imogen, but his ranking of the stories indicates which of them he thought was the most important (the war and recovery of the heirs above Imogen).

The three stories are retold in another way too, divided repeatedly into smaller parts, most times linked causally but not always. The separate parts, set out in clauses and

extended sentences joined together with 'and', don't
follow the division of acts and scenes in the play. The
rearrangement this time suggests that Forman thought of
Cymbeline as an astonishing string of impossibilities,
shocks and outrages. The great army of Roman soldiers
was, against the odds, vanquished,

and Lucius taken prisoner; and all by means of three outlaws
. . . and he kept them as his own sons twenty years with him
in a cave . . . And how one of them slew Cloten that was the
Queen's son . . .

Scandalous and unlikely events are replayed, frame by
frame, out of sequence: the invincible Romans are
defeated by lawbreakers, the kidnapped princes live in a
cave like wild men, the Queen's son is killed by an outlaw,
an Italian tricks his way into Imogen's bedroom,
Posthumus is captured fighting for Britain's enemies, and
the Princess ends up sleeping beside the Queen's dead
son who is dressed in Posthumus' clothes. The things
that audiences shouldn't be aroused by, according to
Jonson – unexpected, gruesome and bizarre scenes as
well as moments of prurience – are the ones that Forman
recalls with excitement (especially 'the Italian' looking at
the naked Princess 'in the deepest of the night'). Forman
tries to set out the stories in a respectable way, starting
with the figures of authority, Caesar, his ambassador and
the British King, but as he goes on his attention is drawn
more and more to the dark bedroom, and to the cave and
the woods, until at last he is looking at the macabre funeral
ceremony, where neither the mourners nor the mourned
are who they appear to be. Fathers, stepfathers and the
father of the Roman Empire are what Forman begins his
account with, but he ends it with their children, bruised

and ungrown, playing out a solemn game, pretending to be adults, on the hard Welsh hills.

Whether Forman saw any deeper into the story that connects fathers and children in *Cymbeline* we don't know. From a modern viewpoint, this is certainly a prime story in the play, one that underpins (and sets in motion) most of the others. It is the story, familiar in all Western literature (in plays, novels and fairy tales), of how children struggle to get free from their parents. The premise of the story is that there are, in real life, customary rites of passage that allow children to detach themselves from their parents without being too damaged in the process. In *Cymbeline* all these rites of passage are abruptly and disastrously interrupted. The mysterious snatching away of the baby boys, Britain's break with Rome, Imogen's sudden wedding and flight from her father, can all be interpreted as grotesque parodies of (or crises in) the normal social and psychological rites of childhood. Seen this way, a good deal of the suffering in *Cymbeline* is attributable to fathers and to father figures, whether it's the kidnapper and substitute-father Belarius, or the Roman Emperor denying Britain full nationhood, or Cymbeline himself, peevishly trying to block his daughter's marriage. This crucial story does not give us the key to everything in the play, but it is certain that fathers fail their children in *Cymbeline*, or get in the way, or simply become unimportant, as they do in most of Shakespeare's work.

The failure to complete a rite of childhood can hurt the father too. Old Cymbeline is so infatuated with his new wife, who is ruling (and probably drugging) him, that he has been persuaded to marry Imogen to Cloten, her horrid, stupid son. This is foolish but it is hinted that even before this the King has somehow lost his way. His sons disappeared twenty years earlier without trace but he survived the loss, unlike Sicilius (Posthumus' father), who simply gave up and died of a broken heart when he lost two of his boys. This parallel poses a question for us, as Shakespeare intended, about whether Cymbeline is still in one piece, emotionally and in his senses, or whether his hidden grief over the lost boys, half a lifetime of it, has left him easily manipulable, functioning only through being petted and flattered by the Queen and by playing the tyrant father with his daughter. Cymbeline's feebleness is in part generic – he is a character in the tradition of the *senex*, the old man in Roman comedies who was thwarted and duped by his relatives – but much of the reason he's silly is that there's something profoundly unfinished in his life.

With his sons, carried off by Belarius into Wales, the rites of maturation have barely begun. Academics and directors have not been very sympathetic to the princes, largely one feels because they are embarrassed by them. Their songs and speeches and ceremonies in Acts III and IV (greeting the morning sun, laying Fidele–Imogen alongside the headless Cloten, speaking the dirge over them) are intense and beautifully sculpted, but they can also seem unbearably arch and precious. The confusion the brothers themselves feel throughout these scenes – one moment veering towards daintiness, the next towards over-manliness – invariably unsettles audiences in the theatre, making them unsure about what their own feelings are, and how they ought to respond to the mix of savagery, desire and anguish shown to them in these young men. Modern critics have offered various explanations of how Shakespeare wanted the brothers to affect us: either as mannequins, or as figures of fun, or as babes in the wood gone native, *Wunderkinder* draped in bloodstained pelts who have regressed to what we (the soft

urban modern sort) always took royal males to be – mad
and sad and not much good for anything except heroics
on the battlefield. What is more likely, however, is that
in Guiderius and Arviragus we have one of Shakespeare's
innovations in *Cymbeline*, the portrayal of children who
have been left emotionally concussed and immobile in
grown-up bodies, left with their feelings trailing behind
as they matured physically. The brothers have remained
stolen children, just as they were twenty years earlier,
swaddled and vulnerable infants abducted from their
nursery. Ungrown boy-men, they are stuck in a childish
trauma, helpless and frustrated, as cruel as kites but as
gentle as summer breezes too.

It is Belarius who has kept them in this repressed state,
and he's used another story to do it. Again and again he
has told them that although their lives are hard and frugal,
and their bodies weary and burnt by the sun, they will
be safe and pure so long as they stay away from the court.
They are unimportant people (beetles rather than eagles)
but at least they have him, an honest though discarded
soldier, as their father. The story has just about kept them
under control until this moment, but their true natures
are irrepressible. The brothers live in a cave but not even
the weight of the hillside above can hold them down any
longer, as Belarius knows. They have seen nothing except
this meagre life, he says, yet

> their thoughts do hit
> The roofs of palaces, and nature prompts them
> In simple and low things to prince it much
> Beyond the trick of others. (III.3.83–6)

The coming of age of the princes, much delayed by
Belarius, coincides, we see, with their sister's, who at the

same time, unknown to them, and hundreds of miles away, is breaking with her father by marrying Posthumus. Like them, Imogen has been stuck in the nursery stage of life for too long, in her case reared with a playmate much beneath her in rank with whom she has fallen in love. The beginning of *Cymbeline* is in this respect like the end of a fairy tale at the point where a sleeping princess is woken by a kiss, and the whole court, slumbering for a hundred years or more, wakes up around her. The shock of Imogen's wedding makes this happen in the British court too, although not to Cymbeline himself (lulled by the Queen), who refuses to wake up and give his daughter to her rescuing prince.

Children must be allowed to grow up, but they mustn't mature too quickly, and they can't grow beyond what they are able to be. This is the other side of the maturation story Shakespeare is concerned with, and which he addresses through the contrasting situations of Posthumus and Cloten. From the outset Posthumus is a fantasy prince, a commoner whose marriage to Imogen functioned as a wish fulfilment for the men in Shakespeare's first audiences. He is *so* talented and virtuous that, as with suitors in fairy tales and romances, he is judged worthy to burst up through the ceiling of rank above him. It is said of him, in a phrase that by now should arouse our suspicions, that in his spring he 'became a harvest' (I.1.46). This is exactly what's wrong with him, and why he behaves so disgracefully. There has been no progress through the seasons for him, no ripening, just an immediate harvest from him before he was ready; Posthumus, in short, is utterly unprepared for adult life and marriage. As for Cloten, the stepson runt among Cymbeline's children, there is no hope of growth in him at all. He can't mature, he can't control his speech or bodily functions, he can't even add up.

Shakespeare makes sure that audiences don't become dewy-eyed about these lost and bewildered children. Puberty rites and the rituals that lead to marriage (bringing jealousy and fear as much as love) are not easy, and if adults won't help them, it will be left to children themselves to break out of the dream they're in. This is especially true of Imogen. She is about sixteen, the same age as the heroines in Shakespeare's other late plays, so perhaps we ought not to be surprised at her girlishness every time she thinks about her new husband. When Posthumus leaves the court, a banished man, she is not permitted to see him off as he sails away. Instead she has to be told how he stood on deck, waving a 'glove or hat or handkerchief' (I.3.11) and calling out his goodbyes to her for as long as possible. Oh, if she'd been there, she says, she would have broken her 'eye-strings, cracked them', just

> To look upon him, till the diminution
> Of space had pointed him sharp as my needle;
> Nay, followed him till he had melted from
> The smallness of a gnat to air; and then
> Have turned mine eye and wept. (17–22)

For these speeches Shakespeare turned to his favourite source, the Roman poet Ovid, drawing on a passage in the *Metamorphoses* (XI.463–72) in which a heroine watches her husband depart. At first, it is said, she could see him

standing on the curved stern, and returned his salute as he waved her good-bye. As the ship drew further away and her eyes could not distinguish his features, her gaze still followed the departing vessel as long as possible. Then, when even the ship was too far away to be clearly seen, she still watched the

sails billowing out from the masthead. Finally not even the
sails were visible, and she sought her empty couch where she
lay down with a heavy heart. (*Metamorphoses*, trans. Mary Innes
(1955), p. 258)

Knowing that Shakespeare is indebted to the *Metamorphoses* is interesting, but it's not as interesting as the
realization that the important borrowings from Ovid are
Imogen's. It is through the conduct of the fictional wife
in the *Metamorphoses* that she imagines how she feels as
Posthumus leaves her, that is, she sees him, in her mind's
eye, in the story she has read in Ovid's poem (which in
Act II, scene 2 she is shown reading for hours at a time).
This aspect of Imogen – her unformed sensibility learning
how to experience things – is communicated throughout
this early scene, from her thrill at the thought of
Posthumus kissing his handkerchief ('Senseless linen!' she
says envyingly, 'happier therein than I') to the 'pretty
things' (I.3.7, 26), the words, that she had been preparing
to say to him before he left; and then there are the overly
pretty things she does manage to say, if only to his servant
Pisanio. Before I was able, she declares, to give him

> that parting kiss which I had set
> Betwixt two charming words, comes in my father,
> And like the tyrannous breathing of the north,
> Shakes all our buds from growing. (34–7)

Imogen is being deliberately exquisite here, lingering on
the fineness of the comparisons, mixing these with her
grief. This is how lovers in chivalric romances address
each other, in metaphors of fabrics (fine 'linen') and
precious ornaments (a 'kiss' between two 'words' is a
jewel within a setting). In the opening scenes of the play

Imogen and Posthumus, despite their wedding and their passion, are still adolescent lovers, childish playfellows, who imagine what their feelings are through the language of poetry, books and courtly games of love (Imogen's allusion to their arrested growth, in the shaken down or perhaps frozen 'buds', is noticeable, as is her blaming it on her father).

In *Cymbeline* susceptibility to stories isn't necessarily a weakness, nor is it confined to young minds. The story of how an older generation of Britons nearly fought off the Roman invasion, even though it is told by Cloten and the Queen, reminds Cymbeline's court that standing up to Julius Caesar was something to be proud of (how prudent it is for Britain to be living on past glories is another matter). In Act III, scene 3, though, Shakespeare goes out of his way to emphasize that it is the young who respond to storytelling without inhibition. Out in Wales, Belarius, who has been feeding the princes sour stories of how wrongly he was treated, knows full well what stories they really want to hear. When he sits and tells them how he fought in this or that battle Guiderius, the elder boy, can barely contain himself:

> . . . his spirits fly out
> Into my story; say 'Thus mine enemy fell,
> And thus I set my foot on's neck', even then
> The princely blood flows in his cheek, he sweats,
> Strains his young nerves, and puts himself in posture
> That acts my words. (90–95)

The younger brother, Arviragus, even more responsive to what he hears, takes up postures 'in as like a figure' but shows 'much more / His own conceiving' (that is, he relives the story but understands what it means too, 96–8).

This part of Belarius' speech is tricky for modern actors to deliver, indeed all of his soliloquy, from when the boys go hunting (III.3.79–107), is difficult to carry off onstage. This is because, as Dr Johnson pointed out, Belarius has robbed the young princes of 'a kingdom only to rob their father of heirs' (Woudhuysen, p. 234), a miserable little revenge, but the old man now speaks so lovingly and so proudly about the boys, his 'sons', that we cannot but feel sympathy for him. The story Belarius himself is susceptible to, although he knows it isn't true, is that by some miracle he really has become their father. Even as he tells it, though, this story starts to come to a bitter-sweet end. The boys go up into the mountains, and when he hears them blow their horn he says, 'Hark, the game is roused!' (98), in other words their prey has been flushed out and the chase has begun. There is no hiding place for the animals any longer, but nowhere that Belarius can hide the boys either. He hears the horn again and tells himself – perhaps pausing as he realizes what he's saying – that 'the game is up', the story of the lost boys is almost over. What the audience knows, but he can't, is that this is because the other world, out of England, is about to arrive in Wales.

The contrasts between England and Wales, separated by the River Severn, are not unlike the contrasts we find in Renaissance pastoral and heroic poems. In *Cymbeline* England is civilized and courtly but going to seed, and it is subordinate to Rome; Wales is a wild green world inhabited by exiles and thieves who have been chased out of England. Shakespeare doesn't make much of the names of the countries because at the time he wrote the play the reigning monarch, King James, had put the creation of Great Britain (Scotland unified with England and Wales) at the top of his agenda. But Wales was a key part of the political iconography of the day for other reasons, as James had to acknowledge. It was where his predecessors, the Tudor monarchs, had come from, and it was the principality he had conferred on his elder son Henry, the heir apparent, when he came of age in 1610 (this is discussed more fully on pp. 157–8). To Shakespeare's English audiences, Wales was also the place of dreamers and bards, and it was associated with Arthur, the most ancient of princes, of whom it was said he was but sleeping and would be king again. So it was to be expected that the dreams in Acts IV and V of *Cymbeline* would be dreamt in Wales: Imogen's dream, that she has found her brothers; Posthumus', that his dead family have found him; the Soothsayer's, that the Roman eagle is heading towards Wales itself, on the western edge of the Empire, to find who knows what.

If we think of the map of *Cymbeline* in these terms, Wales – the place where dreams are dreamt and the dead return to us – is another country, which exists alongside the real world and is sometimes in contact with it. Long before *Cymbeline* this unreal country, in poetry and folklore, was known as the spirit world, the place where all laws were suspended and miracles might happen. It's not by chance that Posthumus, waking from his dream, asks 'what fairies haunt this ground?' (V.4.103), and that Belarius in Act IV, when he first comes upon Imogen in the cave, takes her to be a fairy (by which he means an illusion or enchantment, see the note to III.6.41), and only realizes she isn't one when he sees her eating food. As moderns, we must be careful not to patronize or be impatient about the spirits in *Cymbeline*, at least as a poetic and psychological device within the play. Shakespeare arranges the plot so that the characters and stories all move west out of the real world (where men are jealous imbeciles and knaves, and stepmothers experiment on animals) and converge on Milford Haven. There, the rules of life and history are overturned, if only for a while: four ragged men can defeat the Roman legions, a wife murderer can get his wife back, a girl can turn into a boy and back into a girl, and you can be released from the burden of what you've done, and even be forgiven for it.

There is escape in this, but it is not escapist. In *Cymbeline* the material, visible world – where the characters trust only their envious eyes, the desires of the flesh and the stories they are told – patently fails to protect and nurture by itself. One might argue that the progress the characters make towards the spirit world is the maturation story underlying the whole play, out of which all the other stories flow. Shakespeare didn't need to invent this story, with its parallel kingdoms, he had only to draw on the most powerful literary work of the day, Edmund Spenser's allegorical romance poem *The Faerie Queene* (1590–96), from which he had already borrowed things, especially for *King Lear*. In *The Faerie Queene* Shakespeare could find characters journeying between Britain and Faerie Land, and stories of young boys left in the wilds, and of old soldiers turned into hermits and protectors, and of pubescent girls fearful of the sexual passions of married love. The mysterious theft of the two princes was there as well. Infants in the cradle were believed to be especially vulnerable to fairies, who would steal them from their parents – this had happened to two of Spenser's heroes, Redcross and Artegall – and leave their own ugly unpleasant children in their place.

At one point in *The Faerie Queene*, a few stanzas after the story of King Lear, Spenser refers explicitly to Cymbeline's reign. Cymbeline ruled Britain, he says, at the time of Christ's birth (when the holy ghost or 'heavenly grace' entered human flesh to cleanse men of original sin):

> What time th'eternal Lord in fleshly slime
> Enwombed was, from wretched *Adam's* line
> To purge away the guilt of sinful crime. (II.x.50)

Soon after this the Romans made war on Cymbeline because he refused to pay tribute. He was killed in battle by a treacherous Briton, and succeeded by his brother Arvirage, who fought the Romans until they conceded a peace with Britain. Shakespeare took the germ of the story from Spenser and rearranged some details, but it was probably Christ's incarnation, the meeting of spirit and flesh, which interested him about Cymbeline's reign. This doesn't mean that the play, set in pagan times, has a narrowly Christian meaning, although some critics have indeed interpreted it like this. Rather, it confirms that in *Cymbeline* Shakespeare's sightlines were the creation of 'a system of life' (Dr Johnson's words again) where the limitations of the material world, the here and now, might be reshaped and enriched by the spirit.

ART WORK

We don't learn much about the mental outlook of the social elite in *Cymbeline*, except in one respect, the effect on them of the fine arts, painting and sculpture, as well as poetry, music and song. There are of course references in the play to expensive clothes, gambling, bowls and horse races, as well as to duels, and whoring and drinking, which Shakespeare certainly uses to indicate

what some of the characters are like (Cloten's boorish-
ness, snobbery and intemperance are shown by his binges
at night, for example, and by his touchiness about wearing
the proper clothes, and by his not being able to control
his tongue). Property rights and inheritance are mentioned too, and there is some odd stuff about the Queen
testing drugs on cats and dogs, but in the main it is how
the elite respond to works of art, or at least to aesthetic
experience, that tells us most about them as individuals.
In Act III, scene 4, for instance, when Imogen begins to
be afraid of the strange way Pisanio is staring at her
(it's possible he's just about to murder her), she says to
him:

> One but painted thus
> Would be interpreted a thing perplexed
> Beyond self-explication. (6–7)

The first thing that comes to mind when she sees confusion in his face is a comparison with other faces she has
seen, not in the flesh, but in paintings. A few lines later,
when Pisanio has convinced her that he wants to save
her, he says that she'll have to dress up as a boy, and he
goes into raptures about how awful it will be that the sun
will burn her cheeks when she is not wearing a veil. She'll
have to expose her own beautiful, pale face to

> the greedy touch
> Of common-kissing Titan. (161–2)

She'll also have to do without her 'laboursome and dainty
trims' (her dresses, that is, put on with so much care by
her maids), which in the past have made 'great Juno',
queen of the gods, jealous and angry with her (163–4).

Pisanio is not one of the elite (he is a manservant), but even he, when he thinks of Imogen in all her finery, sees her as a picture, or at least a mythologized image (the sun god wants to kiss her, she is Juno's rival and so forth). Even the parvenu Cloten, who's the person least likely to think of the world in terms of beauty and art, knows that this is how the rest of the court chooses to see it. The aubade he pays musicians to sing and play outside Imogen's bedchamber (the famous song beginning 'Hark, hark, the lark' in Act II, scene 3) is what he knows he must offer her, as a suitor, although to his own ears the singing and music are no more than the fancy outcome of a boy's unbroken voice, and the sounds of a fiddle bow of hair being drawn across strands of dried gut.

Aesthetic experience is important in *Cymbeline* because of the perverted form it takes in Jachimo, the villain of the play. Jachimo isn't perverted because he wants to teach Posthumus a lesson and uses Imogen to do it – this merely shows he is mean and sadistic – but because all the feelings he has about them, and indeed about everything else, are filtered through art and the sentiments associated with art. Jachimo thinks and speaks in the vocabulary of aesthetics, objets d'art and fine judgements. The first time we see him in the play, in Philario's house, he speaks as though he were at an auction checking pictures against a catalogue. Sneering at Posthumus' reputation, he says, 'I could then have looked on him without the help of admiration, though the catalogue of his endowments had been tabled by his side and I to peruse him by items' (I.4.3–6). In the scene that follows, leading up to the bet on Imogen, Jachimo sublimates even the dangerous business of the quarrel (it nearly becomes a duel) into a *conversazione*, an aesthetically pleasing conversation. The language he uses, which he tricks Posthumus into using too, is drawn in part from the business end of the art world: appraisal, valuation, guarantee and verification. Men are weighed to see how they are 'furnished', how they vouch for their ladies 'upon warrant of bloody affirmation', and how their kindnesses are to be paid for or can be rated. Women too, like men and jewels, can be rated, or 'outprized' or over-valued, and of course they can, in this world of prices and comparisons, have less lustre and be of less value than a diamond.

Jachimo's interest in art does not make him an aesthete, but it does make him a collector. What thrills him is the power of art to transform nature into exquisite things (to make a flower into a beautiful memory of a flower), which can then be bought and treasured, or even gambled on. When, in the most famous scene in the play, he gets into Imogen's bedroom, the objects he finds there – tapestries, small statues, an ornate ceiling – are his guides for how to look at Imogen herself. It is midnight, the Princess has fallen asleep, with the taper beside her still alight, and there is a trunk placed nearby in the room. Soon, the spring on the lid of the trunk is released from inside and Jachimo gets out. This should be funny – what is this pathetic little man doing? – but it isn't, and when theatre audiences gasp and giggle, as they often do at this moment, it is because they are not quite sure what he wants from Imogen. Has he really come to rape her? Not at all: Jachimo is there to look at her, to talk about her, to be excited by not being able to touch her. 'The crickets sing,' he says,

> and man's o'er-laboured sense
> Repairs itself by rest. Our Tarquin thus
> Did softly press the rushes ere he wakened
> The chastity he wounded. Cytherea,
> How bravely thou becom'st thy bed; fresh lily,

And whiter than the sheets. That I might touch,
But kiss, one kiss; rubies unparagoned,
How dearly they do't. (II.2.11–18)

One comparison follows another. According to Jachimo,
he is like Tarquin (the Roman lord who raped Lucrece)
and she like Venus (Cytherea is one of the goddess's
lesser-used names), and she's also like a lily, and her skin
is whiter than her sheets, and her red lips are the best
rubies that ever there were. The way he speaks is just as
arty as what he is saying; lush sibilants ('sing', 'sense',
'softly', 'press') introduce a lacework of alliteration that
holds the speech together ('repairs', 'rest', 'rushes', 'rubies';
'wakened', 'wounded', 'whiter'; 'bravery', 'becom'st',
'bed'; 'dearly', 'do't').

Jachimo is a vain Renaissance grandee, a darling
lover-boy who could get any woman into bed, or so he
claims, but what pleases him most, even more than his
rank (his brother is a Duke), is his wit and polished
creative judgement. He is a man of taste, a connoisseur
of the arts, who praises Imogen's body for being delight-
fully in harmony with the furniture and fabrics in her
room. Her lips are jewels, her eyelids are beautiful pale
shutters, with azure lacing (the veins) painted on them
with 'blue of heaven's own tinct'(23). This last bit (just
the right blue) is like something from a sixteenth-century
art handbook, or from one of Vasari's descriptions of
paintings by Raphael or Titian (famous descriptions
that Shakespeare may have known). Jachimo simply
makes an object of Imogen – at one point he wants her
to be so asleep that she is like a monument in a chapel,
a dead image of herself, that is – right down to the
birthmark that makes her unique. 'On her left breast'
he finds a mole

> cinque-spotted, like the crimson drops
> I'th'bottom of a cowslip (II.2.37–9)

and he treats it, not as a natural beauty, but as an artist's mark, a monogram that proves that his image of Imogen, which he is fashioning to show to Posthumus, is authentic.

At the end of the scene, just before he gets back in the trunk, Jachimo looks at the book Imogen was reading when she fell asleep. It is Ovid's *Metamorphoses* (mythological stories about transformations), and she has arrived at the point, in one story, where Philomela has just been raped. Jachimo's speech starts with one rape (of Lucrece) and ends with another. What the audience will ask is whether any harm has been done to Imogen by his gazing at her and turning her into an image, beyond the damage he plans to do to her reputation with Posthumus. Has he in any sense raped her, or transformed her? Shakespeare opens up several disturbing things in this scene about men and their sexual desires, but also about Imogen herself. Jachimo is a voyeur who looks at her and sees a sophisticated dirty picture, which anticipates other sexual pictures of her in the play (Posthumus imagines her being mounted by a boar, Cloten sees himself raping her over a dead body). Imogen is not a helpless victim, though, as she shows earlier when, fully awake at this point, she brushes off Jachimo as he tries to make her think vengeful, dirty thoughts (his speciality) about Posthumus having sex with whores. When she falls asleep Imogen does become vulnerable, but to what? She does have a dream – there is a dream in every other sleep in the play, including two of her own – but is it a dream she can't remember? Is it about a fake picture of her somehow being shown to her husband, in which she has metamorphosed into a lewd, hard-hearted and unfaithful bride?

It is through the arts again, in combination, that the matter is put before us. Jachimo, as we know from the chimes at the close of the scene, is in Imogen's room for three hours past midnight (though the time onstage is only minutes), the same interval she has been reading Ovid until midnight. A connection between these periods is at least implied. Imogen reads a Roman poem about rapes, shape-changers and the metamorphic powers of art. Then, as she sleeps, a Roman lord gets out of a treasure-box (this is what he says it is), recalls two rapes, drools over her body, and transforms her natural beauties, through comparisons, into man-made ones. There is an important pun in this too, whether or not the audience spots it. Jachimo is a phantom come from a box of words (a 'thesaurus', the Latin word for a treasure-box); he is a thing created out of what Imogen has been reading. He is real enough onstage, but Jachimo is also the immaterial thing Imogen prayed to be protected from, the tempter of the night, the demon in her dream. This is why she stays completely asleep, and cannot wake: what the audience is watching is the inside of her nightmare. Shakespeare doesn't mean that this is a repressed sexual fantasy of hers, fed by reading too much Ovid; rather it is a stage in her maturation story. Newly married, Imogen learns that her husband can have ugly, jealous and vicious feelings about her; Jachimo is merely the conduit to convey these feelings between them.

Shakespeare borrowed the bedchamber scene, along with the rest of the wager plot, from Boccaccio's *Decameron*, and from an English version of Boccaccio called *Frederick of Jennen* (see Sources). His inspiration for the art work in it, though, came, once more, from Spenser. All that Boccaccio says about the bedchamber is that the villain prised the chest open from the inside, 'stepped silently forth into the room, where a single lamp was burning,' and started 'to inspect the arrangement of the furniture, the paintings, and everything else of note that the room contained, and committed it all to memory' (*Decameron*, trans. G. H. McWilliam (1972), p. 212). In the play the bedchamber ceiling (Jachimo describes it for Posthumus in Act II, scene 4) is fretted with golden cherubs; her andirons are blind Cupids made of silver; the tapestry on the walls is of Cleopatra at her first meeting with Antony; and carved over the fireplace there is a Diana, the goddess of chastity, bathing. Of the sculpted figures, Jachimo, well versed in judging the best artists, says:

> Never saw I figures
> So likely to report themselves; the cutter
> Was as another Nature, dumb; outwent her,
> Motion and breath left out. (82–5)

The statues, eerily, look as though they are just about to speak, and it is only because they don't move or breathe that we can tell that nature didn't make them. Imogen is asleep in a chamber of erotic art which is pressing towards life, even as Jachimo makes an unliving pornographic image out of her. This was the subject that Spenser had made distinctively his in *The Faerie Queene* in the 1590s. Spenser's allegories of true and false love are conducted in castles and mysterious rooms, where magicians tempt knights and ladies with images from classical mythology while they sleep, or when they enter the underworld or a forest or a wilderness. In one dream a knight is visited by a fantasy of his lady having sex with another man (I.2.2–6); and even when the knights are awake they can't tell the difference between a beautiful lady fleeing from them, and a fake, licentious copy of her made by a witch.

Spenser inspired Shakespeare in another respect too. In *The Faerie Queene* knights and ladies, themselves from different times and places, pass between real and imaginary worlds. They encounter saracens, hermits and classical deities, mixed up with medieval giants, ogres and dragons, and every kind of holy man and magus. The settings include Renaissance palaces, Christian and pagan churches and the pleasure gardens of the ancient world. This eclecticism is a regular feature of Renaissance romance, as it is of great Renaissance paintings, and in *Cymbeline* Shakespeare attempted the same eclectic mixing. Imogen's bedroom has rushes on the floor (the custom in English houses at this date), but its walls are decorated in the finest cinquecento fashion, with *exempla* of profane loves from classical history and mythology, all set beneath a ceiling encrusted with putti. Imogen herself is an Ancient Briton, while Jachimo is an aristocrat from the Rome of the Borgias, who happens to live in the days of the first emperor, Augustus. Jachimo, one of the Renaissance cognoscenti, prides himself on his *virtù*, praising the expressiveness of the art he sees in terms of its *enargia*, the critical concept at the heart of Renaissance theories of artistic imitation (specifically, that art could challenge and even outdo nature).

Modern audiences may agree with neoclassical objections to the mix of time and manners in *Cymbeline*, but they can hardly think, with Dr Johnson, that the mixing happened because Shakespeare was ignorant or careless. It is far too provocative for that. Useful modern thinking has been done about the deliberate uses of anachronism in Shakespeare and in Renaissance art generally, some of which can be applied to *Cymbeline* (see Further Reading). But the reason for the anachronisms in this play in particular (it has more of them than Shakespeare's other plays) is probably the simple one that he used them, as Spenser did, to disrupt the conventions of naturalism. Onstage, psychological and social differences between characters can be signalled by speech or gesture or costume (noblemen are dressed in one way, servants in another), but it is not always easy to mark the different types of existence that characters are living. Anachronism (shuffling times this way and that) is a dramatic device that can be used, alongside others, to convey these differences. Imogen, princess in a Roman province, sleeps among High Renaissance pictures and statues of sexual innocence and experience (Diana and Cleopatra), but the moment Jachimo uses vile whorehouse talk to her, she bristles and says she will ask her father whether he wants

> A saucy stranger in his court to mart
> As in a Romish stew. (I.6.151–2)

In 1610 'Romish' could mean 'Roman' (of classical Rome), but the word was most fully charged when it meant 'Roman Catholic', or popish. English Protestant disgust about papal Rome – sexual as well as religious, since Rome was thought to be filled with 'stews' or brothels – is thus vented by a British princess who is supposed to be alive at the time of Christ. The chronology is impossible but a connection is made nevertheless between Jachimo the adorer of art and filthy images and Jachimo the hypocritical worshipper of relics and idols.

The more closely we examine the artefacts and art in *Cymbeline* (images in pictures and in words) the clearer it becomes that, for Shakespeare, art in elite culture threatened to replace experience, or at least to pasteurize and distort it. As we saw, the princes in their Welsh wilderness, growing up away from the influence of the court, respond directly to the stories of bravery Belarius tells them. It is easy to think them a bit gauche for being so taken up by these stories (assuming the physical postures and so forth), but the immediacy of their feelings shows that they've not been corrupted. At the slightest sign that they are falling in love with beauty, Guiderius warns his brother to stop using 'wench-like words' (IV.2.230). This distrust of counterfeit feelings – ones that high art offers – is Shakespeare's new take on the most ancient of literary genres, the pastoral. How he treats this genre in *Cymbeline*, by exploring originals and counterfeits, is discussed later. Before we turn to that though, we need to consider his general thinking about the dramaturgical art needed to make plays for the public stage.

Fortunately, in *Cymbeline* Shakespeare has left a trail for us, because of the special way he made the battle scene in Act V (shown as a dumb show in V.2, and described by Posthumus in V.3). Shakespeare borrowed the story of the stand against the Romans from Holinshed's history of Scotland, a source he had used to write *Macbeth* a few years earlier. Holinshed tells of a farmer and his two sons working in a field next to a battle between a Scottish army and an army of Danish invaders. The battle was going badly for the Scots, and they were fleeing down 'a long lane fenced on the sides with ditches and walls made of turf'. Seeing the Scottish king 'destitute of the wings' of his army, the farmer and his sons positioned themselves across the lane, and

beat them back whom they met fleeing, and spared neither friend nor foe: but down they went all such as came within their reach, wherewith diverse hardy personages cried unto their fellows to return back unto the battle, for there was a new power of Scottish men come to their succours.

The Danes also believed that Scottish reinforcements had arrived, and they fled 'back in great disorder unto the other of their fellows fighting with the middle ward of the Scots' (quoted from Bullough, *Sources of Shakespeare*, p. 48). The Danes were routed, and for his service the farmer was made a member of the nobility. The episode was a gift for Shakespeare. It provided him with everything needed for a miraculous reversal in a battle, an outcome so wondrous and unexpected as to be laughably unbelievable. In *The Winter's Tale* and *The Tempest* he tested his audience's credulity with marvels and with chance happenings he himself had invented, or had found in novels and romances and travel stories, but here, in Holinshed, he had lighted upon a true miracle that was neither an illusion nor a trick (of the sort that makes Birnam Wood come to Dunsinane in *Macbeth*).

With this material to hand Shakespeare returned to the old problem of stage armies. The notion that Belarius and the princes were an army by themselves is suggested when Posthumus describes them as

> Three thousand confident, in act as many –
> For three performers are the file when all
> The rest do nothing – (V.3.29–31)

He means that the three men accomplished as much as three thousand could, and that they stood in for the many men who had fled or were dying. The vocabulary points to another meaning, however, because Belarius and the brothers are like a small group of players or 'performers', who are 'in act as many' when they march about the stage, inviting the audience to accept them, few as they are, as representing (filling up the file for) a whole army. Shakespeare had used stage armies in his plays in the

1590s, and he persisted with them in the later plays, ignoring or directly challenging neoclassical rules about what should be attempted in the theatre. As we saw earlier, Shakespeare's most severe critic over this was Jonson, who repeatedly jibed at him for taking liberties with nature onstage. In the Prologue to his comedy *Every Man in His Humour* Jonson assured his audience that he would show them 'deeds, and language, such as men do use', and not disregard the unities of time and place. Nor would he (as he thought Shakespeare had done, blunderingly, in his plays about the Wars of the Roses) fight over 'York and Lancaster's long jars' with the help of nothing but big-sounding words, and 'three rusty swords'.

Jonson did not publish this Prologue until 1616, the year Shakespeare died, but he made sure his rival was aware of his opinions long before then. In *The Winter's Tale* Shakespeare responded to Jonson with a series of daring ripostes, where he broke even more of the rules, but knowingly (in one scene a statue comes to life, in another a king and a shepherdess debate art and nature). In *Cymbeline* too, in Act V, there was a reply to neo-classical objections, this time to showing a battle onstage at all. According to Jonson, a three-man army with 'rusty swords' is an absurd and false thing – a charge Shake-speare neatly answers by using a story from history in which a real three-man army, the farmer and his sons, turned a battle from defeat to victory (dressed as wild mountain men, they were 'rusty' in another sense too, as 'rustic, country types'). The refusal to narrow the range of emotions on stage – even if extreme, and hard to repre-sent – is what characterizes Shakespeare's writing at all times, but it is especially true of his last plays. Posthumus' description of the battle in Act V, scene 3 presents the audience with an ampleness, almost an overflow of feeling, which sits uneasily, to neoclassical tastes, on the dividing line between established genres. Is the speech a narrative, in the heroic manner of the epic, or is it an imitation of experience, appropriate to drama? By not sticking to the rules – not keeping the right experience in the right genre, as his critics saw it – Shakespeare risked confusing the audience altogether. In the battle scene they might laugh, wrongly, at the tiny Roman stage army, or cheer, as children do at modern pantomimes, at the impossible British victory.

Shakespeare took these risks consciously. Stage armies were always vulnerable to laughter, as they still are in modern productions, but what the battle scene preserved was a variety of tone and feeling in the play, and also a sense of scale, excitement and energy of body and temperament not entirely under control. Shakespeare knew the distinction between audiences laughing generously, however, even if not always at the right moment, at improbable stage matters, and the kind of disbelief that vents itself in mockery and satire. The exchange between Posthumus and the British Lord in Act V, scene 3 is concerned with this disbelief. Whether through astonishment or envy, the Lord finds it difficult to believe the story he is told, and Posthumus at once interprets this as a sort of effete superiority: the Lord wants to belittle what happened by circulating some smart rhymes about it. Posthumus becomes so angry that, having begun to parody this over-clever manner, which aims to sum up things in a witty jingle, he catches himself speaking in rhyme. Beneath the surface meaning of this exchange (a true gentleman scares off a snob) there is, once again, the larger matter of the relationship between art and experience. Around 1600 Jonson and the poet Donne had started a revival in English of the classical form, the epigram, which in their treatment was compact and pithy, something that mocked and stung its victims. The epigram that Posthumus makes up (57–8) shows that Shakespeare too could write in the new fashion when he wanted to, but evidently he thought the taste for it, spreading quickly among the intellectual elite, led towards a narrowing of feeling and sensibility.

COUNTERFEITS

Modern interpretations of *Cymbeline* often ignore or sideline the emotional density of the play, or are faintly embarrassed by it. This is partly because critics now view the discussion of feeling and sensibility in works of art (even Shakespeare's plays) with suspicion. One effect of this has been to leave whole stretches of *Cymbeline* unaccounted for. A striking instance of something unexamined is the description in Act IV, scene 4 of how the boy Fidele died (he isn't dead of course, simply drugged, and he isn't Fidele but Imogen in disguise). Arviragus returns from the cave '*with Imogen, dead, bearing her in his arms*' – Shakespeare's own stage direction probably (IV.2.194) – and Belarius, aghast, asks, 'How found you him?' (209). The reply is,

> Stark, as you see,
> Thus smiling, as some fly had tickled slumber,
> Not as death's dart being laughed at; his right cheek
> Reposing on a cushion. (209–12)

Fidele appears to have died in his sleep without pain. As Shakespeare intended, he looks like one of the beautiful marble figures that were the fashion on grand funeral monuments. The new emphasis in Jacobean funerary art, breaking with earlier conventions, was on the dead as they had been in life, relaxed and in repose rather than stretched out and stiff with rigor mortis. Fidele has unconsciously assumed the perfect posture in which to be remembered, with his face turned to the right, resting gently on a pillow. When Jachimo looked at Imogen sleeping he wanted her, we recall, to be like a monument in a chapel (II.2.32–3). Arviragus looks at her as Fidele and he too thinks of a monumentalized image, laid out in the new fashion (to make sure we have got the point, Shakespeare makes him refer, seconds later, to monuments that haven't been built because heirs were mean and ungrateful). We might wish to keep them separate, but the voyeur and the princes say the same things about Imogen. Her pale skin lying in white sheets makes Jachimo think of a 'fresh lily' (15) but when Guiderius sees her as Fidele, apparently dead, he too calls her 'sweetest, fairest lily' (IV.2.201). Jachimo describes the delicate veins in her eyelids as 'azure-laced' (II.2.22), and then Arviragus says that her veins are like the 'azured harebell' (IV.2.222).

Disentangling nature from art, and originals from copies and comparisons, isn't easy in *Cymbeline* – there are many other parallels and overlappings like these between Jachimo and the princes – nor is it easy to separate what's real from what's fake. On the Jacobean stage, at this moment of great poignancy, a boy-actor was pretending to be a princess pretending to be a page pretending to be drugged and thought to be dead. And added to the game of impersonations was the real grief – shown by actors who were pretending – for the death of a child, something that the Jacobean elite was beginning to make a cult of (John Donne's clever but mawkish poems, *The Anniversaries*, which commemorated a girl who died when she was eleven, were published at exactly this date). Belarius and the princes grieve because Fidele didn't live the life he deserved, and because he died of melancholy – that is, he sank into gloom and depression, and his body gave way. Melancholy at this date was taken to be a serious medical condition (it could kill), but it was also a pose assumed by people who wanted to be thought refined and special, as the world watched them suffering elegantly. Fidele, whose name means someone true and sincere, is to Belarius the embodiment of what's real and unfeigned, the antithesis of phoney refinement.

What do audiences make of real and fake feelings put together like this? Imogen isn't dead, so how can they possibly feel grief for her death? Indeed if they did feel grief – compelled by the force and vividness of Shakespeare's poetry – wouldn't that make them doubt even more what they were supposed to feel? Audiences may have in mind too the direction in this scene that Arviragus should enter '*with Imogen, dead*' (not 'as if dead'), which looks like a purposeful recollection of Lear carrying in Cordelia, another British princess, who has been hanged and who will come no more again. Can a memory of this tragedy intrude even where there is no tragedy? The sensibility Shakespeare has created in *Cymbeline* is hard to describe, because it's upsetting and it fluctuates (and it is sometimes closer to melodrama than we might like), and because we can't point to a single person in the play who isn't in some way compromised by it, least of all Imogen. Most of the men look at Imogen and see a beautiful corpse, until she ends up wanting to look like a corpse too. The princes lay their sister alongside Cloten (our feelings are complicated even more by this), then speak their dirge and leave. At last Imogen wakes to find she is lying beside a decapitated body wearing her husband's clothes, and the lament that flows from her is as exquisite and heart-rending as any aria in an opera. But the corpse is not her husband's at all, as the audience knows, but that of her enemy, the man who wanted to rape her.

So what is new here? Isn't this simply an extravagant form of dramatic irony, known to writers two millennia before Shakespeare? The new thing is that Imogen, a wife but still a virgin, puts her hands on the headless man and feels his thighs, his muscles and his limbs, and knows by these – but wrongly – that this is indeed her husband. The extremity of her grief drives her to bloody her face from the severed arteries in the man's neck, so that together she and he may seem 'the horrider' (IV.2.331) to those who will chance to find them. This is awful, and it is awful in a way that goes beyond the horrors of classical tragedy, beyond even, say, the moment in Euripides' play *The Bacchae* when a mother sits stupefied, cradling the mangled head and limbs of her son which she and her daughters, in their mad frenzy, have torn from his body. The element that makes this scene in *Cymbeline* different, and much more modern, is that Imogen wants to be seen, with the corpse, as an aesthetic object, a gruesome half-dead and half-alive monument that will arouse the sensibilities of even casual onlookers.

This sensibility certainly won't be to everyone's taste. More than a hundred years ago George Bernard Shaw, in letters to the actress Ellen Terry telling her how to play Imogen at this point, accused Shakespeare of not knowing what he was up to in *Cymbeline*, of letting the emotions in the play get out of hand. We must decide for ourselves whether this is true, but we must also consider the reasons why Shakespeare tackled the

emotions in the first place. One thing he wanted to do –
as did every other Renaissance dramatist who was looking
forward rather than back – was to fuse in a single moment
onstage the sensations of comedy and tragedy. In the
sixteenth century it was the Italian court dramatists, led
by Guarini, who had ventured into this new territory,
arguing, against neoclassical critics, that tragicomedy
was possible in principle, if it was created according to
fixed rules. Shakespeare broke the rules straightaway in
Cymbeline (there weren't supposed to be any deaths in
tragicomedy), but he was clearly trying to mix the anguish
felt by Imogen with the comic consciousness of the audience that she is safe now that the immediate danger has
passed, so long as she isn't tempted to commit suicide.

The other effect Shakespeare was seeking was to make
the fake Fidele and the fake Posthumus (Imogen lying
prostrate over Cloten) part of a fake scene. Imogen thinks
Cloten's body is her husband's so this moment, in a
perverse way, is a recognition scene, but a false one. At
the end of *Cymbeline* there are, famously, multiple
moments of recognition (more than a dozen of them)
where the characters discover who they have been fighting
alongside or who betrayed them or who their brothers
are. Audiences are often charmed by this endless sequence
of reunions and putting right of misunderstandings, but
they are also relieved, as Shakespeare planned, when the
whole business is finally over and done with, so that they
too can be released from the built-up pressure of defer-
rals. Imogen's misrecognition of Posthumus is indeed
horrible to watch, but the moment also has in it, because
we know it is a fake, some promise, after more delays,
of the true reunion that's coming ('The more delayed,
delighted' is how Jupiter puts it (V.4.72), to the ghosts
who have grown impatient with him).

The contribution Cloten made to this sensibility is, for us today, one of the mysteries of *Cymbeline*. By this point in the play, with Imogen weeping over him, Cloten isn't even in one piece, he is just a headless stuffed stage dummy. Where Shakespeare got the idea of Cloten is not clear. He may have borrowed him from Italian tragicomedy (in which there was often an uncivilized brute who attacked the heroine), or copied him from life (he is obviously a court upstart), or he may have dreamt him up as he was devising another monster, Caliban, for *The Tempest*. Whatever his origins, Cloten is one of Shakespeare's most gross characters. His every thought is about parts of the body (sexual ones chiefly, but necks and noses and hands in pockets are there too), he sweats and smells so much that even his minders can't bear it, and the only way he becomes aroused is to imagine himself having sex with a woman while he is dressed in her husband's clothes. What other pleasures the Jacobeans took in him we can't be sure of, but these must have had something to do with smutty schoolboy quibbles and lewd wordplay that he wasn't quite able to understand. At one point he says of himself, bragging, 'I must go up and down like a cock that nobody can match', meaning he's unrivalled (in sex or as a fighting cock), but unknowingly he gives us a truer, phantasmagoric image of himself as a walking phallus, that no one, not even the Queen, can 'match' or marry off to Imogen.

Cloten's main function in the play is to suffer the insults and death that Posthumus deserves. In the source, the *Decameron*, it is the villain who is put to death, and the husband, although he falls on hard times, gets his wife back and she brings him a tidy fortune too. This won't do for Shakespeare and he breaks with the established image of the blameless hero or husband, a character who in all earlier versions of the wager story goes unpunished, even though he plans to have his wife murdered. Posthumus is naive even beyond what normally happens in this type of test-a-wife story, so easily deluded in fact that his outbursts suggest he had never fully trusted Imogen. Later in the play the departure from this convention of the impeccable hero is even more startling when Posthumus repents and feels suicidal that he ordered Pisanio to murder Imogen. Even without knowing this earlier convention, though, modern audiences are aware that Posthumus' hysterical loss of self-control in Rome points to a deep-rooted, almost maniacal distrust of women.

To protect Posthumus from the ultimate penalty for his crime, Shakespeare invented a surrogate for him, and then played a joke on the surrogate by giving him an especially appropriate name, Cloten – the clot, that is, the thick lump, the clodpoll, the blockish head. A small detail in Boccaccio's story, apparently unused, shows what Shakespeare had in mind. The villain, as in the play, taunts the husband until he has got him ready to bet on his wife's chastity, but what the husband offers first as a stake, against a thousand gold florins, is his head. 'I am prepared,' he says, 'in order to convince you of my lady's integrity, to place my head on the block if you ever persuade her to meet your wishes,' to which the villain replies, 'I wouldn't know what to do with your head, if I were to win' (*Decameron*, p. 211). In *Cymbeline* Shakespeare turns the husband's head into a simple pun. Posthumus, when he loses his head in Rome, bets that Imogen will keep her maiden*head* (since she is still a virgin), but when he loses the bet and orders her to be killed, this has to be paid for with a head. And it is Cloten, Lord Stupid-head, named for this sole purpose in life, who ends up with his head cut off while wearing Posthumus' clothes. Puns and playing on names may strike us as a bit strange now, but these were serious things to the Jacobeans: the deciphering of the prophecy at the close of the play may be far-fetched, but Shakespeare's first audiences would not have thought it was trivial.

Cloten is linked to Posthumus by more than his name, as critics and directors have recently come to realize. The characters, significantly, never appear onstage together, and there are disturbing similarities in the things they plan to do to Imogen to take revenge on her. The consensus now is that they are Jeykll and Hyde doubles, and that a single actor, possibly Richard Burbage, may have played both parts on the Jacobean stage. Modern productions, at the Manchester Royal Exchange in 1984 and at Shakespeare's Globe in 2001, confirm that the roles can be played like this, although audiences report being confused by the doubling, as perhaps Forman was in the performance he saw in 1611. How Cloten is played onstage determines the mood of the play out of all proportion to the size of the part (fewer than three hundred lines in all). The more closely he resembles Posthumus, even if he doesn't look like him, the darker the play will be, at least until he is dead: it's a grim thought for an audience that Cloten is Posthumus' other half, his alter ego. Conversely, if he is played as absurdly unlike Posthumus – no more than the reflection we get in a trick mirror – there will probably be a lighter, even comic feel to the scenes he is in. The role of Caliban in *The Tempest*, another smallish part, is a parallel that comes to mind. The extent to which Prospero acknowledges the monster to be his does much to shape our feeling about *The Tempest* as a whole.

Perhaps it was the many fakes and counterfeits in *The Faerie Queene* that prompted Shakespeare to fill *Cymbeline* with imitations. In Spenser the fake is often a degraded copy of some event in antiquity. The famous story of how Paris seduced Helen, for instance, is rewritten as a squalid burlesque: Paridell, a cad, has his way with Hellenore, a drunken middle-class wife, whom he dumps (III.ix–x). In *Cymbeline* there are rewritten stories and untrue histories in every scene. The Queen's tabloid account of the Britons standing up to Julius Caesar is one, and the wager plot is another (the bet on Imogen is a tragicomic imitation of the story of the rape of Lucrece, with the originals, Collatine, Tarquin and Lucrece – boastful husband, envious tyrant and chaste wife – recast as Posthumus, Jachimo and Imogen). To these we could add yet more examples of Imogen fakes (some of them her own), or Jachimo's self-glorifying confessions in the denouement, or Posthumus' counterfeiter speech at the close of Act II, but the point is made. It is easy to create a fake, and even easier to let it replace the original. According to Spenser, the purpose of *The Faerie Queene* was to teach readers how to distinguish images of virtue from the cunning imitations of it that vice could come up with. One problem was that many of the characters, good as well as bad ones, appeared to prefer the imitations; another was that it proved impossible to preserve the distinction between what God had given man, and what man had made – between nature and art, in other words.

Spenser was addressing the moral and religious questions of his own day (among them, Protestant iconophobia), but the literary mode he was writing in was the ancient one known as the pastoral. A Renaissance pastoral poem or play didn't have to have sheep and shepherds

in it, but it did have to have an acute sense of the loss of
Eden, of a lost innocent time when nature supplied man's
needs without him having to work or understand things
through art. After that moment, so the poets and philosophers said, all human beings longed to return to such
primal innocence. Renaissance pastorals showed audiences a glimpse of man's original purity and beauty, but
then left them, saddened, with the thought that there was
no way back to the time that the ancients had called the
Golden Age. In this sense *Cymbeline* is a pastoral lament,
because its counterfeits are constant reminders that there
is no innocent place to escape to (away from the court
and civilization), and no innocent place in the mind either.

Sometimes this lament is the indistinct sound of
mourning that we can hear beneath the surface of other
emotions in the play. One instance of this is the exchange
between the young princes in Wales in Act IV, scene 2,
when they praise the resolved way that Fidele is dealing
with his grief:

ARVIRAGUS   Nobly he yokes
  A smiling with a sigh, as if the sigh
  Was that it was for not being such a smile;
  The smile mocking the sigh that it would fly
  From so divine a temple to commix
  With winds that sailors rail at.
GUIDERIUS   I do note
  That grief and patience, rooted in him both,
  Mingle their spurs together.
ARVIRAGUS   Grow patience,
  And let the stinking elder, grief, untwine
  His perishing root with the increasing vine. (IV.2.51–60)

Modern audiences are right to wonder why Shakespeare has the brothers speak in this mannered way, as if they were performing a duet. Fidele is a temple, Arviragus says, and his smile and sigh are its priests. Outside the temple, as the boy breathes out, the sigh will become impure, mixed with winds that drive ships, and with the breath of sailors, shouting and cursing at the winds. Guiderius responds, in counterpoint, with grief and patience, not as personifications, but as unconscious arboreal or plant life rooted in Fidele, who's imagined as the earth. Arviragus completes the exchange by making his brother's metaphor, of growth in the soil, into a moral and spiritual contrast between evil death and flourishing life (Arviragus is a pagan, but he is thinking of the Judas tree and the vine of Christ).

There is nothing unusual in substance here. Things made by human design (a temple, sailing ships, Fidele's self-control) are set against things that grow without nurture (grief and patience, wild and uncultivated). There are, it's true, two versions of Fidele – one a vessel of air, the other the earth in which roots become tangled and poisoned – but at this date these are no more than conventional symbols of the spirit and human flesh, or soul and body. It's equally to be expected that the princes, in their dialogue, should try to keep things apart and distinguishable – art distinct from nature, air from earth, a smile from a sigh, even the upper classes from their inferiors (a pure boy and common sailors). What they cannot keep separate, though, because they're so in harmony with each other, are the words they are using. In their exchange rhymes and parts of speech flow into each other, mingling, commixing and entwining in the language as inextricably as the roots in the soil. 'Smiling' and 'mocking', noun and verb, merge into the adjectives 'stinking', 'perishing' and 'increasing', as the sounds take over:

> . . . mocking the *sigh*, that it would *fly*
> From so di*vine* a temple to commix
> With *win*ds that *sail*ors *rail* at.

The last phrase confirms that euphony is what dictates the meaning in this: the railing sailors are here as much because of an echoing sound as because of any logical progression within the trope. The studied neatness with which Arviragus takes up 'divine' and makes the closing rhyme 'untwine' and 'vine' out of it completes the impression that, far from being separate and different, everything has its roots deep in something else.

Audiences must be careful not to misunderstand what is happening here. The princes, whom Belarius has trained in all the courtly arts, would have been expected to speak like this in a pastoral. This is how the accomplished courtiers behave in, for example, Sir Philip Sidney's romance novel of 1580, *The Arcadia*, when they compete with each other in songs and poems praising their ladies. In *Cymbeline* this brief dialogue between the princes is in fact a pastoral eclogue, a poem elevated above the commonplaces out of which it is made by the quality of the art that went into its making. Normally the subject of an eclogue is no more important than the layers of words and sounds used to make the poem. To modern audiences this may smack of insincerity and the dialogue may look like yet another fake. Perhaps this is what Shakespeare intended – he certainly makes Guiderius distrustful of sentiments in words – but the message may be simpler, that over-civilized minds, however intensely they love or hate, can only express themselves through exhausted ceremonies and even more tired rhetorical figures from the classical past. The other possibility (opened up in the Renaissance by Italian tragicomedy) is that the dialogue is indeed a simulacrum, but one that imitates what once existed in the Golden Age. Without their knowing it, perhaps the princes speak and act out a beautiful reminder of a time before men and women lost their innocence. Beneath their sympathy for Fidele, which turns into grief as he seems to die, is there a still more profound melancholy that the past we long for is closed off to us for ever?

OLD AND NEW

Critics and audiences have not warmed to *Cymbeline* the way they have to other plays Shakespeare wrote at this date. They have been impressed with it, or they have found fault with it, but still it hasn't engaged them deeply. Directors have come up with brilliant ideas for performing it – Peter Hall made it a weird fairy tale for grown ups, in the manner of Jean Cocteau's film *La Belle et la bête* – but somehow even onstage the play carries on being what we don't want it to be, distant from us. In the final scene, with its brilliant fantasia of recognitions, any doubts we have about the underlying feeling in *Cymbeline* ought by then, surely, to have been put to rest. When, for instance, Belarius gives back the boys he has been father to, his words of parting have him and them in tears, usually along with the audience:

> .... I must lose
> Two of the sweet'st companions in the world.
> The benediction of these covering heavens

Fall on their heads like dew, for they are worthy
To inlay heaven with stars. (V.5.348–52)

Isn't this enough for us? Wasn't this Shakespeare's aim, to show all the children and their fathers waking up, their beautiful and monstrous dream-life over and their real lives about to begin? But no, after so many false feelings and false starts in the play, not even sentiments and metaphors like these can convince us completely.

Much of Shakespeare's technique in *Cymbeline* is primitivist – folksy soliloquies, old-fashioned metres and rhymes, and characters out of folktale – but it is enormously sophisticated too. When people don't like *Cymbeline*, however, it isn't because they don't know how clever the play is, or because they've misunderstood its conventions, it is because they're dissatisfied with what it is, a tragicomic disenchantment with over-civilized life. Shakespeare wasn't the only writer in the Renaissance to feel this disenchantment – it is found in the Italian poet Tasso for instance – and *Cymbeline* isn't the only play in which he explored it. It is here, though, that the disillusionment with the superficiality and petty nastiness of the elite, with their good manners and new taste in art, is most evident. It has become fashionable among modern critics to associate *Cymbeline* closely with the contemporary court (see *Cymbeline* and the Court of King James), in particular with the heir apparent, and to regard the play as another bit of high art quietly propping up the Stuart monarchy. This approach implies that Shakespeare, when he was at court, was so taken with people who had power and rank that he simply had to write smarmy versions of them. An argument like this cannot be maintained for long if we look carefully at the unflattering portraits of everyone in *Cymbeline*, Imogen included.

This disenchantment isn't concerned with just the Jacobean court, but with hyper-civilized life in general. The loss of the Golden Age, the chief theme in pastorals, had been made sharper in the century before *Cymbeline* as Europeans moved west and found people in the New World who weren't civilized at all, but who looked as though they were still living a life of graceful, untroubled innocence. There were no counterfeit feelings there, it seemed, no perverted fantasies and fake art, but a world still in touch with the spirit, and not weighed down with too much thought. It is well known that Shakespeare examined the subject of New World innocence in *The Tempest*, written a few months after *Cymbeline*, and he may have intended the plays to complement each other. Some of Shakespeare's contemporaries believed that the world of Ancient Britain was purer and more primitive than their own (because closer in time to the lost Golden Age and not corrupted by Rome and the Pope), so perhaps in *Cymbeline* he set out to show them just how wrong they were.

Cymbeline ends with pardons, reunions and settled quarrels, and with the prophecy explained. The concluding lines close in a moment of stasis, just before all the good things are about to begin. The gods will forever be pleased by the smell of burnt offerings sacrificed to them, and the smoke from the altars will carry on drifting upwards, crookedly, for ever, because this is an image fixed in time. This is always the case, we say, because it is the end of a play: everything stops, so the images stop. If we go back a little, though, to the reunion that probably matters most to us, between Imogen and Posthumus, we find another image of dependency fixed for ever. When Imogen embraces Posthumus, he lifts her up and says:

> Hang there like fruit, my soul,
>   Till the tree die. (V.5.263–4)

Tennyson wanted these lines with him on his deathbed, he thought them so beautiful, and so they are, but they also tell us something more uncomforting about this couple. Posthumus says he is the tree, and Imogen is the fruit, so she will hang pendant from him for ever, never ripening and falling, always his wife and always his daughter. It won't come as any surprise that the nineteenth-century critics worshipped Imogen, the sylph-like little princess who probably reminded them of the young Victoria, their own queen, before she became a large widowed matriarch. Perhaps it is curmudgeonly to admit it, but disenchantment with over-civilized life, with beauty bought at a high price, seems to reach into these wonderful images as well.

In *Cymbeline* there is, however, a future beyond the smoke of the altars, and there is a new world too, unimaginable to the characters. The point of contact between present and future comes at the most ancient moment in the play, in Act V, scene 4, when the ghosts enter Posthumus' dream. Posthumus has been trying to kill himself on the battlefield, but in the dream he starts shifting the blame, on to his god in heaven and his parents in the grave. After the way he has behaved – believing Imogen has betrayed him and so must be murdered – he doesn't deserve much mercy at all, let alone to have his dead father Sicilius and his superfather Jupiter quarrel about who loves him more. Posthumus does fight against the Romans and rescue Cymbeline, it is true, and he offers his life in recompense for ordering his wife's death. When he falls asleep the dream tells him he was a fool not to trust Imogen, but he wasn't wicked: it was Jachimo's fault, or Sicilius' (for not helping him earlier) or Jupiter's (for not letting on what the divine plan was, and for delaying the happy conclusion).

None of this is easy to swallow – indeed the rehabilitation of Posthumus is the most difficult task Shakespeare set himself in *Cymbeline* – but the dream also has a larger meaning, which becomes intelligible if we take ourselves back to the old order of 1610, to the moment when trust in fathers, especially kings and gods, was challenged conclusively, for the first time, by the evidence of modern experimental science. In that year, because of Galileo, Jupiter, the father of the gods, was unthroned, and the universe was finally proved to be not an enormous glass ball with the earth at its centre but an expanding infinitude of galaxies, each packed with stars. It took a century and more for the old fathers, ruling in European courts and churches, to be unseated by this extraordinary scientific discovery, but everyone in the know realized its significance from the start, including Shakespeare. He explained what it meant by writing a masque.

The dream in *Cymbeline* is a variation on the masques played at the Jacobean court. Masques celebrated royal authority by showing how disorder was expelled and replaced by order. They began in disharmony (satyrs, uncivil behaviour, cacophonous sounds), but ended with graceful songs and dances, stately marches and revelations about the decorous masquers who replaced the ugly, unruly anti-masquers. The chief convention of the masque was that it was performed for a person of high rank with unlimited power. At court it was the King who was at the heart of the masques, though he had played no direct part in them and was seated among the audience. He was an all-powerful offstage figure, who was

presented repeatedly with the story of how his authority
would drive out riot and disharmony; the masques, by
analogy, affirmed his right to control his subjects, merely
by being who he was, God's deputy on earth. In this
sense, masques were the King's own best dreams, fleshed
out for him by writers, musicians and designers.

When Jupiter appears in Posthumus' dream, in
V.4.30–92, a few of the conventions of the masque are
preserved but most are subverted. There is the usual
movement from dissonance to harmony, traced in the
conduct of the Leonati, Posthumus' dead family. The
ghosts, like anti-masquers, threaten to rebel unless Jupiter
answers their petition for justice, but the god frightens
them back into obedience. They speak first in fourteeners,
an old metre from the 1570s, as well as in couplets, broken
half-lines and triple rhymes (less irregular than they seem;
in 57–62, the Mother and Brothers complete triple rhymes
begun by Sicilius, as though the family were a classical
chorus). In response to their threats, Jupiter descends to
scare the ghosts, but also to reassure them. Down he
comes, on his eagle, throwing a thunderbolt and humbling
them, noticeably, in iambic verse and cross rhymes
(63–83). The fate of Posthumus is no care of theirs, he
tells them,

> Whom best I love, I cross, to make my gift
> The more delayed, delighted. (71–2)

At last, in 84–92, as Jupiter returns to heaven, Sicilius
praises him in blank verse, thus completing the progression from the language of the archaic dead to that of the
living, and from protest to awed obedience, patterns
familiar in the masque. Less expected is the condition of
the dreamer Posthumus. By contrast with an all-powerful

ruler watching a masque, Posthumus is an utterly helpless captive, and he is a commoner. He receives help from within the dream in a way that no masque would dare offer help to the King. Because the apparitions reach out to Posthumus from within their dream life – the ghosts risk a rebellion for him, and Jupiter leaves him a prophecy – he comes to believe he is favoured and should not kill himself. When he wakes Posthumus isn't revealed as another hidden powerful figure, like princes and aristocrats in masques, but as a penitent, still a prisoner, chastened but encouraged by what he has been shown.

Even less expected is Jupiter's unimportance. It is no surprise to hear him claim he has everything in hand, guiding and caring for Posthumus, his adopted son, but in truth it is Posthumus himself who has changed the course of his life, long before the dream begins, by acknowledging that he has sinned heinously against Imogen. He does what he can to make amends through confession and self-abasement (as a ragged soldier) and by incredible valour against the Romans. The ghosts speak for him in a solemn and moving way, but when Jupiter appears he roars over the spectres, insisting that he be taken seriously, like some grumpy geriatric, a father figure certainly, but a helpless one. The message might still appear to be benignly authoritarian – do what father Jupiter says and everything will be fine – but for the fact that in the play as a whole not one of the fathers or surrogate fathers can be trusted. In *Cymbeline* parents and step-parents block their children's marriages, or deceive their foster children, or try to poison them, or simply die before their children are born, or only half-recognize them a week after they have gone missing. In all, the message from Jupiter, especially since it ends in a riddling prophecy, doesn't have much fatherly authority about it.

In 1610 the shock of Jupiter divested of his powers was felt outside *Cymbeline* too. This was because of Galileo, who brought something utterly new into the minds of Englishmen, so momentous, and focused on Jupiter, that it made them doubt whether the heavens were still intact, or as under the control of a presiding father as they had once seemed. The event was Galileo's observation early in 1610, through his new instrument the telescope, that the planet Jupiter had four moons in orbit around it, a discovery that carried with it the staggering prospect that the existing closed model of the universe, with the sun and planets going round the Earth, was entirely wrong. Galileo quickly published his findings throughout Europe in a short pamphlet called *Siderius Nuncius*, 'a messenger from the stars'. The pamphlet was remarkably popular and influential, and spoken about everywhere (even the book itself was something new, a scientific publication written in very simple Latin, unimpeded by courtly rhetoric, and illustrated with clear plates). By the second half of 1610, even in England, on the edge of Catholic Europe, scientists, statesmen and writers knew what Galileo had seen, and what it meant: that the planetary system was heliocentric.

Jupiter's descent in *Cymbeline* is related to what Shakespeare too would have known of Galileo's pamphlet. In Act V, scene 4, when the god descends, he comes down through a solid roof that has to be opened before he can enter. When he leaves Jupiter tells his eagle to mount to his crystalline palace, and once the god has gone, Sicilius, enraptured and submissive, declares:

The marble pavement closes, he is entered
His radiant roof. (90–91)

The cosmology is conventional here, and by summer 1610 it must have seemed all too conventional to the elite members of Shakespeare's audience. Jupiter has to come and go through the crystalline spheres that were supposed to be packed tight, in ascending sizes, around the Earth (a globe at the centre of this, the Ptolemaic universe). It was no coincidence that just when Galileo was describing the planet Jupiter, with its four attendant moons, Shakespeare had the old mythological Jupiter come down through fine-cut crystal and hang pendant over four ancient courtly figures. It is evident that Shakespeare intended Jupiter's theophany as a deliberate and subtle twist in the game of old and new being played out constantly in *Cymbeline*. The ancient cosmology of fixed stars and musical spheres, with its roof still secure, was fittingly inhabited by Romans and Ancient Britons, who might dream of and place their trust in even more archaic gods and phantoms. After the *Siderius Nuncius* it simply wasn't possible for Shakespeare's audiences to be secure like this any more. If Galileo's telescope was correct, the crystalline roof had been an illusion all along.

Shakespeare examined the undermining of another omnipotent father, in startling and topical confrontations between old and new, in *The Tempest*, written around the time of *Cymbeline*. Here there are allusions to the most topical of events (the wreck of an English ship off the Bermudas in 1609, at the time mainly known about in manuscript and by word of mouth), while the location and character of Prospero's island are left provocatively inexact – a place where Old World gods are juxtaposed against New World monstrosities and marvels (it is significant that parallels between Galileo's discoveries and ones in the New World were made at once by Shakespeare's contemporaries). Further, Prospero, the father figure, is made to test his own authority in a masque of spirits, which he himself suddenly interrupts when he realizes he has grown too confident of his magic and his power over the destiny of human beings (in marrying his daughter and punishing his enemies).

The dangers of a father in control like this in *The Tempest* should remind us of a corollary to the aims of the Jupiter masque in *Cymbeline*. Shakespeare's own daring and energy, as an artist, complicate considerably the question of paternal authority in the masque, and in *Cymbeline* as a whole. Even as the authority of the old Powerful Ones diminishes *within* the fiction – a superannuated god is shown dangling absurdly over his dead subordinates – so the authority of Shakespeare, the hidden father of the whole play, increases. The Jupiter masque excels, in its ambition and effects, even the sculptures in Imogen's bedchamber, artefacts that were so intensely lifelike but which lacked speech, breath and movement. To make stone speak and move is beyond the powers of Imogen's sculptor, but to put living speech in the mouths of ancient spirits, albeit onstage in a seeming dream-life, is not beyond the artist Shakespeare – as it is not beyond him to make the seeming statue of a dead queen breathe and speak in the famous final moments of another of the late plays, *The Winter's Tale*.

The *Siderius Nuncius* had something else to give Shakespeare. When Galileo looked through the telescope out beyond Jupiter, at the Milky Way, he was astonished to see cluster after cluster of new stars, never visible before. The rudimentary star maps he published in the *Siderius Nuncius*, compiled from just a few weeks of observations, must have given everyone a shock; there were so many stars and they were obviously vast distances from the Earth.

In *Cymbeline* there are signs of this shock in Jachimo's speech in Act I, scene 6, when he feigns amazement that Posthumus prefers common prostitutes over Imogen. 'What, are men mad?' he asks, has Nature given us eyes to see the

> vaulted arch and the rich crop
> Of sea and land, which can distinguish 'twixt
> The fiery orbs above and the twinned stones
> Upon th'unnumbered beach, and can we not
> Partition make with spectacles so precious
> 'Twixt fair and foul? (31–7)

Imogen can't make out what Jachimo is saying, and why he is behaving as though he is thunderstruck. What he wants her to think is that he's been overwhelmed by wonder. In the Renaissance wonder was regarded as a special psychological precondition, often brought about by extreme sensations, which enabled human beings to acquire new knowledge. The reason for his wonder, he pretends, is profound compassion for Imogen, or even sudden love for her, but he also claims to be astonished that, even with the precious gift of human sight, Posthumus can't tell the difference between her beauty and a whore's ugliness ('fair and foul'). He expresses wonder too at what the eye is capable of, its range and powers of distinction. It can look high into the heavens and distinguish between the bright stars ('fiery orbs') but it can also spot the tiny differences between pebbles that look the same, lying among innumerable other pebbles on a beach. Unstated but apparent too is his wonder at the sheer scale and variety of the universe – eyes, stars and stones, sea and land, man-made arches and nature's harvest ('the rich crop').

The striking link between the stars and the beach covered with countless pebbles – possibly a way of saying that the stars too are uncountable – was not Shakespeare's, or at least it wasn't his to begin with. He took it from the Old Testament, from the story of God's promise to Abraham to multiply his children beyond measure. First God said to Abraham, 'Look up now unto heaven, and tell [count] the stars if thou be able to number them; and he said unto him, so shall thy seed be' (Genesis 15:5); and later, when Abraham had proved his faith by offering his son Isaac in sacrifice, God renewed his promise. 'I will greatly multiply thy seed as the stars of the heaven,' he told Abraham, 'and as the sand which is upon the seashore' (22:17). In *Cymbeline* the grains of sand became pebbles (with a memory perhaps of the 'unnumbered idle pebble' in *King Lear*, IV.6.21), and the seed, Abraham's descendants, became a harvest. The underlying meaning of the images may have changed too. In Genesis man can't measure what God has created, but in *Cymbeline* it is not clear whether he can or he can't. Perhaps the new power of sight is so great, that although the stones are not yet numbered, in time they will be, like the stars.

Galileo's discoveries released a stupendous new wonder into the world, and they caused a shift in wonder itself. Formerly, in the Christian West, wonder had been the experience of religious awe at God's covenant with man, as the deity revealed his divine plan to his creatures (the descent of Jupiter comes to mind of course), but now it became the ecstatic experience of understanding the physical world and the laws of the universe. This shift in wonder was completed much later in the seventeenth century, decades after Shakespeare's death, but in *Cymbeline*, as well as in the other late plays, there are signs of its beginning. Shakespeare didn't have an agenda in this – he wasn't a critic of or an apologist for the new science or the new world – but as an artist his eyes were certainly open to imminent change. Much of *Cymbeline* is concerned with wonder in the human heart and mind, as we have seen, so we shouldn't be timid about connecting it to the big new marvels and physical wonders appearing outside it. *Cymbeline* is a threshold play, where the future of human love and art, and various crises in faith and authority, are looked at and drawn out through the thrilling wonder of the Renaissance theatre.

John Pitcher

The Play in Performance

When, in ordinary conversation, we say that something is wonderful – a production of a play perhaps, or an actor's performance – we don't normally mean that it's full of wonder, merely that it's exceptionally good, or that it has excelled our expectations. Four centuries ago, when *Cymbeline* was first played, the notion of wonder, among critics and dramatists, was much more specific than this. Wonder, even more than catharsis, was the crowning experience of the Renaissance theatre. The dramatist, so the critics explained, would present his audience with events that seemed impossible or unpredictable, and give them characters who misunderstood the strange things happening to them. Everything should be designed to stimulate amazement in playgoers, including spectacular stage effects that would astound their senses. Then, when the wonder subsided, reason would reassert itself, and the audience would make sense of the marvels they'd seen (a theophany, say, or a miraculous reunion of parents and children). The aim of wonder, in theory, was to please the mind by engulfing it with new and unexpected sensations and to please it again when what had seemed irrational and inexplicable (twists in the plot or misrecognitions) could be explained and accounted for.

Wonder, in this special sense, was a category of experience that writers had been trying to explain and to recreate ever since the ancient philosophers had given it definition (or part definition) two thousand years before the Renaissance. By Shakespeare's day wonder had become the holy grail of aesthetics, the ultimate proof that the post-classical theatre could create, in pastoral and civic comedy as well as tragedy, an intense and enveloping experience (magical might be the modern word for it). Most of the critical thinking about wonder was done in the sixteenth-century Italian universities, but the theory was tested in practice in the public theatres in England before the Civil War. If we think of *Cymbeline* in these terms, as one of Shakespeare's ventures into wonder, the history of the play on the stage, littered with failures, incomprehension and mistakes, at once becomes intelligible. It is very clearly the history of a retreat from wonder, followed latterly (less than a century ago) by a gradual return to it.

The opening part of this history – performances of *Cymbeline* in Shakespeare's lifetime and immediately after – is largely unknown to us. There was a performance at the Globe in April or May 1611 (the one that Simon Forman saw, see pp. xxv–xxix), and another at court on New Year's Day 1634, played before Charles I. No other references to the play have been traced in the early records. This isn't really a surprise with public performances at the Globe or the Blackfriars, the theatres owned by the King's Men, Shakespeare's company, because many of their records must have been lost or destroyed early on (the Globe was burnt to the ground in 1613 and the company was broken up in the 1640s when the playhouses were shut down). Surviving court records are fuller, because they noted payments to playing compa-

nies from the Exchequer, but they are not always informative about specific plays. When the King's Men played
Cymbeline in 1634 it was said that the performance was
'well liked' by the King, but the absence of other references to the play suggests that it was never as popular at
court as, say, *The Winter's Tale*, which Forman also saw
in 1611, and which was also performed at Whitehall in
January 1634. The figures speak for themselves: from 1611
to 1624, when there is no mention of *Cymbeline*, there
were at least six court performances of *The Winter's Tale*.

Turning back to the early playhouse performances
brings us, once again, to the question of wonder. In
Cymbeline one obvious spectacular effect is the descent
of Jupiter in Act V, scene 3, but we can only guess how
this was managed on the public stage. The play would
have been performed at one of the two theatres owned
by the King's Men, but these differed markedly in design
and social ambience. The Globe was a largish three-
tiered circular structure, standing by itself in marshy fields
surrounding an entertainment district south of the
Thames. Most of its playing area and auditorium were
open to the sky. The Blackfriars, by contrast, was a small
rectangular, roofed, two-floor building on the salubrious
north bank of the river, a former chapel at the heart of
a refurbished shopping and leisure precinct for the elite.
The playing spaces in these venues were markedly
different, as were the acoustics, lighting, performance
times and seating, and probably the styles of acting and
the audiences too (predictably, the Blackfriars was more
expensive and prestigious). Winching Jupiter down in
the Blackfriars, where there was a full roof and a
chiaroscuro provided by candle light, would have been
different from staging the same thing in broad daylight
at the Globe.

Another question follows from this: did these social and technical differences between the theatres allow (or even encourage) different experiences of wonder? It has been claimed that when the King's Men acquired the Blackfriars in 1608 the potential of the new theatre directly affected how Shakespeare wrote his last plays. Indoors, and with artificial lighting and no worries about the weather, he could devise more spectacular entries that would rival those in court entertainments (the descent of Ariel as a harpy in *The Tempest*, for instance), and he could direct his poetry and wit at less boisterous and more sophisticated audiences than those in the Globe, and ones which were camp and self-mocking in their tastes. According to this view, the style and effects in *Cymbeline* were designed to please a coterie of moneyed young men, who would relish the play's old-fashioned manners and staginess as these were sent up for them in an elegant, comfortable auditorium. This argument, developed from the notion of the 'Two Audiences' (the Globe as the theatre for everyone, the Blackfriars as a peep-show for the jaded upper classes), is open to criticism on several grounds. The chief one is that the King's Men carried on playing at the Globe right up to the Civil War, even though they had rich pickings and more homogeneous audiences at court and in the Blackfriars. As we've seen, evidence of early performances has largely disappeared, but what survives does suggest that *Cymbeline*, like Shakespeare's other late plays, was performed before all sorts of audiences. When Forman saw the play at the Globe he obviously loved the wonder of coincidences and grossly mistaken identities (it's true he doesn't mention Jupiter, but he doesn't mention the bear or the statue in *The Winter's Tale* either). Wonder, the capacity to believe first and understand later, wasn't at this date socially stratified. The upper class didn't yet despise it as childish – something to be left to the lower class to take in with open mouths and empty heads – but this would happen soon enough, at least as regards the staging of *Cymbeline*.

After 1634 *Cymbeline* seems to have slipped out of sight for almost fifty years. When it next appeared onstage, at the Theatre Royal in Drury Lane in 1682, it had been altered in various ways by Thomas D'Urfey (1653–1723), who renamed it *The Injured Princess*, and implied that it was his own (he certainly didn't say it came from Shakespeare). D'Urfey changed the names of the principal characters – Imogen became Eugenia (meaning 'well-born') and Posthumus became Ursaces – and he made the Italian villain into a French one, Shattillion. He kept the wager plot, the flight of the princess into Wales and most of the story-line that leads to the reunions in the final scene. His most drastic cuts were in Act IV, where he disposed of the funeral dirge and Imogen waking beside the headless corpse, and in Act V, from which he removed the whole dream vision, with its ghosts, the appearance of Jupiter and the prophecy (he also dispensed with several of the revelations in V.4). The material he'd taken out of Act IV he replaced with a sub-plot of his own, in which Pisanio, an entirely rewritten role, kills a servant of Cloten's for trying to rape his daughter Clarinda, and is then blinded for it by Cloten.

Shakespeare's plays were frequently adapted for the Restoration stage, but the changes were not always improvements (Nahum Tate (1652–1715) famously re-wrote *King Lear* with a happy ending). D'Urfey's version of *Cymbeline*, however, even by Restoration standards, was unusually perverse. Because he misunderstood or couldn't tolerate the element of wonder in Acts IV and V, he simply eliminated it, leaving the play emotionally unintelligible. Regrettably, this has happened many times with *Cymbeline* since. The play, to be coherent, has to have the three scenes in which sleep is associated with death and with amazement: Imogen in her bedchamber (II.2), Imogen waking after her funeral (IV.2) and Posthumus dreaming of his dead family (V.4). Breaking or interrupting this sequence of wonder – which builds towards a climax with the startling descent of Jupiter – stimulates the feelings and expectations of an audience but leaves it unsatisfied (one might compare how, at a simpler level, a trick in stage magic needs an opening, a middle and an end which leaves us, at the least, impressed and gasping at the magician's skill and sleight of hand). The knowledge that this is the only way *Cymbeline* can be held together as a whole was forgotten, even in the theatre, for about another 250 years, until the 1920s in fact, when directors started to play the whole text, or at least to keep in the dirge, the ghosts and the Jupiter theophany.

The Injured Princess was probably a moderate success in the theatre. It was revived in 1718 and performed a dozen times or so in the next twenty years until *Cymbeline* spluttered back into life in 1746, in a production mounted at Covent Garden by Theophilus Cibber (1703–58). It was not until November 1761, however, when the actor-manager David Garrick (1717–79) put it on, that *Cymbeline* re-established itself securely in the theatre (there had been another hopeless stage adaptation in 1759, this time by William Hawkins, the Professor of Poetry at Oxford). Garrick's *Cymbeline* was enormously popular. In the fifteen years from 1761 to 1776, when Garrick retired, there were 132 performances. At one performance at Drury Lane in 1787 – the Benefit Night for Sarah Siddons, the great actress who had starred as Imogen – the box office takings were £650, a considerable sum at this date. Garrick himself played Posthumus for the first two seasons. It was a role his contemporaries thought was perfect for him: 'the pathos of his grief', one reviewer wrote, 'the fire of his rage, and the distraction of his jealousy, have never been surpassed, and possibly will never be equalled' (cited in Stone, 'A Century of *Cymbeline*'). Garrick was praised too for the changes he had made to the text of the play, shortening it (especially in Act V, where he omitted 500 lines), and repositioning the act divisions and some of the scenes. Once more, the opportunities for creating wonder in the play were consciously rejected. The funeral dirge was shortened and changed, and a brief scene was inserted immediately after it (moved from elsewhere in the play); this presumably made the pathos of Imogen's waking up easier to bear, but it must have broken the concentration and flow of feeling that Shakespeare was looking for from the audience. The dream vision was of course dropped. In the theatre the English middle class, in the latter half of the eighteenth century, didn't have much time for dead folk and pagan deities, and the marvellous, explosive element in Jupiter coming down from heaven was, for them, out of place in a serious play about noble and ignoble male passions and the sublime sufferings of a princess. Intriguingly, these incongruous elements were present in the theatre when Garrick's *Cymbeline* was performed, though they weren't inside the play but in the entertainment that regularly accompanied it. This was made up of short, jolly musicals, sentimental one-act plays, farces, pantomimes and topical pieces. Wonder, by now regarded as light relief for middlebrows, remained subdued at the heart of the play, but flourished, in this supplementary entertainment, just outside its precincts. If we ask ourselves what *Cymbeline* might have been like at this date, had the amazement, the poetry and music, and the disconcerting shifts of mood all been left in and mixed up, the answer is probably something like Mozart's final opera, *buffa* and *seria*, *The Magic Flute*.

Cymbeline had nothing of this about it in the Victorian theatre. The actor-managers, in the middle and at the end of the nineteenth century, William Macready and Henry Irving, kept to Garrick's formula for their productions (a virtuoso male lead, expensive and sumptuous sets, large numbers of extras, large amounts of text omitted), though they never enjoyed the same measure of popular success. In their hands the play became tamer and duller. In Macready's production of 1843 Cloten's severed head was not shown at all (it was replaced by his sword), and his corpse was covered entirely by a huge cloak, making nonsense of Imogen's handling and misrecognition of the dead body (it was too indelicate to be staged). Henry Irving was a very accomplished actor, and he put this to good and bad effect in his production at the Lyceum in 1896 by casting himself as Jachimo. As Shaw observed, in a famous review, Irving's Jachimo was a 'true impersonation, unbroken in its life-current from end to end', but it wasn't Shakespeare's Jachimo. Irving made the role into a character from a melodramatic novel, a 'handsome, bland and deadly seducer', as another (anonymous) reviewer put it (in the 1896 *Athenæum*, p. 428), who was 'spectral and ghoul-like' in the bedroom scene. Overplaying the part like this upset the balance of the play (Posthumus became little more than a foil to Jachimo), but Irving didn't care about *Cymbeline* anyway: it wasn't 'worth a damn' on the stage, he said, except for Imogen

(cited in Winter, *Shakespeare on the Stage*). The cult of
Imogen – which confused the role, the actress and Ideal
Womanhood – had reached its highest point by this date.
It had started with Sarah Siddons as Imogen in the Garrick
productions, passed to Helen Faucit (four productions in
ten years with Macready, the last in 1847), and was
bestowed, in 1896, on Ellen Terry. These were excellent
actresses (Terry's exchange of letters with Shaw just
before she played the part shows how talented she was),
but there was obviously something larger at work in the
fulsome praise that men of letters heaped on their
performances. In 1880 the poet Swinburne, risking sacri-
lege, declared that Imogen was 'woman above all
Shakespeare's women' – an idea and a phrase normally
reserved for the Virgin Mary herself (cited in the Arden
edition of *Cymbeline*, p. xliii). The worship of Imogen,
in truth, is less to do with the history of *Cymbeline* on
stage than the stage of history which men and women
had arrived at by 1900.

The temptation to turn *Cymbeline* into a star vehicle
for the actress playing Imogen (by sidelining the war plot
and by ignoring much of Act V) persisted into the twentieth century. Perhaps there was a feeling, obscure and
unsettling, that there was indeed something of wonder
in the play, so directors continued to look for it in
Imogen's wonderful character. By the 1920s and 1930s,
though, there were new thoughts about *Cymbeline*. G.
Wilson Knight, an academic, showed that, contrary to
what people had believed for about three centuries, the
dream vision in Act V – the ghosts, Jupiter and the
prophecy – was all Shakespeare's, and none of it could
be explained away as written by somebody else. This was
liberating because it meant that if Shakespeare wasn't
embarrassed by this strange stuff, there was no reason

why directors should be. New findings about the Jacobean theatre (how plays were performed on the open apron stage at the Globe and so forth) also helped shift attention to *Cymbeline* as a whole (new things could be tried out on stage the moment the mental frame of the proscenium arch was removed for instance). Even Shaw, who in 1896 had described the play as trashy and the final act as unplayable, came to realize he was wrong (his famous rewriting of Act V was really only a spoof, written decades after).

Audiences in the second half of the twentieth century were shown *Cymbeline* as never before, or not since 1634 perhaps. The breakthrough was in 1957 with Peter Hall's production at the Shakespeare Memorial Theatre in Stratford. Instead of apologizing for the heterogeneous elements in the play, Hall made the most of them. In his account *Cymbeline* began as a fairy tale (the sets were an enchanted castle and a dark forest) that had buried in it the most profound truths of good and evil. The action of the play worked to open the fairy tale so that the audience could see these truths. Hall's interpretation was a therapeutic one – how dreams, fantasies and visions may come to make sense to us and heal us – and this is perhaps as close to Renaissance wonder as modern minds, ruled by Freud, can manage at present. Reviewers thought that some of the 1957 production was too ornamented and fussy (especially the designs and costumes), but the cast, headed by Peggy Ashcroft in outstanding form as Imogen, kept the whole experience disciplined and precise, and very moving in places (the princes' speeches in Act IV, scene 4, often under-rated, were widely praised for their poignancy and beauty). Even the ghosts in Act V, scene 4, usually omitted, were allowed to speak, or rather chant, their eerie incantation.

Five years later, for the Royal Shakespeare Company
where he was now Artistic Director, Peter Hall made
possible another innovative production of *Cymbeline*.
Directed by William Gaskill, the 1962 *Cymbeline* literally
astonished its audience, because it was played in a vast
cleared space with a simple white set (we're used to such
things now, but they were very new then). Human
motives and conduct, measured against this capacious-
ness, looked small and often petty, and the breathtaking
descent of Jupiter overwhelmed everyone (no half meas-
ures with the eagle, since its wing-span was a third of
the width of the stage). Gaskill's production made the
audience look for connections between small interiors
and large exteriors – a private bedroom and an open
Welsh hillside – and to examine more closely, because of
the many changes in scale, the detail of the text. The
accomplished ensemble cast, with Vanessa Redgrave as
a primavera Imogen and Eric Porter as a subtle Jachimo,
proved that at the level of vocabulary and verse too
Cymbeline can be astonishing.

Productions after 1962 have become still more adven-
turous with scale and astonishing effects (Jean Gascon
in 1970 and Robin Phillips in 1986, both on the large
open stage at Stratford, Ontario), and more keen to
grapple with the strange moral world and genre of
Cymbeline. The BBC television version, directed by
Elijah Moshinsky in 1982, took the play closer to neurosis
and tragedy, and Peter Hall, in his 1988 production at
the National Theatre, eschewed fairy tale and reread the
play as a hard romance, the entwined stories of how
Imogen and Posthumus grow to full adulthood. What
lies ahead for *Cymbeline* onstage is not clear – wonder
has moved pretty much to the US cinema, with scale and
sensation in Steven Spielberg and engaging narratives

and recognitions in Robert Altman – but it will be interesting to see whether directors in the future can strike the balance this play needs between delight and wisdom, and wonder and knowledge.

John Pitcher

Further Reading

THE TEXT AND MODERN EDITIONS

There is a full-size facsimile of the text of *Cymbeline* in
The First Folio of Shakespeare, prepared by Charlton
Hinman, second edition with a new introduction by Peter
W. M. Blayney (1996). Blayney gives an authoritative
account of how the Folio was printed in *The First Folio
of Shakespeare* (1991). An energetic re-examination of
the text of *Cymbeline* is undertaken in *William Shakespeare: A Textual Companion*, by Stanley Wells and Gary
Taylor, with John Jowett and William Montgomery
(1987), pp. 604–11. Modern scholarly editions of
Cymbeline, all with reliable introductions to the text, are
available in the Arden Shakespeare (ed. J. M. Nosworthy,
1955; rev. 1960), the New Cambridge Shakespeare (ed.
J. C. Maxwell, 1960) and the Oxford Shakespeare (ed.
Roger Warren, 1998). Warren presents evidence that
Ralph Crane was the scribe whose manuscript was used
to print *Cymbeline*, and he sets out the debate about how
the characters' names should be spelt in a modern edition.
Warren's discussion of the date of the play is particularly valuable. Each of these editions has useful glosses
and line-by-line explanations, which can be supplemented
by C. T. Onions, *A Shakespeare Glossary*, revised by

Robert D. Eagleson (1986; corrected reprint, 1988), N. F. Blake, *A Grammar of Shakespeare's Language* (2002) and David and Ben Crystal, *Shakespeare's Words* (2002).

STUDIES OF SOURCES

The most complete collection of sources of *Cymbeline* is in volume VIII (1975) of *Narrative and Dramatic Sources of Shakespeare*, edited by Geoffrey Bullough.

In *Shakespeare and Multiplicity* (1993), pp. 29–35 and 217–19, Brian Gibbons writes very well about Shakespeare's indebtedness to Edmund Spenser in *Cymbeline*. The passages about the reigns of Kimbeline and his ancestors can be read in the Penguin edition of *The Faerie Queene*, ed. Thomas P. Roche, Jr., and C. Patrick O'Donnell, Jr. (1978). The best way to understand the masques written for the Jacobean court is to read Stephen Orgel's *The Illusion of Power* (1977), and the World's Classics selection of *Court Masques*, ed. David Lindley (1995). Galileo's *Siderius Nuncius*, translated as 'The Starry Messenger', is included in *Discoveries and Opinions of Galileo*, a collection of major works translated by Stillman Drake (1957). Marjorie Hope Nicolson examines the general impact of scientific discoveries on poets in seventeenth-century England in *The Breaking of the Circle* (1950). For the evidence of Shakespeare's debate with Ben Jonson, see E. A. J. Honigmann, *Shakespeare's Impact on His Contemporaries* (1982), pp. 40–45, 109–20; Anne Barton examines Jonson's changing views on Shakespeare in *Ben Jonson* (1984), esp. pp. 258 ff.

Another subsidiary but important influence on *Cymbeline* was the ancient Greek novel *The Aethiopica*, written by Heliodorus in the third or fourth century AD, translated into English in the middle of the sixteenth century. Carol Gesner gives a good description of what the novel is, and how the Elizabethans read it, in *Shakespeare and the Greek Romance* (1970). The standard account of Ovid's influence is Jonathan Bate, *Shakespeare and Ovid* (1993). In *Myth, Emblem, and Music in Shakespeare's 'Cymbeline'* (1992), Peggy Muñoz Simonds offers a large number of interesting visual sources for images and themes throughout the play. The recapitulative element in *Cymbeline* – where Shakespeare draws on passages and scenes in his earlier plays, or alludes to them – has not yet been dealt with as a whole, but a good example of what can be done is the essay by Ann Thompson on 'Philomel in *Titus Andronicus* and *Cymbeline*', *Shakespeare Survey 31* (1978), pp. 23–32.

CRITICAL APPROACHES

The major critics have said next to nothing about *Cymbeline*. The views of Dr Johnson and George Bernard Shaw, referred to in the Introduction, can be found in the Penguin Shakespeare Library editions, *Samuel Johnson on Shakespeare*, ed. H. R. Woudhuysen (1989), and *Shaw on Shakespeare*, ed. Edwin Wilson (1962). The modern critic who did most to rehabilitate *Cymbeline*, and to make sense of it, was G. Wilson Knight. As early as 1928 he set out to show that the entire play was Shakespeare's and that there was a wholeness to the design of it. The chapter in *The Crown of Life* (1947; reprinted many times) is still one of the most important discussions of *Cymbeline*. There is much in it to disagree with (his views on the British Empire and the Christian faith now look faded), but his understanding of the play's themes and his sensitivity to its poetry make the chapter indispensable.

Modern critical discussion of *Cymbeline* begins at the turn of the twentieth century. There are helpful surveys of what has been written on the play since then in Philip Edwards, 'Shakespeare's Romances: 1900–1957', *Shakespeare Survey 11* (1958), pp. 1–18; and F. David Hoeniger, 'Shakespeare's Romances since 1958', *Shakespeare Survey 29* (1976), pp. 1–10. Michael Taylor provides an introduction to a list of critical writing on the late plays in *Shakespeare: A Bibliographical Guide*, ed. Stanley Wells (1990), pp. 159–79. An extensive and annotated list of editions, critical essays and stage history (1378 items) is available in the Garland Shakespeare Bibliographies, *Cymbeline*, compiled by Henry E. Jacobs (1982). *Shakespeare: The Last Plays* (1999) is an anthology of essays edited by Kiernan Ryan, which concludes with an annotated list of modern discussions, more than twenty of them devoted to *Cymbeline*. Another useful collection, in the Penguin Shakespeare Library, is *Shakespeare's Later Comedies: An Anthology of Modern Criticism*, ed. D. J. Palmer (1971). An earlier anthology, *Later Shakespeare*, Stratford-upon-Avon Studies 8, ed. John Russell Brown and Bernard Harris (1966), contains essays referred to below. Frank Kermode's short but incisive study, *Shakespeare and the Final Plays* (1963), remains a useful introduction.

The formal shape of *Cymbeline* is a key critical issue. One approach to its form is through genre: how Shakespeare fused comedy with romance or, if we prefer, how he developed comedy so that it became romance. The standard work in this area is Northrop Frye's *A Natural Perspective: The Development of Shakespearean Comedy and Romance* (1965). Frye's anthropology is out of date, and his view that the world has a structure is presently

unfashionable, but he still offers an outstanding description of how ancient and modern men tried, in comedy, to
relate their wishes and desires to the natural world, of
growth and decay and of the contest of the seasons (spring
replacing winter, youth set against age). The best introduction to Roman comedy and its descendants in sixteenth-
century Italy and England is Leo Salingar, *Shakespeare and
the Traditions of Comedy* (1974). Romance is a notoriously
slippery term, but there are useful comments and caveats
in Stanley Wells, 'Shakespeare and Romance', first
published in the Russell Brown and Harris collection, but
available too in the Palmer anthology. Tragicomedy is also
difficult to define, but there are reliable discussions by
Joseph Loewenstein, 'Guarini and the Presence of Genre',
and by Barbara Mowat, 'Shakespearean Tragicomedy', in
Renaissance Tragicomedy, ed. Nancy Klein Maguire (1987).
Guarini's famous tragicomedy, *Il Pastor Fido* ('The Faithful
Shepherd'), is translated in the Penguin Classics anthology
Five Italian Renaissance Comedies, ed. Bruce Penman
(1990). The function of pastoral in *Cymbeline* is considered by Michael Taylor in 'The Pastoral Reckoning in
Cymbeline', *Shakespeare Survey 36* (1983), pp. 97–106.
Phyllis Rackin's chapter 'Anachronism and Nostalgia'
in her *Stages of History: Shakespeare's English Chronicles*
(1991), pp. 86–145, is a good introduction to this
difficult subject.

The question of the type of characters Shakespeare
created in *Cymbeline*, and the language he gave them to
speak, is addressed by Anne Barton in 'Leontes and the
Spider: Language and Speaker in Shakespeare's Last
Plays', in *Essays, Mainly Shakespearean* (1994), pp.
161–81. R. A. Foakes, in *Shakespeare: The Dark Comedies
to the Last Plays* (1971), explores the detached style of
characterization in all the late plays, particularly in

Cymbeline. In *Shakespeare's Language* (2000) Frank Kermode is quietly unhappy with the verse in *Cymbeline* (he thinks it is overworked in places) and with the tone, and he is dismissive about the difficulties of the language and the misplaced energy, as he sees it, in the syntax. There are more sympathetic and persuasive readings in Brian Gibbons, *Shakespeare and Multiplicity* (1993), pp. 37–44. For the many sexual quibbles and allusions in the play, which Kermode ignores, one can turn to Eric Partridge, *Shakespeare's Bawdy* (3rd edn, 1968), and to Gordon Williams, *A Glossary of Shakespeare's Sexual Language* (1997).

Critics have dealt with the sexual and familial issues in *Cymbeline* in different ways. Anne Barton considers, with careful delicacy, whether Imogen and Posthumus have consummated their marriage (which is crucial to our understanding of the end of Act II and much else in the play), in '"Wrying but a little": Marriage, Law and Sexuality in the Plays of Shakespeare', in *Essays, Mainly Shakespearean* (1994), pp. 3–30. There is a wide-ranging discussion of the problems and anxieties of maturation in Marjorie Garber, *Coming of Age in Shakespeare* (1981), while in *Suffocating Mothers* (1992), pp. 200–219 (reprinted in the Ryan anthology), Janet Adelman advances the proposition that fathers in *Cymbeline* are never mature enough to realize that it is women who give birth, not them (that is, they suffer from delusional, parthenogenetic fantasies, designed to protect them against the threat of the female). Other psychoanalytic interpretations seem tame in comparison with Adelman's, but two earlier essays are well worth reading: Ruth Nevo, *Shakespeare's Other Language*, (1987), pp. 62–94, and Murray M. Schwartz, 'Between Fantasy and Imagination: A Psychological Exploration

of *Cymbeline*', in *Psychoanalysis and Literary Process*, ed.
F. C. Crews (1970), pp. 219–83. The same Freudian
approach taken by Bruno Bettleheim in *The Uses of
Enchantment: The Meaning and Importance of Fairy Tales*
(1978) may be of particular interest to students of
Cymbeline. Studies of the sexual politics of the late plays
are listed and commented on in the Ryan anthology, pp.
281–5. The extraordinary literary convention by which
husbands were allowed to have their unfaithful wives
killed is the subject of a good article by Homer Swander,
'*Cymbeline* and the "Blameless Hero"', *English Literary
History* 31 (1964), pp. 249–70.

Political readings of *Cymbeline* have shifted in the past
fifty years. To begin with they were centripetal – the play
was pointing, Wilson Knight claimed, towards a big spiritual unity in the British state, or it contained a smaller
message, according to critics from the 1960s to the 1980s,
about King James's plans for the union of Scotland and
England. In the 1990s, however, political readings became
centrifugal, perhaps because real political life was
changing in the United Kingdom (with devolution in
Scotland and the disestablishment of the Church of
England a real possibility). Shakespeare was now said to
be interested, not in the centre of power, but in periph-
eral, local issues, not in the equilibrium of union but in
its disequilibrium. Useful starting points for these positions are Wilson Knight, *The Crown of Life* (1947); Leah
Marcus, '*Cymbeline* and the Unease of Topicality',
in *Puzzling Shakespeare: Local Reading and Its Discontents*
(1988), reprinted, in a shorter version, in the Ryan
anthology (see above); Jodi Mikalachki, 'The Masculine
Romance of Roman Britain and Early Modern English
Nationalism', *Shakespeare Quarterly* 46 (1995), pp. 301–22;
and Willy Maley, 'Postcolonial Shakespeare: British

Identity Formation and *Cymbeline*', in *Shakespeare's Late Plays: New Readings*, ed. Jennifer Richards and James Knowles (1999), pp. 145–57.

THE PLAY IN PERFORMANCE

There is no full-length history of *Cymbeline* on the stage, but C. B Young offers a concise survey in the 1960 New Cambridge Shakespeare edition. Simon Forman's description of the King's Men production in 1611 is available in all modern editions of *Cymbeline* (see above). For the view that *Cymbeline* was a self-conscious toy play for audiences in the Jacobean private playhouses, see Arthur C. Kirsch, '*Cymbeline* and Coterie Dramaturgy', *English Literary History* 34 (1967), pp. 285–306, reprinted in the Palmer anthology (see above). Garrick's productions of the 1760s and 1770s are well described by George Winchester Stone, Jr., in 'A Century of *Cymbeline*; or Garrick's Magic Touch', *Philological Quarterly* 54 (1975), pp. 310–22. For a vivid reconstruction of Macready's 1843 *Cymbeline*, see Carol J. Carlisle, 'Macready's Production of *Cymbeline*', in *Shakespeare and the Victorian Stage*, ed. Richard Foulkes (1986), pp. 138–52. There is a great deal to be learnt about the 1896 Irving production in *Shaw on Shakespeare* (1962), and *Ellen Terry and Bernard Shaw: A Correspondence*, ed. Christopher St John (1931). Further information about nineteenth-century productions of *Cymbeline*, including Irving's, can be found in William Winter, *Shakespeare on the Stage*, third series (1916), though one should be aware that Winter was highly conservative in outlook (he thought the Jupiter masque (V.4) couldn't possibly be by Shakespeare, and that directors ought to cut all the indecencies out of the play). Turning to *Cymbeline* on the stage in the first half of the twentieth century, the key discussions are Arthur Quiller-Couch, *Shakespeare's Workmanship* (1917), pp. 259–81 (good on the recognitions in V.5), and Harley Granville-Barker, *Prefaces to Shakespeare*, second series (1930), pp. 234–345 (good on many things). In *Cymbeline* (1989), a volume in the Shakespeare in Performance series, Roger Warren provides a vigorous account of selected productions in England and Canada, beginning with Peter Hall's at the Shakespeare Memorial Theatre in 1957. Warren's 'Spiritual Journeys: *Cymbeline*', a chapter in his *Staging Shakespeare's Late Plays* (1990), pp. 25–94, is a valuable commentary on the production that Hall directed at the National Theatre in 1988. The finale in *Cymbeline* has aroused different responses (even in the eighteenth century the scholar George Steevens praised it as 'a catastrophe which is intricate without confusion, and not more rich in ornament than in nature'). For an informative account of the cuts and revisions that have been made to the final scene over the years, see Ann Thompson, '*Cymbeline*'s Other Endings', in *The Appropriation of Shakespeare: Post-Renaissance Reconstructions of the Works and the Myth* (1991), pp. 203–20. There is an intelligent book on Renaissance theories of stage wonder, relevant to the finale, by T. G. Bishop, *Shakespeare and the Theatre of Wonder* (1996). In *Shakespeare's Tragicomic Vision* (1972), pp. 70–81, Joan Hartwig identifies significant connections between Posthumus and Cloten, and in 'Speculations on Doubling in Shakespeare's Plays', *Shakespeare: The Theatrical Dimension*, ed. Philip McGuire and David A. Samuelson (1979), pp. 103–31 (esp. pp. 121–5), Stephen Booth shows that Shakespeare may have written the roles so that they could be doubled.

CYMBELINE, KING OF BRITAIN

The Characters in the Play

The British Royal Family
CYMBELINE, King of Britain

GUIDERIUS, known as Polydore ⎱ Cymbeline's sons,
ARVIRAGUS, known as Cadwal ⎰ abducted to Wales
in their infancy by
Belarius

Princess IMOGEN, Cymbeline's daughter, later
disguised as a boy called Fidele
The QUEEN, Cymbeline's wife, Imogen's stepmother
Lord CLOTEN, her son, the King's stepson

The Britons
POSTHUMUS Leonatus, a Gentleman, banished for
marrying Imogen
PISANIO, his servant
BELARIUS, a banished Lord, disguised as Morgan,
supposed father of Polydore and Cadwal (Guiderius
and Arviragus)
CORNELIUS, a doctor
A LADY, attending on Imogen, called Helen
Two LORDS, attending on Cloten
A LORD, who flees the battlefield in Wales
Two GENTLEMEN, one a stranger to Britain
Two CAPTAINS
Two JAILERS

Philario's Guests in Rome
PHILARIO, an Italian, friend of Posthumus
JACHIMO, an Italian nobleman, brother to the Duke of
    Siena
A FRENCHMAN
A Dutchman
A Spaniard

The Romans
Caius LUCIUS, Ambassador to Britain, later commander
    of the Roman army
A SOOTHSAYER, called Philharmonus
Two SENATORS
A TRIBUNE
A CAPTAIN

Apparitions
JUPITER
SICILIUS Leonatus, father of Posthumus ⎫ Ghosts of
MOTHER of Posthumus   ⎬ the dead
Two BROTHERS of Posthumus   ⎭ Leonati

MESSENGERS
MUSICIANS attending on Cloten
Lords attending on Cymbeline, ladies attending on the
    Queen and on Imogen
Roman tribunes, British and Roman captains and
    soldiers

Enter two Gentlemen

FIRST GENTLEMAN
You do not meet a man but frowns. Our bloods
No more obey the heavens than our courtiers
Still seem as does the King.

SECOND GENTLEMAN   But what's the matter?

FIRST GENTLEMAN
His daughter, and the heir of's kingdom, whom
He purposed to his wife's sole son – a widow
That late he married – hath referred herself
Unto a poor but worthy gentleman. She's wedded,
Her husband banished, she imprisoned. All
Is outward sorrow, though I think the King
Be touched at very heart.

SECOND GENTLEMAN   None but the King?   10

FIRST GENTLEMAN
He that hath lost her too; so is the Queen,
That most desired the match. But not a courtier,
Although they wear their faces to the bent
Of the King's looks, hath a heart that is not
Glad of the thing they scowl at.

SECOND GENTLEMAN   And why so?

FIRST GENTLEMAN
He that hath missed the Princess is a thing

Too bad for bad report, and he that hath her,
I mean that married her – alack, good man,
And therefore banished – is a creature such
20   As to seek through the regions of the earth
For one his like, there would be something failing
In him that should compare. I do not think
So fair an outward and such stuff within
Endows a man but he.

SECOND GENTLEMAN   You speak him far.

FIRST GENTLEMAN
I do extend him, sir, within himself,
Crush him together rather than unfold
His measure duly.

SECOND GENTLEMAN What's his name and birth?

FIRST GENTLEMAN
I cannot delve him to the root. His father
Was called Sicilius, who did join his honour
30   Against the Romans with Cassibelan
But had his titles by Tenantius, whom
He served with glory and admired success,
So gained the sur-addition Leonatus;
And had, besides this gentleman in question,
Two other sons, who in the wars o'th'time
Died with their swords in hand; for which their father,
Then old and fond of issue, took such sorrow
That he quit being, and his gentle lady,
Big of this gentleman, our theme, deceased
40   As he was born. The King he takes the babe
To his protection, calls him Posthumus Leonatus,
Breeds him and makes him of his Bedchamber,
Puts to him all the learnings that his time
Could make him the receiver of, which he took
As we do air, fast as 'twas minist'red,
And in's spring became a harvest; lived in court –

Which rare it is to do – most praised, most loved;
A sample to the youngest, to th'more mature
A glass that feated them, and to the graver
A child that guided dotards. To his mistress,   50
For whom he now is banished, her own price
Proclaims how she esteemed him; and his virtue
By her election may be truly read
What kind of man he is.
SECOND GENTLEMAN   I honour him
   Even out of your report. But pray you tell me,
   Is she sole child to th'King?
FIRST GENTLEMAN   His only child.
   He had two sons – if this be worth your hearing,
   Mark it – the eldest of them at three years old,
   I'th'swathing clothes the other, from their nursery
   Were stol'n, and to this hour no guess in knowledge   60
   Which way they went.
SECOND GENTLEMAN   How long is this ago?
FIRST GENTLEMAN
   Some twenty years.
SECOND GENTLEMAN
   That a king's children should be so conveyed,
   So slackly guarded, and the search so slow
   That could not trace them!
FIRST GENTLEMAN   Howsoe'er 'tis strange,
   Or that the negligence may well be laughed at,
   Yet is it true, sir.
SECOND GENTLEMAN I do well believe you.
FIRST GENTLEMAN
   We must forbear. Here comes the gentleman,
   The Queen, and Princess.   *Exeunt*
      Enter the Queen, Posthumus, and Imogen
QUEEN
   No, be assured you shall not find me, daughter,   70

After the slander of most stepmothers,
Evil-eyed unto you. You're my prisoner, but
Your jailer shall deliver you the keys
That lock up your restraint. For you, Posthumus,
So soon as I can win th'offended King,
I will be known your advocate. Marry, yet
The fire of rage is in him, and 'twere good
You leaned unto his sentence with what patience
Your wisdom may inform you.

POSTHUMUS   Please your highness,
80   I will from hence today.

QUEEN   You know the peril.
I'll fetch a turn about the garden, pitying
The pangs of barred affections, though the King
Hath charged you should not speak together.   *Exit*

IMOGEN   O
Dissembling courtesy! How fine this tyrant
Can tickle where she wounds! My dearest husband,
I something fear my father's wrath, but nothing –
Always reserved my holy duty – what
His rage can do on me. You must be gone,
And I shall here abide the hourly shot
90   Of angry eyes, not comforted to live
But that there is this jewel in the world
That I may see again.

POSTHUMUS   My queen, my mistress.
O lady, weep no more, lest I give cause
To be suspected of more tenderness
Than doth become a man. I will remain
The loyal'st husband that did e'er plight troth.
My residence in Rome at one Philario's,
Who to my father was a friend, to me
Known but by letter; thither write, my queen,
100 And with mine eyes I'll drink the words you send,

Though ink be made of gall.
   Enter Queen

QUEEN   Be brief, I pray you.
If the King come, I shall incur I know not
How much of his displeasure. (*Aside*) Yet I'll move him
To walk this way. I never do him wrong
But he does buy my injuries, to be friends,
Pays dear for my offences.   *Exit*

POSTHUMUS   Should we be taking leave
As long a term as yet we have to live,
The loathness to depart would grow. Adieu.

IMOGEN
Nay, stay a little.
Were you but riding forth to air yourself,   110
Such parting were too petty. Look here, love:
This diamond was my mother's; take it, heart;
   She gives him a ring
But keep it till you woo another wife,
When Imogen is dead.

POSTHUMUS   How, how? another?
You gentle gods, give me but this I have,
And cere up my embracements from a next
With bonds of death. Remain, remain thou here
   He puts on the ring
While sense can keep it on. And, sweetest, fairest,
As I my poor self did exchange for you
To your so infinite loss, so in our trifles   120
I still win of you. For my sake wear this.
It is a manacle of love. I'll place it
Upon this fairest prisoner.
   He puts a bracelet on her arm

IMOGEN   O the gods!
When shall we see again?
   Enter Cymbeline and Lords

POSTHUMUS   Alack, the King!

CYMBELINE

Thou basest thing, avoid hence, from my sight!
If after this command thou fraught the court
With thy unworthiness, thou diest. Away!
Thou'rt poison to my blood.

POSTHUMUS   The gods protect you,
And bless the good remainders of the court.

130   I am gone.   *Exit*

IMOGEN   There cannot be a pinch in death
More sharp than this is.

CYMBELINE   O disloyal thing,
That shouldst repair my youth, thou heap'st
A year's age on me.

IMOGEN   I beseech you sir,
Harm not yourself with your vexation.
I am senseless of your wrath; a touch more rare
Subdues all pangs, all fears.

CYMBELINE   Past grace? Obedience?

IMOGEN

Past hope, and in despair; that way past grace.

CYMBELINE

That mightst have had the sole son of my queen!

IMOGEN

O blessed that I might not! I chose an eagle
140   And did avoid a puttock.

CYMBELINE

Thou took'st a beggar, wouldst have made my throne
A seat for baseness.

IMOGEN   No, I rather added
A lustre to it.

CYMBELINE   Oh thou vile one!

IMOGEN   Sir,
It is your fault that I have loved Posthumus.

You bred him as my playfellow, and he is
A man worth any woman, overbuys me
Almost the sum he pays.

CYMBELINE   What, art thou mad?

IMOGEN

Almost, sir. Heaven restore me! Would I were
A neatherd's daughter, and my Leonatus
Our neighbour shepherd's son.

Enter Queen

CYMBELINE   Thou foolish thing!   150
(*To the Queen*) They were again together; you have done
Not after our command. Away with her,
And pen her up.

QUEEN   Beseech your patience. Peace,
Dear lady daughter, peace. Sweet sovereign,
Leave us to ourselves, and make yourself some comfort
Out of your best advice.

CYMBELINE   Nay, let her languish
A drop of blood a day; and, being aged,
Die of this folly.   *Exit with Lords*

QUEEN   Fie, you must give way.

Enter Pisanio

Here is your servant. How now, sir? What news?

PISANIO

My lord your son drew on my master.

QUEEN   Ha!   160
No harm, I trust, is done?

PISANIO   There might have been,
But that my master rather played than fought,
And had no help of anger; they were parted
By gentlemen at hand.

QUEEN   I am very glad on't.

IMOGEN

Your son's my father's friend; he takes his part

To draw upon an exile. O brave sir!
I would they were in Afric both together,
Myself by with a needle, that I might prick
The goer-back. (*To Pisanio*) Why came you from your
        master?

PISANIO
170   On his command. He would not suffer me
To bring him to the haven; left these notes
Of what commands I should be subject to
When't pleased you to employ me.

QUEEN   This hath been
Your faithful servant. I dare lay mine honour
He will remain so.

PISANIO   I humbly thank your highness.

QUEEN
Pray walk a while.   *Exit*

IMOGEN
About some half-hour hence, pray you speak with me.
You shall at least go see my lord aboard.
For this time leave me.   *Exeunt*

I.2   *Enter Cloten and the two Lords*

FIRST LORD Sir, I would advise you to shift a shirt; the
violence of action hath made you reek as a sacrifice.
Where air comes out, air comes in; there's none abroad
so wholesome as that you vent.

CLOTEN If my shirt were bloody, then to shift it. Have I
hurt him?

SECOND LORD (*aside*) No, faith, not so much as his patience.

FIRST LORD Hurt him? His body's a passable carcass if
10   he be not hurt. It is a thoroughfare for steel if it be not
hurt.

SECOND LORD (*aside*) His steel was in debt — it went o'th'backside the town.

CLOTEN The villain would not stand me.

SECOND LORD (*aside*) No, but he fled forward still, toward your face.

FIRST LORD Stand you? You have land enough of your own, but he added to your having, gave you some ground.

SECOND LORD (*aside*) As many inches as you have oceans.   20
Puppies!

CLOTEN I would they had not come between us.

SECOND LORD (*aside*) So would I, till you had measured how long a fool you were upon the ground.

CLOTEN And that she should love this fellow and refuse me.

SECOND LORD (*aside*) If it be a sin to make a true election, she is damned.

FIRST LORD Sir, as I told you always, her beauty and her brain go not together. She's a good sign, but I have   30
seen small reflection of her wit.

SECOND LORD (*aside*) She shines not upon fools, lest the reflection should hurt her.

CLOTEN Come, I'll to my chamber. Would there had been some hurt done.

SECOND LORD (*aside*) I wish not so, unless it had been the fall of an ass, which is no great hurt.

CLOTEN You'll go with us?

FIRST LORD I'll attend your lordship.

CLOTEN Nay, come, let's go together.   40

SECOND LORD Well, my lord.   *Exeunt*

I.3   *Enter Imogen and Pisanio*

IMOGEN
       I would thou grew'st unto the shores o'th'haven
       And questioned'st every sail. If he should write
       And I not have it, 'twere a paper lost
       As offered mercy is. What was the last
       That he spake to thee?
PISANIO   It was his queen, his queen.
IMOGEN
       Then waved his handkerchief?
PISANIO   And kissed it, madam.
IMOGEN
       Senseless linen, happier therein than I.
       And that was all?
PISANIO   No, madam. For so long
       As he could make me with this eye or ear
10   Distinguish him from others, he did keep
       The deck, with glove or hat or handkerchief
       Still waving, as the fits and stirs of 's mind
       Could best express how slow his soul sailed on,
       How swift his ship.
IMOGEN   Thou shouldst have made him
       As little as a crow, or less, ere left
       To after-eye him.
PISANIO   Madam, so I did.
IMOGEN
       I would have broke mine eye-strings, cracked them, but
       To look upon him, till the diminution
       Of space had pointed him sharp as my needle;
20   Nay, followed him till he had melted from
       The smallness of a gnat to air; and then
       Have turned mine eye and wept. But good Pisanio,
       When shall we hear from him?
PISANIO   Be assured, madam,

With his next vantage.

IMOGEN

I did not take my leave of him, but had
Most pretty things to say. Ere I could tell him
How I would think on him at certain hours,
Such thoughts and such; or I could make him swear
The shes of Italy should not betray
Mine interest and his honour; or have charged him   30
At the sixth hour of morn, at noon, at midnight
T'encounter me with orisons, for then
I am in heaven for him; or ere I could
Give him that parting kiss which I had set
Betwixt two charming words, comes in my father,
And like the tyrannous breathing of the north,
Shakes all our buds from growing.

Enter a Lady

LADY   The Queen, madam,
Desires your highness' company.

IMOGEN (*to Pisanio*)

Those things I bid you do, get them dispatched.
I will attend the Queen.

PISANIO   Madam, I shall.   *Exeunt* 40

Enter Philario, Jachimo, a Frenchman, a Dutchman,   I.4
and a Spaniard

JACHIMO Believe it, sir, I have seen him in Britain. He
was then of a crescent note, expected to prove so worthy
as since he hath been allowed the name of. But I could
then have looked on him without the help of admiration, though the catalogue of his endowments had been
tabled by his side and I to peruse him by items.

PHILARIO You speak of him when he was less furnished

than now he is, with that which makes him both without and within.

FRENCHMAN I have seen him in France. We had very many there could behold the sun with as firm eyes as he.

JACHIMO This matter of marrying his king's daughter, wherein he must be weighed rather by her value than his own, words him, I doubt not, a great deal from the matter.

FRENCHMAN And then his banishment.

JACHIMO Ay, and the approbation of those that weep this lamentable divorce under her colours are wonderfully to extend him, be it but to fortify her judgement, which else an easy battery might lay flat for taking a beggar without less quality. But how comes it he is to sojourn with you? How creeps acquaintance?

PHILARIO His father and I were soldiers together, to whom I have been often bound for no less than my life.

Enter Posthumus

Here comes the Briton. Let him be so entertained amongst you as suits with gentlemen of your knowing to a stranger of his quality. I beseech you all, be better known to this gentleman, whom I commend to you as a noble friend of mine. How worthy he is I will leave to appear hereafter, rather than story him in his own hearing.

FRENCHMAN (*to Posthumus*) Sir, we have known together in Orléans.

POSTHUMUS Since when I have been debtor to you for courtesies which I will be ever to pay, and yet pay still.

FRENCHMAN Sir, you o'er-rate my poor kindness; I was glad I did atone my countryman and you. It had been pity you should have been put together with so mortal a purpose as then each bore, upon importance of so slight and trivial a nature.

POSTHUMUS By your pardon, sir, I was then a young trav-
eller – rather shunned to go even with what I heard
than in my every action to be guided by others' experiences – but upon my mended judgement, if I offend
not to say it is mended, my quarrel was not altogether
slight.

FRENCHMAN Faith, yes, to be put to the arbitrement of
swords, and by such two that would by all likelihood
have confounded one the other, or have fall'n both.

JACHIMO Can we with manners ask what was the dif-   50
ference?

FRENCHMAN Safely, I think. 'Twas a contention in public,
which may without contradiction suffer the report. It
was much like an argument that fell out last night, where
each of us fell in praise of our country mistresses; this
gentleman at that time vouching – and upon warrant
of bloody affirmation – his to be more fair, virtuous,
wise, chaste, constant, qualified, and less attemptable
than any the rarest of our ladies in France.

JACHIMO That lady is not now living, or this gentleman's   60
opinion, by this, worn out.

POSTHUMUS She holds her virtue still, and I my mind.

JACHIMO You must not so far prefer her 'fore ours of Italy.

POSTHUMUS Being so far provoked as I was in France, I
would abate her nothing, though I profess myself her
adorer, not her friend.

JACHIMO As fair and as good – a kind of hand-in-hand
comparison – had been something too fair and too good
for any lady in Britain. If she went before others I have
seen, as that diamond of yours outlustres many I   70
have beheld, I could not but believe she excelled many;
but I have not seen the most precious diamond that is,
nor you the lady.

POSTHUMUS I praised her as I rated her; so do I my stone.

JACHIMO What do you esteem it at?

POSTHUMUS More than the world enjoys.

JACHIMO Either your unparagoned mistress is dead, or
  she's outprized by a trifle.

POSTHUMUS You are mistaken. The one may be sold or
80 given, or if there were wealth enough for the purchase
  or merit for the gift. The other is not a thing for sale,
  and only the gift of the gods.

JACHIMO Which the gods have given you?

POSTHUMUS Which by their graces I will keep.

JACHIMO You may wear her in title yours; but you know
  strange fowl light upon neighbouring ponds. Your ring
  may be stolen too; so your brace of unprizable estima-
  tions, the one is but frail, and the other casual. A cunning
  thief, or a that way accomplished courtier, would hazard
90 the winning both of first and last.

POSTHUMUS Your Italy contains none so accomplished a
  courtier to convince the honour of my mistress, if in
  the holding or loss of that you term her frail. I do
  nothing doubt you have store of thieves; notwith-
  standing, I fear not my ring.

PHILARIO Let us leave here, gentlemen.

POSTHUMUS Sir, with all my heart. This worthy signor, I
  thank him, makes no stranger of me; we are familiar at
  first.

100 JACHIMO With five times so much conversation I should
  get ground of your fair mistress, make her go back even
  to the yielding, had I admittance and opportunity to
  friend.

POSTHUMUS No, no.

JACHIMO I dare thereupon pawn the moiety of my estate
  to your ring, which in my opinion o'ervalues it something. But I make my wager rather against your confidence than her reputation; and, to bar your offence

herein too, I durst attempt it against any lady in the
world.   110

POSTHUMUS You are a great deal abused in too bold a
persuasion, and I doubt not you sustain what you're
worthy of by your attempt.

JACHIMO What's that?

POSTHUMUS A repulse; though your attempt, as you call
it, deserve more – a punishment too.

PHILARIO Gentlemen, enough of this. It came in too
suddenly; let it die as it was born, and I pray you be
better acquainted.

JACHIMO Would I had put my estate and my neighbour's   120
on th'approbation of what I have spoke.

POSTHUMUS What lady would you choose to assail?

JACHIMO Yours, whom in constancy you think stands so
safe. I will lay you ten thousand ducats to your ring
that, commend me to the court where your lady is, with
no more advantage than the opportunity of a second
conference, and I will bring from thence that honour
of hers which you imagine so reserved.

POSTHUMUS I will wage against your gold, gold to it. My
ring I hold dear as my finger, 'tis part of it.   130

JACHIMO You are a friend, and therein the wiser. If you
buy ladies' flesh at a million a dram, you cannot preserve
it from tainting; but I see you have some religion in
you, that you fear.

POSTHUMUS This is but a custom in your tongue. You
bear a graver purpose, I hope.

JACHIMO I am the master of my speeches, and would
undergo what's spoken, I swear.

POSTHUMUS Will you? I shall but lend my diamond till
your return. Let there be covenants drawn between's.   140
My mistress exceeds in goodness the hugeness of your

unworthy thinking. I dare you to this match. Here's my
ring.

PHILARIO I will have it no lay.

JACHIMO By the gods, it is one. If I bring you no sufficient testimony that I have enjoyed the dearest bodily
part of your mistress, my ten thousand ducats are yours;
so is your diamond too. If I come off, and leave her in
such honour as you have trust in, she your jewel, this
150 your jewel, and my gold are yours – provided I have
your commendation for my more free entertainment.

POSTHUMUS I embrace these conditions; let us have articles betwixt us. Only, thus far you shall answer: if you
make your voyage upon her, and give me directly to
understand you have prevailed, I am no further your
enemy; she is not worth our debate. If she remain un-
seduced, you not making it appear otherwise, for your
ill opinion and th'assault you have made to her chastity,
you shall answer me with your sword.

160 JACHIMO Your hand – a covenant. We will have these
things set down by lawful counsel, and straight away
for Britain, lest the bargain should catch cold and starve.
I will fetch my gold, and have our two wagers recorded.

POSTHUMUS Agreed.

FRENCHMAN Will this hold, think you?

PHILARIO Signor Jachimo will not from it. Pray let us
follow 'em.   *Exeunt*

I.5   *Enter Queen, Ladies, and Cornelius*

QUEEN
Whiles yet the dew's on ground, gather those flowers.
Make haste. Who has the note of them?

LADY   I, madam.

QUEEN

    Dispatch.   *Exeunt Ladies*

    Now, master doctor, have you brought those drugs?

CORNELIUS

    Pleaseth your highness, ay. Here they are, madam.

    He gives her a small box

    But I beseech your grace, without offence –

    My conscience bids me ask – wherefore you have

    Commanded of me these most poisonous compounds,

    Which are the movers of a languishing death,

    But though slow, deadly.

QUEEN   I wonder, doctor,   10

    Thou ask'st me such a question. Have I not been

    Thy pupil long? Hast thou not learned me how

    To make perfumes, distil, preserve? Yea, so

    That our great King himself doth woo me oft

    For my confections? Having thus far proceeded,

    Unless thou think'st me devilish, is't not meet

    That I did amplify my judgement in

    Other conclusions? I will try the forces

    Of these thy compounds on such creatures as

    We count not worth the hanging – but none human –   20

    To try the vigour of them, and apply

    Allayments to their act, and by them gather

    Their several virtues and effects.

CORNELIUS   Your highness

    Shall from this practice but make hard your heart.

    Besides, the seeing these effects will be

    Both noisome and infectious.

QUEEN   Oh, content thee.

    Enter Pisanio

    (*Aside*) Here comes a flattering rascal; upon him

    Will I first work. He's factor for his master,

    And enemy to my son. (*Aloud*) How now, Pisanio?

30   Doctor, your service for this time is ended;
       Take your own way.
CORNELIUS (*aside*)   I do suspect you, madam.
       But you shall do no harm.
QUEEN (*to Pisanio*)   Hark thee, a word.
CORNELIUS (*aside*)
       I do not like her. She doth think she has
       Strange ling'ring poisons. I do know her spirit,
       And will not trust one of her malice with
       A drug of such damned nature. Those she has
       Will stupefy and dull the sense a while,
       Which first perchance she'll prove on cats and dogs,
       Then afterward up higher; but there is
40   No danger in what show of death it makes,
       More than the locking up the spirits a time,
       To be more fresh, reviving. She is fooled
       With a most false effect, and I the truer
       So to be false with her.
QUEEN   No further service, doctor,
       Until I send for thee.
CORNELIUS   I humbly take my leave.   *Exit*
QUEEN (*to Pisanio*)
       Weeps she still, sayst thou? Dost thou think in time
       She will not quench, and let instructions enter
       Where folly now possesses? Do thou work.
       When thou shalt bring me word she loves my son,
50   I'll tell thee on the instant thou art then
       As great as is thy master – greater, for
       His fortunes all lie speechless, and his name
       Is at last gasp. Return he cannot, nor
       Continue where he is. To shift his being
       Is to exchange one misery with another,
       And every day that comes comes to decay
       A day's work in him. What shalt thou expect

To be depender on a thing that leans,
Who cannot be new built, nor has no friends
So much as but to prop him?
She drops the box, and Pisanio picks it up
                                        Thou tak'st up   60
Thou know'st not what, but take it for thy labour.
It is a thing I made, which hath the King
Five times redeemed from death. I do not know
What is more cordial. Nay, I prithee take it,
It is an earnest of a farther good
That I mean to thee. Tell thy mistress how
The case stands with her; do't as from thyself.
Think what a chance thou changest on, but think
Thou hast thy mistress still; to boot, my son,
Who shall take notice of thee. I'll move the King   70
To any shape of thy preferment, such
As thou'lt desire; and then myself, I chiefly,
That set thee on to this desert, am bound
To load thy merit richly. Call my women.
Think on my words.   *Exit Pisanio*
                        A sly and constant knave,
Not to be shaked; the agent for his master,
And the remembrancer of her to hold
The hand-fast to her lord. I have given him that
Which, if he take, shall quite unpeople her
Of liegers for her sweet, and which she after,   80
Except she bend her humour, shall be assured
To taste of too.
Enter Pisanio and Ladies
                    So, so; well done, well done.
The violets, cowslips, and the primroses
Bear to my closet. Fare thee well, Pisanio.
Think on my words.
                                Exeunt Queen and Ladies

PISANIO   And shall do.
But when to my good lord I prove untrue,
I'll choke myself – there's all I'll do for you.   *Exit*

I.6   *Enter Imogen*

IMOGEN
    A father cruel and a stepdame false,
    A foolish suitor to a wedded lady
    That hath her husband banished. O, that husband,
    My supreme crown of grief, and those repeated
    Vexations of it! Had I been thief-stol'n,
    As my two brothers, happy; but most miserable
    Is the desire that's glorious. Blest be those,
    How mean soe'er, that have their honest wills,
    Which seasons comfort.
        Enter Pisanio and Jachimo
                                Who may this be? Fie!

PISANIO
10 Madam, a noble gentleman of Rome
    Comes from my lord with letters.

JACHIMO   Change you, madam:
    The worthy Leonatus is in safety,
    And greets your highness dearly.
        He gives her a letter

IMOGEN   Thanks, good sir.
    You're kindly welcome.

JACHIMO (*aside, as she reads*)
    All of her that is out of door most rich!
    If she be furnished with a mind so rare,
    She is alone th'Arabian bird, and I
    Have lost the wager. Boldness be my friend;
    Arm me audacity from head to foot,

Or, like the Parthian, I shall flying fight;   20
Rather, directly fly.

IMOGEN (*reads aloud*)

He is one of the noblest note, to whose kindnesses I am
most infinitely tied. Reflect upon him accordingly, as you
value your trust. Leonatus.

So far I read aloud,
But even the very middle of my heart
Is warmed by th'rest, and takes it thankfully.
You are as welcome, worthy sir, as I
Have words to bid you, and shall find it so
In all that I can do.

JACHIMO   Thanks, fairest lady.   30
What, are men mad? Hath Nature given them eyes
To see this vaulted arch and the rich crop
Of sea and land, which can distinguish 'twixt
The fiery orbs above and the twinned stones
Upon th'unnumbered beach, and can we not
Partition make with spectacles so precious
'Twixt fair and foul?

IMOGEN   What makes your admiration?

JACHIMO

It cannot be i'th'eye, for apes and monkeys,
'Twixt two such shes, would chatter this way and
Contemn with mows the other; nor i'th'judgement,   40
For idiots in this case of favour would
Be wisely definite; nor i'th'appetite –
Sluttery, to such neat excellence opposed,
Should make desire vomit emptiness,
Not so allured to feed.

IMOGEN

What is the matter, trow?

JACHIMO   The cloyèd will,
That satiate yet unsatisfied desire, that tub

Both filled and running, ravening first the lamb,
Longs after for the garbage.

IMOGEN   What, dear sir,
50 Thus raps you? Are you well?

JACHIMO   Thanks, madam, well.
(*To Pisanio*) Beseech you, sir,
Desire my man's abode where I did leave him.
He's strange and peevish.

PISANIO   I was going, sir,
To give him welcome.   *Exit*

IMOGEN
Continues well my lord? His health, beseech you?

JACHIMO
Well, madam.

IMOGEN
Is he disposed to mirth? I hope he is.

JACHIMO
Exceeding pleasant, none a stranger there
So merry and so gamesome: he is called
60 The Briton Reveller.

IMOGEN   When he was here
He did incline to sadness, and oft-times
Not knowing why.

JACHIMO   I never saw him sad.
There is a Frenchman his companion, one
An eminent monsieur, that, it seems, much loves
A Gallian girl at home. He furnaces
The thick sighs from him, whiles the jolly Briton –
Your lord, I mean – laughs from's free lungs, cries 'O,
Can my sides hold, to think that man, who knows
By history, report, or his own proof,
70 What woman is, yea, what she cannot choose
But must be, will's free hours languish for
Assured bondage?'

IMOGEN   Will my lord say so?
JACHIMO
  Ay, madam, with his eyes in flood with laughter.
  It is a recreation to be by
  And hear him mock the Frenchman. But heavens know
  Some men are much to blame.
IMOGEN   Not he, I hope.
JACHIMO
  Not he;
  But yet heaven's bounty towards him might
  Be used more thankfully. In himself 'tis much;
  In you, which I account his, beyond all talents.   80
  Whilst I am bound to wonder, I am bound
  To pity too.
IMOGEN   What do you pity, sir?
JACHIMO
  Two creatures heartily.
IMOGEN   Am I one, sir?
  You look on me: what wreck discern you in me
  Deserves your pity?
JACHIMO   Lamentable! What,
  To hide me from the radiant sun, and solace
  I'th'dungeon by a snuff?
IMOGEN   I pray you, sir,
  Deliver with more openness your answers
  To my demands. Why do you pity me?
JACHIMO
  That others do –   90
  I was about to say, enjoy your – but
  It is an office of the gods to venge it,
  Not mine to speak on't.
IMOGEN   You do seem to know
  Something of me, or what concerns me. Pray you,
  Since doubting things go ill often hurts more

Than to be sure they do – for certainties
Either are past remedies, or, timely knowing,
The remedy then born – discover to me
What both you spur and stop.

JACHIMO   Had I this cheek
100   To bathe my lips upon; this hand whose touch,
Whose every touch, would force the feeler's soul
To th'oath of loyalty; this object which
Takes prisoner the wild motion of mine eye,
Fixing it only here: should I, damned then,
Slaver with lips as common as the stairs
That mount the Capitol; join grips with hands
Made hard with hourly falsehood – falsehood as
With labour; then by-peeping in an eye
Base and illustrous as the smoky light
110   That's fed with stinking tallow – it were fit
That all the plagues of hell should at one time
Encounter such revolt.

IMOGEN   My lord, I fear,
Has forgot Britain.

JACHIMO   And himself. Not I,
Inclined to this intelligence, pronounce
The beggary of his change, but 'tis your graces
That from my mutest conscience to my tongue
Charms this report out.

IMOGEN   Let me hear no more.

JACHIMO
O dearest soul, your cause doth strike my heart
With pity that doth make me sick. A lady
120   So fair, and fastened to an empery
Would make the great'st king double, to be partnered
With tomboys hired with that self exhibition
Which your own coffers yield; with diseased ventures
That play with all infirmities for gold

Which rottenness can lend nature; such boiled stuff
As well might poison poison! Be revenged,
Or she that bore you was no queen, and you
Recoil from your great stock.

IMOGEN   Revenged?
How should I be revenged? If this be true –
As I have such a heart that both mine ears   130
Must not in haste abuse – if it be true,
How should I be revenged?

JACHIMO   Should he make me
Live like Diana's priest betwixt cold sheets
Whiles he is vaulting variable ramps,
In your despite, upon your purse – revenge it.
I dedicate myself to your sweet pleasure,
More noble than that runagate to your bed,
And will continue fast to your affection,
Still close as sure.

IMOGEN   What ho, Pisanio!

JACHIMO
Let me my service tender on your lips.   140

IMOGEN
Away, I do condemn mine ears that have
So long attended thee. If thou wert honourable
Thou wouldst have told this tale for virtue, not
For such an end thou seek'st, as base as strange.
Thou wrong'st a gentleman who is as far
From thy report as thou from honour, and
Solicits here a lady that disdains
Thee and the devil alike. What ho, Pisanio!
The King my father shall be made acquainted
Of thy assault. If he shall think it fit   150
A saucy stranger in his court to mart
As in a Romish stew, and to expound
His beastly mind to us, he hath a court

He little cares for, and a daughter who
He not respects at all. What ho, Pisanio!

JACHIMO

O happy Leonatus! I may say
The credit that thy lady hath of thee
Deserves thy trust, and thy most perfect goodness
Her assured credit. Blessèd live you long,
160   A lady to the worthiest sir that ever
Country called his; and you his mistress, only
For the most worthiest fit. Give me your pardon.
I have spoke this to know if your affiance
Were deeply rooted, and shall make your lord
That which he is new o'er; and he is one
The truest mannered, such a holy witch
That he enchants societies into him;
Half all men's hearts are his.

IMOGEN   You make amends.

JACHIMO

He sits 'mongst men like a descended god.
170   He hath a kind of honour sets him off
More than a mortal seeming. Be not angry,
Most mighty princess, that I have adventured
To try your taking of a false report, which hath
Honoured with confirmation your great judgement
In the election of a sir so rare,
Which you know cannot err. The love I bear him
Made me to fan you thus, but the gods made you,
Unlike all others, chaffless. Pray, your pardon.

IMOGEN

All's well, sir. Take my power i'th'court for yours.

JACHIMO

180   My humble thanks. I had almost forgot
T'entreat your grace but in a small request,
And yet of moment too, for it concerns

Your lord; myself and other noble friends
Are partners in the business.

IMOGEN   Pray what is't?

JACHIMO

Some dozen Romans of us, and your lord –
The best feather of our wing – have mingled sums
To buy a present for the Emperor,
Which I, the factor for the rest, have done
In France. 'Tis plate of rare device, and jewels
Of rich and exquisite form; their value's great,   190
And I am something curious, being strange,
To have them in safe stowage. May it please you
To take them in protection?

IMOGEN   Willingly,
And pawn mine honour for their safety; since
My lord hath interest in them, I will keep them
In my bedchamber.

JACHIMO   They are in a trunk
Attended by my men. I will make bold
To send them to you, only for this night.
I must aboard tomorrow.

IMOGEN   O no, no.

JACHIMO

Yes, I beseech, or I shall short my word   200
By length'ning my return. From Gallia
I crossed the seas on purpose and on promise
To see your grace.

IMOGEN   I thank you for your pains;
But not away tomorrow.

JACHIMO   O, I must, madam.
Therefore I shall beseech you, if you please
To greet your lord with writing, do't tonight.
I have outstood my time, which is material
To th'tender of our present.

IMOGEN   I will write.
Send your trunk to me; it shall safe be kept,
And truly yielded you. You're very welcome. *Exeunt*

*

II.1   *Enter Cloten and the two Lords*

CLOTEN Was there ever man had such luck? When I kissed
the jack, upon an upcast to be hit away! I had a hundred
pound on't, and then a whoreson jackanapes must take
me up for swearing, as if I borrowed mine oaths of
him, and might not spend them at my pleasure.

FIRST LORD What got he by that? You have broke his
pate with your bowl.

SECOND LORD (*aside*) If his wit had been like him that
broke it, it would have run all out.

CLOTEN When a gentleman is disposed to swear it is not
for any standers-by to curtail his oaths. Ha?

SECOND LORD No, my lord (*aside*) – nor crop the ears of
them.

CLOTEN Whoreson dog! I give him satisfaction? Would
he had been one of my rank.

SECOND LORD (*aside*) To have smelled like a fool.

CLOTEN I am not vexed more at anything in th'earth. A
pox on't! I had rather not be so noble as I am; they dare
not fight with me because of the Queen my mother.
Every jack-slave hath his bellyful of fighting, and I
must go up and down like a cock that nobody can match.

SECOND LORD (*aside*) You are cock and capon too, and
you crow cock with your comb on.

CLOTEN Sayest thou?

SECOND LORD It is not fit your lordship should undertake
every companion that you give offence to.

CLOTEN No, I know that, but it is fit I should commit
offence to my inferiors.

SECOND LORD Ay, it is fit for your lordship only.

CLOTEN Why, so I say.   30

FIRST LORD Did you hear of a stranger that's come to
court tonight?

CLOTEN A stranger, and I not know on't?

SECOND LORD (*aside*) He's a strange fellow himself and
knows it not.

FIRST LORD There's an Italian come, and 'tis thought,
one of Leonatus' friends.

CLOTEN Leonatus? A banished rascal; and he's another,
whatsoever he be. Who told you of this stranger?

FIRST LORD One of your lordship's pages.   40

CLOTEN Is it fit I went to look upon him? Is there no
derogation in't?

SECOND LORD You cannot derogate, my lord.

CLOTEN Not easily, I think.

SECOND LORD (*aside*) You are a fool granted, therefore
your issues, being foolish, do not derogate.

CLOTEN Come, I'll go see this Italian. What I have lost
today at bowls I'll win tonight of him. Come, go.

SECOND LORD I'll attend your lordship.

Exeunt Cloten and the First Lord

That such a crafty devil as is his mother   50
Should yield the world this ass! A woman that
Bears all down with her brain, and this her son
Cannot take two from twenty, for his heart,
And leave eighteen. Alas, poor princess,
Thou divine Imogen, what thou endur'st,
Betwixt a father by thy stepdame governed,
A mother hourly coining plots, a wooer
More hateful than the foul expulsion is
Of thy dear husband, than that horrid act

60   Of the divorce he'd make. The heavens hold firm
        The walls of thy dear honour; keep unshaked
        That temple, thy fair mind, that thou mayst stand
        T'enjoy thy banished lord and this great land!   *Exit*

II.2   *Imogen is in bed, reading. There is a trunk in the room.*
            Enter a Lady, called Helen

IMOGEN
        Who's there? My woman Helen?

LADY   Please you, madam.

IMOGEN
        What hour is it?

LADY   Almost midnight, madam.

IMOGEN
        I have read three hours then. Mine eyes are weak.
        Fold down the leaf where I have left. To bed.
        Take not away the taper, leave it burning,
        And if thou canst awake by four o'th'clock,
        I prithee call me. Sleep hath seized me wholly.
                                            Exit Helen

        To your protection I commend me, gods.
        From fairies and the tempters of the night
10   Guard me, beseech ye.   *She sleeps*
            Jachimo gets out of the trunk

JACHIMO
        The crickets sing, and man's o'er-laboured sense
        Repairs itself by rest. Our Tarquin thus
        Did softly press the rushes ere he wakened
        The chastity he wounded. Cytherea,
        How bravely thou becom'st thy bed; fresh lily,
        And whiter than the sheets. That I might touch,
        But kiss, one kiss; rubies unparagoned,
        How dearly they do't. 'Tis her breathing that

Perfumes the chamber thus. The flame o'th'taper
Bows toward her, and would underpeep her lids   20
To see th' enclosèd lights, now canopied
Under these windows, white and azure-laced
With blue of heaven's own tint. But my design –
To note the chamber. I will write all down.

He writes notes

Such and such pictures; there the window; such
Th'adornment of her bed; the arras, figures,
Why, such and such; and the contents o'th'story.
Ah, but some natural notes about her body
Above ten thousand meaner movables
Would testify, t'enrich mine inventory.   30
O sleep, thou ape of death, lie dull upon her,
And be her sense but as a monument,
Thus in a chapel lying. Come off, come off;
As slippery as the Gordian knot was hard.

He takes the bracelet from her arm

'Tis mine, and this will witness outwardly,
As strongly as the conscience does within,
To th'madding of her lord. On her left breast
A mole, cinque-spotted, like the crimson drops
I'th'bottom of a cowslip. Here's a voucher
Stronger than ever law could make: this secret   40
Will force him think I have picked the lock and ta'en
The treasure of her honour. No more. To what end?
Why should I write this down that's riveted,
Screwed to my memory? She hath been reading late
The tale of Tereus. Here the leaf's turned down
Where Philomel gave up. I have enough.
To th'trunk again, and shut the spring of it.
Swift, swift, you dragons of the night, that dawning
May bare the raven's eye! I lodge in fear;
Though this a heavenly angel, hell is here.   50

Clock strikes
One, two, three. Time, time!
　　Exit into the trunk, which is removed, with the bed

II.3　　*Enter Cloten and the two Lords, outside Imogen's rooms*

FIRST LORD Your lordship is the most patient man in loss,
　　the most coldest that ever turned up ace.

CLOTEN It would make any man cold to lose.

FIRST LORD But not every man patient after the noble
　　temper of your lordship. You are most hot and furious
　　when you win.

CLOTEN Winning will put any man into courage. If I
　　could get this foolish Imogen, I should have gold
　　enough. It's almost morning, is't not?

10 FIRST LORD Day, my lord.

CLOTEN I would this music would come. I am advised to
　　give her music o'mornings; they say it will penetrate.
　　　　Enter Musicians
　　Come on, tune. If you can penetrate her with your
　　fingering, so; we'll try with tongue too. If none will
　　do, let her remain; but I'll never give o'er. First, a very
　　excellent good-conceited thing; after, a wonderful sweet
　　air, with admirable rich words to it; and then let her
　　consider.

MUSICIAN (*sings, with music*)
Hark, hark, the lark at heaven's gate sings,
20　　And Phoebus 'gins arise,
His steeds to water at those springs
　　On chaliced flowers that lies;
And winking Mary-buds begin to ope their golden eyes;
With every thing that pretty is, my lady sweet arise:
　　Arise, arise!

CLOTEN So, get you gone. If this penetrate, I will consider

your music the better; if it do not, it is a vice in her
ears which horse hairs and calves' guts, nor the voice
of unpaved eunuch to boot, can never amend.

Exeunt Musicians

Enter Cymbeline and the Queen

SECOND LORD Here comes the King.   30

CLOTEN I am glad I was up so late, for that's the reason
I was up so early. He cannot choose but take this service
I have done fatherly. Good morrow to your majesty,
and to my gracious mother.

CYMBELINE
Attend you here the door of our stern daughter?
Will she not forth?

CLOTEN   I have assailed her
With musics, but she vouchsafes no notice.

CYMBELINE
The exile of her minion is too new,
She hath not yet forgot him. Some more time
Must wear the print of his remembrance out,   40
And then she's yours.

QUEEN (*to Cloten*)   You are most bound to th'King,
Who lets go by no vantages that may
Prefer you to his daughter. Frame yourself
To orderly solicits, and be friended
With aptness of the season; make denials
Increase your services; so seem as if
You were inspired to do those duties which
You tender to her; that you in all obey her,
Save when command to your dismission tends,
And therein you are senseless.

CLOTEN   Senseless? Not so.   50

Enter a Messenger

MESSENGER
So like you, sir, ambassadors from Rome;

The one is Caius Lucius.
CYMBELINE   A worthy fellow,
Albeit he comes on angry purpose now;
But that's no fault of his. We must receive him
According to the honour of his sender,
And towards himself, his goodness forespent on us,
We must extend our notice. Our dear son,
When you have given good morning to your mistress,
Attend the Queen and us. We shall have need
60   T'employ you towards this Roman. Come, our queen.
                                        Exeunt all but Cloten

CLOTEN
If she be up, I'll speak with her; if not,
Let her lie still and dream.   *He knocks*
                        By your leave, ho!
I know her women are about her; what
If I do line one of their hands? 'Tis gold
Which buys admittance – oft it doth – yea, and makes
Diana's rangers false themselves, yield up
Their deer to th'stand o'th'stealer; and 'tis gold
Which makes the true man killed and saves the thief,
Nay, sometime hangs both thief and true man. What
70   Can it not do and undo? I will make
One of her women lawyer to me, for
I yet not understand the case myself.   *He knocks*
By your leave.
    Enter a Lady

LADY
Who's there that knocks?
CLOTEN   A gentleman.
LADY   No more?
CLOTEN
Yes, and a gentlewoman's son.
LADY (*aside*)   That's more

Than some whose tailors are as dear as yours
Can justly boast of. (*Aloud*) What's your lordship's
    pleasure?

CLOTEN

Your lady's person. Is she ready?

LADY   Ay.

(*Aside*) To keep her chamber.

CLOTEN   There is gold for you.

Sell me your good report.   80

LADY

How, my good name? or to report of you
What I shall think is good?

    Enter Imogen

                The Princess.   *Exit*

CLOTEN

Good morrow, fairest sister, your sweet hand.

IMOGEN

Good morrow, sir. You lay out too much pains
For purchasing but trouble. The thanks I give
Is telling you that I am poor of thanks,
And scarce can spare them.

CLOTEN   Still I swear I love you.

IMOGEN

If you but said so, 'twere as deep with me.
If you swear still, your recompense is still
That I regard it not.

CLOTEN   This is no answer.   90

IMOGEN

But that you shall not say I yield being silent,
I would not speak. I pray you, spare me. Faith,
I shall unfold equal discourtesy
To your best kindness. One of your great knowing
Should learn, being taught, forbearance.

CLOTEN

    To leave you in your madness, 'twere my sin.
    I will not.

IMOGEN   Fools cure not mad folks.

CLOTEN

    Do you call me fool?

IMOGEN   As I am mad, I do.
    If you'll be patient, I'll no more be mad;
100   That cures us both. I am much sorry, sir,
    You put me to forget a lady's manners
    By being so verbal; and learn now for all
    That I, which know my heart, do here pronounce
    By th'very truth of it, I care not for you,
    And am so near the lack of charity
    To accuse myself I hate you; which I had rather
    You felt than make't my boast.

CLOTEN   You sin against
    Obedience, which you owe your father. For
    The contract you pretend with that base wretch,
110   One bred of alms and fostered with cold dishes,
    With scraps o'th'court, it is no contract, none.
    And though it be allowed in meaner parties –
    Yet who than he more mean? – to knit their souls,
    On whom there is no more dependency
    But brats and beggary, in self-figured knot,
    Yet you are curbed from that enlargement by
    The consequence o'th' crown, and must not foil
    The precious note of it with a base slave,
    A hilding for a livery, a squire's cloth,
120   A pantler – not so eminent.

IMOGEN   Profane fellow,
    Wert thou the son of Jupiter, and no more
    But what thou art besides, thou wert too base
    To be his groom; thou wert dignified enough,

Even to the point of envy, if 'twere made
Comparative for your virtues to be styled
The under-hangman of his kingdom, and hated
For being preferred so well.

CLOTEN   The south fog rot him!

IMOGEN

He never can meet more mischance than come
To be but named of thee. His meanest garment
That ever hath but clipped his body is dearer   130
In my respect than all the hairs above thee,
Were they all made such men. How now, Pisanio!

    Enter Pisanio

CLOTEN

'His garment'? Now the devil –

IMOGEN (*to Pisanio*)

To Dorothy my woman hie thee presently.

CLOTEN

'His garment'?

IMOGEN   I am sprited with a fool,
Frighted, and angered worse. Go bid my woman
Search for a jewel that too casually
Hath left mine arm. It was thy master's. 'Shrew me
If I would lose it for a revenue
Of any king's in Europe! I do think   140
I saw't this morning; confident I am
Last night 'twas on mine arm; I kissed it.
I hope it be not gone to tell my lord
That I kiss aught but he.

PISANIO   'Twill not be lost.

IMOGEN

I hope so. Go and search.   *Exit Pisanio*

CLOTEN   You have abused me.
'His meanest garment'?

IMOGEN   Ay, I said so, sir.

    If you will make't an action, call witness to't.

CLOTEN

    I will inform your father.

IMOGEN   Your mother too.

    She's my good lady, and will conceive, I hope,

150   But the worst of me. So I leave you, sir,

    To th'worst of discontent.   *Exit*

CLOTEN   I'll be revenged.

    'His meanest garment'! Well.   *Exit*

II.4   *Enter Posthumus and Philario*

POSTHUMUS

    Fear it not, sir. I would I were so sure

    To win the King as I am bold her honour

    Will remain hers.

PHILARIO   What means do you make to him?

POSTHUMUS

    Not any; but abide the change of time,

    Quake in the present winter's state, and wish

    That warmer days would come. In these feared hopes

    I barely gratify your love; they failing,

    I must die much your debtor.

PHILARIO

    Your very goodness and your company

10   O'erpays all I can do. By this, your king

    Hath heard of great Augustus. Caius Lucius

    Will do's commission throughly. And I think

    He'll grant the tribute, send th'arrearages,

    Or look upon our Romans, whose remembrance

    Is yet fresh in their grief.

POSTHUMUS   I do believe,

    Statist though I am none, nor like to be,

    That this will prove a war, and you shall hear

The legions now in Gallia sooner landed
In our not-fearing Britain than have tidings
Of any penny tribute paid. Our countrymen   20
Are men more ordered than when Julius Caesar
Smiled at their lack of skill but found their courage
Worthy his frowning at. Their discipline,
Now mingled with their courages, will make known
To their approvers they are people such
That mend upon the world.

    Enter Jachimo

PHILARIO   See, Jachimo!
POSTHUMUS
The swiftest harts have posted you by land,
And winds of all the corners kissed your sails
To make your vessel nimble.
PHILARIO   Welcome, sir.
POSTHUMUS
I hope the briefness of your answer made   30
The speediness of your return.
JACHIMO   Your lady
Is one of the fairest that I have looked upon.
POSTHUMUS
And therewithal the best, or let her beauty
Look through a casement to allure false hearts,
And be false with them.
JACHIMO   Here are letters for you.
POSTHUMUS
Their tenor good, I trust.

    He reads the letters

JACHIMO   'Tis very like.
PHILARIO
Was Caius Lucius in the Briton court
When you were there?
JACHIMO   He was expected then,

But not approached.

POSTHUMUS   All is well yet.
40 Sparkles this stone as it was wont, or is't not
Too dull for your good wearing?

JACHIMO   If I have lost it,
I should have lost the worth of it in gold.
I'll make a journey twice as far t'enjoy
A second night of such sweet shortness which
Was mine in Britain; for the ring is won.

POSTHUMUS
The stone's too hard to come by.

JACHIMO   Not a whit,
Your lady being so easy.

POSTHUMUS   Make not, sir,
Your loss your sport. I hope you know that we
Must not continue friends.

JACHIMO   Good sir, we must,
50 If you keep covenant. Had I not brought
The knowledge of your mistress home, I grant
We were to question farther; but I now
Profess myself the winner of her honour,
Together with your ring, and not the wronger
Of her or you, having proceeded but
By both your wills.

POSTHUMUS   If you can make't apparent
That you have tasted her in bed, my hand
And ring is yours. If not, the foul opinion
You had of her pure honour gains or loses
60 Your sword or mine, or masterless leaves both
To who shall find them.

JACHIMO   Sir, my circumstances,
Being so near the truth as I will make them,
Must first induce you to believe; whose strength
I will confirm with oath, which I doubt not

You'll give me leave to spare when you shall find
You need it not.

POSTHUMUS   Proceed.

JACHIMO   First, her bedchamber –
Where I confess I slept not, but profess
Had that was well worth watching – it was hanged
With tapestry of silk and silver; the story
Proud Cleopatra when she met her Roman,   70
And Cydnus swelled above the banks, or for
The press of boats or pride: a piece of work
So bravely done, so rich, that it did strive
In workmanship and value; which I wondered
Could be so rarely and exactly wrought,
Since the true life on't was –

POSTHUMUS   This is true,
And this you might have heard of here, by me
Or by some other.

JACHIMO   More particulars
Must justify my knowledge.

POSTHUMUS   So they must,
Or do your honour injury.

JACHIMO   The chimney   80
Is south the chamber, and the chimney-piece
Chaste Dian bathing. Never saw I figures
So likely to report themselves; the cutter
Was as another Nature, dumb; outwent her,
Motion and breath left out.

POSTHUMUS   This is a thing
Which you might from relation likewise reap,
Being, as it is, much spoke of.

JACHIMO   The roof o'th'chamber
With golden cherubins is fretted. Her andirons –
I had forgot them – were two winking Cupids
Of silver, each on one foot standing, nicely   90

Depending on their brands.

POSTHUMUS   This is her honour!
Let it be granted you have seen all this – and praise
Be given to your remembrance – the description
Of what is in her chamber nothing saves
The wager you have laid.

JACHIMO   Then, if you can
Be pale, I beg but leave to air this jewel. See!

He shows the bracelet

And now 'tis up again; it must be married
To that your diamond. I'll keep them.

POSTHUMUS   Jove!
Once more let me behold it. Is it that
100   Which I left with her?

JACHIMO   Sir, I thank her, that.
She stripped it from her arm. I see her yet.
Her pretty action did outsell her gift,
And yet enriched it too. She gave it me,
And said she prized it once.

POSTHUMUS   May be she plucked it off
To send it me.

JACHIMO   She writes so to you, doth she?

POSTHUMUS
O, no, no, no, 'tis true! Here, take this too.

He gives Jachimo the ring

It is a basilisk unto mine eye,
Kills me to look on't. Let there be no honour
Where there is beauty, truth where semblance, love
110   Where there's another man. The vows of women
Of no more bondage be to where they are made
Than they are to their virtues, which is nothing.
O, above measure false!

PHILARIO   Have patience, sir,
And take your ring again; 'tis not yet won.

It may be probable she lost it, or
Who knows if one her women, being corrupted,
Hath stol'n it from her?
POSTHUMUS   Very true,
And so I hope he came by't. Back my ring.
Render to me some corporal sign about her
More evident than this; for this was stol'n.   120
JACHIMO
By Jupiter, I had it from her arm.
POSTHUMUS
Hark you, he swears, by Jupiter he swears.
'Tis true, nay, keep the ring, 'tis true. I am sure
She would not lose it. Her attendants are
All sworn and honourable. They induced to steal it?
And by a stranger? No, he hath enjoyed her.
The cognizance of her incontinency
Is this: she hath bought the name of whore thus dearly.
There, take thy hire, and all the fiends of hell
Divide themselves between you!
PHILARIO   Sir, be patient.   130
This is not strong enough to be believed
Of one persuaded well of.
POSTHUMUS   Never talk on't.
She hath been colted by him.
JACHIMO   If you seek
For further satisfying, under her breast –
Worthy the pressing – lies a mole, right proud
Of that most delicate lodging. By my life,
I kissed it, and it gave me present hunger
To feed again, though full. You do remember
This stain upon her?
POSTHUMUS   Ay, and it doth confirm
Another stain, as big as hell can hold,   140
Were there no more but it.

JACHIMO   Will you hear more?

POSTHUMUS

Spare your arithmetic, never count the turns.
Once, and a million!

JACHIMO   I'll be sworn.

POSTHUMUS   No swearing.
If you will swear you have not done't, you lie,
And I will kill thee if thou dost deny
Thou'st made me cuckold.

JACHIMO   I'll deny nothing.

POSTHUMUS

O that I had her here to tear her limb-meal!
I will go there and do't i'th'court, before
Her father. I'll do something.   *Exit*

PHILARIO   Quite besides
150   The government of patience! You have won.
Let's follow him and pervert the present wrath
He hath against himself.

JACHIMO   With all my heart.   *Exeunt*

        Enter Posthumus

POSTHUMUS

Is there no way for men to be, but women
Must be half-workers? We are all bastards,
And that most venerable man which I
Did call my father was I know not where
When I was stamped. Some coiner with his tools
Made me a counterfeit; yet my mother seemed
The Dian of that time: so doth my wife
160   The nonpareil of this. O vengeance, vengeance!
Me of my lawful pleasure she restrained,
And prayed me oft forbearance; did it with
A pudency so rosy the sweet view on't
Might well have warmed old Saturn; that I thought her
As chaste as unsunned snow. O all the devils!

This yellow Jachimo in an hour, was't not?
Or less – at first? Perchance he spoke not, but
Like a full-acorned boar, a German one,
Cried 'O!' and mounted; found no opposition
But what he looked for should oppose and she   170
Should from encounter guard. Could I find out
The woman's part in me – for there's no motion
That tends to vice in man but I affirm
It is the woman's part: be it lying, note it,
The woman's; flattering, hers; deceiving, hers;
Lust and rank thoughts, hers, hers; revenges, hers;
Ambitions, covetings, change of prides, disdain,
Nice longing, slanders, mutability,
All faults that name, nay, that hell knows, why, hers
In part or all, but rather all. For even to vice   180
They are not constant, but are changing still,
One vice but of a minute old for one
Not half so old as that. I'll write against them,
Detest them, curse them; yet 'tis greater skill
In a true hate, to pray they have their will:
The very devils cannot plague them better.   *Exit*

*

Enter in state, Cymbeline, the Queen, Cloten, and   III.1
Lords at one door, and at another, Caius Lucius and
attendants

CYMBELINE

Now say, what would Augustus Caesar with us?

LUCIUS

When Julius Caesar – whose remembrance yet
Lives in men's eyes, and will to ears and tongues
Be theme and hearing ever – was in this Britain,

And conquered it, Cassibelan, thine uncle,
Famous in Caesar's praises no whit less
Than in his feats deserving it, for him
And his succession granted Rome a tribute,
Yearly three thousand pounds, which by thee lately
Is left untendered.

10

QUEEN   And to kill the marvel,
Shall be so ever.

CLOTEN   There be many Caesars
Ere such another Julius. Britain's a world
By itself, and we will nothing pay
For wearing our own noses.

QUEEN   That opportunity
Which then they had to take from's, to resume
We have again. Remember, sir, my liege,
The kings your ancestors, together with
The natural bravery of your isle, which stands
As Neptune's park, ribbèd and palèd in

20

With oaks unscalable and roaring waters,
With sands that will not bear your enemies' boats,
But suck them up to th'topmast. A kind of conquest
Caesar made here, but made not here his brag
Of 'came and saw and overcame'. With shame –
The first that ever touched him – he was carried
From off our coast, twice beaten; and his shipping,
Poor ignorant baubles, on our terrible seas
Like eggshells moved upon their surges, cracked
As easily 'gainst our rocks: for joy whereof

30

The famed Cassibelan, who was once at point –
O giglot fortune! – to master Caesar's sword,
Made Lud's Town with rejoicing fires bright,
And Britons strut with courage.

CLOTEN Come, there's no more tribute to be paid. Our
kingdom is stronger than it was at that time, and, as I

said, there is no more such Caesars. Other of them may
have crooked noses, but to owe such straight arms, none.

CYMBELINE Son, let your mother end.

CLOTEN We have yet many among us can grip as hard as
   Cassibelan. I do not say I am one, but I have a hand.   40
   Why tribute? Why should we pay tribute? If Caesar
   can hide the sun from us with a blanket, or put the moon
   in his pocket, we will pay him tribute for light; else, sir,
   no more tribute, pray you now.

CYMBELINE (*to Lucius*)
            You must know,
   Till the injurious Romans did extort
   This tribute from us, we were free. Caesar's ambition,
   Which swelled so much that it did almost stretch
   The sides o'th'world, against all colour here
   Did put the yoke upon's, which to shake off   50
   Becomes a warlike people, whom we reckon
   Ourselves to be. We do say then to Caesar,
   Our ancestor was that Mulmutius which
   Ordained our laws, whose use the sword of Caesar
   Hath too much mangled, whose repair and franchise
   Shall, by the power we hold, be our good deed,
   Though Rome be therefore angry. Mulmutius made
         our laws,
   Who was the first of Britain which did put
   His brows within a golden crown and called
   Himself a king.

LUCIUS   I am sorry, Cymbeline,   60
   That I am to pronounce Augustus Caesar –
   Caesar, that hath more kings his servants than
   Thyself domestic officers – thine enemy.
   Receive it from me, then: war and confusion
   In Caesar's name pronounce I 'gainst thee. Look
   For fury not to be resisted. Thus defied,

I thank thee for myself.

CYMBELINE   Thou art welcome, Caius.
Thy Caesar knighted me; my youth I spent
Much under him; of him I gathered honour,
70   Which he to seek of me again, perforce,
Behoves me keep at utterance. I am perfect
That the Pannonians and Dalmatians for
Their liberties are now in arms, a precedent
Which not to read would show the Britons cold;
So Caesar shall not find them.

LUCIUS   Let proof speak.

CLOTEN His majesty bids you welcome. Make pastime with us
a day or two, or longer. If you seek us afterwards in other
terms, you shall find us in our salt-water girdle. If you
beat us out of it, it is yours; if you fall in the adventure,
80   our crows shall fare the better for you, and there's an end.

LUCIUS So, sir.

CYMBELINE
I know your master's pleasure, and he mine.
All the remain is 'Welcome'.   *Exeunt*

III.2   *Enter Pisanio, with letters, reading one of them*

PISANIO
How? Of adultery? Wherefore write you not
What monster's her accuser? Leonatus,
O master, what a strange infection
Is fall'n into thy ear! What false Italian,
As poisonous-tongued as handed, hath prevailed
On thy too ready hearing? Disloyal? No.
She's punished for her truth, and undergoes,
More goddess-like than wife-like, such assaults
As would take in some virtue. O my master,
10   Thy mind to hers is now as low as were

Thy fortunes. How? That I should murder her,
Upon the love and truth and vows which I
Have made to thy command? I her? Her blood?
If it be so to do good service, never
Let me be counted serviceable. How look I,
That I should seem to lack humanity
So much as this fact comes to? (*Reads aloud*) *Do't. The*
      letter
That I have sent her, by her own command
Shall give thee opportunity. O damned paper,
Black as the ink that's on thee! Senseless bauble,   20
Art thou a fedary for this act, and look'st
So virgin-like without? Lo, here she comes.
      Enter Imogen
I am ignorant in what I am commanded.

IMOGEN

How now, Pisanio?

PISANIO

Madam, here is a letter from my lord.

IMOGEN

Who, thy lord? That is my lord, Leonatus?
O learned indeed were that astronomer
That knew the stars as I his characters –
He'd lay the future open. You good gods,
Let what is here contained relish of love,   30
Of my lord's health, of his content – yet not
That we two are asunder, let that grieve him;
Some griefs are med'cinable, that is one of them,
For it doth physic love – of his content
All but in that. Good wax, thy leave. Blest be
You bees that make these locks of counsel. Lovers
And men in dangerous bonds pray not alike;
Though forfeiters you cast in prison, yet
You clasp young Cupid's tables. Good news, gods!

She opens the letter and reads aloud

40 *Justice and your father's wrath, should he take me in his*
dominion, could not be so cruel to me as you, O the dearest of
creatures, would even renew me with your eyes. Take notice
that I am in Cambria, at Milford Haven. What your own love
will out of this advise you, follow. So he wishes you all happi-
ness, that remains loyal to his vow, and your increasing in love,
                                          Leonatus Posthumus.

O for a horse with wings! Hear'st thou, Pisanio?
He is at Milford Haven. Read, and tell me
How far 'tis thither. If one of mean affairs
50 May plod it in a week, why may not I
Glide thither in a day? Then, true Pisanio,
Who long'st like me to see thy lord, who long'st –
O let me bate – but not like me; yet long'st
But in a fainter kind; O, not like me,
For mine's beyond beyond; say, and speak thick –
Love's counsellor should fill the bores of hearing,
To th'smothering of the sense – how far it is
To this same blessed Milford. And by th'way
Tell me how Wales was made so happy as
60 T'inherit such a haven. But first of all,
How we may steal from hence; and for the gap
That we shall make in time from our hence-going
And our return, to excuse; but first, how get hence.
Why should excuse be born or ere begot?
We'll talk of that hereafter. Prithee speak,
How many score of miles may we well ride
'Twixt hour and hour?
PISANIO   One score 'twixt sun and sun,
Madam, 's enough for you, and too much too.
IMOGEN
Why, one that rode to's execution, man,
70 Could never go so slow. I have heard of riding wagers

Where horses have been nimbler than the sands
That run i'th'clock's behalf. But this is fool'ry.
Go bid my woman feign a sickness, say
She'll home to her father; and provide me presently
A riding-suit, no costlier than would fit
A franklin's housewife.

PISANIO   Madam, you're best consider.

IMOGEN

I see before me, man. Nor here, nor here,
Nor what ensues, but have a fog in them
That I cannot look through. Away, I prithee,
Do as I bid thee. There's no more to say: 80
Accessible is none but Milford way.   *Exeunt*

Enter Belarius, Guiderius, and Arviragus   III.3

BELARIUS

A goodly day, not to keep house with such
Whose roof's as low as ours. Stoop, boys; this gate
Instructs you how t'adore the heavens, and bows you
To a morning's holy office. The gates of monarchs
Are arched so high that giants may jet through
And keep their impious turbans on, without
Good morrow to the sun. Hail, thou fair heaven!
We house i'th'rock, yet use thee not so hardly
As prouder livers do.

GUIDERIUS   Hail, heaven!

ARVIRAGUS   Hail, heaven!

BELARIUS

Now for our mountain sport. Up to yon hill.   10
Your legs are young; I'll tread these flats. Consider,
When you above perceive me like a crow,
That it is place which lessens and sets off,
And you may then revolve what tales I have told you

Of courts, of princes, of the tricks in war;
This service is not service, so being done,
But being so allowed. To apprehend thus
Draws us a profit from all things we see,
And often to our comfort shall we find
20   The sharded beetle in a safer hold
Than is the full-winged eagle. O, this life
Is nobler than attending for a check,
Richer than doing nothing for a babe,
Prouder than rustling in unpaid-for silk;
Such gain the cap of him that makes him fine,
Yet keeps his book uncrossed. No life to ours.

GUIDERIUS

Out of your proof you speak: we poor unfledged
Have never winged from view o'th'nest, nor know not
What air's from home. Haply this life is best,
30   If quiet life be best; sweeter to you
That have a sharper known; well corresponding
With your stiff age; but unto us it is
A cell of ignorance, travelling abed,
A prison, or a debtor that not dares
To stride a limit.

ARVIRAGUS   What should we speak of
When we are old as you? When we shall hear
The rain and wind beat dark December, how,
In this our pinching cave, shall we discourse
The freezing hours away? We have seen nothing.
40   We are beastly: subtle as the fox for prey,
Like warlike as the wolf for what we eat;
Our valour is to chase what flies; our cage
We make a choir, as doth the prisoned bird,
And sing our bondage freely.

BELARIUS   How you speak!
Did you but know the city's usuries,

And felt them knowingly; the art o'th'court,
As hard to leave as keep, whose top to climb
Is certain falling, or so slipp'ry that
The fear's as bad as falling; the toil o'th'war,
A pain that only seems to seek out danger   50
I'th'name of fame and honour, which dies i'th'search
And hath as oft a sland'rous epitaph
As record of fair act; nay, many times
Doth ill deserve by doing well; what's worse,
Must curtsy at the censure. O boys, this story
The world may read in me. My body's marked
With Roman swords, and my report was once
First with the best of note. Cymbeline loved me,
And when a soldier was the theme, my name
Was not far off. Then was I as a tree   60
Whose boughs did bend with fruit; but in one night
A storm, or robbery, call it what you will,
Shook down my mellow hangings, nay, my leaves,
And left me bare to weather.

GUIDERIUS   Uncertain favour!
BELARIUS
My fault being nothing, as I have told you oft,
But that two villains, whose false oaths prevailed
Before my perfect honour, swore to Cymbeline
I was confederate with the Romans. So
Followed my banishment, and this twenty years
This rock and these demesnes have been my world,   70
Where I have lived at honest freedom, paid
More pious debts to heaven than in all
The fore-end of my time. But up to th'mountains!
This is not hunters' language. He that strikes
The venison first shall be the lord o'th'feast,
To him the other two shall minister,
And we will fear no poison which attends

In place of greater state. I'll meet you in the valleys.
                        Exeunt Guiderius and Arviragus
How hard it is to hide the sparks of nature!
80 These boys know little they are sons to th'King,
Nor Cymbeline dreams that they are alive.
They think they are mine, and though trained up thus
        meanly
I'th'cave wherein they bow, their thoughts do hit
The roofs of palaces, and nature prompts them
In simple and low things to prince it much
Beyond the trick of others. This Polydore,
The heir of Cymbeline and Britain, who
The King his father called Guiderius – Jove!
When on my three-foot stool I sit and tell
90 The warlike feats I have done, his spirits fly out
Into my story; say 'Thus mine enemy fell,
And thus I set my foot on's neck', even then
The princely blood flows in his cheek, he sweats,
Strains his young nerves, and puts himself in posture
That acts my words. The younger brother, Cadwal,
Once Arviragus, in as like a figure
Strikes life into my speech, and shows much more
His own conceiving.
    A hunting horn sounds
                        Hark, the game is roused!
O Cymbeline, heaven and my conscience knows
100 Thou didst unjustly banish me, whereon
At three and two years old I stole these babes,
Thinking to bar thee of succession as
Thou reft'st me of my lands. Euriphile,
Thou wast their nurse; they took thee for their mother,
And every day do honour to her grave.
Myself, Belarius, that am Morgan called,

They take for natural father.
The horn sounds again

                              The game is up.   *Exit*

Enter Pisanio and Imogen   III.4
IMOGEN
    Thou told'st me when we came from horse, the place
    Was near at hand. Ne'er longed my mother so
    To see me first as I have now. Pisanio, man,
    Where is Posthumus? What is in thy mind
    That makes thee stare thus? Wherefore breaks that sigh
    From th'inward of thee? One but painted thus
    Would be interpreted a thing perplexed
    Beyond self-explication. Put thyself
    Into a haviour of less fear, ere wildness
    Vanquish my staider senses. What's the matter?   10
    Why tender'st thou that paper to me with
    A look untender? If't be summer news,
    Smile to't before; if winterly, thou need'st
    But keep that count'nance still.
        Pisanio gives her a letter

                              My husband's hand?
    That drug-damned Italy hath out-craftied him,
    And he's at some hard point. Speak, man; thy tongue
    May take off some extremity, which to read
    Would be even mortal to me.
PISANIO   Please you read,
    And you shall find me, wretched man, a thing
    The most disdained of fortune.   20
IMOGEN (*reads aloud*)
    Thy mistress, Pisanio, hath played the strumpet in my bed,
    the testimonies whereof lie bleeding in me. I speak not out of
    weak surmises, but from proof as strong as my grief and as

certain as I expect my revenge. That part thou, Pisanio, must
act for me, if thy faith be not tainted with the breach of hers.
Let thine own hands take away her life. I shall give thee oppor-
tunity at Milford Haven. She hath my letter for the purpose,
where, if thou fear to strike and to make me certain it is done,
thou art the pander to her dishonour, and equally to me disloyal.

PISANIO

30   What shall I need to draw my sword? The paper
      Hath cut her throat already. No, 'tis slander,
      Whose edge is sharper than the sword, whose tongue
      Outvenoms all the worms of Nile, whose breath
      Rides on the posting winds and doth belie
      All corners of the world. Kings, queens, and states,
      Maids, matrons, nay, the secrets of the grave
      This viperous slander enters. What cheer, madam?

IMOGEN

      False to his bed? What is it to be false?
      To lie in watch there and to think on him?
40   To weep 'twixt clock and clock? If sleep charge nature,
      To break it with a fearful dream of him
      And cry myself awake? That's false to's bed, is it?

PISANIO

      Alas, good lady.

IMOGEN

      I false? Thy conscience witness. Jachimo,
      Thou didst accuse him of incontinency;
      Thou then look'dst like a villain; now, methinks,
      Thy favour's good enough. Some jay of Italy,
      Whose mother was her painting, hath betrayed him.
      Poor I am stale, a garment out of fashion,
50   And for I am richer than to hang by th'walls
      I must be ripped. To pieces with me! O,
      Men's vows are women's traitors! All good seeming,
      By thy revolt, O husband, shall be thought

Put on for villainy; not born where't grows,
But worn a bait for ladies.

PISANIO   Good madam, hear me.

IMOGEN

True honest men, being heard like false Aeneas,
Were in his time thought false, and Sinon's weeping
Did scandal many a holy tear, took pity
From most true wretchedness. So thou, Posthumus,
Wilt lay the leaven on all proper men: 60
Goodly and gallant shall be false and perjured
From thy great fail. Come, fellow, be thou honest,
Do thou thy master's bidding. When thou seest him,
A little witness my obedience. Look,
I draw the sword myself; take it, and hit
The innocent mansion of my love, my heart.
Fear not, 'tis empty of all things but grief;
Thy master is not there, who was indeed
The riches of it. Do his bidding; strike.
Thou mayst be valiant in a better cause,   70
But now thou seem'st a coward.

PISANIO   Hence, vile instrument,
Thou shalt not damn my hand!

IMOGEN   Why, I must die,
And if I do not by thy hand, thou art
No servant of thy master's. Against self-slaughter
There is a prohibition so divine
That cravens my weak hand. Come, here's my heart.
Something's afore't.

    She takes letters from her bosom
                        Soft, soft, we'll no defence,
Obedient as the scabbard. What is here?
The scriptures of the loyal Leonatus,
All turned to heresy? Away, away,   80
Corrupters of my faith, you shall no more

Be stomachers to my heart. Thus may poor fools
Believe false teachers. Though those that are betrayed
Do feel the treason sharply, yet the traitor
Stands in worse case of woe.
And thou, Posthumus, thou that didst set up
My disobedience 'gainst the King my father,
And make me put into contempt the suits
Of princely fellows, shalt hereafter find
90   It is no act of common passage, but
A strain of rareness; and I grieve myself
To think, when thou shalt be disedged by her
That now thou tirest on, how thy memory
Will then be panged by me. Prithee, dispatch.
The lamb entreats the butcher. Where's thy knife?
Thou art too slow to do thy master's bidding
When I desire it too.

PISANIO   O gracious lady,
Since I received command to do this business
I have not slept one wink.

IMOGEN   Do't, and to bed then.

PISANIO
100   I'll wake mine eyeballs out first.

IMOGEN   Wherefore then
Didst undertake it? Why hast thou abused
So many miles with a pretence? This place?
Mine action, and thine own? Our horses' labour?
The time inviting thee? The perturbed court,
For my being absent, whereunto I never
Purpose return? Why hast thou gone so far,
To be unbent when thou hast ta'en thy stand,
Th'elected deer before thee?

PISANIO   But to win time
To lose so bad employment, in the which
110   I have considered of a course. Good lady,

Hear me with patience.
IMOGEN   Talk thy tongue weary, speak.
I have heard I am a strumpet, and mine ear,
Therein false struck, can take no greater wound,
Nor tent, to bottom that. But speak.
PISANIO   Then, madam,
I thought you would not back again.
IMOGEN   Most like,
Bringing me here to kill me.
PISANIO   Not so, neither.
But if I were as wise as honest, then
My purpose would prove well. It cannot be
But that my master is abused. Some villain,
Ay, and singular in his art, hath done you both   120
This cursèd injury.
IMOGEN
Some Roman courtesan.
PISANIO   No, on my life.
I'll give but notice you are dead, and send him
Some bloody sign of it, for 'tis commanded
I should do so. You shall be missed at court,
And that will well confirm it.
IMOGEN   Why, good fellow,
What shall I do the while? Where bide? How live?
Or in my life what comfort, when I am
Dead to my husband?
PISANIO   If you'll back to th'court –
IMOGEN
No court, no father, nor no more ado   130
With that harsh, churlish noble, simple nothing,
That Cloten, whose love suit hath been to me
As fearful as a siege.
PISANIO   If not at court,
Then not in Britain must you bide.

IMOGEN   Where then?
Hath Britain all the sun that shines? Day, night,
Are they not but in Britain? I'th'world's volume
Our Britain seems as of it, but not in't,
In a great pool a swan's nest. Prithee, think
There's livers out of Britain.

PISANIO   I am most glad
140   You think of other place. Th'ambassador,
Lucius the Roman, comes to Milford Haven
Tomorrow. Now if you could wear a mind
Dark as your fortune is, and but disguise
That which t'appear itself must not yet be
But by self-danger, you should tread a course
Pretty and full of view; yea, haply, near
The residence of Posthumus; so nigh, at least,
That though his actions were not visible, yet
Report should render him hourly to your ear
150   As truly as he moves.

IMOGEN   O, for such means,
Though peril to my modesty, not death on't,
I would adventure.

PISANIO   Well then, here's the point:
You must forget to be a woman; change
Command into obedience, fear and niceness –
The handmaids of all women, or more truly
Woman it pretty self – into a waggish courage,
Ready in gibes, quick-answered, saucy and
As quarrelous as the weasel. Nay, you must
Forget that rarest treasure of your cheek,
160   Exposing it – but O, the harder heart!
Alack, no remedy – to the greedy touch
Of common-kissing Titan, and forget
Your laboursome and dainty trims, wherein
You made great Juno angry.

IMOGEN   Nay, be brief.
  I see into thy end, and am almost
  A man already.
PISANIO   First, make yourself but like one.
  Forethinking this, I have already fit –
  'Tis in my cloak-bag – doublet, hat, hose, all
  That answer to them. Would you in their serving,
  And with what imitation you can borrow   170
  From youth of such a season, 'fore noble Lucius
  Present yourself, desire his service, tell him
  Wherein you're happy – which will make him know
  If that his head have ear in music – doubtless
  With joy he will embrace you, for he's honourable,
  And, doubling that, most holy. Your means abroad –
  You have me rich, and I will never fail
  Beginning nor supplyment.
IMOGEN   Thou art all the comfort
  The gods will diet me with. Prithee away.
  There's more to be considered, but we'll even   180
  All that good time will give us. This attempt
  I am soldier to, and will abide it with
  A prince's courage. Away, I prithee.
PISANIO
  Well, madam, we must take a short farewell,
  Lest being missed I be suspected of
  Your carriage from the court. My noble mistress,
  Here is a box – I had it from the Queen –
  What's in't is precious. If you are sick at sea,
  Or stomach-qualmed at land, a dram of this
  Will drive away distemper. To some shade,   190
  And fit you to your manhood. May the gods
  Direct you to the best.
IMOGEN   Amen. I thank thee.   *Exeunt*

III.5   *Enter Cymbeline, the Queen, Cloten, Lucius, Lords,*
            and attendants

CYMBELINE
    Thus far, and so farewell.
LUCIUS   Thanks, royal sir.
    My emperor hath wrote I must from hence;
    And am right sorry that I must report ye
    My master's enemy.
CYMBELINE   Our subjects, sir,
    Will not endure his yoke, and for ourself
    To show less sovereignty than they, must needs
    Appear unkinglike.
LUCIUS   So, sir. I desire of you
    A conduct over land to Milford Haven.
    (*To the Queen*) Madam, all joy befall your grace, and
        you.
CYMBELINE
10 My lords, you are appointed for that office:
    The due of honour in no point omit.
    So farewell, noble Lucius.
LUCIUS   Your hand, my lord.
CLOTEN
    Receive it friendly, but from this time forth
    I wear it as your enemy.
LUCIUS   Sir, the event
    Is yet to name the winner. Fare you well.
CYMBELINE
    Leave not the worthy Lucius, good my lords,
    Till he have crossed the Severn. Happiness!
                                Exeunt Lucius and Lords
QUEEN
    He goes hence frowning, but it honours us
    That we have given him cause.
CLOTEN   'Tis all the better.

Your valiant Britons have their wishes in it.   20
CYMBELINE
   Lucius hath wrote already to the Emperor
   How it goes here. It fits us therefore ripely
   Our chariots and our horsemen be in readiness.
   The powers that he already hath in Gallia
   Will soon be drawn to head, from whence he moves
   His war for Britain.
QUEEN   'Tis not sleepy business,
   But must be looked to speedily and strongly.
CYMBELINE
   Our expectation that it would be thus
   Hath made us forward. But, my gentle queen,
   Where is our daughter? She hath not appeared   30
   Before the Roman, nor to us hath tendered
   The duty of the day. She looks us like
   A thing more made of malice than of duty.
   We have noted it. Call her before us, for
   We have been too slight in sufferance.

Exit an attendant

QUEEN   Royal sir,
   Since the exile of Posthumus, most retired
   Hath her life been, the cure whereof, my lord,
   'Tis time must do. Beseech your majesty,
   Forbear sharp speeches to her. She's a lady
   So tender of rebukes that words are strokes,   40
   And strokes death to her.

Enter an attendant

CYMBELINE   Where is she, sir? How
   Can her contempt be answered?
MESSENGER   Please you, sir,
   Her chambers are all locked, and there's no answer
   That will be given to th'loud'st of noise we make.

QUEEN
    My lord, when last I went to visit her
    She prayed me to excuse her keeping close,
    Whereto constrained by her infirmity
    She should that duty leave unpaid to you,
    Which daily she was bound to proffer. This
50   She wished me to make known, but our great court
    Made me to blame in memory.

CYMBELINE   Her doors locked?
    Not seen of late? Grant heavens that which I fear
    Prove false!   *Exit*

QUEEN   Son, I say, follow the King.

CLOTEN
    That man of hers, Pisanio, her old servant,
    I have not seen these two days.

QUEEN   Go, look after.
                                Exit Cloten

    Pisanio, thou that stand'st so for Posthumus!
    He hath a drug of mine. I pray his absence
    Proceed by swallowing that, for he believes
    It is a thing most precious. But for her,
60   Where is she gone? Haply despair hath seized her,
    Or, winged with fervour of her love, she's flown
    To her desired Posthumus. Gone she is
    To death or to dishonour, and my end
    Can make good use of either. She being down,
    I have the placing of the British crown.
      Enter Cloten
    How now, my son?

CLOTEN   'Tis certain she is fled.
    Go in and cheer the King; he rages, none
    Dare come about him.

QUEEN   All the better. May
    This night forestall him of the coming day.   *Exit*

CLOTEN

    I love and hate her. For she's fair and royal,   70
    And that she hath all courtly parts more exquisite
    Than lady, ladies, woman, from every one
    The best she hath, and she, of all compounded,
    Outsells them all. I love her therefore; but
    Disdaining me, and throwing favours on
    The low Posthumus, slanders so her judgement
    That what's else rare is choked; and in that point
    I will conclude to hate her, nay, indeed,
    To be revenged upon her. For when fools
    Shall –

     Enter Pisanio

        Who is here? What, are you packing, sirrah?   80
    Come hither. Ah, you precious pander! Villain,
    Where is thy lady? In a word, or else
    Thou art straightway with the fiends.

PISANIO   O good my lord!

CLOTEN

    Where is thy lady? Or, by Jupiter,
    I will not ask again. Close villain,
    I'll have this secret from thy heart or rip
    Thy heart to find it. Is she with Posthumus,
    From whose so many weights of baseness cannot
    A dram of worth be drawn?

PISANIO   Alas, my lord,
    How can she be with him? When was she missed?   90
    He is in Rome.

CLOTEN   Where is she, sir? Come nearer.
    No farther halting. Satisfy me home
    What is become of her.

PISANIO

    O my all-worthy lord!

CLOTEN   All-worthy villain,

Discover where thy mistress is at once,
At the next word. No more of 'worthy lord'.
Speak, or thy silence on the instant is
Thy condemnation and thy death.

PISANIO   Then, sir,
This paper is the history of my knowledge
100 Touching her flight.

He gives Cloten a letter

CLOTEN   Let's see't. I will pursue her
Even to Augustus' throne.

Cloten reads

PISANIO (*aside*)   Or this or perish.
She's far enough, and what he learns by this
May prove his travel, not her danger.

CLOTEN   Hum!

PISANIO (*aside*)
I'll write to my lord she's dead. O Imogen,
Safe mayst thou wander, safe return again!

CLOTEN
Sirrah, is this letter true?

PISANIO   Sir, as I think.

CLOTEN It is Posthumus' hand, I know't. Sirrah, if thou
wouldst not be a villain, but do me true service, undergo
those employments wherein I should have cause to use
110 thee with a serious industry – that is, what villainy soe'er
I bid thee do, to perform it directly and truly – I would
think thee an honest man. Thou shouldst neither want
my means for thy relief, nor my voice for thy preferment.

PISANIO Well, my good lord.

CLOTEN Wilt thou serve me? For since patiently and constantly thou hast stuck to the bare fortune of that beggar
Posthumus, thou canst not in the course of gratitude but
be a diligent follower of mine. Wilt thou serve me?

PISANIO Sir, I will.

CLOTEN Give me thy hand. Here's my purse. Hast any of   120
  thy late master's garments in thy possession?

PISANIO I have, my lord, at my lodging the same suit he
  wore when he took leave of my lady and mistress.

CLOTEN The first service thou dost me, fetch that suit
  hither. Let it be thy first service. Go.

PISANIO I shall, my lord.   *Exit*

CLOTEN Meet thee at Milford Haven! I forgot to ask him
  one thing; I'll remember't anon. Even there, thou villain
  Posthumus, will I kill thee. I would these garments were
  come. She said upon a time – the bitterness of it I now   130
  belch from my heart – that she held the very garment
  of Posthumus in more respect than my noble and natural
  person, together with the adornment of my qualities.
  With that suit upon my back will I ravish her; first kill
  him, and in her eyes; there shall she see my valour, which
  will then be a torment to her contempt. He on the ground,
  my speech of insultment ended on his dead body, and
  when my lust hath dined – which, as I say, to vex her I
  will execute in the clothes that she so praised – to the
  court I'll knock her back, foot her home again. She hath   140
  despised me rejoicingly, and I'll be merry in my revenge.

  Enter Pisanio, with Posthumus' clothes
  Be those the garments?

PISANIO   Ay, my noble lord.

CLOTEN
  How long is't since she went to Milford Haven?

PISANIO She can scarce be there yet.

CLOTEN Bring this apparel to my chamber. That is the
  second thing that I have commanded thee. The third
  is that thou wilt be a voluntary mute to my design. Be
  but duteous, and true preferment shall tender itself to
  thee. My revenge is now at Milford; would I had wings
  to follow it! Come, and be true.   *Exit*   150

PISANIO
 Thou bidd'st me to my loss, for true to thee
 Were to prove false, which I will never be
 To him that is most true. To Milford go,
 And find not her whom thou pursuest. Flow, flow,
 You heavenly blessings, on her. This fool's speed
 Be crossed with slowness; labour be his meed. *Exit*

III.6 *Enter Imogen, dressed as a boy*

IMOGEN
 I see a man's life is a tedious one.
 I have tired myself, and for two nights together
 Have made the ground my bed. I should be sick,
 But that my resolution helps me. Milford,
 When from the mountain-top Pisanio showed thee,
 Thou wast within a ken. O Jove, I think
 Foundations fly the wretched: such, I mean,
 Where they should be relieved. Two beggars told me
 I could not miss my way. Will poor folks lie,
10 That have afflictions on them, knowing 'tis
 A punishment or trial? Yes; no wonder,
 When rich ones scarce tell true. To lapse in fullness
 Is sorer than to lie for need, and falsehood
 Is worse in kings than beggars. My dear lord,
 Thou art one o'th'false ones. Now I think on thee
 My hunger's gone; but even before I was
 At point to sink for food. But what is this?
 Here is a path to't. 'Tis some savage hold.
 I were best not call; I dare not call; yet famine,
20 Ere clean it o'erthrow nature, makes it valiant.
 Plenty and peace breeds cowards, hardness ever
 Of hardiness is mother. Hoa! Who's here?
 If anything that's civil, speak; if savage,

Take or lend. Ho! No answer? Then I'll enter.
Best draw my sword, and if mine enemy
But fear the sword like me he'll scarcely look on't.
Such a foe, good heavens!   *Exit into the cave*
    Enter Belarius, Guiderius, and Arviragus

BELARIUS

You, Polydore, have proved best woodman and
Are master of the feast. Cadwal and I
Will play the cook and servant; 'tis our match.   30
The sweat of industry would dry and die
But for the end it works to. Come, our stomachs
Will make what's homely savoury. Weariness
Can snore upon the flint when resty sloth
Finds the down pillow hard. Now peace be here,
Poor house, that keep'st thyself.

GUIDERIUS   I am throughly weary.

ARVIRAGUS

I am weak with toil, yet strong in appetite.

GUIDERIUS

There is cold meat i'th'cave; we'll browse on that
Whilst what we have killed be cooked.

BELARIUS (*looks into the cave*)   Stay, come not in.
But that it eats our victuals, I should think   40
Here were a fairy.

GUIDERIUS   What's the matter, sir?

BELARIUS

By Jupiter, an angel! – or, if not,
An earthly paragon. Behold divineness
No elder than a boy.

    Enter Imogen from the cave

IMOGEN   Good masters, harm me not.
Before I entered here I called, and thought
To have begged or bought what I have took. Good
    truth,

I have stol'n naught, nor would not, though I had found
Gold strewed i'th'floor. Here's money for my meat.
I would have left it on the board so soon
50   As I had made my meal, and parted
With prayers for the provider.

GUIDERIUS   Money, youth?

ARVIRAGUS
All gold and silver rather turn to dirt,
As 'tis no better reckoned but of those
Who worship dirty gods.

IMOGEN   I see you're angry.
Know, if you kill me for my fault, I should
Have died had I not made it.

BELARIUS   Whither bound?

IMOGEN
To Milford Haven.

BELARIUS   What's your name?

IMOGEN
Fidele, sir. I have a kinsman who
Is bound for Italy. He embarked at Milford,
60   To whom being going, almost spent with hunger,
I am fall'n in this offence.

BELARIUS   Prithee, fair youth,
Think us no churls, nor measure our good minds
By this rude place we live in. Well encountered.
'Tis almost night; you shall have better cheer
Ere you depart, and thanks to stay and eat it.
Boys, bid him welcome.

GUIDERIUS   Were you a woman, youth,
I should woo hard but be your groom in honesty;
I bid for you as I do buy.

ARVIRAGUS   I'll make't my comfort
He is a man, I'll love him as my brother:
70   And such a welcome as I'd give to him

After long absence, such is yours. Most welcome.
Be sprightly, for you fall 'mongst friends.

IMOGEN   'Mongst friends?
If brothers. (*Aside*) Would it had been so, that they
Had been my father's sons; then had my prize
Been less, and so more equal ballasting
To thee, Posthumus.

    Belarius and the brothers speak apart

BELARIUS   He wrings at some distress.

GUIDERIUS
Would I could free't.

ARVIRAGUS   Or I, whate'er it be,
What pain it cost, what danger. Gods!

BELARIUS   Hark, boys.

    They whisper

IMOGEN (*aside*)
Great men
That had a court no bigger than this cave,   80
That did attend themselves, and had the virtue
Which their own conscience sealed them, laying by
That nothing-gift of differing multitudes,
Could not outpeer these twain. Pardon me, gods,
I'd change my sex to be companion with them,
Since Leonatus' false.

BELARIUS (*aloud*)   It shall be so.
Boys, we'll go dress our hunt. Fair youth, come in.
Discourse is heavy, fasting. When we have supped
We'll mannerly demand thee of thy story,
So far as thou wilt speak it.

GUIDERIUS   Pray draw near.   90

ARVIRAGUS
The night to th'owl and morn to th'lark less welcome.

IMOGEN
Thanks, sir.

ARVIRAGUS I pray draw near.   *Exeunt*

III.7   *Enter two Roman Senators, and Tribunes*

FIRST SENATOR
      This is the tenor of the Emperor's writ:
      That since the common men are now in action
      'Gainst the Pannonians and Dalmatians,
      And that the legions now in Gallia are
      Full weak to undertake our wars against
      The fall'n-off Britons, that we do incite
      The gentry to this business. He creates
      Lucius proconsul, and to you the tribunes,
      For this immediate levy, he commends
10   His absolute commission. Long live Caesar!

TRIBUNE
      Is Lucius general of the forces?

SECOND SENATOR   Ay.

TRIBUNE
      Remaining now in Gallia?

FIRST SENATOR   With those legions
      Which I have spoke of, whereunto your levy
      Must be supplyant. The words of your commission
      Will tie you to the numbers and the time
      Of their dispatch.

TRIBUNE   We will discharge our duty. *Exeunt*

*

IV.I   *Enter Cloten, wearing Posthumus' clothes*

CLOTEN I am near to th'place where they should meet, if
      Pisanio have mapped it truly. How fit his garments serve
      me! Why should his mistress, who was made by him that
      made the tailor, not be fit too? The rather – saving rever-
      ence of the word – for 'tis said a woman's fitness comes
      by fits. Therein I must play the workman. I dare speak it

to myself, for it is not vainglory for a man and his glass
to confer in his own chamber. I mean, the lines of my
body are as well drawn as his: no less young, more
strong, not beneath him in fortunes, beyond him in the   10
advantage of the time, above him in birth, alike conver-
sant in general services, and more remarkable in single
oppositions; yet this imperceiverant thing loves him in
my despite. What mortality is! Posthumus, thy head,
which now is growing upon thy shoulders, shall within
this hour be off, thy mistress enforced, thy garments cut
to pieces before her face; and all this done, spurn her
home to her father, who may haply be a little angry for
my so rough usage; but my mother, having power of his
testiness, shall turn all into my commendations. My   20
horse is tied up safe. Out, sword, and to a sore purpose!
Fortune put them into my hand. This is the very description of their meeting-place, and the fellow dares not
deceive me.   *Exit*

Enter Belarius, Guiderius, and Arviragus, and   IV.2
Imogen, dressed as the boy Fidele, from the cave

BELARIUS (*to Imogen*)
You are not well. Remain here in the cave.
We'll come to you after hunting.

ARVIRAGUS (*to Imogen*)   Brother, stay here.
Are we not brothers?

IMOGEN   So man and man should be,
But clay and clay differs in dignity,
Whose dust is both alike. I am very sick.

GUIDERIUS (*to Belarius and Arviragus*)
Go you to hunting. I'll abide with him.

IMOGEN
So sick I am not, yet I am not well;

But not so citizen a wanton as
To seem to die ere sick. So please you, leave me.
10   Stick to your journal course: the breach of custom
Is breach of all. I am ill, but your being by me
Cannot amend me. Society is no comfort
To one not sociable. I am not very sick,
Since I can reason of it. Pray you, trust me here.
I'll rob none but myself; and let me die,
Stealing so poorly.

GUIDERIUS   I love thee: I have spoke it.
How much the quantity, the weight as much,
As I do love my father.

BELARIUS   What? How, how?

ARVIRAGUS
If it be sin to say so, sir, I yoke me
20   In my good brother's fault. I know not why
I love this youth, and I have heard you say
Love's reason's without reason. The bier at door
And a demand who is't shall die, I'd say
'My father, not this youth.'

BELARIUS (aside)   O noble strain!
O worthiness of nature, breed of greatness!
Cowards father cowards, and base things sire base;
Nature hath meal and bran, contempt and grace.
I'm not their father, yet who this should be
Doth miracle itself, loved before me.
30   (Aloud) 'Tis the ninth hour o'th'morn.

ARVIRAGUS (to Imogen)   Brother, farewell.

IMOGEN
I wish ye sport.

ARVIRAGUS   You health – so please you, sir.

IMOGEN (aside)
These are kind creatures. Gods, what lies I have heard.
Our courtiers say all's savage but at court:

Experience, O thou disprov'st report.
Th'imperious seas breeds monsters, for the dish,
Poor tributary rivers as sweet fish.
I am sick still, heart-sick. Pisanio,
I'll now taste of thy drug.
            She swallows the drug. The men speak apart
GUIDERIUS   I could not stir him.
He said he was gentle, but unfortunate,
Dishonestly afflicted, but yet honest.   40
ARVIRAGUS
Thus did he answer me, yet said hereafter
I might know more.
BELARIUS   To th'field, to th'field.
(*To Imogen*) We'll leave you for this time. Go in and rest.
ARVIRAGUS
We'll not be long away.
BELARIUS (*to Imogen*)   Pray be not sick,
For you must be our housewife.
IMOGEN   Well or ill,
I am bound to you.   *Exit into the cave*
BELARIUS   And shalt be ever.
This youth, howe'er distressed, appears he hath had
Good ancestors.
ARVIRAGUS   How angel-like he sings!
GUIDERIUS
But his neat cookery! He cut our roots in characters,
And sauced our broths as Juno had been sick,   50
And he her dieter.
ARVIRAGUS   Nobly he yokes
A smiling with a sigh, as if the sigh
Was that it was for not being such a smile;
The smile mocking the sigh that it would fly
From so divine a temple to commix
With winds that sailors rail at.

GUIDERIUS   I do note
That grief and patience, rooted in them both,
Mingle their spurs together.

ARVIRAGUS   Grow patience,
And let the stinking elder, grief, untwine
60 His perishing root with the increasing vine.

BELARIUS
It is great morning. Come away. Who's there?
Enter Cloten

CLOTEN
I cannot find those runagates. That villain
Hath mocked me. I am faint.

BELARIUS (*aside to the brothers*) 'Those runagates'?
Means he not us? I partly know him; 'tis
Cloten, the son o'th'Queen. I fear some ambush.
I saw him not these many years, and yet
I know 'tis he. We are held as outlaws. Hence!

GUIDERIUS
He is but one. You and my brother search
What companies are near. Pray you, away.
70 Let me alone with him.
                        Exeunt Belarius and Arviragus

CLOTEN   Soft, what are you
That fly me thus? Some villain mountaineers?
I have heard of such. What slave art thou?

GUIDERIUS   A thing
More slavish did I ne'er than answering
A slave without a knock.

CLOTEN   Thou art a robber,
A law-breaker, a villain. Yield thee, thief.

GUIDERIUS
To who? To thee? What art thou? Have not I
An arm as big as thine, a heart as big?
Thy words, I grant, are bigger, for I wear not

My dagger in my mouth. Say what thou art,
Why I should yield to thee.

CLOTEN   Thou villain base,   80
Know'st me not by my clothes?

GUIDERIUS   No, nor thy tailor, rascal,
Who is thy grandfather. He made those clothes,
Which, as it seems, make thee.

CLOTEN   Thou precious varlet,
My tailor made them not.

GUIDERIUS   Hence then, and thank
The man that gave them thee. Thou art some fool.
I am loath to beat thee.

CLOTEN   Thou injurious thief,
Hear but my name and tremble.

GUIDERIUS   What's thy name?

CLOTEN
Cloten, thou villain.

GUIDERIUS
Cloten, thou double villain, be thy name,
I cannot tremble at it. Were it Toad or Adder, Spider,   90
'Twould move me sooner.

CLOTEN   To thy further fear,
Nay, to thy mere confusion, thou shalt know
I am son to th'Queen.

GUIDERIUS   I am sorry for't, not seeming
So worthy as thy birth.

CLOTEN   Art not afeard?

GUIDERIUS
Those that I reverence, those I fear, the wise.
At fools I laugh, not fear them.

CLOTEN   Die the death.
When I have slain thee with my proper hand
I'll follow those that even now fled hence,
And on the gates of Lud's Town set your heads.

100   Yield, rustic mountaineer.   *They fight and exeunt*
            Enter Belarius and Arviragus

BELARIUS

No company's abroad?

ARVIRAGUS

None in the world. You did mistake him, sure.

BELARIUS

I cannot tell. Long is it since I saw him,
But time hath nothing blurred those lines of favour
Which then he wore. The snatches in his voice,
And burst of speaking were as his; I am absolute
'Twas very Cloten.

ARVIRAGUS   In this place we left them.
I wish my brother make good time with him,
You say he is so fell.

BELARIUS   Being scarce made up,

110   I mean to man, he had not apprehension
Of roaring terrors; for defect of judgement
Is oft the cease of fear.
            Enter Guiderius with Cloten's head
                        But see, thy brother.

GUIDERIUS

This Cloten was a fool, an empty purse,
There was no money in't. Not Hercules
Could have knocked out his brains, for he had none.
Yet I not doing this, the fool had borne
My head as I do his.

BELARIUS   What hast thou done?

GUIDERIUS

I am perfect what: cut off one Cloten's head,
Son to the Queen after his own report,

120   Who called me traitor, mountaineer, and swore
With his own single hand he'd take us in,
Displace our heads where – thank the gods – they grow,

And set them on Lud's Town.

BELARIUS   We are all undone.

GUIDERIUS

Why, worthy father, what have we to lose
But that he swore to take, our lives? The law
Protects not us; then why should we be tender
To let an arrogant piece of flesh threat us,
Play judge and executioner all himself,
For we do fear the law? What company
Discover you abroad?

BELARIUS   No single soul   130
Can we set eye on, but in all safe reason
He must have some attendants. Though his humour
Was nothing but mutation, ay, and that
From one bad thing to worse, not frenzy,
Not absolute madness, could so far have raved
To bring him here alone. Although perhaps
It may be heard at court that such as we
Cave here, hunt here, are outlaws, and in time
May make some stronger head, the which he hearing –
As it is like him – might break out, and swear   140
He'd fetch us in, yet is't not probable
To come alone, either he so undertaking,
Or they so suffering. Then on good ground we fear,
If we do fear this body hath a tail
More perilous than the head.

ARVIRAGUS   Let ord'nance
Come as the gods foresay it; howsoe'er,
My brother hath done well.

BELARIUS   I had no mind
To hunt this day. The boy Fidele's sickness
Did make my way long forth.

GUIDERIUS   With his own sword,
Which he did wave against my throat, I have ta'en   150

His head from him. I'll throw't into the creek
Behind our rock, and let it to the sea
And tell the fishes he's the Queen's son, Cloten.
That's all I reck.   *Exit with Cloten's head*

BELARIUS   I fear 'twill be revenged.
Would, Polydore, thou hadst not done't, though valour
Becomes thee well enough.

ARVIRAGUS   Would I had done't,
So the revenge alone pursued me. Polydore,
I love thee brotherly, but envy much
Thou hast robbed me of this deed. I would revenges
160 That possible strength might meet would seek us
      through
And put us to our answer.

BELARIUS   Well, 'tis done.
We'll hunt no more today, nor seek for danger
Where there's no profit. I prithee, to our rock.
You and Fidele play the cooks. I'll stay
Till hasty Polydore return, and bring him
To dinner presently.

ARVIRAGUS   Poor sick Fidele,
I'll willingly to him. To gain his colour
I'd let a parish of such Clotens blood,
And praise myself for charity.   *Exit into the cave*

BELARIUS   O thou goddess,
170 Thou divine Nature, how thyself thou blazon'st
In these two princely boys! They are as gentle
As zephyrs blowing below the violet,
Not wagging his sweet head; and yet as rough,
Their royal blood enchafed, as the rud'st wind
That by the top doth take the mountain pine
And make him stoop to th'vale. 'Tis wonder
That an invisible instinct should frame them
To royalty unlearned, honour untaught,

Civility not seen from other, valour
That wildly grows in them, but yields a crop   180
As if it had been sowed. Yet still it's strange
What Cloten's being here to us portends,
Or what his death will bring us.

    Enter Guiderius

GUIDERIUS   Where's my brother?
  I have sent Cloten's clotpoll down the stream
In embassy to his mother. His body's hostage
For his return.

    Solemn music

BELARIUS   My ingenious instrument!
  Hark, Polydore, it sounds. But what occasion
Hath Cadwal now to give it motion? Hark!

GUIDERIUS
  Is he at home?

BELARIUS   He went hence even now.

GUIDERIUS
  What does he mean? Since death of my dear'st mother 190
It did not speak before. All solemn things
Should answer solemn accidents. The matter?
Triumphs for nothing and lamenting toys
Is jollity for apes and grief for boys.
Is Cadwal mad?

    *Enter Arviragus with Imogen, dead, bearing her in
    his arms*

BELARIUS   Look, here he comes,
  And brings the dire occasion in his arms
Of what we blame him for.

ARVIRAGUS   The bird is dead
  That we have made so much on. I had rather
Have skipped from sixteen years of age to sixty,
To have turned my leaping time into a crutch,   200
Than have seen this.

GUIDERIUS *(to Imogen)* O sweetest, fairest lily,
   My brother wears thee not the one half so well
   As when thou grew'st thyself.

BELARIUS   O melancholy,
   Who ever yet could sound thy bottom? Find
   The ooze, to show what coast thy sluggish crare
   Might easiliest harbour in? Thou blessed thing,
   Jove knows what man thou mightst have made; but I,
   Thou diedst, a most rare boy, of melancholy.
   How found you him?

ARVIRAGUS   Stark, as you see,
210   Thus smiling, as some fly had tickled slumber,
   Not as death's dart being laughed at; his right cheek
   Reposing on a cushion.

GUIDERIUS   Where?

ARVIRAGUS   O'th'floor,
   His arms thus leagued. I thought he slept, and put
   My clouted brogues from off my feet, whose rudeness
   Answered my steps too loud.

GUIDERIUS   Why, he but sleeps.
   If he be gone, he'll make his grave a bed;
   With female fairies will his tomb be haunted,
   (to Imogen) And worms will not come to thee.

ARVIRAGUS   With fairest flowers
   Whilst summer lasts, and I live here, Fidele,
220   I'll sweeten thy sad grave. Thou shalt not lack
   The flower that's like thy face, pale primrose, nor
   The azured harebell, like thy veins; no, nor
   The leaf of eglantine, whom not to slander,
   Outsweet'ned not thy breath. The ruddock would
   With charitable bill – O bill sore shaming
   Those rich-left heirs that let their fathers lie
   Without a monument – bring thee all this,
   Yea, and furred moss besides, when flowers are none,

To winter-ground thy corpse —
GUIDERIUS   Prithee, have done,
And do not play in wench-like words with that   230
Which is so serious. Let us bury him,
And not protract with admiration what
Is now due debt. To th'grave.
ARVIRAGUS   Say, where shall's lay him?
GUIDERIUS
By good Euriphile, our mother.
ARVIRAGUS   Be't so,
And let us, Polydore, though now our voices
Have got the mannish crack, sing him to th'ground
As once our mother; use like note and words,
Save that Euriphile must be Fidele.
GUIDERIUS
Cadwal,
I cannot sing. I'll weep, and word it with thee,   240
For notes of sorrow out of tune are worse
Than priests and fanes that lie.
ARVIRAGUS   We'll speak it then.
BELARIUS
Great griefs, I see, med'cine the less, for Cloten
Is quite forgot. He was a queen's son, boys,
And though he came our enemy, remember
He was paid for that. Though mean and mighty rotting
Together have one dust, yet reverence,
That angel of the world, doth make distinction
Of place 'tween high and low. Our foe was princely,
And though you took his life as being our foe,   250
Yet bury him as a prince.
GUIDERIUS   Pray you, fetch him hither.
Thersites' body is as good as Ajax'
When neither are alive.
ARVIRAGUS (to Belarius) If you'll go fetch him,

We'll say our song the whilst.   *Exit Belarius*
                                    Brother begin.

GUIDERIUS
  Nay, Cadwal, we must lay his head to th'east.
  My father hath a reason for't.

ARVIRAGUS   'Tis true.

GUIDERIUS
  Come on, then, and remove him.

ARVIRAGUS   So, begin.

GUIDERIUS
                Fear no more the heat o'th'sun,
                Nor the furious winter's rages.
260   Thou thy worldly task hast done,
                Home art gone and ta'en thy wages.
                Golden lads and girls all must,
                As chimney-sweepers, come to dust.

ARVIRAGUS
                Fear no more the frown o'th'great,
                Thou art past the tyrant's stroke.
                Care no more to clothe and eat,
                To thee the reed is as the oak.
                The sceptre, learning, physic, must
                All follow this and come to dust.

GUIDERIUS
270   Fear no more the lightning flash,

ARVIRAGUS
                Nor th'all-dreaded thunder-stone.

GUIDERIUS
                Fear not slander, censure rash.

ARVIRAGUS
                Thou hast finished joy and moan.

GUIDERIUS *and* ARVIRAGUS
                All lovers young, all lovers must
                Consign to thee and come to dust.

GUIDERIUS
        No exorciser harm thee,
ARVIRAGUS
        Nor no witchcraft charm thee.
GUIDERIUS
        Ghost unlaid forbear thee.
ARVIRAGUS
        Nothing ill come near thee.
GUIDERIUS *and* ARVIRAGUS
            Quiet consummation have,   280
            And renownèd be thy grave.
        Enter Belarius with the body of Cloten
GUIDERIUS
    We have done our obsequies. Come, lay him down.
BELARIUS
    Here's a few flowers, but 'bout midnight more;
    The herbs that have on them cold dew o'th'night
    Are strewings fitt'st for graves. Upon their faces.
    You were as flowers, now withered; even so
    These herblets shall, which we upon you strew.
    Come on, away; apart, upon our knees.
    The ground that gave them first has them again.
    Their pleasures here are past, so is their pain.   290
                        Exeunt Belarius and the brothers
IMOGEN (*awakes*)
    Yes, sir, to Milford Haven. Which is the way?
    I thank you. By yon bush? Pray, how far thither?
    'Ods pittikins, can it be six mile yet?
    I have gone all night. Faith, I'll lie down and sleep.
        She sees Cloten's body
    But soft, no bedfellow. O gods and goddesses!
    These flowers are like the pleasures of the world,
    This bloody man the care on't. I hope I dream;
    For so I thought I was a cavekeeper,

And cook to honest creatures. But 'tis not so;
'Twas but a bolt of nothing, shot of nothing,
Which the brain makes of fumes. Our very eyes
Are sometimes like our judgements, blind. Good faith,
I tremble still with fear; but if there be
Yet left in heaven as small a drop of pity
As a wren's eye, feared gods, a part of it!
The dream's here still: even when I wake it is
Without me as within me; not imagined, felt.
A headless man? The garments of Posthumus?
I know the shape of 's leg; this is his hand,
His foot Mercurial, his Martial thigh,
The brawns of Hercules; but his Jovial face –
Murder in heaven! How? 'Tis gone. Pisanio,
All curses madded Hecuba gave the Greeks,
And mine to boot, be darted on thee! Thou,
Conspired with that irregulous devil Cloten,
Hath here cut off my lord. To write and read
Be henceforth treacherous! Damned Pisanio
Hath with his forgèd letters – damned Pisanio –
From this most bravest vessel of the world
Struck the main-top! O Posthumus, alas,
Where is thy head? Where's that? Ay me, where's that?
Pisanio might have killed thee at the heart,
And left this head on. How should this be? Pisanio?
'Tis he and Cloten; malice and lucre in them
Have laid this woe here. O, 'tis pregnant, pregnant!
The drug he gave me, which he said was precious
And cordial to me, have I not found it
Murd'rous to th'senses? That confirms it home.
This is Pisanio's deed, and Cloten's. O!
Give colour to my pale cheek with thy blood,
That we the horrider may seem to those
Which chance to find us.

300

310

320

330

She falls on the body, and smears her face with blood
                              O my lord, my lord!
        Enter Lucius, Captains, and a Soothsayer
CAPTAIN (*to Lucius*)
    To them the legions garrisoned in Gallia
    After your will have crossed the sea, attending
    You here at Milford Haven with your ships.
    They are here in readiness.
LUCIUS   But what from Rome?
CAPTAIN
    The senate hath stirred up the confiners
    And gentlemen of Italy, most willing spirits
    That promise noble service; and they come
    Under the conduct of bold Jachimo,   340
    Siena's brother.
LUCIUS   When expect you them?
CAPTAIN
    With the next benefit o'th'wind.
LUCIUS   This forwardness
    Makes our hopes fair. Command our present numbers
    Be mustered; bid the captains look to't. (*To the
        Soothsayer*) Now, sir,
    What have you dreamed of late of this war's purpose?
SOOTHSAYER
    Last night the very gods showed me a vision –
    I fast, and prayed for their intelligence – thus:
    I saw Jove's bird, the Roman eagle, winged
    From the spongy south to this part of the west,
    There vanished in the sunbeams; which portends,   350
    Unless my sins abuse my divination,
    Success to th'Roman host.
LUCIUS   Dream often so,
    And never false.
        He sees Cloten's body

               Soft, ho, what trunk is here
Without his top? The ruin speaks that sometime
It was a worthy building. How, a page?
Or dead or sleeping on him? But dead rather,
For nature doth abhor to make his bed
With the defunct, or sleep upon the dead.
Let's see the boy's face.

CAPTAIN   He's alive, my lord.

LUCIUS

360   He'll then instruct us of this body. Young one,
Inform us of thy fortunes, for it seems
They crave to be demanded. Who is this
Thou mak'st thy bloody pillow? Or who was he
That, otherwise than noble Nature did,
Hath altered that good picture? What's thy interest
In this sad wreck? How came't? Who is't?
What art thou?

IMOGEN   I am nothing; or if not,
Nothing to be were better. This was my master,
A very valiant Briton, and a good,

370   That here by mountaineers lies slain. Alas,
There is no more such masters. I may wander
From east to occident, cry out for service,
Try many, all good; serve truly, never
Find such another master.

LUCIUS   'Lack, good youth,
Thou mov'st no less with thy complaining than
Thy master in bleeding. Say his name, good friend.

IMOGEN
Richard du Champ. (*Aside*) If I do lie, and do
No harm by it, though the gods hear, I hope
They'll pardon it. (*Aloud*) Say you, sir?

LUCIUS   Thy name?

IMOGEN   Fidele, sir.

LUCIUS

    Thou dost approve thyself the very same: 380
    Thy name well fits thy faith, thy faith thy name.
    Wilt take thy chance with me? I will not say
    Thou shalt be so well mastered, but be sure,
    No less beloved. The Roman Emperor's letters
    Sent by a consul to me should not sooner
    Than thine own worth prefer thee. Go with me.

IMOGEN

    I'll follow, sir. But first, an't please the gods,
    I'll hide my master from the flies, as deep
    As these poor pickaxes can dig; and when
    With wild wood-leaves and weeds I ha' strewed his grave   390
    And on it said a century of prayers,
    Such as I can, twice o'er, I'll weep and sigh,
    And leaving so his service, follow you,
    So please you entertain me.

LUCIUS   Ay, good youth,
    And rather father thee than master thee.
    My friends,
    The boy hath taught us manly duties. Let us
    Find out the prettiest daisied plot we can,
    And make him with our pikes and partisans
    A grave. Come, arm him. Boy, he is preferred   400
    By thee to us, and he shall be interred
    As soldiers can. Be cheerful; wipe thine eyes.
    Some falls are means the happier to arise.

                        Exeunt with Cloten's body

    Enter Cymbeline, Lords, and Pisanio   IV.3

CYMBELINE

    Again, and bring me word how 'tis with her.
                        Exit one of the Lords

A fever with the absence of her son;
A madness of which her life's in danger. Heavens,
How deeply you at once do touch me. Imogen,
The great part of my comfort, gone; my queen
Upon a desperate bed, and in a time
When fearful wars point at me; her son gone,
So needful for this present. It strikes me past
The hope of comfort. (*To Pisanio*) But for thee, fellow,
10 Who needs must know of her departure and
Dost seem so ignorant, we'll enforce it from thee
By a sharp torture.

PISANIO   Sir, my life is yours;
I humbly set it at your will. But for my mistress,
I nothing know where she remains, why gone,
Nor when she purposes return. Beseech your highness,
Hold me your loyal servant.

LORD   Good my liege,
The day that she was missing he was here.
I dare be bound he's true, and shall perform
All parts of his subjection loyally. For Cloten,
20 There wants no diligence in seeking him,
And will no doubt be found.

CYMBELINE   The time is troublesome.
(*To Pisanio*) We'll slip you for a season, but our jealousy
Does yet depend.

LORD   So please your majesty,
The Roman legions, all from Gallia drawn,
Are landed on your coast, with a supply
Of Roman gentlemen by the Senate sent.

CYMBELINE
Now for the counsel of my son and queen!
I am amazed with matter.

LORD   Good my liege,
Your preparation can affront no less

Than what you hear of. Come more, for more you're   30
    ready.
The want is but to put those powers in motion
That long to move.

CYMBELINE   I thank you. Let's withdraw,
And meet the time as it seeks us. We fear not
What can from Italy annoy us, but
We grieve at chances here. Away.

                 Exeunt Cymbeline with Lords

PISANIO
I heard no letter from my master since
I wrote him Imogen was slain. 'Tis strange.
Nor hear I from my mistress, who did promise
To yield me often tidings. Neither know I
What is betid to Cloten, but remain   40
Perplexed in all. The heavens still must work.
Wherein I am false I am honest; not true, to be true.
These present wars shall find I love my country,
Even to the note o'th'King, or I'll fall in them.
All other doubts, by time let them be cleared:
Fortune brings in some boats that are not steered. *Exit*

   Enter Belarius, Guiderius, and Arviragus   IV.4
GUIDERIUS
The noise is round about us.

BELARIUS   Let us from it.

ARVIRAGUS
What pleasure, sir, find we in life, to lock it
From action and adventure?

GUIDERIUS   Nay, what hope
Have we in hiding us? This way the Romans
Must or for Britons slay us, or receive us
For barbarous and unnatural revolts

During their use, and slay us after.

BELARIUS   Sons,
We'll higher to the mountains; there secure us.
To the King's party there's no going. Newness
Of Cloten's death — we being not known, not mustered
Among the bands — may drive us to a render
Where we have lived, and so extort from's that
Which we have done, whose answer would be death
Drawn on with torture.

GUIDERIUS   This is, sir, a doubt
In such a time nothing becoming you,
Nor satisfying us.

ARVIRAGUS   It is not likely
That when they hear the Roman horses neigh,
Behold their quartered fires, have both their eyes
And ears so cloyed importantly as now,
That they will waste their time upon our note,
To know from whence we are.

BELARIUS   O, I am known
Of many in the army. Many years,
Though Cloten then but young, you see, not wore him
From my remembrance. And besides, the King
Hath not deserved my service nor your loves,
Who find in my exile the want of breeding,
The certainty of this hard life; aye hopeless
To have the courtesy your cradle promised,
But to be still hot summer's tanlings, and
The shrinking slaves of winter.

GUIDERIUS   Than be so
Better to cease to be. Pray, sir, to th'army.
I and my brother are not known; yourself
So out of thought, and thereto so oe'rgrown,
Cannot be questioned.

ARVIRAGUS   By this sun that shines,

I'll thither. What thing is't that I never
Did see man die, scarce ever looked on blood
But that of coward hares, hot goats, and venison,
Never bestrid a horse save one that had
A rider like myself, who ne'er wore rowel
Nor iron on his heel. I am ashamed   40
To look upon the holy sun, to have
The benefit of his blest beams, remaining
So long a poor unknown.

GUIDERIUS   By heavens, I'll go.
If you will bless me, sir, and give me leave,
I'll take the better care; but if you will not,
The hazard therefore due fall on me by
The hands of Romans.

ARVIRAGUS   So say I, amen.

BELARIUS
No reason I, since of your lives you set
So slight a valuation, should reserve
My cracked one to more care. Have with you, boys!   50
If in your country wars you chance to die,
That is my bed, too, lads, and there I'll lie.
Lead, lead. (*Aside*) The time seems long; their blood
    thinks scorn
Till it fly out and show them princes born.   *Exeunt*

*

Enter Posthumus, dressed as an Italian gentleman,   V.I
carrying a blood-stained cloth

POSTHUMUS
Yea, bloody cloth, I'll keep thee, for I wished
Thou shouldst be coloured thus. You married ones,
If each of you should take this course, how many

Must murder wives much better than themselves
For wrying but a little. O Pisanio,
Every good servant does not all commands;
No bond but to do just ones. Gods, if you
Should have ta'en vengeance on my faults, I never
Had lived to put on this: so had you saved
The noble Imogen to repent, and struck
Me, wretch, more worth your vengeance. But alack,
You snatch some hence for little faults; that's love,
To have them fall no more; you some permit
To second ills with ills, each elder worse,
And make them dread it, to the doers' thrift.
But Imogen is your own: do your best wills,
And make me blest to obey. I am brought hither
Among th'Italian gentry, and to fight
Against my lady's kingdom. 'Tis enough
That, Britain, I have killed thy mistress; peace,
I'll give no wound to thee. Therefore, good heavens,
Hear patiently my purpose. I'll disrobe me
Of these Italian weeds, and suit myself
As does a Briton peasant.

He changes clothes

                              So I'll fight
Against the part I come with; so I'll die
For thee, O Imogen, even for whom my life
Is every breath a death; and thus, unknown,
Pitied nor hated, to the face of peril
Myself I'll dedicate. Let me make men know
More valour in me than my habits show.
Gods, put the strength o'th'Leonati in me.
To shame the guise o'th'world, I will begin
The fashion – less without and more within.   *Exit*

Enter Lucius, Jachimo, and the Roman army at one   V.2
door, and the Briton army at another, Leonatus
Posthumus following, like a poor soldier. They march
over and go out.
Alarums, and the battle begins.
Then enter again, in skirmish, Jachimo and
Posthumus: he vanquisheth and disarmeth Jachimo,
and then leaves him

JACHIMO

The heaviness and guilt within my bosom
Takes off my manhood. I have belied a lady,
The princess of this country, and the air on't
Revengingly enfeebles me; or could this carl,
A very drudge of Nature's, have subdued me
In my profession? Knighthoods and honours borne
As I wear mine are titles but of scorn.
If that thy gentry, Britain, go before
This lout as he exceeds our lords, the odds
Is that we scarce are men and you are gods.   *Exit*   10

The battle continues. Alarums and excursions. A retreat
is sounded. The Britons fly, Cymbeline is taken.
Then enter to his rescue Belarius, Guiderius, and
Arviragus

BELARIUS

Stand, stand, we have th'advantage of the ground.
The lane is guarded. Nothing routs us but
The villainy of our fears.

GUIDERIUS *and* ARVIRAGUS Stand, stand, and fight.

Enter Posthumus and seconds the Britons. They rescue
Cymbeline and exeunt.

Then enter Lucius, Jachimo, and Imogen, as the boy Fidele

LUCIUS (*to Imogen*)

Away, boy, from the troops, and save thyself;
For friends kill friends, and the disorder's such

As war were hoodwinked.

JACHIMO   'Tis their fresh supplies.

LUCIUS

It is a day turned strangely; or betimes
Let's reinforce, or fly.   *Exeunt*

V.3   *Enter Posthumus, like a poor soldier, and a Briton Lord*

LORD

Cam'st thou from where they made the stand?

POSTHUMUS   I did,
Though you, it seems, come from the fliers.

LORD   I did.

POSTHUMUS

No blame be to you, sir, for all was lost,
But that the heavens fought. The King himself
Of his wings destitute, the army broken,
And but the backs of Britons seen, all flying
Through a strait lane; the enemy full-hearted,
Lolling the tongue with slaught'ring, having work
More plentiful than tools to do't, struck down
Some mortally, some slightly touched, some falling
Merely through fear, that the strait pass was dammed
With dead men hurt behind, and cowards living
To die with length'ned shame.

LORD   Where was this lane?

POSTHUMUS

Close by the battle, ditched, and walled with turf;
Which gave advantage to an ancient soldier,
An honest one, I warrant, who deserved
So long a breeding as his white beard came to,
In doing this for's country. Athwart the lane
He with two striplings – lads more like to run
The country base than to commit such slaughter;

With faces fit for masks, or rather fairer
Than those for preservation cased, or shame –
Made good the passage, cried to those that fled,
'Our Britain's harts die flying, not our men.
To darkness fleet souls that fly backwards. Stand,
Or we are Romans, and will give you that
Like beasts which you shun beastly, and may save
But to look back in frown. Stand, stand.' These three,
Three thousand confident, in act as many –
For three performers are the file when all   30
The rest do nothing – with this word 'Stand, stand',
Accommodated by the place, more charming
With their own nobleness, which could have turned
A distaff to a lance, gilded pale looks;
Part shame, part spirit renewed, that some, turned
        coward
But by example – O, a sin in war,
Damned in the first beginners – 'gan to look
The way that they did and to grin like lions
Upon the pikes o'th'hunters. Then began
A stop i'th'chaser, a retire; anon   40
A rout, confusion thick; forthwith they fly
Chickens, the way which they stooped eagles; slaves,
The strides they victors made; and now our cowards,
Like fragments in hard voyages, became
The life o'th'need. Having found the back door open
Of the unguarded hearts, heavens, how they wound!
Some slain before, some dying, some their friends
O'erborne i'th'former wave, ten chased by one,
Are now each one the slaughterman of twenty.
Those that would die or ere resist are grown   50
The mortal bugs o'th'field.
LORD   This was strange chance.
    A narrow lane, an old man, and two boys.

POSTHUMUS

    Nay, do not wonder at it. You are made
    Rather to wonder at the things you hear
    Than to work any. Will you rhyme upon't,
    And vent it for a mock'ry? Here is one:
      'Two boys, an old man twice a boy, a lane,
      Preserved the Britons, was the Romans' bane.'

LORD

    Nay, be not angry, sir.

POSTHUMUS   'Lack, to what end?

60   Who dares not stand his foe, I'll be his friend,
    For if he'll do as he is made to do,
    I know he'll quickly fly my friendship too.
    You have put me into rhyme.

LORD   Farewell; you're angry.

Exit

POSTHUMUS

    Still going? This is a lord! O noble misery,
    To be i'th'field and ask 'what news?' of me.
    Today how many would have given their honours
    To have saved their carcasses, took heel to do't,
    And yet died too! I, in mine own woe charmed,
    Could not find death where I did hear him groan,
70   Nor feel him where he struck. Being an ugly monster,
    'Tis strange he hides him in fresh cups, soft beds,
    Sweet words, or hath more ministers than we
    That draw his knives i'th'war.

    He dresses again as an Italian gentleman

                       Well, I will find him,
    For being now a favourer to the Briton,
    No more a Briton, I have resumed again
    The part I came in. Fight I will no more,
    But yield me to the veriest hind that shall
    Once touch my shoulder. Great the slaughter is

Here made by th'Roman; great the answer be
Britons must take. For me, my ransom's death;   80
On either side I come to spend my breath,
Which neither here I'll keep nor bear again,
But end it by some means for Imogen.
    Enter two Briton Captains, and soldiers

FIRST CAPTAIN
    Great Jupiter be praised, Lucius is taken.
    'Tis thought the old man and his sons were angels.

SECOND CAPTAIN
    There was a fourth man, in a silly habit,
    That gave th'affront with them.

FIRST CAPTAIN   So 'tis reported,
    But none of 'em can be found. Stand, who's there?

POSTHUMUS
    A Roman,
    Who had not now been drooping here if seconds   90
    Had answered him.

SECOND CAPTAIN (*to soldiers*) Lay hands on him: a dog!
    A leg of Rome shall not return to tell
    What crows have pecked them here. He brags his service
    As if he were of note. Bring him to th'King. *Exeunt*

    Enter Cymbeline, Belarius, Guiderius, Arviragus,   V.4
    Pisanio, and Roman captives, guarded by soldiers.
    Enter the two Captains, with Posthumus. They present
    him to Cymbeline, who delivers him over to a Jailer.
                Exeunt all but Posthumus and two Jailers,
                        who put manacles on him

FIRST JAILER
    You shall not now be stol'n, you have locks upon you,
    So graze as you find pasture.

SECOND JAILER   Ay, or a stomach.
                        Exeunt Jailers

POSTHUMUS

Most welcome bondage, for thou art a way,
I think, to liberty. Yet am I better
Than one that's sick o'th'gout, since he had rather
Groan so in perpetuity than be cured
By th'sure physician, death, who is the key
T'unbar these locks. My conscience, thou art fettered
More than my shanks and wrists. You good gods give me
The penitent instrument to pick that bolt,
Then free for ever. Is't enough I am sorry?
So children temporal fathers do appease;
Gods are more full of mercy. Must I repent,
I cannot do it better than in gyves –
Desired more than constrained. To satisfy,
If of my freedom 'tis the main part, take
No stricter render of me than my all.
I know you are more clement than vile men
Who of their broken debtors take a third,
A sixth, a tenth, letting them thrive again
On their abatement; that's not my desire.
For Imogen's dear life take mine, and though
'Tis not so dear, yet 'tis a life; you coined it.
'Tween man and man they weigh not every stamp;
Though light, take pieces for the figure's sake;
You rather mine, being yours. And so, great powers,
If you will take this audit, take this life,
And cancel these cold bonds. O Imogen,
I'll speak to thee in silence!   *He sleeps.*
    Solemn music.

*Enter, as in an apparition, Sicilius Leonatus, father to
Posthumus, an old man, attired like a warrior, leading
in his hand an ancient matron, his wife, and mother to
Posthumus, with music before them. Then, after other
music, follow the two young Leonati, brothers to*

Posthumus, with wounds as they died in the wars. They
circle Posthumus round as he lies sleeping

SICILIUS

No more, thou thunder-master, show thy spite on mortal flies;   30
With Mars fall out, with Juno chide, that thy adulteries
Rates and revenges.
Hath my poor boy done aught but well, whose face I never saw?
I died whilst in the womb he stayed, attending Nature's law.
Whose father then – as men report, thou orphans' father art –
Thou shouldst have been, and shielded him from this earth-vexing
       smart.

MOTHER

Lucina lent not me her aid, but took me in my throes,
That from me was Posthumus ripped, came crying 'mongst his foes,
A thing of pity.

SICILIUS

Great Nature like his ancestry moulded the stuff so fair,   40
That he deserved the praise o'th'world, as great Sicilius' heir.

FIRST BROTHER

When once he was mature for man, in Britain where was he,
That could stand up his parallel, or fruitful object be
In eye of Imogen, that best could deem his dignity?

MOTHER

With marriage wherefore was he mocked, to be exiled and thrown
From Leonati seat, and cast from her, his dearest one,
Sweet Imogen?

SICILIUS

Why did you suffer Jachimo, slight thing of Italy,
To taint his nobler heart and brain, with needless jealousy,
And to become the geck and scorn o'th'other's villainy?   50

SECOND BROTHER

For this, from stiller seats we came, our parents and us twain,
That striking in our country's cause, fell bravely and were slain,
Our fealty, and Tenantius' right, with honour to maintain.

FIRST BROTHER

Like hardiment Posthumus hath to Cymbeline performed:
Then Jupiter, thou king of gods, why hast thou thus adjourned
The graces for his merits due, being all to dolours turned?

SICILIUS

Thy crystal window ope, look out, no longer exercise
Upon a valiant race, thy harsh and potent injuries.

MOTHER

Since, Jupiter, our son is good, take off his miseries.

SICILIUS

60 Peep through thy marble mansion, help, or we poor ghosts will
        cry
To th'shining synod of the rest, against thy deity.

BROTHERS

Help, Jupiter, or we appeal, and from thy justice fly.

*Jupiter descends in thunder and lightning, sitting upon an
eagle.*

He throws a thunderbolt. The ghosts fall on their knees

JUPITER

No more, you petty spirits of region low,
Offend our hearing. Hush! How dare you ghosts
Accuse the thunderer, whose bolt, you know,
Sky-planted, batters all rebelling coasts?
Poor shadows of Elysium, hence, and rest
Upon your never-withering banks of flowers.
Be not with mortal accidents oppressed;
70 No care of yours it is; you know 'tis ours.
Whom best I love, I cross, to make my gift,
The more delayed, delighted. Be content,
Your low-laid son our godhead will uplift.
His comforts thrive, his trials well are spent.
Our Jovial star reigned at his birth, and in
Our temple was he married. Rise, and fade.
He shall be lord of Lady Imogen

And happier much by his affliction made.
This tablet lay upon his breast, wherein
Our pleasure his full fortune doth confine.   80

The ghosts receive a book, which they place on
Posthumus' breast

And so away. No farther with your din
Express impatience, lest you stir up mine.
Mount, eagle, to my palace crystalline.

He ascends into the heavens

SICILIUS

He came in thunder; his celestial breath
Was sulphurous to smell; the holy eagle
Stooped, as to foot us. His ascension is
More sweet than our blest fields. His royal bird
Prunes the immortal wing and claws his beak
As when his god is pleased.

ALL THE GHOSTS   Thanks, Jupiter.

SICILIUS

The marble pavement closes, he is entered   90
His radiant roof. Away, and, to be blest,
Let us with care perform his great behest.

The ghosts vanish. Posthumus wakes

POSTHUMUS

Sleep, thou hast been a grandsire, and begot
A father to me; and thou hast created
A mother and two brothers. But, O scorn,
Gone! They went hence so soon as they were born;
And so I am awake. Poor wretches that depend
On greatness' favour dream as I have done,
Wake and find nothing. But, alas, I swerve.
Many dream not to find, neither deserve,   100
And yet are steeped in favours; so am I,
That have this golden chance and know not why.
What fairies haunt this ground? A book? O rare one,

Be not, as is our fangled world, a garment
Nobler than that it covers. Let thy effects
So follow to be most unlike our courtiers,
As good as promise. (*Reads aloud*)
Whenas a lion's whelp shall, to himself unknown, without
seeking find, and be embraced by a piece of tender air; and
when from a stately cedar shall be lopped branches which,
being dead many years, shall after revive, be jointed to
the old stock, and freshly grow; then shall Posthumus end his
miseries, Britain be fortunate and flourish in peace and plenty.
'Tis still a dream, or else such stuff as madmen
Tongue, and brain not; either both, or nothing,
Or senseless speaking, or a speaking such
As sense cannot untie. Be what it is,
The action of my life is like it, which I'll keep,
If but for sympathy.
    Enter Jailer
JAILER Come, sir, are you ready for death?
POSTHUMUS Over-roasted rather; ready long ago.
JAILER Hanging is the word, sir. If you be ready for that,
    you are well cooked.
POSTHUMUS So, if I prove a good repast to the spectators,
    the dish pays the shot.
JAILER A heavy reckoning for you, sir. But the comfort is,
    you shall be called to no more payments, fear no more
    tavern bills, which are as often the sadness of parting as
    the procuring of mirth. You come in faint for want of
    meat, depart reeling with too much drink, sorry that you
    have paid too much and sorry that you are paid too much;
    purse and brain both empty; the brain the heavier for
    being too light, the purse too light, being drawn of heavi-
    ness. Of this contradiction you shall now be quit. O the
    charity of a penny cord! It sums up thousands in a trice.
    You have no true debitor-and-creditor but it: of what's

past, is, and to come the discharge. Your neck, sir, is pen,
book, and counters; so the acquittance follows.

POSTHUMUS I am merrier to die than thou art to live.

JAILER Indeed, sir, he that sleeps feels not the toothache;   140
but a man that were to sleep your sleep, and a hangman
to help him to bed, I think he would change places with
his officer; for look you, sir, you know not which way
you shall go.

POSTHUMUS Yes, indeed do I, fellow.

JAILER Your death has eyes in's head, then. I have not seen
him so pictured. You must either be directed by some
that take upon them to know, or take upon yourself that
which I am sure you do not know, or jump the after-
enquiry on your own peril; and how you shall speed in   150
your journey's end I think you'll never return to tell on.

POSTHUMUS I tell thee, fellow, there are none want eyes to
direct them the way I am going, but such as wink and
will not use them.

JAILER What an infinite mock is this, that a man should
have the best use of eyes to see the way of blindness! I
am sure hanging's the way of winking.

Enter a Messenger

MESSENGER Knock off his manacles: bring your prisoner
to the King.

POSTHUMUS Thou bring'st good news, I am called to be   160
made free.

JAILER I'll be hanged then.

POSTHUMUS Thou shalt be then freer than a jailer; no bolts
for the dead.

JAILER (*aside*) Unless a man would marry a gallows and
beget young gibbets, I never saw one so prone. Yet,
on my conscience, there are verier knaves desire to live,
for all he be a Roman; and there be some of them, too,
that die against their wills; so should I, if I were one.

170   I would we were all of one mind, and one mind good.
        O, there were desolation of jailers and gallowses!
        I speak against my present profit, but my wish hath
        a preferment in't.   *Exeunt*

V.5   *Enter Cymbeline, Belarius, Guiderius, Arviragus,*
            Pisanio, and Lords
        CYMBELINE (*to Belarius and the brothers*)
            Stand by my side, you whom the gods have made
            Preservers of my throne. Woe is my heart
            That the poor soldier that so richly fought,
            Whose rags shamed gilded arms, whose naked breast
            Stepped before targes of proof, cannot be found.
            He shall be happy that can find him, if
            Our grace can make him so.
        BELARIUS   I never saw
            Such noble fury in so poor a thing,
            Such precious deeds in one that promised naught
10   But beggary and poor looks.
        CYMBELINE   No tidings of him?
        PISANIO
            He hath been searched among the dead and living,
            But no trace of him.
        CYMBELINE   To my grief, I am
            The heir of his reward, which I will add
                (*to Belarius and the brothers*)
            To you, the liver, heart, and brain of Britain,
            By whom I grant she lives. 'Tis now the time
            To ask of whence you are. Report it.
        BELARIUS   Sir,
            In Cambria are we born, and gentlemen.
            Further to boast were neither true nor modest,
            Unless I add we are honest.

CYMBELINE   Bow your knees.
  They kneel, and he knights them
  Arise, my knights o'th'battle. I create you   20
  Companions to our person, and will fit you
  With dignities becoming your estates.
    Enter Cornelius and Ladies
  There's business in these faces. Why so sadly
  Greet you our victory? You look like Romans,
  And not o'the court of Britain.
CORNELIUS   Hail, great King.
  To sour your happiness, I must report
  The Queen is dead.
CYMBELINE   Who worse than a physician
  Would this report become? But I consider
  By med'cine life may be prolonged, yet death
  Will seize the doctor too. How ended she?   30
CORNELIUS
  With horror, madly dying, like her life,
  Which, being cruel to the world, concluded
  Most cruel to herself. What she confessed
  I will report, so please you. These her women
  Can trip me if I err, who with wet cheeks
  Were present when she finished.
CYMBELINE   Prithee, say.
CORNELIUS
  First, she confessed she never loved you; only
  Affected greatness got by you, not you;
  Married your royalty, was wife to your place;
  Abhorred your person.
CYMBELINE   She alone knew this;   40
  And but she spoke it dying, I would not
  Believe her lips in opening it. Proceed.
CORNELIUS
  Your daughter, whom she bore in hand to love

With such integrity, she did confess
Was as a scorpion to her sight; whose life,
But that her flight prevented it, she had
Ta'en off by poison.

CYMBELINE   O most delicate fiend!
Who is't can read a woman? Is there more?

CORNELIUS

More, sir, and worse. She did confess she had
50   For you a mortal mineral which, being took,
Should by the minute feed on life, and, ling'ring,
By inches waste you. In which time she purposed
By watching, weeping, tendance, kissing, to
O'ercome you with her show; and in time,
When she had fitted you with her craft, to work
Her son into th'adoption of the crown;
But failing of her end by his strange absence,
Grew shameless-desperate; opened, in despite
Of heaven and men, her purposes, repented
60   The evils she hatched were not effected; so
Despairing died.

CYMBELINE   Heard you all this, her women?

LADIES

We did, so please your highness.

CYMBELINE   Mine eyes
Were not in fault, for she was beautiful;
Mine ears that heard her flattery, nor my heart
That thought her like her seeming. It had been vicious
To have mistrusted her. Yet, O my daughter,
That it was folly in me thou mayst say,
And prove it in thy feeling. Heaven mend all.

Enter Lucius, Jachimo, the Soothsayer, and other
Roman prisoners, with Posthumus behind, dressed as
an Italian gentleman, and Imogen as the boy Fidele,
all guarded by soldiers

Thou com'st not, Caius, now for tribute: that
The Britons have razed out, though with the loss   70
Of many a bold one; whose kinsmen have made suit
That their good souls may be appeased with slaughter
Of you their captives, which ourself have granted.
So think of your estate.

LUCIUS

Consider, sir, the chance of war. The day
Was yours by accident; had it gone with us,
We should not, when the blood was cool, have threatened
Our prisoners with the sword. But since the gods
Will have it thus, that nothing but our lives
May be called ransom, let it come. Sufficeth   80
A Roman with a Roman's heart can suffer:
Augustus lives to think on't. And so much
For my peculiar care. This one thing only
I will entreat: my boy, a Briton born,
Let him be ransomed. Never master had
A page so kind, so duteous, diligent,
So tender over his occasions, true,
So feat, so nurse-like; let his virtue join
With my request, which I'll make bold your highness
Cannot deny. He hath done no Briton harm,   90
Though he have served a Roman. Save him, sir,
And spare no blood beside.

CYMBELINE   I have surely seen him.
His favour is familiar to me. (*To Imogen*) Boy,
Thou hast looked thyself into my grace,
And art mine own. I know not why, wherefore,
To say, 'Live, boy'. Ne'er thank thy master; live,
And ask of Cymbeline what boon thou wilt;
Fitting my bounty and thy state, I'll give it,
Yea though thou do demand a prisoner,
The noblest ta'en.

100 IMOGEN   I humbly thank your highness.

LUCIUS
I do not bid thee beg my life, good lad,
And yet I know thou wilt.

IMOGEN   No, no; alack,
There's other work in hand. I see a thing
Bitter to me as death. Your life, good master,
Must shuffle for itself.

LUCIUS   The boy disdains me.
He leaves me, scorns me. Briefly die their joys
That place them on the truth of girls and boys.
Why stands he so perplexed?

CYMBELINE   What wouldst thou, boy?
I love thee more and more; think more and more
110 What's best to ask. Know'st him thou look'st on? Speak,
Wilt have him live? Is he thy kin? Thy friend?

IMOGEN
He is a Roman, no more kin to me
Than I to your highness; who, being born your vassal,
Am something nearer.

CYMBELINE   Wherefore ey'st him so?

IMOGEN
I'll tell you, sir, in private, if you please
To give me hearing.

CYMBELINE   Ay, with all my heart,
And lend my best attention. What's thy name?

IMOGEN
Fidele, sir.

CYMBELINE   Thou'rt my good youth. My page,
I'll be thy master. Walk with me, speak freely.
              Cymbeline and Imogen speak apart
BELARIUS (*aside to Guiderius and Arviragus*)
120 Is not this boy revived from death?

ARVIRAGUS   One sand another

Not more resembles that sweet rosy lad
Who died, and was Fidele. What think you?

GUIDERIUS
The same dead thing alive.

BELARIUS
Peace, peace, see further. He eyes us not, forbear;
Creatures may be alike. Were't he, I am sure
He would have spoke to us.

GUIDERIUS   But we see him dead.

BELARIUS
Be silent; let's see further.

PISANIO (*aside*)   It is my mistress.
Since she is living, let the time run on
To good or bad.

CYMBELINE (*to Imogen*) Come, stand thou by our side,
Make thy demand aloud. (*To Jachimo*) Sir, step you forth.   130
Give answer to this boy, and do it freely,
Or, by our greatness and the grace of it,
Which is our honour, bitter torture shall
Winnow the truth from falsehood. (*To Imogen*) On,
    speak to him.

IMOGEN
My boon is that this gentleman may render
Of whom he had this ring.

POSTHUMUS (*aside*)   What's that to him?

CYMBELINE (*to Jachimo*)
That diamond upon your finger, say,
How came it yours?

JACHIMO
Thou'lt torture me to leave unspoken that
Which, to be spoke, would torture thee.

CYMBELINE   How? me?   140

JACHIMO
I am glad to be constrained to utter that

Which torments me to conceal. By villainy
I got this ring; 'twas Leonatus' jewel,
Whom thou didst banish and – which more may grieve
      thee,
As it doth me – a nobler sir ne'er lived
'Twixt sky and ground. Wilt thou hear more, my lord?

CYMBELINE
All that belongs to this.

JACHIMO   That paragon, thy daughter,
For whom my heart drops blood, and my false spirits
Quail to remember – give me leave, I faint.

CYMBELINE
150   My daughter? What of her? Renew thy strength.
I had rather thou shouldst live while nature will
Than die ere I hear more. Strive, man, and speak.

JACHIMO
Upon a time – unhappy was the clock
That struck the hour; it was in Rome – accursed
The mansion where; 'twas at a feast – O, would
Our viands had been poisoned, or at least
Those which I heaved to head; the good Posthumus –
What should I say? He was too good to be
Where ill men were, and was the best of all,
160   Amongst the rar'st of good ones – sitting sadly,
Hearing us praise our loves of Italy
For beauty that made barren the swelled boast
Of him that best could speak; for feature, laming
The shrine of Venus or straight-pight Minerva,
Postures beyond brief Nature; for condition,
A shop of all the qualities that man
Loves woman for; besides that hook of wiving,
Fairness which strikes the eye –

CYMBELINE   I stand on fire.
Come to the matter.

JACHIMO   All too soon I shall,
  Unless thou wouldst grieve quickly. This Posthumus,   170
  Most like a noble lord in love and one
  That had a royal lover, took his hint,
  And not dispraising whom we praised – therein
  He was as calm as virtue – he began
  His mistress' picture, which by his tongue being made,
  And then a mind put in't, either our brags
  Were cracked of kitchen-trulls, or his description
  Proved us unspeaking sots.
CYMBELINE   Nay, nay, to th'purpose.
JACHIMO
  Your daughter's chastity – there it begins.
  He spake of her as Dian had hot dreams   180
  And she alone were cold; whereat I, wretch,
  Made scruple of his praise, and wagered with him
  Pieces of gold 'gainst this which then he wore
  Upon his honoured finger, to attain
  In suit the place of 's bed and win this ring
  By hers and mine adultery. He, true knight,
  No lesser of her honour confident
  Than I did truly find her, stakes this ring –
  And would so had it been a carbuncle
  Of Phoebus' wheel, and might so safely had it   190
  Been all the worth of 's car. Away to Britain
  Post I in this design. Well may you, sir,
  Remember me at court, where I was taught
  Of your chaste daughter the wide difference
  'Twixt amorous and villainous. Being thus quenched
  Of hope, not longing, mine Italian brain
  'Gan in your duller Britain operate
  Most vilely; for my vantage, excellent.
  And, to be brief, my practice so prevailed
  That I returned with simular proof enough   200

To make the noble Leonatus mad,
By wounding his belief in her renown
With tokens thus and thus; averring notes
Of chamber-hanging, pictures, this her bracelet –
O cunning, how I got it – nay, some marks
Of secret on her person, that he could not
But think her bond of chastity quite cracked,
I having ta'en the forfeit. Whereupon –
Methinks I see him now –

POSTHUMUS (*coming forward*) Ay, so thou dost,
210   Italian fiend! Ay me, most credulous fool,
Egregious murderer, thief, anything
That's due to all the villains past, in being,
To come! O, give me cord, or knife, or poison,
Some upright justicer! Thou, King, send out
For torturers ingenious. It is I
That all th'abhorrèd things o'th'earth amend
By being worse than they. I am Posthumus,
That killed thy daughter – villain-like, I lie –
That caused a lesser villain than myself,
220   A sacrilegious thief, to do't. The temple
Of virtue was she; yea, and she herself.
Spit and throw stones, cast mire upon me, set
The dogs o'th'street to bay me. Every villain
Be called Posthumus Leonatus, and
Be villainy less than 'twas! O Imogen!
My queen, my life, my wife, O Imogen,
Imogen, Imogen!

IMOGEN (*approaching him*) Peace, my lord; hear, hear.
POSTHUMUS
Shall's have a play of this? Thou scornful page,
There lie thy part.
    He strikes her and she falls
PISANIO (*coming forward*) O gentlemen, help

Mine and your mistress! O my lord Posthumus,   230
You ne'er killed Imogen till now. Help, help!
(*To Imogen*) Mine honoured lady.

CYMBELINE   Does the world go round?

POSTHUMUS
How comes these staggers on me?

PISANIO   Wake, my mistress.

CYMBELINE
If this be so, the gods do mean to strike me
To death with mortal joy.

PISANIO   How fares my mistress?

IMOGEN
O, get thee from my sight!
Thou gav'st me poison. Dangerous fellow, hence!
Breathe not where princes are.

CYMBELINE   The tune of Imogen.

PISANIO
Lady,
The gods throw stones of sulphur on me if   240
That box I gave you was not thought by me
A precious thing. I had it from the Queen.

CYMBELINE
New matter still.

IMOGEN   It poisoned me.

CORNELIUS   O gods!
I left out one thing which the Queen confessed,
Which must approve (*to Pisanio*) thee honest. 'If Pisanio
Have,' said she, 'given his mistress that confection
Which I gave him for cordial, she is served
As I would serve a rat.'

CYMBELINE   What's this, Cornelius?

CORNELIUS
The Queen, sir, very oft importuned me
To temper poisons for her, still pretending   250

The satisfaction of her knowledge only
In killing creatures vile, as cats and dogs
Of no esteem. I, dreading that her purpose
Was of more danger, did compound for her
A certain stuff which, being ta'en, would cease
The present power of life, but in short time
All offices of nature should again
Do their due functions. (*To Imogen*) Have you ta'en of it?

IMOGEN
Most like I did, for I was dead.

BELARIUS (*aside to Guiderius and Arviragus*) My boys,
260   There was our error.

GUIDERIUS   This is sure Fidele.

IMOGEN (*to Posthumus*)
Why did you throw your wedded lady from you?
Think that you are upon a rock, and now
Throw me again.
    She embraces him

POSTHUMUS   Hang there like fruit, my soul,
Till the tree die.

CYMBELINE (*to Imogen*) How now, my flesh? My child?
What, mak'st thou me a dullard in this act?
Wilt thou not speak to me?

IMOGEN   Your blessing, sir.

BELARIUS (*aside to Guiderius and Arviragus*)
Though you did love this youth, I blame ye not.
You had a motive for't.

CYMBELINE   My tears that fall
Prove holy water on thee! Imogen,
270   Thy mother's dead.

IMOGEN   I am sorry for't, my lord.

CYMBELINE
O, she was naught, and 'long of her it was
That we meet here so strangely. But her son

Is gone, we know not how nor where.

PISANIO   My lord,
Now fear is from me I'll speak truth. Lord Cloten,
Upon my lady's missing, came to me
With his sword drawn, foamed at the mouth, and swore
If I discovered not which way she was gone,
It was my instant death. By accident
I had a feignèd letter of my master's
Then in my pocket, which directed him   280
To seek her on the mountains near to Milford;
Where, in a frenzy, in my master's garments,
Which he enforced from me, away he posts
With unchaste purpose, and with oath to violate
My lady's honour. What became of him
I further know not.

GUIDERIUS   Let me end the story.
I slew him there.

CYMBELINE   Marry, the gods forfend!
I would not thy good deeds should from my lips
Pluck a hard sentence. Prithee, valiant youth,
Deny't again.

GUIDERIUS   I have spoke it, and I did it.   290

CYMBELINE
He was a prince.

GUIDERIUS
A most incivil one. The wrongs he did me
Were nothing prince-like, for he did provoke me
With language that would make me spurn the sea
If it could so roar to me. I cut off's head,
And am right glad he is not standing here
To tell this tale of mine.

CYMBELINE   I am sorrow for thee.
By thine own tongue thou art condemned, and must
Endure our law. Thou'rt dead.

IMOGEN   That headless man
300   I thought had been my lord.
CYMBELINE (*to soldiers*)   Bind the offender,
   And take him from our presence.
BELARIUS   Stay, sir King.
   This man is better than the man he slew,
   As well descended as thyself, and hath
   More of thee merited than a band of Clotens
   Had ever scar for. (*To soldiers*) Let his arms alone,
   They were not born for bondage.
CYMBELINE   Why, old soldier,
   Wilt thou undo the worth thou art unpaid for,
   By tasting of our wrath? How of descent
   As good as we?
ARVIRAGUS   In that he spake too far.
CYMBELINE
310   And thou shalt die for't.
BELARIUS   We will die all three,
   But I will prove that two on's are as good
   As I have given out him. My sons, I must
   For mine own part unfold a dangerous speech,
   Though haply well for you.
ARVIRAGUS   Your danger's ours.
GUIDERIUS
   And our good his.
BELARIUS   Have at it then; by leave,
   Thou hadst, great King, a subject who
   Was called Belarius.
CYMBELINE   What of him? He is
   A banished traitor.
BELARIUS   He it is that hath
   Assumed this age: indeed a banished man,
320   I know not how a traitor.
CYMBELINE (*to soldiers*)   Take him hence.

The whole world shall not save him.

BELARIUS   Not too hot.
First pay me for the nursing of thy sons,
And let it be confiscate all, so soon
As I have received it.

CYMBELINE   Nursing of my sons?

BELARIUS
I am too blunt and saucy. (*Kneeling*) Here's my knee.
Ere I arise I will prefer my sons,
Then spare not the old father. Mighty sir,
These two young gentlemen that call me father,
And think they are my sons, are none of mine.
They are the issue of your loins, my liege,   330
And blood of your begetting.

CYMBELINE   How? My issue?

BELARIUS
So sure as you your father's. I, old Morgan,
Am that Belarius whom you sometime banished.
Your pleasure was my mere offence, my punishment
Itself, and all my treason; that I suffered
Was all the harm I did. These gentle princes –
For such and so they are – these twenty years
Have I trained up: those arts they have as I
Could put into them. My breeding was, sir,
As your highness knows. Their nurse Euriphile,   340
Whom for the theft I wedded, stole these children
Upon my banishment. I moved her to't,
Having received the punishment before
For that which I did then. Beaten for loyalty
Excited me to treason. Their dear loss,
The more of you 'twas felt, the more it shaped
Unto my end of stealing them. But, gracious sir,
Here are your sons again, and I must lose
Two of the sweet'st companions in the world.

350   The benediction of these covering heavens
   Fall on their heads like dew, for they are worthy
   To inlay heaven with stars.

CYMBELINE   Thou weep'st, and speak'st.
   The service that you three have done is more
   Unlike than this thou tell'st. I lost my children.
   If these be they, I know not how to wish
   A pair of worthier sons.

BELARIUS   Be pleased awhile.
   This gentleman, whom I call Polydore,
   Most worthy prince, as yours, is true Guiderius.
   This gentleman, my Cadwal, Arviragus,
360   Your younger princely son. He, sir, was lapped
   In a most curious mantle, wrought by th'hand
   Of his queen mother, which for more probation
   I can with ease produce.

CYMBELINE   Guiderius had
   Upon his neck a mole, a sanguine star.
   It was a mark of wonder.

BELARIUS   This is he,
   Who hath upon him still that natural stamp.
   It was wise Nature's end in the donation,
   To be his evidence now.

CYMBELINE   O, what am I?
   A mother to the birth of three? Ne'er mother
370   Rejoiced deliverance more. Blest pray you be,
   That, after this strange starting from your orbs,
   You may reign in them now. O Imogen,
   Thou hast lost by this a kingdom.

IMOGEN   No, my lord,
   I have got two worlds by't. O my gentle brothers,
   Have we thus met? O, never say hereafter
   But I am truest speaker. You called me brother,
   When I was but your sister; I you brothers,
   When ye were so indeed.

CYMBELINE   Did you e'er meet?

ARVIRAGUS

  Ay, my good lord.

GUIDERIUS   And at first meeting loved,

  Continued so until we thought he died.   380

CORNELIUS

  By the Queen's dram she swallowed.

CYMBELINE   O rare instinct!

  When shall I hear all through? This fierce abridgement

  Hath to it circumstantial branches which

  Distinction should be rich in. Where? How lived you?

  And when came you to serve our Roman captive?

  How parted with your brothers? How first met them?

  Why fled you from the court? And whither? These,

  And your three motives to the battle, with

  I know not how much more, should be demanded,

  And all the other by-dependences,   390

  From chance to chance. But nor the time nor place

  Will serve our long inter'gatories. See,

  Posthumus anchors upon Imogen,

  And she, like harmless lightning, throws her eye

  On him, her brothers, me, her master, hitting

  Each object with a joy: the counterchange

  Is severally in all. Let's quit this ground,

  And smoke the temple with our sacrifices.

  (*To Belarius*) Thou art my brother; so we'll hold thee ever.

IMOGEN (*to Belarius*)

  You are my father too, and did relieve me   400

  To see this gracious season.

CYMBELINE   All o'erjoyed,

  Save these in bonds. Let them be joyful too,

  For they shall taste our comfort.

IMOGEN (*to Lucius*)   My good master,

  I will yet do you service.

LUCIUS   Happy be you!

CYMBELINE
The forlorn soldier that so nobly fought,
He would have well becomed this place, and graced
The thankings of a king.

POSTHUMUS   I am, sir,
The soldier that did company these three
In poor beseeming. 'Twas a fitment for
410 The purpose I then followed. That I was he,
Speak, Jachimo; I had you down, and might
Have made you finish.

JACHIMO (*kneeling*)   I am down again,
But now my heavy conscience sinks my knee
As then your force did. Take that life, beseech you,
Which I so often owe; but your ring first,
And here the bracelet of the truest princess
That ever swore her faith.

POSTHUMUS   Kneel not to me.
The power that I have on you is to spare you,
The malice towards you to forgive you. Live,
420 And deal with others better.

CYMBELINE   Nobly doomed.
We'll learn our freeness of a son-in-law.
Pardon's the word to all.

ARVIRAGUS (*to Posthumus*) You holp us, sir,
As you did mean indeed to be our brother;
Joyed are we that you are.

POSTHUMUS
Your servant, princes. (*To Lucius*) Good my lord of Rome,
Call forth your soothsayer. As I slept, methought
Great Jupiter, upon his eagle backed,
Appeared to me with other spritely shows
Of mine own kindred. When I waked, I found
430 This label on my bosom, whose containing

Is so from sense in hardness that I can
Make no collection of it. Let him show
His skill in the construction.

LUCIUS   Philharmonus.

SOOTHSAYER
Here, my good lord.

LUCIUS   Read, and declare the meaning.

SOOTHSAYER (*reads aloud*)
Whenas a lion's whelp shall, to himself unknown, without
seeking find, and be embraced by a piece of tender air; and
when from a stately cedar shall be lopped branches which,
being dead many years, shall after revive, be jointed to the
old stock, and freshly grow: then shall Posthumus end his
miseries, Britain be fortunate and flourish in peace and plenty.   440
Thou, Leonatus, art the lion's whelp;
The fit and apt construction of thy name,
Being 'Leo-natus', doth import so much.
(*To Cymbeline*) The piece of tender air, thy virtuous
          daughter,
Which we call 'mollis aer', and 'mollis aer'
We term it 'mulier'; which 'mulier' I divine
Is this most constant wife, who even now,
Answering the letter of the oracle,
Unknown (*to Posthumus*) to you, unsought, were
          clipped about
With this most tender air.

CYMBELINE   This hath some seeming.   450

SOOTHSAYER
The lofty cedar, royal Cymbeline,
Personates thee; and thy lopped branches point
Thy two sons forth, who, by Belarius stol'n,
For many years thought dead, are now revived,
To the majestic cedar joined, whose issue
Promises Britain peace and plenty.

CYMBELINE   Well,
My peace we will begin; and, Caius Lucius,
Although the victor, we submit to Caesar
And to the Roman empire, promising
460   To pay our wonted tribute, from the which
We were dissuaded by our wicked queen,
Whom heavens in justice both on her and hers
Have laid most heavy hand.

SOOTHSAYER
The fingers of the powers above do tune
The harmony of this peace. The vision,
Which I made known to Lucius ere the stroke
Of this yet scarce-cold battle, at this instant
Is full accomplished. For the Roman eagle,
From south to west on wing soaring aloft,
470   Lessened herself, and in the beams o'th'sun
So vanished; which foreshowed our princely eagle,
Th'imperial Caesar, should again unite
His favour with the radiant Cymbeline,
Which shines here in the west.

CYMBELINE   Laud we the gods,
And let our crooked smokes climb to their nostrils
From our blest altars. Publish we this peace
To all our subjects. Set we forward, let
A Roman and a British ensign wave
Friendly together. So through Lud's Town march,
480   And in the temple of great Jupiter
Our peace we'll ratify, seal it with feasts.
Set on there. Never was a war did cease,
Ere bloody hands were washed, with such a peace.

                                          Exeunt

An Account of the Text

Cymbeline was first printed in 1623, in Shakespeare's *Comedies, Histories, and Tragedies*, the collected edition of the three dozen plays known as F, the first Folio. F was reprinted, again in folio (F2), in 1632, with tiny changes in wording, chiefly modernizations made by the printer. The ownership of *Cymbeline* was entered, with fifteen other plays in F, in the Stationers' Register in November 1623. *Cymbeline* is the final play in the book, placed among the Tragedies, immediately after *Antony and Cleopatra*. In F the title above the text of the play and the running head on each page is 'THE TRAGEDIE OF CYMBELINE', but in the Catalogue (or contents page) the play, last in the list of Tragedies, is called '*Cymbeline, King of Britaine*'. The notion that *Cymbeline* is a tragedy is puzzling to modern minds, since the play has more of the characteristics of Renaissance tragicomedy (the generic hybrid of tragedy and comedy) than of tragedy proper. It is notable that *The Tempest* and *The Winter's Tale*, which have certain features of tragicomedy in common with *Cymbeline*, are not listed among the Tragedies in F, but placed, respectively, at the beginning and the end of the Comedies. Why *Cymbeline* is where it is, and why it is called a tragedy, is not likely to be accounted for conclusively. It is possible that the printer Jaggard received the manuscript for the play (perhaps with the title 'Cymbeline, King of Britain') later than was planned, and that by then there was nowhere else to put it but at the very end. Or perhaps the editors of F, Hemmings and Condell, having denied themselves the useful category of tragicomedy, felt that *Cymbeline*, with its Roman and British war and diplomacy, was close enough to a tragedy of state to justify placing it with *King Lear* and *Antony and Cleopatra*.

Jaggard printed the plays in F from different kinds of manuscripts. Some manuscripts were copied directly from the theatre prompt books, while others were transcripts of manuscripts that had never been used for the theatre (the one for *Antony and Cleopatra*, for instance, was Shakespeare's own fair copy, without any of the marking up needed to make it the prompter's copy). The current view of the manuscript for *Cymbeline* is that it was a copy prepared by a professional scribe, either from Shakespeare's own papers, possibly a working draft, or from an earlier copy of these papers. The older view, that the manuscript was a copy of the prompt book, has now been discarded, since there are no signs that the text in F was prepared for performance (F retains the mutes, the Dutchman and Spaniard, in the opening stage direction to I.4, for instance, a superfluity that a prompter in the theatre would have got rid of). There is some evidence that the scribe who copied the manuscript for F was Ralph Crane, the scrivener who prepared the manuscripts of *The Tempest* and *The Winter's Tale* used in F. It has been argued that the longer stage directions in these plays, and ones in *Cymbeline* too, especially in Act V, are Crane's 'literary' sophistications of what Shakespeare wrote, possibly after the scribe had seen the plays in production. This claim is far from being proven, since it takes no account of Shakespeare's mind at work, imagining new scenes and new effects through the writing itself, and at a point in composition when he may not have been particularly concerned with the requirements of staging. For now, it is probably safer to assume that Shakespeare himself wrote nearly everything in *Cymbeline*, except the act and scene divisions, with Latin headings ('*Actus Primus. Scaena Prima.*' for I.1, and so on), which were added either by the scribe or by someone in the printing house.

By the standards of the day F was well printed. The text of *Cymbeline*, while it is not free from misprints and small errors (about three a page), does not need much correction. The printer set out the lines of verse systematically, only relining where the width of the column demanded it, and there are only a few instances of verse set as prose. There is some confusion with one stage direction in Act V, but the problem may have been in Shakespeare's manuscript, or in the scribal manuscript from which the printer was working (see above). For modern editors of

Cymbeline the only contentious issue is how to spell the names of the characters, especially that of the heroine. The spellings for Cymbeline, Lucius and Pisanio are uncontested – and even for Cloten, spelt like this most times in F but probably pronounced 'Clotten', the spelling in a few cases – but each of these names is from a clearly defined time (Ancient British, Roman, Italian). With Imogen and Jachimo the situation is different. In three recent Oxford editions these names have been changed, against F, to Innogen and Giacomo, so making them distinctly British and Italian. The editors conclude that 'Imogen' was a misprint or scribal minim error for 'Innogen' ('m' for 'nn'), the name Simon Forman used when he described the performance he saw in 1611. It is argued that 'Innogen', a name Shakespeare had already used in *Much Ado About Nothing*, is close in sound to 'innocence', and so comparable to Perdita (meaning 'lost') and Miranda ('wonderful'), the names of the heroines in *The Winter's Tale* and *The Tempest*. The case for making this change is not decisive. Forman got other details wrong, and he may have mistaken the unusual name 'Imogen' for the more common one 'Innogen'. As for sounds and meanings, 'Imogen' is close to 'image' and 'imagine' (an Elizabethan noun stressed on the first syllable), which are key words in *Cymbeline*, as the Introduction explains. Perhaps Shakespeare found a powerful Italian meaning within an Ancient British name, and mixed them, like much else in the play. The change of 'Jachimo' to 'Giacomo' is open to challenge on similar grounds. It may be that 'Jachimo' is an English and Italian hybrid, 'jack-imo' or little jack (a petty knave). Until a more compelling case has been made against them it is, once again, safer to regard the spellings of these names in F as Shakespeare's.

In the present edition, vocabulary has been modernized silently ('murder' for F's 'murther', 'yon' for 'yond', 'truth' for 'troth', and so forth), and normalized too in most cases (always 'Briton(s)' for 'Britaine(s)' for instance). Other verbal alterations, including changes to scene divisions and speech-prefixes, are recorded in the first list of collations (the reading to the right of the lemma is that of F). Alterations in punctuation, where there are substantial changes in meaning, are also recorded in this list. Shakespeare wrote quite a few short lines in *Cymbeline*, especially in V.4, for special effects (extended pauses, heightening of feeling); all changes to F's lineation, since short lines are often involved, are listed too ('I.5.46] *two lines*, thou? | Dost' means that in F line 46 divided at 'thou?' and started a second line with 'Dost'). In the second list of collations there is a selection of emendations (to the right of the lemma) that have been made to the text of *Cymbeline* since 1623, but not incorporated here. Stage directions in the present edition are based on F, although some have been modified and others have been added to clarify the action. The more important changes and additions are included in the third list of collations. Asides and indications of the person addressed are not marked in F; they are only added to the present text where other action is taking place.

COLLATIONS

1 Alterations of F

Title: Cymbeline, King of Britain] The Tragedie of Cymbeline
The Characters in the Play] *heading and list of roles not in* F

I.1

      1–3] *four lines* (see Commentary)
        1 FIRST GENTLEMAN] 1. *Gent.* (*and* '1')
        2 than] Then
        3 does the King] do's the Kings
        3 SECOND GENTLEMAN] 2 *Gent.* (*and* '2')
       15 of] at
       45 minist'red] ministred
    53–6] *four lines*, By . . . is. | I . . . report. | But . . .
              th'King? | His
      70] *new scene*, Scena Secunda.
      83 O] *at the beginning of* 84
    116 cere] seare
    138] *two lines*, had | The
  141–3] *three lines*, my | Throne . . . basenesse. | No . . . it
    177] *two lines*, hence, | Pray

I.2

      0] *Scena Tertia.*
      1 FIRST LORD] 1.

7 SECOND LORD] 2.
10 thoroughfare] through-fare

I.3

0] *Scena Quarta.*
9 this] his
17 cracked them, but] *at the beginning of* 18

I.4

0] *Scena Quinta.*
44–5 offend not] offend
55 country mistresses] Country-Mistresses
69 Britain] Britanie
71 not but] not
80 purchase] purchases
97, 166 signor] Signior
112 you're] y'are
120 neighbour's] Neighbors
124 thousand] thousands
131 therein] there in
132 ladies'] Ladies

I.5

0] *Scena Sexta.*
1] *two lines,* ground, | Gather
28 factor for] for
46] *two lines,* thou? | Dost

I.6

0] *Scena Septima.*
7 desire] desires
8 soe'er] so ere
27 takes] take
35 th'unnumbered] the number'd
36 spectacles] Spectales
51 Beseech you, sir,] *at the end of* 50
55] *two lines,* Lord? | His
75 But heavens know] *at the beginning of* 76
76 to] too
98 born] borne
104 Fixing] Fiering
106 grips] gripes
109 illustrous] illustrious

169 descended] defended
179] *two lines*, Sir: | Take
190 value's] valewes

II.1

6 FIRST LORD] 1.
8 SECOND LORD] 2.
11 curtail] curtall
14 give] gaue
25 your] you
32 tonight] night
59 husband, than] Husband. Then
60 he'd make. The] hee'ld make the

II.2

3] *two lines*, then: | Mine
49 bare] beare

II.3

1 FIRST LORD] 1.
7 CLOTEN] *not in* F
12 o'mornings] a mornings
18 MUSICIAN] SONG.
26 CLOTEN] *not in* F
27 vice] voyce
30 SECOND LORD] 2.
36–7 I . . . notice] *as prose*
40 out] on't
44 solicits] solicity
60] *two lines*, Romane. | Come
78 Ay] I, *at the beginning of* 79
83 fairest sister] fairest, Sister
97 cure] are
131 hairs] Heires
133 garment] Garments
150 you] your
152 meanest] mean'st

II.4

6 hopes] hope
18 legions] Legion
24 mingled] wing-led
34 through] thorough

36 tenor] tenure
37 PHILARIO] *Post.*
47 not] note
60 leaves] leaue
135 the] her
142 never . . . turns] *at the beginning of* 143
164] *two lines*, Saturne; | That
168 German one] Iarmen on
179 why, hers] *at the beginning of* 180

III.1

36 more] mo
39 grip] gripe
52 be. We do say] be, we do. Say
62 more] moe

III.2

2 monster's her accuser] Monsters her accuse
10 hers] her
21 fedary] Foedarie
45 *love,*] *Loue.*
55 beyond beyond] beyond, beyond
66 score] store; ride] rid
72 clock's] Clocks
77 nor] not

III.3

2 Stoop] Sleepe
28 know] knowes
33 travelling abed] trauailing a bed
43 choir] Quire
45 city's] Citties
74 hunters'] Hunters
78] *two lines*, State: | Ile meete
82] *two lines*, mine, | And though
83 cave wherein they bow,] Caue, whereon the Bowe
103 reft'st] refts

III.4

22 *lie*] *lyes*
47 favour's] fauours
77 afore't] a-foot
85–8] *three lines*, Posthumus, | That . . . King | My

86 Posthumus, thou] *Posthumus*
88 make] makes
93 tirest] tyrest
100 out first] first
131 churlish noble] noble
146 haply] happily
166–7 one. . . . this,] one, . . . this.
183 prince's] Princes

III.5

32 looks] looke
44 loud'st] lowd
51 to] too
52 fear] *at the beginning of* 53
80 Shall] *at the end of* 79

III.6

2 tired] tyr'd
28] *new scene*, Scena Septima.
32 to] too
86 Leonatus'] *Leonatus*
91] *two lines,* th'Owle, | And

III.7

0] *Scena Octava.*
1, 12 FIRST SENATOR] *1.Sen.*
9 commends] commands
11 SECOND SENATOR] *2.Sen.*
14 supplyant] suppliant

IV.1

13 imperceiverant] imperseuerant
17 her face] thy face
18 haply] happily

IV.2

22 bier] Beere
26, 27] *in inverted commas*
32] *two lines,* Creatures. | Gods
46 shalt] shal't
47 howe'er] how ere
49 *two lines,* cookerie | He
49–51 He . . . dieter.] *assigned to Arviragus*
58 patience] patient

112 cease] cause
122 thank] thanks
132 humour] Honor
154 reck] reake
170 how] thou
186 ingenious] ingenuous
190] *two lines*, meane? | Since
205 crare] care
206 Might easiliest] Might'st easilest
219 Whilst] Whil'st
224 ruddock] Raddocke
229 corpse] Coarse
237 our] to our
258–81] *headed* SONG
274, 280 GUIDERIUS *and* ARVIRAGUS] Both.
282] *two lines*, obsequies: | Come
290 is] are
329 Cloten's] *Cloten*
387 an't] and't
396 My friends] *at the end of* 395
400 he is] hee's

IV.3

40 betid] betide

IV.4

2 find we] we find
17 the] their
27 hard] heard
30 Than] Then
54 born] borne

V.1

1 wished] am wisht
15 doers'] dooers

V.3

24 harts] hearts
42 stooped] stopt
43 they] the
65 'what news?'] what newes
72 more] moe
84, 87 FIRST CAPTAIN] I.

86, 91 SECOND CAPTAIN] 2.

V.4

1 FIRST JAILER] *Gao.*

1–2] *three lines*, stolne, | You . . . you: | So

2 SECOND JAILER] 2. *Gao.*

25 figure's] figures

29 *follow*] followes

30] *two lines*, Thunder-Master | Shew

33–6] *eight lines*, well, | whose . . . saw: | I . . . staide, | attending . . . Law. | Whose . . . report, | thou . . . art) | Thou . . . him, | from

35 orphans'] Orphanes

37–8] *four lines*, ayde, | but . . . Throwes, | That . . . ript, | came

40–41] *four lines*, Ancestrie, | moulded . . . faire: | That . . . o'th'World, | as

42, 54 FIRST BROTHER] 1. *Bro.*

42–6] *ten lines*, man, | in . . . hee | that . . . paralell? | Or . . . bee? | In . . . deeme | his dignitie. | With . . . mockt | to . . . throwne | From . . . her, | his

50 geck] geeke

51 SECOND BROTHER] 2 *Bro.*

51–2] *four lines*, came, | our . . . twaine, | That . . . cause, | fell

54] *two lines*, hath | To

57 *two lines*, ope; looke, | looke out
   look out] looke, looke out

59–60] *four lines*, good, | take . . . miseries. | Peepe . . . helpe, | or

62] *two lines*, appeale, | and

88 claws] cloyes

89 ALL THE GHOSTS] *All.*

96 born] borne

98 greatness'] Greatnesse

128 are as] are

134 Of] Oh, of

148 take] to take

151 on] one

V.5

58 shameless-desperate] shamelesse desperate
62 LADIES] *La.*
64 heard] heare
70 razed] rac'd
116 Ay] I
134 On,] One
177 cracked] crak'd
205 got it] got
228 Thou scornful page,] *at the beginning of* 229
239 Lady] *at the beginning of* 240
259 My boys,] *at the beginning of* 260
261 from] fro
287 I . . . there] *at the end of* 286
300 I . . . lord] *at the end of* 299
311 on's] one's
318 A banished traitor] *at the end of* 317
334 mere] neere
351 like] liks
378 ye] we
386 brothers] Brother
387 whither? These] whether these
392 inter'gatories] Interrogatories
395 me, her master,] Me: her Master
404 I . . . service] *at the end of* 403
405 so] no
435 SOOTHSAYER] *not in* F
443 'Leo-natus'] Leonatus
467 this yet] yet this

2 Rejected Emendations

I.1

2 than our courtiers] then, our courtiers; than our courtiers'
29 join] joy in
49 feated] featur'd

I.5

85 words] words, Pisanio

I.6

186 The best] Best

II.1

23 and] an (*meaning* if)

II.2

18 they do't] they'd do't
26 arras, figures] arras-figures

II.3

117 foil] soil] 'file (*for* defile)

II.4

6 feared] seared
14 Or] Ere
32 one of] one
41 have] had
43 I'll] I'ld (*for* I'd)
76 Since] Such
    on't was –] on't was.] was out on't.
154 all bastards] bastards all
179 name] may be nam'd] man may name] earth may
    name] have a name

III.1

11–14] There . . . noses] *arranged as prose*
11 There] There'll
13 By] Unto
19 Neptune's] the great Neptunes
    ribbèd and palèd] were ribbed and paled
20 oaks] rocks
52 We do] *attributed to Cloten and Lords, as an interjection*

III.2

37 And] Till

III.3

16 This] That
23 babe] bauble] bribe] robe
25 him] them] 'em
34 prison, or] prison for] prison of
40 beastly: subtle] beastly-subtle
87 who] whom

III.4

> 46 look'dst] lookst
> 83 teachers] treachers
> 146 Pretty] Privy

III.5

> 86 heart] tongue

III.6

> 2 tired] 'tired (*for* attired)
> 24 or] ere
> 67 but be] but t'be
> 68 I bid] And bid] Aye, bid] Bid
>   I do] I'd
> 74 prize] price

IV.2

> 57 them] him
> 111 defect] th'effect
> 135 Not] *at the end of* 134
> 145 ord'nance] ordinance
> 195 *dead*] *as dead*
> 202 not the] not
> 218 to thee] there
> 229 winter-ground] winter gown] winter-green
> 285 their faces.] th'earth's face,
> 323 this head] thy head
> 332 *Soothsayer*] *Soothsayer to them*
> 336 are here] are
> 373 many,] many and] many men,
> 375 mov'st] movest

IV.4

> 18 fires] files
> 35 is't] is it

V.1

> 15 dread it] dreaded] dread ill
> 16 best] blessed (*one syllable*)
> 20 mistress; peace] mistress-piece

V.3

> 1 I did] I (*meaning* Aye *or* I *or* I?)
> 24 our] her
> 53 not] but] you (*making a question with* it?)

53 You] yet you] though you
72 words] viands

V.4

16 main part] mainport (*meaning* offering *or* tribute)
27 take] make
51 came] come
88 Prunes] Preens
119 *Enter Jailer*] *Re-enter Jailers*

V.5

54 in time] so in time] in due time] in fine
55 fitted] fit
126 see] saw
142 Which torments] Torments
225 villainy] 'villain'
233 comes] come
260 is sure] is, sure,
262 rock] lock
292 incivil] uncivil
297 sorrow] sorry
302 man is] boy is

3 Stage Directions

I.1

106 *Exit*] *not in* F
112 *She gives him a ring*] *not in* F
117 *He puts on the ring*] *not in* F
123 *He puts a bracelet on her arm*] *not in* F
158 *Exit with Lords*] *Exit*

I.2

0 *the two Lords*] *two Lords*

I.5

5 *He gives her a small box*] *not in* F
60 *She drops the box, and Pisanio picks it up*] *not in* F

I.6

0 *Imogen*] *Imogen alone*
13 *He gives her a letter*] *not in* F
15 *(aside, as she reads)*] *not in* F
22 *(reads aloud)*] *reads*

II.1

    49 *Exeunt Cloten and the First Lord*] *Exit*

II.2

    0 *Imogen is in bed . . . Helen*] *Enter Imogen, in her Bed, and a Lady*
      Exit Helen] *not in* F
    10 *gets out of the trunk*] *from the Trunke*
    24 *He writes notes*] *not in* F
    34 *He takes the bracelet from her arm*] *not in* F
    51 *Exit into the trunk, which is removed, with the bed*] *Exit*

II.3

    0 *the two Lords, outside Imogen's rooms*] *Lords*
    19 *(sings, with music)*] *not in* F
    29 *Exeunt Musicians*] *not in* F
    50 *Enter a Messenger*] *not in* F
    60 *Exeunt all but Cloten*] *Exeunt*
    62 *He knocks*] *not in* F
    82 *Exit*] *not in* F
    145 *Exit Pisanio*] *not in* F

II.4

    36 *He reads the letters*] *not in* F
    96 *He shows the bracelet*] *not in* F
    106 *He gives Jachimo the ring*] *not in* F

III.2

    0 *Enter Pisanio . . . them*] *Enter Pisanio reading of a Letter*
    17 *(Reads aloud)*] *not in* F
    39 *She opens the letter and reads aloud*] *not in* F

III.3

    78 *Exeunt Guiderius and Arviragus*] *Exeunt*
    98 *A hunting horn sounds*] *not in* F
    107 *The horn sounds again*] *not in* F

III.4

    14 *Pisanio gives her a letter*] *not in* F
    21 *(reads aloud)*] *reades*
    77 *She takes letters from her bosom*] *not in* F

III.5

    0 *and attendants*] *not in* F
    17 *and Lords*] *&c*

35   *Exit an attendant*] *not in* F
41   *an attendant*] *a Messenger*
100 *He gives Cloten a letter*] *not in* F
101 *Cloten reads*] *not in* F
141 *Enter Pisanio, with Posthumus' clothes*] *Enter Pisanio*

III.6

0   *Enter Imogen, dressed as a boy*] *Enter Imogen alone*
27   *Exit into the cave*] *Exit*
39   *(looks into the cave)*] *not in* F
44   *Enter Imogen from the cave*] *Enter Imogen*
76   *Belarius and the brothers speak apart*] *not in* F
78   *They whisper*] *not in* F

IV.1

0   *Enter Cloten, wearing Posthumus' clothes*] *Enter Clotten
     alone*

IV.2

0   *Imogen, dressed as the boy Fidele*] *Imogen*
38   *She swallows the drug. The men speak apart*] *not in* F
46   *Exit into the cave*] *Exit*
70   *Exeunt Belarius and Arviragus*] *not in* F
112 *Enter Guiderius with Cloten's head*] *Enter Guiderius*
154 *Exit with Cloten's head*] *Exit*
169 *Exit into the cave*] *Exit*
254 *Exit Belarius*] *not in* F
290 *Exeunt Belarius and the brothers*] *Exeunt*
295 *She sees Cloten's body*] *not in* F
332 *She falls on the body, and smears her face with blood*]
     not in F
353 *He sees Cloten's body*] *not in* F
403 *Exeunt with Cloten's body*] *Exeunt*

IV.3

1   *Exit one of the Lords*] *not in* F
35   *Exeunt Cymbeline with Lords*] *Exeunt*

V.1

0   *Enter Posthumus . . . cloth*] *Enter Posthumus alone*
24   *He changes clothes*] *not in* F

V.2

0   *Alarums, and the battle begins*] *not in* F
10   *Alarums and excursions. A retreat is sounded.*] *not in* F
13   *Imogen, as the boy Fidele*] *Imogen*

V.3

    0 *Posthumus, like a poor soldier*] Posthumus
   73 *He dresses again as an Italian gentleman*] not in F
   83 *Briton*] not in F
   94 *Exeunt*] not in F

V.4

    0 *guarded by soldiers*] not in F
     Enter the two Captains . . . him] The Captains present
     Posthumus
     Exeunt all but Posthumus . . . him] Enter Posthumus,
     and Gaoler
    2 *Exeunt Jailers*] not in F
   29 *He sleeps*] not in F
   80 *The ghosts receive a book . . . Posthumus' breast*] not in F
   83 *He ascends into the heavens*] Ascends
   92 *The ghosts vanish. Posthumus wakes*] Vanish
 107 *(Reads aloud)*] Reads

V.5

   19 *They kneel, and he knights them*] not in F
   68 *the Soothsayer*] not in F
     with Posthumus behind . . . Soldiers] Leonatus behind,
     and Imogen
 119 *Cymbeline and Imogen speak apart*] not in F
 209 *(coming forward)*] not in F
 227 *(approaching him)*] not in F
 229 *He strikes her and she falls*] not in F
     (coming forward)] not in F
 263 *She embraces him*] not in F
 325 *(Kneeling)*] not in F
 412 *(kneeling)*] not in F
 435 *(reads aloud)*] Reades

Music and Songs

Shakespeare uses music sparingly in *Cymbeline*. Modern productions sometimes add offstage music and even voices to create or to intensify particular moods (especially in poignant moments in the Welsh scenes in Act IV), and nowadays music is often played between the acts, or at least between the end of Act III and the beginning of Act IV, the most usual place for an interval in the modern theatre. It has been claimed, though not universally accepted, that music was played between the acts in other plays on the Jacobean stage too. Trumpet fanfares (or flourishes) to herald the formal entry of important people – Cymbeline and his court receiving the Roman ambassador Lucius in III.1, for instance – would have been standard in the public theatre at the date of *Cymbeline*. The notes blown on the hunting horn at the end of III.3, that are supposed to come from the mountain tops, would have been recognized immediately as a signal that hunted animals had been flushed out of hiding.

There are two songs in *Cymbeline*: the first, 'Hark, hark, the lark', is the aubade (or dawn song) played and sung outside Imogen's bedchamber in II.3, while the second is the dirge, 'Fear no more the heat', spoken by the brothers over the bodies of Imogen and Cloten at IV.2.258–81. A seventeenth-century setting of the aubade survives in a manuscript collection of songs by composers who wrote for the Jacobean and Caroline courts. One of these was Robert Johnson, lutenist to King James at the date of *Cymbeline*, to whom the setting for the aubade has been attributed by modern scholars (there is no attribution in the manuscript). It is possible that Johnson's setting was used for the first performances of *Cymbeline*, since he is believed to have written other music for the King's Men, including songs for *The Winter's Tale* and *The Tempest*. Two lines of the aubade are missing from the manuscript text:

> His steeds to water at those springs
> On chaliced flowers that lies. (II.3.21–2)

It has been said that these were omitted because the cluster of sibilants in them made them difficult to sing, but other songs of Johnson's have lines that are just as demanding for a singer. The manuscript lyrics and setting of the aubade are reproduced on p. 150, in a slightly edited form.

The funeral dirge, shared between Guiderius and Arviragus at IV.2.258–81, has the heading 'SONG' in the Folio text of 1623. At 235–8 Arviragus proposes that they sing the same dirge they sang when their mother Euriphile died, even though their voices have broken since then. Guiderius says he can't sing because he'll be out of tune, so they agree to speak the words rather than to sing them. Some scholars see this as an expedient: Shakespeare intended the dirge to be sung, but the actor playing Guiderius did not have a good enough voice, so it was necessary to make up an excuse. A simpler explanation is that Shakespeare thought the effect of the words would be more powerful (because clearer) if they were spoken.

One thing Shakespeare did not want was a musical accompaniment to the dirge. In *Cymbeline* music does not simply come out of nowhere, like an offstage soundtrack, but is explicable within the setting and the story. When Arviragus finds Fidele (Imogen) in the cave, apparently dead, he sets off Belarius's 'ingenious instrument' (IV.2.186), which has not been sounded since Euriphile died. The instrument, some kind of automaton, produces '*solemn music*' for his entry with Imogen lifeless in his arms. In the Jacobean theatre the music was created offstage, perhaps by a consort of viols, with or without other instruments, but in the story the source of the music is explained as a marvellous mechanical contrivance (Shakespeare's audiences were familiar with musical automata, the early ancestors of the pianola). Shakespeare was not being literal-minded in this, nor over-exact about making the action plausible. He was preparing the audience for a special moment of music later in the play. The full impact of the great entry at V.4.29, when the ghosts arrive to call down Jupiter, depends on their being introduced with music. First there is '*solemn music*', then Sicilius and his wife enter, with (as the stage direction puts it), '*music before them. Then, after other music, follow the two young Leonati, brothers to Posthumus*'. We do not know for sure what this means, perhaps simply that music was played offstage before and as each pair entered (father and mother, brother with brother), the pairs either coming from different sides of the stage or one after another, as in a pageant or a Renaissance triumph. If this is what Shakespeare did intend, one function of the music was to emphasize the mysteriousness of the dead. The music of the ghosts, by contrast with the aubade and the automaton, was not human at all, but supernatural and to be heard only during a vision. An alternative explanation is that in this stage direction, *music* means musicians, that is, the family of ghosts had spectral attendants who led them onstage, playing instruments as they entered. In this explanation too, however, there is a contrast Shakespeare has prepared us for between the sounds that human voices and instruments can produce and the ethereal music of the dead.

'Hark, hark, the lark' (II.3.19–25)

Sources

Shakespeare arranged the story-lines of *Cymbeline* in three over-lapping plots: the wager between Posthumus and Jachimo on Imogen's chastity; the royal brothers abducted to Wales twenty years before the beginning of the play, but found by Imogen; and the refusal of Britain to pay tribute to imperial Rome, and the war that follows from this.

The source material for the first two plots was very old indeed. In the assault on Imogen we can see the medieval motifs of the Slandered but Innocent Bride, and the Chaste but Chastised Wife (or Patient Griselda), and in the story of her two brothers, carried off to the mountains from the court, there is the very stuff of fairy tales about foster-parents, and kind and cruel fathers, and how royal blood will always reveal itself, however deeply buried it is in adversity and rags. The story which connects these two plots appears to be a variation on the fairy tale known to us now as Snow White: Imogen flees from her cruel stepmother to the Welsh mountains, dressed as a boy, finds her lost brothers by chance but does not know them (nor they her), lives with them in their cave as housekeeper, takes a drug which her stepmother hopes will kill her but which is harmless, then seems to die, and so forth. The third plot, the war with Rome, is a pseudo-history which Shakespeare made up, largely from passages in Ralph Holinshed's sixteenth-century histories of England and Scotland and in Edmund Spenser's epic poem, *The Faerie Queene* (1590–96). As one might expect, the immediate sources for the traditional folk material, in the stories of the stolen princes and the fleeing princess, are less easy to identify. Suggestions have included a post-Reformation miracle play, a popular novella, a couple of old-fashioned 1580s stage plays (the important one is the anonymous *The Rare Triumphs of Love and Fortune*), and Sir Philip Sidney's prose romance *The Arcadia* (1580). Further exploration of (say) Renaissance Italian epic and romance, and into ancient Roman comedy, is only likely to confirm that Shakespeare's reading was at its most richly entangled as he worked on *Cymbeline*. Attempting to disentangle the sources, so as to separate the more recent growths and borrowings from earlier ones, is impracticable, at least as regards the dominant plot, the chastity wager.

The chief source for the wager story is in Giovanni Boccaccio's *Decameron* (Second Day, Ninth Story). Most scholars now believe that Shakespeare read this story in the original Italian, supplementing and varying it, at least in detail, with help from a version in English, *Frederick of Jennen* (that is, of Genoa). The latter was a sixteenth-century translation of a German version, much elaborated, of the story as it is told in the *Decameron*. This mixture is complicated enough, but it is by no means the full genealogy. The wager story had literary analogues in high and low culture, in verse and prose, and in drama and romance, and a complete account of its genesis and descent, traced back through its various forms to some archetype at origin, is not really possible.

Two scenes in particular, I.6 and II.2, show how Shakespeare modified and fused the materials he found in the *Decameron* and *Frederick of Jennen*. I.6 is the scene in which Jachimo tries to seduce Imogen. In Boccaccio there is nothing about a meeting between the seducer and lady, while in *Frederick of Jennen* the villain has to walk about the town, hoping for a chance meeting with the lady. When he does, and realizes how good a woman she is, he feels ashamed. To win the bet he decides he will have to sneak into her bedroom. The means by which the villain does this is much the same in Boccaccio and *Frederick of Jennen*: he bribes an old woman to have a chest, in which he is hidden, conveyed into the lady's house. In *Frederick of Jennen*, when the old woman asks her to take care of the chest, said to contain jewels and plate, the wife agrees to take it into her bedroom for safe keeping. Shakespeare dispenses with the old woman, but retains the heroine's offer to keep the chest in her bedchamber, as well as a description of what the chest is supposed to contain. Neither the offer nor the chest's contents is mentioned by Boccaccio.

In both sources the villain thinks up the idea of the chest, and of using the old woman, *after* he has realized that he cannot succeed against such a virtuous wife. By contrast, Jachimo arrives in Britain with a trunk big enough to hold him – and one which opens with an interior lock – and with an excuse for leaving it with Imogen (I.6.185–92); presumably he fears or expects that he won't be able to seduce her. After all, this is not his first visit to Britain (I.4.1), even if he hasn't met the princess before, and he does know something of her character by general report (12 ff.). It is this preparedness which distinguishes Jachimo from Iago, with whom he is often compared. In *Othello* Iago's opportunism – his ability to exploit new circumstances and to relish taking a risk, even after a temporary setback – differs from the subtle and cautious planning implied by Jachimo arriving with a conjurer's trick box and a fancy explanation about a gift for the Emperor (at I.6.156–78, his way of handling Imogen seems entirely rehearsed). Both men are villains who know how to manipulate their victims' insecurity and jealousy, but Jachimo's villainy looks more like the careful instrument of some design than the embodiment of a capricious and anarchic malice.

The other scene, II.2, is the famous one in which Jachimo gets out of the trunk in Imogen's bedroom. This time Shakespeare drew on the *Decameron* for the details of the taper, the paintings and tapestries, and for the idea that the intruder sees the lady naked; in *Frederick of Jennen*, by contrast, the room is lit by moonlight, there is nothing said about the decor, and the mole (there said to be a black wart) is on the heroine's arm, which lies exposed above the bedclothes. In Boccaccio no reason is given for the light left burning, although Zinevra does have a little girl sleeping in bed with her, who is perhaps afraid of the dark. Shakespeare dispensed with the child, but he may have transferred the fears of the night to Imogen (see line 5).

Another small but crucial rendering of Boccaccio is Shakespeare's word for the Italian '*cassa*', which in *Frederick of Jennen* is given as 'chest'. Shakespeare avoids 'chest' altogether in *Cymbeline* and uses instead *trunk*, a word with a lot of sexual force for a Jacobean audience. In a contemporary ballad, 'The Married Man's Misery', it is said that a woman who gets drunk will easily be unfaithful, 'For when her wits are sunk | All keys will fit her trunk', and in the same ballad, cuckolded husbands are told that 'Italian locks' can't keep 'Hens from Cocks'. Jachimo uses much the same vocabulary (II.2.41–2 and 47), where the *trunk* has a special Italian *spring*-lock, and where it is implied that Imogen too is a trunk, full of treasure, the lock of which can be picked. Throughout his speech Jachimo refers to Imogen as a series of objects, sealed up, closed off or hidden away (her eyes are shuttered windows, her body is a sepulchred statue, her birthmark is the corolla of a cowslip, concealed by petals). Likening her to a trunk is the most important comparison because it joins with the series of puns on the word *head*, which is fundamental to the play (discussed in the Introduction, pp. lix–lx). Some of these puns are explicit, others are unsaid. Here in II.2 the trunk is a trick box and the head is Imogen's virginity (or maiden*head*); in IV.2 the trunk is the decapitated body of Cloten, the clot whose head has been cut off; and in V.5 the trunk is the cedar tree, said to signify Cymbeline, the head of Britain.

The *Decameron* and *Frederick of Jennen* can be read in the standard collection of sources of *Cymbeline*, volume VIII (1975) of *Narrative and Dramatic Sources of Shakespeare*, edited by Geoffrey Bullough. This collection also prints passages from Holinshed's histories, extracts from some of the secondary sources, and analogues from episodes in Spanish and Italian romances. Studies of the sources are listed in Further Reading.

Cymbeline *and the Court of King James*

In 1974 the director John Barton attempted something unusual in his Royal Shakespeare Company production of *Cymbeline* at Stratford. The vision, or Jupiter masque, in Act V, was the centre of the play. Peter Hall and William Gaskill, in their RSC productions in 1957 and 1962, had restored the vision to the stage, but they hadn't gone as far as this. Following the lead of G. Wilson Knight and other critics, Barton took the vision to be the culminating moment in the story of empire Shakespeare was trying to tell us in *Cymbeline*. The vision, for him, was the key to the lost allegorical meaning of the play. In 1610 King James had been trying to bring about a political union of Scotland, England and Wales, which, although it didn't happen in his lifetime, became the foundation of the British Empire. According to this argument, Shakespeare wrote *Cymbeline* to praise the origins of this fledgeling empire, destined to replace and to outdo the empire of classical Rome. This meant that onstage in 1974 there was a really spectacular show for Jupiter, who came out of a golden egg, and a great moment too for Cymbeline who, in the finale, as reviewer Frank Kermode put it, was 'dressed in gold as a version of *rex oriens*, endowed with the solar attributes of the *Augusti*, ancestor of the imperial James' ('*Cymbeline* at Stratford', *Times Literary Supplement*, 5 July 1974, p. 710).

The reviewers, when they noticed it, were not persuaded that Barton's emphasis on Jupiter and empire made much difference to how the audience understood the rest of the play. Directors since 1974 have steered away from interpreting *Cymbeline* like this, but outside the theatre, in the academy, imperial interpretations continue to be influential. It is telling that of the two essays devoted to *Cymbeline* in a recent anthology for students (Ryan, *Shakespeare: The Last Plays* (1999)), one was concerned with finding topical allusions to Jacobean parliamentary debates and to James's political plans in the first years of his reign. The general conclusion drawn from this approach is that Shakespeare wrote *Cymbeline* as propaganda for the crown. To decide how true this is, we need to ask a few questions, about Shakespeare allusions in general, about the date of the play (does it fit the argument?), and about the likelihood that Shakespeare would show his hand as fully as the critics suggest, and if so, to what audience he would show it.

Shakespeare certainly alludes to contemporaries and contemporary events. In *King Lear*, 1.2.131–2, when Edgar refers to the 'maidenliest star of the firmament', scholars think that this is an allusion to the new star observed by Kepler in 1604, which shone brightly for most of 1605 and 1606. In *Henry V*, when the Chorus refers to the 'general of our gracious empress' returning from Ireland with 'rebellion broached upon his sword' (V. Chorus. 30, 32), this is taken to be a reference to Queen Elizabeth, and the 'general' is believed to be either the Earl of Essex or Baron Mountjoy, commanders-in-chief in the campaigns against the Irish from 1598 to 1603. Often topical allusions are only of interest to scholars, who use them to establish when plays were written, but more has been made of the ones detected in *Cymbeline*. Some critics have used these to argue that *Cymbeline* is a royal play or panegyric that celebrates King James and the House of Stuart, rather as the court masques written by Ben Jonson did. This celebration, it is claimed, is connected to the date of the play.

It is generally agreed that when Simon Forman saw *Cymbeline* in spring 1611 it was a new play Shakespeare had finished no more than a year or so earlier, and possibly as late as winter 1610. Because of the plague, the public theatres were shut for most of 1608 and 1609, and for half of 1610, during which time – the longest interval the playhouses had been closed since the 1590s – Shakespeare was reading for, planning and writing *Cymbeline*, *The Winter's Tale* and *The Tempest*. We know that *The Winter's Tale* was played at the Globe in May 1611, and at court six months later when it was presented, along with *The Tempest*, in the winter festivities. The surviving evidence suggests that all three plays were written and performed between 1609 and 1611 (tests of the vocabulary and verse – incidence of rare words, and high percentages of lines longer than pentameters – tend to corroborate this).

An even more precise date is possible for *Cymbeline*. There are parallels in phrasing between lines in *Cymbeline* and in *The Golden Age*, a play of 1610 by Thomas Heywood, and scholars have also linked *The Golden Age* with *The Winter's Tale* (parallel scenes as well as phrases in this case). The direction of influence – from Shakespeare to Heywood or vice versa – is difficult to establish, but all the connections point to 1610 as the year Shakespeare wrote *Cymbeline*. Evidence presented in the Introduction – that when he wrote the play he had in mind a pamphlet published by Galileo in Italy in March 1610 – suggests a date in the second half of the year.

Cymbeline can be assigned to 1610 for another reason too, namely that much of the action (most of Acts IV and V) is located around the port of Milford Haven in Wales. In June 1610, when the court marked the investiture of the heir apparent Henry as Prince of Wales, Milford Haven was celebrated, in shows and entertainments, as the place where the Welsh nobleman Henry Tudor had landed in 1485 on his way to defeat Richard III, and place himself, as Henry VII, on the English throne. The House of Tudor had begun at Milford Haven, so it was necessary for its successor, the House of Stuart (James and his son Henry), to incorporate the place into the royal mythology of rightful succession. How far Shakespeare intended *Cymbeline* to mark the accession of the Stuart monarchy is a matter for debate, but it would be perverse to argue that the prominence of Milford Haven in the play is unconnected to these celebrations. Shakespeare was at court regularly enough to be aware, months before the investiture, that Milford Haven was to be fêted in this way, so he may have started writing *Cymbeline* in the spring of 1610. It is equally possible that it wasn't until later in the year, when he saw the fuss being made of the place, that he decided to locate the play in Wales.

We don't know whether Shakespeare had any private views about this Stuart mythology, but performances at court were an important source of income for his company, the King's Men, so if a play with a Welsh setting was what the elite called for, or would be happy to have sprung on them, no doubt he could write it. In *Cymbeline* the themes of princes coming into their true inheritance, and having to fight for it, and it all starting at Milford Haven, had obvious points of contact with the story of Henry Tudor in 1485. But Shakespeare was too canny to go much further. The parallels that critics have urged (both Cymbeline and James had two sons and a daughter, and so forth) aren't fully convincing because Shakespeare took care to keep imaginary and real lives apart. Cymbeline, for instance, is regal on occasions, but most often he is weak and led by the nose by his wife. Would Shakespeare have dared to suggest such a parallel with James?

Some critics have gone too far in the opposite direction, declaring that there are no topical references in *Cymbeline* at all – Milford Haven is the location only because invading armies always landed there – but we don't need to be as sceptical as this. Shakespeare's plays do contain personal compliments, and it's not impossible he was paid for them (one aristocrat, the Earl of Rutland, paid him for writing an *impresa*, a sort of motto, in March 1613). In Act V of *Cymbeline* there is probably a compliment embedded in the story of the heroic defeat of the Romans. In the source in Holinshed's history of Scotland the farmer and his sons who stood up to the Danes were ancestors of Sir James Hay, a Scots courtier and favourite of King James. Hay came to the English court as a gentleman in 1603, but he was elevated to the Scottish peerage by 1606. It is conceivable that by using this episode, in a far from disguised form, Shakespeare intended, at some court performance of *Cymbeline*, a small compliment to Hay on having such distinguished ancestors.

There is no sign that *Cymbeline* was played at the Jacobean court, so the compliment may never have reached Hay in public. This is true of course of any larger political message the play is supposed to communicate, which also raises the thorny question, not explicitly addressed by advocates of this way of reading *Cymbeline*: what sort of audience was the propaganda intended for? Was it the King himself, so that he could bask in praise, or was it the elite court audience, who already knew what they were supposed to believe but went through it again for pleasure, or was it the mixed crowd in the public theatres? (Wilson Knight in his transcendental, trans-historical way, thought that the audience were the unborn generations of Britons who would in time come to run the British Empire, and of whom Shakespeare, as a genius and divinely prescient, was aware.) In all, until this vexed question of audience(s) has been more adequately answered, serious doubts about the supposed propaganda and political allegory in *Cymbeline* must remain.

Commentary

Biblical references are to the Geneva Bible (1560).

I.I

The scene is Cymbeline's palace in Lud's Town (London) in Ancient Britain. The Second Gentleman is a stranger to the court, and perhaps to Britain as well (he knows nothing of Posthumus or the abduction of the princes). The social status of the Gentlemen is important, because they are the same rank as Posthumus. Perhaps the prospect of a dangerous, upward mobility (of being advanced from a commoner's modest beginnings to marry the heir apparent) is what agitates the First Gentleman as he describes Posthumus. He certainly becomes insistent that what he is saying isn't exaggerated or untrue, even if the Second Gentleman appears to find it hyperbolic (24), or laughable (66), or difficult to follow (notice his reminder, *our theme*, in 39). This uneasy distance between commoners and the royal family becomes apparent as the scene progresses. Cymbeline had reared Posthumus as Imogen's *playfellow* (145), a word which could mean a childhood companion or a mature sexual partner. Either the King was blind to the love and desire which might grow when the children were brought up together, or he had been fully aware that it might happen, and at one stage even intended it (perhaps there was a late change of favour away from Posthumus, formerly his favourite in the Bedchamber; see note to 42).

1–3 *You do not . . . the King*: Editors have not agreed on a
satisfactory text for these lines. In F they are like this:

> You do not meet a man but Frownes.
> Our bloods no more obey the Heauens
> Then our Courtiers:
> Still seeme, as do's the Kings.

The difficulty in construing the lines is to know what
is being compared with what. In their emended form
in the present edition, the lines can be paraphrased as
'You don't meet anyone who isn't frowning. Our
temperaments are ruled by heavenly influences to the
degree that our courtiers continue to wear the same
outward expression that the King does.' Some of this
gloss is confirmed by the First Gentleman himself, a
few lines later, when he says that *not a courtier,* |
Although they wear their faces to the bent | *Of the King's
looks, hath a heart that is not* | *Glad of the thing they
scowl at* (12–15). This return to what he has said, so as
to clarify and qualify it, is characteristic of the First
Gentleman's speeches (for instance, the way he tact-
fully modifies the verbs *hath* to *married* in 17–18).

4 *of's*: Of his.

5 *purposed to*: Planned to (marry).

5–6 *his wife's sole son . . . late he married*: Shakespeare invites
the audience to note a double standard in this.
Cymbeline's new wife is not of royal birth, nor even
an aristocrat. Cloten gives this away when he speaks
to Imogen's lady-in-waiting, Helen, at II.3.74–5: when
asked who he is, he replies *A gentleman* and, more, *a
gentlewoman's son*. This is the assertiveness and compla-
cency of a parvenu, who has not adjusted to his new
rank. Cymbeline is so besotted with the gentlewoman
(because of her beauty, V.5.63) that he has done the
very thing he is punishing his daughter for; he has
married a commoner.

6 *late*: Recently, but also 'late in his life'.

referred: (1) Given *or* (2) entrusted (with the suggestion of bestowing herself on a social inferior, marrying beneath her).

10 *touched at very heart*: Deeply hurt.

13 *bent*: Inclination.

16 *He*: Cloten.

17 *he*: Posthumus.

19 *creature*: The nuances of this word were considerable at this date. Posthumus is a unique being, without peer, and in his own right always distinguishable from all others (19–21); but he is still only a social dependant, whose position was created by Cymbeline (40–41).

22 *that should compare*: Who was chosen for comparison (with Posthumus).

23 *outward*: External appearance.

stuff: Substance.

24 *Endows*: Furnishes.

speak him far: Praise him lavishly.

25–7 *I do extend him . . . measure duly*: The sense of the lines is: 'My praise of him, however extensive it seems, is yet within the limits of his worth: if anything, I have given an ungenerous account of him, rather than the fuller one he deserves.'

28 *delve him to the root*: Dig to the root of his family tree (*birth*, 27). The *root* of his name is given at 28–33 and 39–40.

28–40 *His father . . . was born*: Shakespeare arranged Post-humus' family to mirror Imogen's, gathering the names and genealogy from various places in Holinshed (printed in Bullough, see Sources).

The names in italic type are of people alive at the beginning of the play.

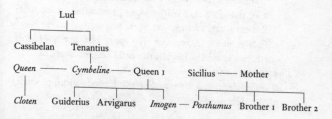

King *Tenantius* (31) was Cymbeline's father, who
succeeded to Lud's throne after the death of *Cassibelan*
(30), Cymbeline's uncle (III.1.5). Sicilius *did join his
honour* (gave his service and reputation as a soldier) to
Cassibelan, but received *his titles* from Tenantius. One
of these was *Leonatus* ('Lion-born'), a *sur-addition*, or
additional name awarded to him for success in battle
(there may be a pun on *sur*/sir). It is worth noting that
Shakespeare's own claim to be a gentleman rested, in
large part, on service done by his ancestors, as soldiers
under Henry VII. His coat of arms was a reminder of
this – a spear brandished by a falcon (a shake-spear) –
but his origin, at least on his father's side, was as obscure
and undistinguished at its *root* as that of Posthumus.

30 *Cassibelan*: Pronounced 'Cas-*sib*-e-lan'.

37 *fond of issue*: (1) Doting on his sons *or* (2) past hope
of further children.

38 *quit being*: Died.

39 *Big of this gentleman*: Pregnant with Posthumus.

41 *Posthumus*: The name signifies that he was born after
his parents' deaths (his mother died giving birth to him).
Shakespeare may have derived the name from Silvius
Posthumus, the grandfather of Brute, the legendary
founder of Britain.

42 *Bedchamber*: The most important office in the Jacobean
court, because it comprised the King's entourage,
through whom he governed personally. This was an
innovation in the English court, introduced from
Scotland by King James in 1603, which shifted power
from the bureaucrats in the Privy Chamber (the Tudor
arrangement) to a select group of royal favourites.
Cymbeline had swept Posthumus upwards in the same
way that James, by 1611, was promoting his courtier
Robert Carr, future Earl of Somerset.

43–4 *Puts to him . . . receiver of*: Offers him every kind of
education which his youth could benefit from.

45 *fast*: As fast.

46 *spring became a harvest*: See the Introduction, p. xxxii.

47 *rare*: Unusual.

48–9 *A sample . . . feated them*: An example to the youngest
people at court, to older ones a mirror which reflected
(*feated*) the perfect shape they ought to have attained
(but could not); the verb *feated* may mean 'showed them
how to behave properly'.

50 *To his mistress*: This conflates two constructions: 'To
his mistress, Posthumus was', and 'As regards his
mistress (to move on from describing Posthumus)';
mistress here refers to Imogen as a wife as well as a
princess, but it does not mean a sexual partner outside
marriage.

51 *her own price*: (1) What she is prepared to pay (endure)
to marry Posthumus (imprisonment and her father's
anger) *or* (2) her own value (as heir to the British
throne).

53 *election*: Choice (to marry him).

55 *Even out of your report*: (1) On your account alone *or*
(2) even beyond what you have told me.

57–8 *two sons . . . three years old*: Guiderius is thus twenty-
three and Arviragus a year younger: Jacobean children
were swaddled (*swathing clothes*, 59) until they were at
least two. Shakespeare took the names from Holinshed
(see Sources, p. 151).

60 *stol'n*: The mysterious theft of the princes may have a
trace of popular magic about it; see the Introduction,
p. xxxviii.

60 *no guess in knowledge*: (1) No informed guess *or* (2) no
conjecture which has informed us (where they are).

63 *conveyed*: Carried off, stolen.

68 *We must forbear*: Perhaps simply 'we must withdraw'
(or 'be quiet'), since the Queen and the others are
approaching, but it may mean instead, or as well, 'we
gentlemen must show forbearance, put up with things',
despite Cymbeline's injustice to Posthumus and negligence over the care of the princes.

70 *No, be assured . . . daughter*: F at this point marks a new
scene; this is abandoned here, as in most modern
editions, even though the stage is briefly cleared.

71–2 *After the slander . . . Evil-eyed unto you*: Intending you harm, as stepmothers are generally reputed (but falsely) to wish their stepchildren. For some of the Queen's cruelties, see headnote to I.5. *Evil* is pronounced as a monosyllable, with *v* elided.

74 *your restraint*: Imogen is evidently under house arrest, so the *keys* that the Queen refers to, as her *jailer* (73), are real enough. The vocabulary of advocacy, judgement, imprisonment and bars (70–83) amounts to a witty and cruel conceit, but the Queen may also be pretending, conspiratorially, that she will help free Imogen from her sexual *restraint* (she'll let the lovers be together so that they can have sex).

75 *win*: Win over.

76 *Marry*: Indeed (from the mild oath, 'By Mary', the Holy Mother); but perhaps also a sly reminder from the Queen, with a pause and a smile (see 84–5), that Cymbeline is furious because Imogen has dared to 'marry'.

78 *leaned unto*: Deferred to.

79 *inform*: (1) Equip *or* (2) teach.
   Please: If it please you.

80 *peril*: Penalty (of not leaving).

81 *fetch*: Take.

82 *barred*: Banned, forbidden (literally, separated by bars).

85 *tickle*: (1) Pretend to please *or* (2) play with (a victim).

86 *something*: To some extent.

87 *my holy duty*: Imogen means her *duty* either (1) to the marriage bond, since Cymbeline can do *nothing* (86) to hurt her if she can but preserve this, by refusing to divorce Posthumus and marry Cloten; *or* (2) to her father, who will not harm her, whatever his anger, so long as she obeys the Fifth Commandment, to honour her father and mother.

89 *hourly*: Continual.

91 *jewel*: Wonderful treasure (that is, their love).

96 *plight troth*: This phrase has misled some critics into thinking that Imogen's marriage was an Elizabethan spousal, or betrothal, in which the parties were joined by private agreement (*de praesenti* contract) but which was not yet blessed by the Church. The opposite is

true: Imogen is a *wedded lady* (I.6.2, V.5.261), and
Posthumus was married in Jupiter's temple (V.4.75–6).
Yet it is odd that Posthumus, so completely a husband,
should *plight troth*, a phrase normally associated with
an engagement. This is probably relevant to the question of whether the marriage has been consummated;
see headnote to II.4 and note to II.4.169–71.

97 *Philario's*: The name means 'lover of the air'.

101 *Though . . . of gall*: Even though the ink is bitter.

103 *move*: Encourage, prompt.

104–5 *I never . . . to be friends:* Whenever I wrong him
(Cymbeline), he accepts it just to stay friends with me;
or he mistakes my wrongs for good deeds (that is, I can
do nothing wrong in his eyes).

110 *to air yourself*: For exercise.

111 *too petty*: Inadequate.

112 *heart*: Darling (a term of endearment).

113 *But*: Only.

116 *cere up*: Shroud (wrap in waxed cloth).

117 *bonds*: Constraints (perhaps winding bands used in
burials; there may be a pun which connects the waxed
cloth (116) to the wax used to seal legal bonds).

117–18 *remain thou . . . keep it on*: Posthumus addresses the
ring directly in 117, and then refers to it in 118 as he
speaks to Imogen (*sweetest*), or thinks aloud.

118 *sense*: The capacity to feel (that is, for as long as I live).

121 *still win of you*: Always do better than you in our
exchanges.

124 *see*: Meet.

125 *avoid hence*: Get out of here.

126 *fraught*: Burden.

129 *good remainders of*: (1) Good people I leave behind at
or (2) (whatever) good people survive; in either case,
perhaps said with irony.

130 *cannot be a pinch in death*: Could be no pain in death.

132 *repair*: Restore.

132–3 *thou heap'st . . . A year's age*: Equivalent to 'you're
putting years on me'.

135 *senseless of . . . touch more rare*: Unaffected, unmoved

by your anger, an anguish deeper and more painful (at parting from Posthumus).

136–7 *Past grace . . . way past grace*: Cymbeline says Imogen is behaving ungraciously by not showing him filial respect (possibly her *holy duty* of 87), but in 137 she uses *grace* figuratively, with a specific, religious meaning. Her despair (at losing Posthumus) has placed her beyond God's grace, so she is damned. The quibble continues in 139–40: even though she is damned, she is also *blessed* because she has chosen Posthumus (the *eagle*) rather than Cloten (the *puttock*). This is anachronistic, but intentionally so. Imogen is a pagan princess living just before the birth of Christ, yet she puns in the language of Christian theology.

that way: Because of that.

140 *puttock*: Kite, a bird of prey (in Shakespeare's time, thought to be much inferior to the supreme bird, the *eagle*); also an insulting term for a greedy, ignoble person, or even a prostitute.

146–7 *overbuys me . . . he pays*: He exceeds my worth by almost as much as the price he has paid for me (that is, his banishment).

149 *neatherd*: Cowherd ('neat' was another word for cattle).

152 *after*: According to.

153 *pen her up*: Imprison her (with a quibble on an animal pen, the King's rejoinder to Imogen's romantic pastoral fantasy in 148–9, wanting to be a cowherd's daughter).

Beseech: I beseech.

156 *best advice*: Settled reflection.

158 *Fie, you must give way*: The Queen probably addresses this to Cymbeline rather than to Imogen, either just before the King exits, so as to thwart and infuriate him still further, or once he has left, with the hope of ingratiating herself with the princess.

160 *your son drew on*: Cloten drew his sword against Posthumus.

163 *no help of anger*: Got no help from his anger, wasn't angry enough (to fight in earnest).

164 *on't*: Of it.

165 *he takes his part*: (1) He behaves as expected (in attacking an exiled and apparently vulnerable man) *or* (2) he challenges Posthumus on behalf of the King.

167 *in Afric*: That is, in some desert place outside Cymbeline's territory, where Cloten would have no protection in a duel (probably an allusion to the many duels of the Jacobean court; see the headnote to I.2).

168 *needle*: Pronounced as a monosyllable, 'neel'.

169 *goer-back*: One who backs away, retreats.

170 *suffer*: Permit.

171 *haven*: Harbour.

notes: Instructions.

174 *lay*: Wager.

177–9 *About some half-hour . . . leave me*: Four lines in F, with 178 divided in two. Editors usually reline the speech as it is in the present edition, and take it to be addressed to Pisanio (Imogen exits following the Queen, and Pisanio leaves on the other side of the stage). Another possibility might be:

QUEEN

Pray, walk awhile.

IMOGEN   About some half-hour hence.

Pray you speak with me. You shall at least go see
My lord aboard. For this time leave me.

Imogen, anxious to keep out of the Queen's clutches, promises to join her shortly, but not just yet (the Queen is still trying to get hold of her at I.3.37–8). She calls Pisanio to her, tells him to go to the harbour, and dismisses him. She exits in the opposite direction to the Queen. Interpreted like this, the lines are part of the cat-and-mouse game being played out between princess and stepmother. This reading would allow Pisanio more time than half an hour to get down to the harbour, watch Posthumus' ship into the distance (8–16), and return to the court; it would also end the scene on a rhyme.

I.2

The scene is Cymbeline's palace. The name *Cloten*, not spoken onstage until III.4.132, rhymes with 'rotten'. Shakespeare probably derived the name from Cloton who, according to Holinshed, was an ancient prince of Cornwall and the father of Mulmutius (at III.1.53–4 said to be the king who gave the Britons their laws). The special meaning Shakespeare gave the name is discussed in the Introduction, pp. lix–lx.

Cloten's exchanges with the Lords, here and in II.1 and II.3, are often trimmed or disposed of in modern productions. Few reasons have been suggested for the coarseness and triviality of the speeches, beyond their confirmation that Cloten is a vile boor. The scenes have more purpose than this, however, even if the jokes and lewdness have gone flat, or become partly unintelligible. One thing they do is to show Cloten as the dark side of Posthumus. In I.1 and I.2 the First Gentleman and Imogen emphasize how unalike the men are, and their differences apparently extend into the next three scenes, where Cloten is all earth (a clot or clod who gives ground) while Posthumus melts into air, at least in Imogen's description (I.3.20–21), and is befriended by Philario. The parallels between the men are unmistakable, however, as is explained in the Introduction, pp. lviii–lx.

Aspects of Cloten's behaviour in these scenes (gambling, quarrelsomeness, swearing) allude to a contemporary concern at the Jacobean court to reform personal manners and to forbid duelling among courtiers. By 1610 there were so many duels, and so much insistence on the protocol of honour, that King James had to issue an edict against them (this has a bearing on how Posthumus conducts himself in I.4 and how Cloten and Guiderius fight in IV.2). The King was less critical about his courtiers' personal behaviour, though it was widely known that his son Henry disapproved of the moral laxity in his father's court, and especially the King's own foulmouthedness (consider Cloten's remark about swearing at II.1.10–11).

1–4 *Sir, I would . . . that you vent*: The First Lord urges Cloten to change (to *shift*) his shirt because he is sweating and smelly after the offstage encounter with Posthumus, I.1.160–64 (the exertion (*violence of action*), and perhaps fear, makes him give off vapours (*reek*) like a slaughtered animal). Unless Cloten strips off, the Lord tells him, the air in his body, lost through overheating, will be replaced by less *wholesome* air outside him (*abroad*).

9 *passable*: Penetrable (without causing the body to rupture), with quibbles on 'run through with thrusts of a sword', and 'tolerably good'.

12–13 *His steel . . . the town*: His sword was like a debtor evading his creditors by going through the town's back streets (avoiding the main *thoroughfare*); Cloten's sword strokes missed Posthumus' body altogether.

14 *stand*: Stand his ground against.

15 *still*: Continually.

18–19 *gave you some ground*: Gave way, retired (with a play on handing over *land*, which Cloten already owns *enough* of).

20 *As many inches . . . oceans*: Just as Cloten has no oceans, so Posthumus did not budge an inch (there is a quibble on *oceans* and *inches*, which could also mean 'small islands').

21 *Puppies*: Fops (silly, pampered creatures, full of big talk): perhaps the Second Lord is older than Cloten and the First Lord, and he regards them as spoilt and degenerate, unworthy successors to earlier generations of young British warriors (Posthumus' brothers, for example).

22 *come between*: Parted (see I.1.163–4).

23–4 *till you . . . the ground*: Until you, fool that you are, were laid out full length on the ground (presumably a long fool is the antithesis of a 'tall man', Shakespeare's phrase for someone who is upright, valiant, and admirable).

27–8 *a true election, she is damned*: A theological allusion, probably to the Calvinist doctrine of *election* (choice) in which only the few souls selected by Christ will be saved from destruction.

29–30 *her beauty ... together*: Her intelligence does not match her looks.

30 *She's*: (1) She is *or* (2) she has.

a good sign: (1) Physically attractive *or* (2) (born under) a favourable constellation or sign (in the Zodiac) *or* (3) a good picture (alluding to signs on taverns and other buildings, which were painted with a motto, or a piece of *wit*, that accompanied the picture).

31 *small reflection of her wit*: Little evidence of her judgement.

32–3 *lest the reflection should hurt her*: In case she should be harmed by her own brilliant light being reflected back (from their polished surfaces, which have no depth beneath them).

37 *the fall of an ass*: (Cloten) being dumped on his backside (*ass*) *or* his come-uppance as a proud fool (*ass*). Perhaps there is also a bawdy quibble, 'the dung from an ass (arse)', which causes *no great hurt* (is not that painful): this would conclude the Second Lord's attacks on Cloten's bluster and cowardice (that is, he would have shit himself with fear had Posthumus really fought back).

1.3

The scene is Cymbeline's palace. The intimacy of the moment, where Pisanio is more of a confidant than a servant, is marked by Imogen addressing him with the familiar pronouns, *thou* (1 and 14) and *thee* (5); when the Lady enters, the Princess reverts to the more distant and formal *you* (39).

For the description of how Posthumus left the shore (8–22) Shakespeare turned to Ovid's *Metamorphoses*, in which Alcyone watches her husband, Ceyx, depart (the borrowing is discussed in the Introduction, pp. xxxiii–xxxiv). He also returned to what he had done in *King Lear*, IV.6.17–20, in Edgar's account of the height of the cliff at Dover. There the fishermen walking on the beach

> Appear like mice, and yon tall anchoring bark
> Diminished to her cock; her cock, a buoy
> Almost too small for sight.

The life-size figure of Posthumus similarly gives way
to crow, crow to gnat, and gnat to thin air. It is also
possible that Inigo Jones had some influence on both
these speeches, given the startling effects he was
achieving in the Jacobean court masques, with his inno-
vatory use of perspective and scenic design. Yet another
influence, at least on *Cymbeline*, may have been the
discoveries Galileo had made with the telescope in 1610
(see the Introduction, pp. lxxii–lxxvii).

2 *write*: Write a letter.

3–4 *'twere a paper . . . offered mercy is*: The loss of the letter
would be as great as losing (1) divine mercy *or* (2) a
pardon from a king

7 *Senseless*: Without feeling (because inanimate).

10 *keep*: Stay on.

12 *as*: (1) As if *or* (2) so that.
fits and stirs of's mind: His mental turmoil.

15–16 *ere left . . . him*: Before you stopped watching him as
he departed (*after-eye him*).

17 *eye-strings*: It was thought that the nerves and muscles
of the eye *broke* or *cracked* when a person died or went
blind; Imogen is saying that she would have sacrificed
her eyesight just to catch the last glimpses of
Posthumus.

19 *Of space*: That is, caused by the distance increasing.

24 *vantage*: Opportunity.

29 *shes*: Women.

30 *Mine interest*: What is rightfully mine (as his wife).
honour: (1) Reputation *or* (2) chastity.

31–3 *At the sixth hour . . . in heaven for him*: To join me in
prayers (*orisons*) at six in the morning, and at noon and
midnight, because at these times I shall be praying for
him (*or* because then we may meet in heaven, although
we are separated in this world). The times Imogen

mentions are three of the hours specified for worship
by the Christian Church (presumably she prays for her
husband at midnight in II.2, but the *encounter* is with
Jachimo, not Posthumus).

34 *set*: Placed.

35 *charming words*: Words which would ward off evil, like
a magic spell.

36 *north*: North wind.

I.4

The scene is Philario's house in Rome. In Boccaccio's
Decameron and *Frederick of Jennen*, the English version
(see Sources), the encounter between the Posthumus
and Jachimo characters, who are rich merchants, takes
place after supper, at an inn in Paris. In *Frederick of
Jennen* two other merchants are present, one a
Frenchman, the other a Spaniard; in Boccaccio the
group is larger, and the men are all Italians. The
Dutchman (a German) and *Spaniard* listed in the
opening stage direction are not given any lines to speak;
it is possible that Shakespeare, prompted by the setting
in *Frederick of Jennen*, intended them to play a larger
part in the scene, but subsequently changed his mind.
As national stereotypes, they may have communicated
important things to Shakespeare's first audiences. A
Spaniard would probably have been characterized as
haughty and overproud, and a German as an utter
drunkard. A Jacobean audience may also have per-
ceived a contrast, perhaps in dress and behaviour as
well, between Jachimo and Philario – that is, between
one of the modern Italians, notorious for their crafti-
ness and supposed lasciviousness with boys and women,
and one of the ancient Romans, soldiers renowned for
virtue, loyalty and gravity.

Shakespeare changes the rank of the men (courtiers
rather than merchants), as well as the preliminaries to
the wager, and some of the reasons for it. In the sources
there is nothing premeditated about the way the Jachimo
character taunts the husband for trusting his wife, and
lauding her virtues. By contrast, even before Posthumus

enters, it is clear that Jachimo intends to prove to Philario that the Briton has too high a reputation. Quarrels and debates over women are evidently a regular thing among men of rank (according to the Frenchman, 53–9, there had been *an argument* over ladies the night before), and Posthumus is known already to have come close to a duel over Imogen's fidelity (47–9). Jachimo sets a trap for Posthumus by making it impossible for him not to defend his wife's good name. The conditions here are those of a Renaissance honour culture, which insisted that reputation was to be valued above everything: not to fight for Imogen would be an unspeakable dishonour for Posthumus. The stages by which the men make claims and counterclaims about Imogen, and finally arrive at the bet itself, have parallels in the procedure leading to a duel.

1 *him*: Posthumus.

2 *of a crescent note*: Growing in reputation.

4–5 *without ... admiration*: Without feeling wonder and awe.

5 *though*: Even if.

5–6 *the catalogue ... items*: His abilities had been set down in a list (*tabled*) for me to examine them, item by item, against the man himself (the act of a connoisseur considering a portrait against a catalogue of its qualities).

7 *furnished*: Equipped.

8–9 *makes him ... within*: Is the making of him (makes him a substantial man), in his bearing and his place in the world, and in his character (an echo of the First Gentleman's praise at I.1.23–4).

10–11 *many there ... as he*: Many others there who could gaze at the sun without blinking just as easily as he could. To look directly into the sun was, by tradition, the prerogative of the eagle, the noblest of birds (Imogen calls Posthumus *an eagle* at I.1.139); the Frenchman is saying that in France there were many young men (eagles) of as much distinction as Posthumus.

13 *value*: Valuation (referring to Imogen's rank, wealth and personal worth).

14-15 *words him . . . the matter*: Gives an account of him, I
    have no doubt, which goes far beyond the facts (that
    is, makes him out to be much better than he really is).

17 *approbation*: (1) Testimony *or* (2) approval.

18 *under her colours*: Under her banner (that is, her sup-
    porters).

18-19 *are wonderfully to extend him*: His *banishment* and their
    approbation are the kind of things that exaggerate his
    worth and reputation (*to extend* is another echo of the
    First Gentleman's praise of Posthumus; see I.1.25).

19 *be it but*: If only.

20 *an easy battery might lay flat*: That is, a simple assault
    would level the walls of her (reputation for) *judgement*,
    were it not that her supporters, *under her colours*, support
    or *fortify* it. The vocabulary is that of a besieged city,
    of an attack with guns or a battering-ram, and of an
    army bringing relief (Imogen is also spoken of as a
    besieged temple at II.1.60–62). Jachimo means that
    Imogen's choice of Posthumus would be indefensible,
    were it not that her friends maintain that she was right
    to marry him.

20-21 *a beggar without less quality*: (1) A beggar without more
    status and talent (*without less* is a double negative,
    frequent in Shakespeare's grammar) *or* (2) a beggar,
    leaving aside the question of his lower rank.

22 *How creeps acquaintance*: (1) How has he wormed his
    way into an acquaintance with you? *or* (2) how low
    acquaintance has sunk, or can grovel, that you can admit
    a beggar like him into your company! (a reading which
    assumes that the phrase was intended as an exclama-
    tion rather than a question, something possible in F's
    punctuation).

24 *bound*: Obliged.

25 *entertained*: Welcomed.

26 *suits*: Is suitable.
    knowing: Experience in the world, *savoir-faire*.

27 *stranger of his quality*: Foreigner of his social position
    and ability.

30 *story him*: Give an account of him.

32 *known together*: Been acquainted with one another.

33 *Orléans*: A city on the River Loire, south of Paris, famous for the siege raised by Joan of Arc (Shakespeare had treated this in *Henry VI, Part I*); pronounced 'Or-*le*-ans' (*Orleance* in F).

35 *courtesies . . . yet pay still*: Kindnesses which will leave me always in your debt, even though I go on repaying them for ever.

37 *atone*: Reconcile.

38 *put together*: Set against one another (in a duel).

38–9 *so mortal a purpose . . . bore*: So deadly an intention as each of you then had (to kill the other).

39 *importance*: A matter.

42–4 *rather shunned . . . experiences*: I avoided agreeing (*to go even*) with anything that I was told rather than allow myself to be guided, in all of my actions, by the experience of other people.

44 *mended*: Corrected, improved.

47 *Faith, yes*: Indeed it was (an exclamation to contradict Posthumus).

47–8 *be put to the arbitrement of swords*: Test the rights and wrongs of the quarrel by a duel, *the arbitrement of* meaning 'settlement by'.

49 *confounded . . . fall'n both*: That is, one of them would have destroyed the other, or they would have killed each other.

50 *with manners*: Without being rude or presumptuous.

53 *may . . . report*: May be reported without fear of contradiction or objection (even though in 44–6 Posthumus has already, and at once, disputed what the Frenchman claimed in 39–40).

55 *country mistresses*: (1) The ladies of our own nations *or* (2) our girlfriends back home (the Frenchman also quibbles on *country*, female genitals; these mistresses were being praised for what was between their legs, how good they were in bed).

56–7 *vouching . . . his*: Affirming with great certainty – and with a pledge to back up his claim by shedding the blood of anyone who contested it – his lady.

58 *qualified*: Accomplished, perfect.

  attemptable: Open to attempts (to seduce her).

59 *any the rarest*: Any of the most exquisite.

61 *by this, worn out*: By now is out of use (that is, he no longer holds this opinion).

62 *I my mind*: I (still) have the same estimate (of her).

63 *prefer her 'fore*: Advance her claims against, put her ahead of (*'fore*, before).

65 *would . . . nothing*: That is, Posthumus would not acknowledge that Imogen was anything less than perfect.

65–6 *though I profess . . . friend*: Although (*or* since) I declare myself to be her devoted servant, and true love, rather than merely her boy*friend* or casual lover (Posthumus is in part correcting the Frenchman for implying that Imogen is his mistress in the sense of *country mistresses*).

67 *hand-in-hand*: A comparison, that is, which claimed only that she was the equal of (*As fair, as good*), not superior to (Italian and French ladies).

68 *something*: Somewhat.

69 *Britain*: F has *Britainie*, at this date a spelling used indiscriminately with 'Britain'.

  went before: Surpassed (in beauty and virtue).

71 *not but*: F has *not* (the omission of *but* was probably the scribe's or the printer's error). Jachimo is saying here that if Imogen outshines other ladies to the same extent that the diamond on Posthumus' finger *outlustres* many other diamonds, then he would have to *believe that she excelled many* ladies: but equally because he has not seen the *most precious diamond* that exists in the world (and it would be an exaggeration for anyone to claim that they had), he will not concede that Imogen is a matchless beauty (Jachimo implies that Posthumus is making unconsidered and hyperbolic claims for her).

74 *rated*: Estimated.

75 *esteem*: Value.

76 *enjoys*: Possesses.

77–8 *Either . . . a trifle*: Jachimo makes a feeble and tasteless reply which means: if you value your diamond more than anything in the world (that is, more than what it *enjoys*), that must include your lady because she is part of the world, and so you are admitting that you value the diamond more than you do her (*she's outprized by a trifle*); this is true unless your lady is dead, and so not part of the world (it cannot *enjoy* her).

80 *or if*: Either if.

82 *only the gift of the gods*: The gift of the gods alone.

84 *graces*: Shakespeare borrowed the word *graces*, which means 'favour', and the notion of a *gift of the gods* from the *Decameron*. Benarbo (Posthumus) first boasts that he received his wife by the special favour of God ('di spezial grazia da Dio'); then, when Ambroguiolo asks him, mockingly, whether it was the Emperor who gave him such a unique lady, Benarbo repeats that the favour came from God not an emperor. There is nothing like this in *Frederick of Jennen*.

85 *wear her in title yours*: You may possess her as your legal right, have title to her in name (she is yours nominally).

86 *strange fowl . . . ponds*: This is a sequence of lewd references: lustful strangers (*strange fowl*) may discover and come to rest on (*light upon*) the genitals of women who belong to other men (*neighbouring ponds*). There is another lewd quibble in *Your ring*, the circle or hole (vagina) given to Posthumus by Imogen, into which he has put his finger, and which a *cunning thief* might steal and use in the same way.

87-8 *so your brace . . . casual*: So, of your pair of inestimably valuable objects, the one (your lady) is merely frail, while the other (your ring) is subject to mischance (*casual*, subject to accident). The suggestion that Imogen is *but frail* may have been prompted by the passage in the *Decameron* in which the Jachimo character repeats commonplaces about the physical and moral inferiority of women, and says they can be seduced easily because they are 'naturalmente mobile', frail and changeable by nature.

89 *that way*: That is, a courtier accomplished in persuading

women to be unfaithful; Jachimo is being provocatively coy by not quite saying what the *way* is (presumably, to have polish, charm, daring).

89 *hazard*: Venture (with the idea of betting).

91-3 *Italy contains . . . frail*: Italy contains no courtier so *accomplished* (Posthumus returns Jachimo's word to him) as to be able to conquer the chastity (*convince the honour*) of my lady, if it is by this – the preservation or loss of her chastity – *that you term her frail*.

95 *I fear not*: I am not uneasy or anxious about.

96 *leave here*: Leave the matter now, drop the subject.

97 *signor*: Gentleman, sir (anglicized from the Italian 'signore').

98-9 *familiar at first*: (We are) on familiar terms right from the start (*too* familiar is what Posthumus means).

100 *so much conversation*: As much familiar talk (as we have been having); but *conversation* was also a colloquialism for sexual intercourse.

101 *get ground of*: Gain an advantage over (a term from duelling, as are the phrases *go back* and the *yielding*; all of these are used as metaphors for sexual advances and intimacy).

102-3 *to friend*: Like a friend (Jachimo repeats the word, tauntingly, which Posthumus had used at 66 to mean a boy*friend*, or a casual sexual lover; see the note to 131 below).

105 *pawn the moiety*: Stake half.

106 *to*: Against.

106-7 *something*: Somewhat.

108 *to bar your offence*: To prevent your displeasure, resentment.

109 *herein too*: (1) In this, moreover *or* (2) in this case as well (Jachimo may be alluding to the offence done to Posthumus when he was in France).

111 *abused*: Deceived.

112 *persuasion*: Opinion.

112-13 *you sustain . . . worthy of*: You will receive what you deserve.

120 *put*: Bet.

neighbour's: Jachimo means 'everything I own, and what
my friends own too'.

121 *th'approbation*: The proof.

124 *lay*: Bet.

ten thousand ducats: See note to 147–50.

125 *commend me*: Recommend me, give me an introduction.

127 *conference*: Meeting (with the suggestion of a sexual
encounter).

128 *reserved*: Secure, invulnerable.

129 *wage*: Wager.

gold to it: An equal sum in gold.

131 *You are a friend*: (1) You are intimate with the lady (and
know she is indeed *frail*, 88, or seducible) *or* (2) you are
only her *friend* not her *adorer*, whatever you claimed earlier
(see 65–6 and note), and you don't feel much for her *or*
(3) you are a friend to me, that is, you are of my *persuasion*, 112, or opinion, about her and women in general.
and therein the wiser: And because of this you are smart
enough to know the danger of such a bet.

131–3 *If you buy ladies' flesh . . . from tainting*: That is, nothing
can prevent female flesh from going rotten (since all
women are unfaithful), even when the woman is the
most expensive one you can buy (even if she costs a
million ducats for a *dram*, a very tiny amount).

133–4 *you have some religion . . . you fear*: You are religious,
and in one way her *adorer*, because, like all believers
who only fear god through superstition, you too are
fearful, but still don't trust your goddess enough to bet
on her. Jachimo is perhaps alluding, cynically, to Psalm
111:10: 'the fear of the Lord is the beginning of
wisdom'; like the Machiavel, the Elizabethan stage-
villain, Jachimo is contemptuous of religion.

135–6 *This is but a custom . . . I hope*: The view (*or* the bet)
you are putting forward is only your way of speaking,
and you can't mean it seriously; I hope that you have
a more sensible notion in mind.

137 *I am the master of my speeches*: I am in charge of
(I meant) everything I said.

138 *undergo*: Undertake.

140 *covenants drawn between's*: A legal agreement drawn up between us.

142 *match*: Contest.

144 *have it no lay*: (I will) not permit this wager.

147–50 *my ten thousand . . . gold are yours*: Jachimo tells Posthumus twice over what he stands to win from the wager (a wife whose chastity is confirmed, the diamond ring and ten thousand ducats in gold); he is shrewd enough not to remind him that he might lose them all.

148 *come off*: Fail.

151 *your commendation . . . entertainment*: (A letter of) introduction to her from you, so that I am welcomed as a guest more easily (than a complete stranger would be).

152 *embrace*: Accept.

152–3 *articles*: A contract (drawn up to define the terms of the bet).

153 *thus far you shall answer*: You would have to settle matters with me to this extent. Posthumus is stipulating the condition that Jachimo must fight a duel with him if he fails to seduce Imogen.

154 *your voyage upon her*: (1) Make a predatory expedition (like a pirate ship) and capture her as a prize *or* (2) sail upon her waters (perhaps recalling the lewd meaning of *ponds* in 86).
     directly: Plainly.

159 *answer me with your sword*: You will render an account for the harm you have done her by fighting me.

160 *Your hand – a covenant*: Shake hands on it; it's a deal.

161 *lawful counsel*: Lawyers. In Boccaccio the merchants draw up a form of contract with their own hands, which is binding on both parties.
     straight away: (I shall) leave at once.

162 *catch cold and starve*: In case, as you cool down, you change your mind about the bet and want it to be cancelled (because it will *starve* to death if Posthumus is no longer feeding it with his anger).

165 *Will this hold*: Will they stick to this bet?

166 *will not from it*: Will not give it up.

1.5

The scene is Cymbeline's palace, presumably before dawn (Friar Laurence, in *Romeo and Juliet*, II.3.1–8, is anxious, like the Queen, to gather flowers before the sun comes up and dries the dew). The Queen wants the flowers of spring – violets, cowslips and primroses (83) – from which she can make oils, medicines and perhaps something worse: according to Belarius, *herbs that have on them cold dew o'th'night | Are strewings fitt'st for graves* (IV.2.284–5).

It has been suggested that Shakespeare modelled the Queen's character on Cecropia, the ambitious, cruel and treacherous mother of Amphialus in Sir Philip Sidney's *The Arcadia* (c. 1583), or on the wife of Augustus, the Empress Livia, whose cruelty and manoeuvring are described by Plutarch (*The Lives of the Noble Grecians and Romans*, trans. Sir Thomas North, 1579). Cymbeline's Queen is in fact cruel in a more modern way. In 1611 there was nothing new about a powerful woman trying to poison an opponent (in a notorious case in 1613 Sir Thomas Overbury died from a slow poison given to him in his food, on the orders of Lady Essex). Nor is her contempt for animals unusual at this date. What is modern about the Queen is that she purports to be, in a modest way, an experimental scientist: she claims to want drugs to test them on animals and study the effects (18–23). Her insincerity and real purpose (to kill Pisanio, Imogen and Cymbeline) are not surprising; but it is remarkable at this date, given her gender and rank, that she should try to pass off her murderous plans as scientific experiments.

Equally unusual is the doctor's warning that these experiments would be dangerous to her moral and physical health. The debate about vivisection, and opposition to it, lay a century and more ahead. In *The New Atlantis*, begun around 1614, Francis Bacon describes research on animals and plant life without a jot of unease. His fictional scientists have parks in which mutations of fertility, growth, size and behaviour are achieved by experiments on live animals. Poisons and surgery are used on them to 'learn what may be wrought upon the body of man'. It is this disinterested search for knowledge which the Queen claims as her defence. Cornelius' response – that seeing these practices will harden her heart (23–4) – points to a contrast between old and new sensibilities as much as between techniques in medical science. By 1765 Dr Johnson, in his notes on these lines, could assure readers that Cornelius' remarks would 'have been more amplified' had Shakespeare lived 'to be shocked with such experiments as have been published in later times by a race of men that have practised tortures without pity and related them without shame' (Woudhuysen, *Johnson on Shakespeare*, p. 232). One classical model for the Queen, in this scene at least, may have been Cleopatra. As her doctor told Caesar, before her suicide Cleopatra had 'pursued conclusions infinite | Of easy ways to die' (*Antony and Cleopatra*, V.2.353–4), a reference to experiments on condemned prisoners: she had them poisoned, or made them die by snake-bite, in order to find out the least painful way to take her own life.

2 *note*: List.

3 *Dispatch*: Get it done at once.

5 *Pleaseth*: May it please.

5 *He gives her a small box*: F has no stage direction at this point. Some eighteenth-century editors added a direction in which Cornelius began the scene with a phial (a small glass bottle); others had him present some papers or a small box to the Queen. The last is verbally correct (see III.4.187), but a box was originally a small receptacle of any material for drugs, ointments or valuables. Onstage, its size and shape depend on how Imogen takes the drug it contains (as a liquid, a powder or pills).

7 *wherefore*: Why.

8 *compounds*: Compounded drugs.

9 *are the movers of*: Cause.

12 *learned*: Taught.

13 *distil*: Extract the essence from the flowers.

15 *confections*: Compounded drugs (other contemporary meanings included sweetmeats, sugary preserves and poison).

16 *meet*: Appropriate.

17 *did*: Should.

   amplify my judgement: Increase my knowledge and understanding.

18 *conclusions*: Experiments.

21–3 *try the vigour . . . effects*: The pronouns here are as unclear as the Queen can make them. She may mean simply 'test the potency of the drugs (*them*, 21) and apply antidotes to their action (*Allayments to their act*), and from these experiments (*them*, 22) deduce how the drugs work (*several virtues and effects*)'; but another, more repulsive meaning would be 'test the strength of the animals (*them*, 21), and administer drugs which paralyse them or retard their movement (*Allayments to their act*), and from these reactions (*them*, 22) make observations about the different physical characteristics (*several virtues and effects*) of the animals'. The poison the Queen believes she has obtained is supposed to cause its victims to die a *ling'ring* (34) and *languishing death* (9), perhaps immobilizing them (*Allayments*) before the very end.

25 *seeing these effects*: Sight of (1) the effects of the drugs *or* (2) the reality of the animals' suffering (*effects* also meant 'facts' at this time).

26 *noisome and infectious*: Literally, noxious and physically contagious, but also figuratively, harmful and unhealthy (to the Queen's mind and soul).

   content thee: (1) Don't worry yourself *or* (2) just shut up and do it.

28 *factor*: Agent.

38 *prove*: Test.

39 *up higher*: On superior, more complex species (that is, on human beings ultimately).

40 *it*: The working of the benign drugs (*Those she has*, 36).

44 *So to be*: For being.

47 *quench*: Cool down; perhaps another of the Queen's jokes (hasn't darling Imogen cried enough tears to put out the flames of love?).

instructions: Warnings, sound advice.

52–3 *his name . . . last gasp*: Probably another cruel witticism (Posthumus had of course received his name *at last gasp*, after his mother had died giving birth to him).

54 *shift his being*: (1) Change the place where he is living or (2) alter his way of life.

56–7 *comes to decay . . . him*: (1) Brings a day to nought for him *or* (2) destroys a day of the work it took to make him (his birth and education); *decay* is either a noun or a transitive verb.

58 *depender*: A dependant (since Pisanio relies on Posthumus), but also, figuratively, something which is suspended or hangs down.

leans: Is leaning (and about to fall).

64 *What is more cordial*: Anything which is more restorative (health-giving).

68 *Think what . . . but think*: (1) Consider what a golden opportunity presents itself as (*or* if) you change your loyalties; just think *or* (2) weigh up what a risk you will be taking if you switch sides: but also weigh in the balance. These lines have been emended in various ways, including the simple transposition to *what a change thou chancest on*, that is, what a change in fortune you have come upon.

69 *to boot*: To your advantage (*or* as well).

71 *To . . . thy preferment*: (To give you) any kind of advancement you wish.

73 *desert*: Action which will deserve reward.

74 *load*: Reward.

76 *shaked*: Shaken (from his allegiance to Posthumus).

77 *remembrancer*: Person whose duty it is to remind someone of something (a legal term).

78 *hand-fast*: Marriage contract.

79–80 *quite unpeople . . . her sweet*: Remove all the people who represent (*liegers*, or resident ambassadors) Posthumus

(Imogen's *sweet*, or lover) in his absence; Pisanio is the solitary representative.

81 *bend her humour*: (1) Change her mind *or* (2) alter her outlook (to suit mine).

82 *So, so*: A term of approval; or perhaps the Queen checks the flowers against the note she gave the Ladies at the beginning of the scene.

84 *closet*: Private room.

I.6

The setting is Cymbeline's palace, probably in the evening (at II.1.32, Jachimo is said to have arrived at *court tonight*). See Sources, pp. 152–3, for details of how Shakespeare drew on the *Decameron* and *Frederick of Jennen* for this scene.

4 *My supreme crown of grief*: Who is (or whose absence is) the crowning sorrow of my grief.

4–5 *those . . . Vexations of it*: (1) The things which constantly exacerbate it (the grief), that is, cruelty, falsity and foolishness *or* (2) those frequent vexations, the three people I have just mentioned, a cruel father, a false stepmother and a foolish suitor.

6–7 *happy . . . that's glorious*: (I'd have been) happy (because no longer a princess), but the wishes and needs of people of high birth and status are most unhappy. Imogen, as a princess, is not permitted to love anyone she pleases, certainly not someone beneath her in rank (Cloten reminds her of this at II.3.108–20). Her *desire* for Posthumus, a commoner, is more miserable than that of ordinary people who can marry without considerations of state.

7–9 *Blest be . . . comfort*: These people are lucky who, however humble their social status, have their own free choice in things, a condition that sweetens (*seasons*) whatever comfort they take in life. The phrase *seasons comfort* is perhaps a noun followed by a verb, in which case it means 'which the passing of time, marked by the seasons, gives comfort to' (an appropriate pointer to the humble lives her brothers are living in the Welsh mountains, subject to seasons of rain and blistering heat).

9 *Fie*: An exclamation of surprise, or annoyance at being disturbed.

11 *letters*: One of the conditions of the wager is that Posthumus supply Jachimo with *commendation* for *more free entertainment* with Imogen (1.4.151), that is, he should supply him with *letters* of introduction. In Boccaccio, but not in *Frederick of Jennen*, the villain stipulates that the husband must *not* write any letters which would be a hindrance to his attempt on the wife.

Change you, madam: At first Imogen looks startled, or annoyed, or anxious and uncertain what news a stranger from Rome might be bringing about her husband; Jachimo urges her to change her expression and be cheerful because the news is good. Some editors emend F's *madam:* to 'madam?', so that Jachimo can ask Imogen why her expression has changed, or whether she is momentarily unwell ('are you well, madam?').

15 *out of door*: External, visible.

16 *furnished*: Equipped.

rare: Exceptional.

17 *alone th'Arabian bird*: This is the phoenix, a mythical bird which was said to perch on a tree in Arabia, to live for hundreds of years, and at its death to be consumed in fire, out of the ashes of which it would be born again. Only one example of the species existed at a time, so to describe someone as a phoenix was to say that they were unique (*alone* may be a tautology, or Jachimo may mean '(she is) beyond all others the phoenix').

19 *Arm me audacity*: (1) Let me be audacious *or* (2) audacity arm me.

20 *the Parthian*: The mounted archers of Parthia were famous for the way they shot their arrows behind them while in flight from an enemy; Jachimo probably means (1) he will have to resort to an indirect and deceptive assault on Imogen *or* (2) if he gets caught, he'll have to make a quick getaway.

22 *note*: (1) Distinction *or* (2) reputation.

23 *Reflect upon him*: (1) Regard him *or* (2) bestow your

attention on him *or* (3) show him the radiance of your favour (cf. I.2.32–3). Posthumus may also be signalling privately to Imogen to think about what type of man Jachimo is ('ask yourself what kindnesses I could possibly owe this man, and don't be taken in by him').

24 *trust*: Some modern editors alter this to 'truest', and read 'Your truest Leonatus' as the phrase subscribed, as a farewell, at the end of the letter.

31–49 *What, are men . . . for the garbage*: Jachimo feigns something like a reverie, occasioned by his supposed incredulity that Posthumus has sex with whores when he has a wife like Imogen.

32 *vaulted arch*: The heavens (imagined as in a picture in a medieval Book of Hours, of an arch).

32–3 *rich crop . . . land*: (1) Harvest of all the life on the earth and in the seas *or* (2) harvest which the eyes gather in, that is, the sea and land.

33–5 *distinguish . . . beach*: See the Introduction, pp. lxxv–lxxvi.

34 *orbs*: Heavenly bodies.

36–7 *Partition make . . . foul*: Distinguish between fair and foul (1) with such precious organs of vision as our eyes (*spectacles*) *or* (2) when we are presented with such precious sights (*spectacles*) as this Imogen.

37 *admiration*: Wonder.

39 *two such shes*: Two such women (one of them Imogen, the other, a foul slut whom, Jachimo suggests, Posthumus has taken up with).

   chatter this way: That is, voice their gibberish sounds in favour of Imogen.

40 *Contemn*: Scorn.

   mows: Grimaces (of dislike, disapproval).

41 *case of favour*: (1) Question of beauty *or* (2) question of which to prefer.

42 *definite*: Decisive, sure which to choose.

   appetite: Physical desire.

43 *neat*: Elegant, refined.

44 *vomit emptiness*: Feel sick, but with an empty stomach (not *allured* or attracted *to feed*, 45, by *Sluttery*), and so cast up nothing: that is, desire would turn to loathing.

46 *What . . . trow*: What on earth is the matter? (*trow* is an intensifier).

46–7 *cloyèd will . . . desire*: Lust wearied with excess, that kind of sexual desire which is insatiable even when it is surfeiting (*will* is contrasted with the normal physical *appetite* (42) and *desire* (44), that gags at the prospect of *Sluttery*).

47–8 *tub . . . running*: Both filled to the brim and emptying away. This may be a classical allusion (the Danaides, wives who were punished in hell for murdering their husbands, were condemned to pour water into an ever-emptying vessel), but there were other associations at this date: one treatment for venereal disease was to sweat it out in a *tub*; and the phrase 'a tale of a tub' was proverbial for something that was empty and a cheat.

48 *ravening*: Devouring voraciously; there is perhaps a pun on 'raven', the bird that feeds on lambs and pecks out their eyes.
lamb: The Christian and pastoral symbol of innocent purity (here, a virtuous woman as opposed to *garbage*, stale, thrown-away food, or prostitutes).

49 *garbage*: General refuse (filthy and used in contrast with the white purity of the lamb). An older meaning of *garbage* was offal, used for cooking, which may be connected, through a series of puns, with *boiled stuff* (125), prostitutes, that is, who sweat in a *stew* (152) or brothel, or in a *tub* (47).

50 *Thus raps you*: Has possessed you in such a way.

52–3 *Desire . . . peevish*: Request my servant to wait for me where I left him; he is a stranger (to Britain) and easily distressed.

53 *peevish*: Temperamental.

58 *none a stranger*: (1) (There is) no foreigner *or* (2) he is not at all a stranger.

59 *gamesome*: Sportive.

60 *Briton*: British.

61 *sadness*: Gravity, serious thoughtfulness.

62 *sad*: Serious (perhaps melancholy).

65 *Gallian*: French.

65-6 *furnaces . . . him*: Breathes out hot, passionate sighs, in
      quick succession (like the blasts from a furnace); *thick*
      means 'close together'.

66 *jolly*: Jovial (but with connotations of licentiousness).

67 *from's free lungs*: Without restraint (the equivalent of
      belly-laughs).

69 *proof*: Experience.

71 *will's*: Will his.

71-2 *will's free hours . . . bondage*: Will spend the time that
      he is free from her pining away (1) for a most certain
      slavery *or* (2) for the restrictions which are placed on
      an engaged (*Assured*) man.

78 *bounty towards him*: Generous gifts to him – first, his
      own endowments, and second, Imogen as his wife
      (*himself* and *you*, 79-80).

80 *account*: Reckon.

    all talents: (1) All the natural abilities bestowed on
      Posthumus *or* (2) all the gifts or wealth (*talents* were
      also coins) which anyone could ever receive (that is,
      Imogen is inestimable).

81 *wonder*: Marvel at (Posthumus' behaviour and ingrati-
      tude).

83 *Two creatures*: Jachimo is deliberately unclear about
      who these two are; they may be (1) Imogen and
      Posthumus (whom he pretends to be sorry for, despite
      the Briton's deplorable conduct in Rome) *or* (2) Imogen
      and himself (as he begins to insinuate that he has fallen
      for her, and that she should have pity on his love).

84 *wreck*: Disaster.

86 *solace*: To take pleasure or comfort.

87 *a snuff*: (The light from) a candle.

92 *office . . . venge it*: Duty of the gods to take revenge
      for it.

93 *on't*: About it.

95 *doubting things go ill*: Fearing (*or* suspecting) that
      matters are going badly.

97 *timely knowing*: If one knows in time.

98 *born*: Is born.

98–9 *discover to me . . . stop*: Let me know what it is you (1) both urge yourself to say and then rein back from *or* (2) both force on me and then withhold.

101 *feeler's*: That is, the person whom she touched.

102 *th'oath of loyalty*: In Elizabethan and Jacobean England oaths of allegiance were enforced on Roman Catholics to ensure their loyalty to the Protestant monarch. Jachimo means that Imogen's *touch* (100) would compel even someone of a different faith (even himself, a Roman playboy who has never been faithful to a woman) to pledge fidelity to her.

this object: That is, Imogen's eye (Jachimo contrasts her cheek, hand and eye, 99–104, with the lips, hands and eye of her sluttish rival, 105–10).

103–4 *the wild motion . . . only here*: The erratic motion of my eye which Imogen's eye alone captivates (*Takes prisoner*) and holds here in its place. *Fixing*, the reading in F2, replaces *Fiering* in F, which some editors retain, with the gloss 'the wild passion of my eye catches fire from her alone'.

105 *Slaver with lips*: Set slobbery kisses on the lips (of prostitutes).

105–6 *as common as . . . Capitol*: Contemporary proverbs about whores and promiscuous women included 'as common as the highway' (or the cartway, or the barber's chair). The stairway to the Capitol, or the Temple of Jupiter in Rome, had a hundred steps: like the *lips* in 105, the stairs were used by everyone. Shakespeare perhaps intended a contrast between this temple in Rome and the one dedicated to Jupiter in Britain, in which Imogen and Posthumus were married (see V.4.75–6).

106–8 *join grips . . . labour*: Take hold of hands (a synecdoche for the prostitute's heart and body) coarsened by the constant pretence (of feeling desire for customers) – a pretence that hardens her as much as the sexual work (*labour*) itself. There is a pun in *hourly* ('whore-ly', like a whore).

108–9 *by-peeping . . . illustrous*: Sidelong (lascivious) glances with eyes that are mean and vulgar, and dulled (lack-lustre); *illustrious* in F is obviously inappropriate.

110 *tallow*: Tallow candle.

112 *Encounter such revolt*: Come upon as a punishment for (1) such inconstancy and casting off of allegiance *or* (2) such a revulsion of appetite.

113–17 *Not I . . . report out*: It is not my inclination to tell tales (*intelligence* about Posthumus) which makes me declare the meanness (the *beggary*) of his change (in behaviour, taste in women); rather (*but*) it is your demeanour and person which charm this report out of my innermost and silent keeping (*mutest conscience*) and into words (from *my tongue*). The F reading *And himself*, in 113, here emended to *And himself.*, could give another interpretation: 'And it is his own behaviour, not my inclination to talk about it, which reveals the meanness (the *beggary*) of his change.'

120–21 *an empery . . . double*: (1) An empire which would make double (the power and wealth of) the greatest of kings (were he able to marry Imogen) *or* (2) a kingdom twice as powerful and wealthy as one ruled over by the greatest king. Either of these, in the setting of the play, Ancient Britain, is gross hyperbole (see III.1.62–3); but there is probably an anachronistic allusion here to the political aims of King James in 1610 (see *Cymbeline and the Court of King James*).

121–2 *partnered . . . tomboys*: (Imogen is) (1) made the same as *or* (2) debased to sharing her husband with whores (or sexual playthings: *tomboys* was contemporary slang for the female genitals and for prostitutes).

122 *self exhibition*: Self-same supply of money, or allowance.

123 *ventures*: Adventuresses, prostitutes paid to take risks with, or venture their bodies.

124 *play with*: (1) Gamble with *or* (2) toy with *or* (3) mock at.

125 *boiled stuff*: See notes to 47–8 and 49 above.

128 *Recoil from . . . stock*: Prove degenerate, fall away from the standards and royal blood of your progenitors.

132 *Should he*: If he should (the beginning of a clause which Jachimo leaves unfinished at *purse* – (135), with

the sense 'need I say more?'; F has *purse:*).

133 *Diana's priest*: Priestess, a chaste votary dedicated to the goddess of chastity.

134 *vaulting variable ramps*: A 'vaulting school' (like a 'leaping house') was a Jacobean colloquialism for a whorehouse; *ramps* were crude, wild-living and immodest prostitutes (the word later became British Army slang for a brothel); *variable* means (1) that there were various ones *or* (2) that they were fickle *or* (3) that they could be vaulted over in various positions *or* (4) that they were used by various men.

135 *In your despite*: In contempt of you.
upon your purse: Out of the money you've given him; but the word was also a low colloquialism for a woman's or a man's genitalia; Posthumus is using (1) other women's purses rather than Imogen's, to insult her *or* (2) his purse – which is hers by right of marriage – over the ramps.

137 *runagate to*: Traitor to, deserter from.

138 *fast to your affection*: Constant to your loving feeling (but also, sexual passion).

139 *close*: Secret.

140 *Let me . . . your lips*: That is, kiss you; once again, there is a lewd suggestion beneath the more polite one (*service* could mean the sexual act).

142 *attended thee*: Listened or paid any attention to you. In her anger at what Jachimo has been suggesting, Imogen drops the polite pronoun *you* (used in 14–99), suitable for addressing an equal, and uses instead *thou* and *thee*, pronouns normally reserved for social inferiors. She reverts to *you* at 168, when she accepts his apology. Jachimo uses *thee* and *thy* in his exclamatory address to Posthumus at 156–9, perhaps to give Imogen the impression that he is particularly intimate with him.

147 *Solicits*: This, the reading in F, is a third rather than a second person singular, something that was still grammatically permissible at this date. F2 has *Solicit'st*, which is more proper, but difficult to pronounce.

151–2 *A saucy stranger . . . Romish stew*: That an impudent foreigner should bargain and trade (*mart*) in Cymbeline's court as (if he were) in a brothel in Rome (*saucy* is connected to *stew*, a brothel, and *boiled stuff* at 125).

157–9 *The credit . . . assured credit*: The trust which your lady places in you deserves your trust, and your entirely perfect integrity (deserves) her unshakeable trust; *credit* has connotations of good opinion, high estimate.

161 *called his*: Claimed as its own.

his mistress: (1) His (Posthumus') lady *or* (2) its (Britain's) princess.

163 *affiance*: Loyalty (to Posthumus; specifically her marriage vows to him).

164–5 *shall make . . . new o'er*: (I will) confirm to your husband (*lord*), what he knows already (that he has a faithful wife).

165–6 *is one . . . mannered*: He (Posthumus), above all others, is the most honourable and faithful (man) in his conduct.

166–7 *such a holy witch . . . into him*: Such a charmer (but a righteous one) that he draws (whole) groups of people to him, as if by enchantment. Jachimo elides magical terms, figuratively, into social ones.

societies: Groups of people.

169 *a descended god*: This is one of Jachimo's hyperboles, but perhaps he (or Shakespeare) already has in mind Augustus, the Roman emperor for whom the gifts in the trunk are supposed to be intended (see 185–96); Augustus was a human being deified, or made into a god, by state decree. This line may also anticipate Posthumus' dream in V.4, in which Jupiter, who is truly immortal, descends among the Leonati.

171 *More than a mortal seeming*: (1) More than a human appearance *or* (2) seeming to be more than a human being.

173 *try your taking of*: Test your reaction to.

175 *election . . . so rare*: Choice of such an unusual (*or* wonderful) man.

176 *Which*: Who (Posthumus is the sir who *cannot err*).

177 *to fan*: To winnow (that is, separate the wheat from the chaff); Jachimo came to test whether Imogen had imperfections, but she was faultless (*chaffless*, 178).

182 *moment*: Importance.

183 *lord,*: F has *Lord,,* so perhaps the line should be construed 'it concerns your lord, myself, and other noble friends (who) are partners in the business'.

186 *best feather of our wing*: Most remarkable member of our company.

188 *factor*: Agent.

191 *something curious, being strange*: Rather anxious, being a stranger.

195 *interest*: Share.

200 *short my word*: Not live up to my promise.

201 *Gallia*: France.

202 *on promise*: Because I had promised Posthumus.

203 *your grace*: (1) Your graciousness *or* (2) your gracefulness. It is possible that it's also a courtesy title, the equivalent of 'your highness' or 'your majesty' (F has *Grace*).

206 *do't*: Do it.

207 *outstood*: Outstayed.

    is material: (1) Is important *or* (2) causes a delay.

208 *th'tender of our present*: The presentation of our gift (to the Emperor).

210 *truly yielded you*: Faithfully returned to you.

II.1

The setting is Cymbeline's palace in the evening, shortly after or perhaps at the same time as Jachimo attempts to seduce Imogen in I.6.

The puns and quibbles in this scene and in II.2 and 3 look inexplicably weak, but they do have a purpose even if they are too obscure and fantastical for modern tastes. Consider, for instance, the puns in the first speech, 1–2: *Was there ever man had such luck? When I kissed the jack, upon an upcast to be hit away!* The literal meaning is that Cloten, in a game of bowls, had thrown his ball so that it *kissed* (lay just beside) the *jack*, the small white target ball, but another player's lucky *upcast* (final shot) had

knocked his bowl away. Clustered around this kiss,
however, are puns that refigure the action of the adja-
cent scenes. Other names for the target ball were the
'mistress' and the 'block', and the game of bowls in
general, with its balls, and its terms – 'cheek', 'jump'
and 'rubbing' – was a much-used source for sexual innu-
endo and coarseness. Here, what only the audience can
recognize (it is signalled to them by Cloten's iterated
jack, *jackanapes* and *jack-slave*, 2, 3 and 20), are the allusions to the game that *Jach*imo has been playing in the
previous scene, in his attempt on Imogen. There are no
one-for-one correspondences, word for word, but instead
a convoluted realignment of meaning, in effect a conver-
sion of the story into words. In I.6 Jachimo (the jack or
knave) had almost laid himself beside, and tried to kiss
his target, Imogen (the pure white mistress), but her
resistance (an *upcast*) had deflected him away. In the
subsequent scenes, II.2 and 3, first Jachimo, the jack, and
then Cloten, the *block*head, will try to bowl or rub up
close to her, but with no better luck.

3 *on't*: (Wagered) on it (that is, bet on (1) the outcome
  of the game *or* (2) this particular cast of the bowl).
  jackanapes: Impertinent creature.

3–4 *must take me up*: Felt he had to tell me off.

11 *curtail his oaths*: Restrict his swearing. Here, as in 4,
   Cloten probably speaks the word *oaths* as it's spelt, but
   it could also be pronounced as 'oats', with a sexual pun
   (as in 'sowing one's wild oats'). In a quibbling aside
   the Second Lord takes *curtail his oaths* to mean *crop the
   ears* or dock Cloten's 'oats' (*ears* of corn), that is,
   castrate him: in other words, it is not for gentlemen
   bystanders, however much they are tempted, to geld a
   lord who is also a foul-mouthed fool (ear cropping was
   also a real punishment at this date). The Second Lord
   carries over the pun into 16, with *fool* (for 'fowl' and
   'foul'), and into 22, with *capon* (a male fowl that has
   been castrated).

14 *I give him satisfaction*: F has *I gave him satisfaction*,
   which means simply 'I dealt with him (by banging him

on the head)!' F2's *give* is more convincing. Cloten is
recalling, with characteristic bluster, funk and annoyance, that the bystander had challenged him to a duel,
had asked *him* for satisfaction (that is, the cheeky creature dared to challenge me, merely because I hit him:
if only *he had been one of my rank*, my social equal, so
that I could have answered him in a duel).

16 *smelled like a fool*: (1) To smell like a fowl *and* (2) to
be foul-smelling, to smell *rank* (a quibbling response
to what Cloten means by *rank*, his elevated position in
the social hierarchy).

20 *Every jack-slave . . . fighting*: Every inferior lout has
ample opportunity to fight duels.

20–21 *I must go up . . . match*: Cloten reveals much more about
himself than he intends; see the next two notes.

22 *You are cock and capon too*: Cloten's unconscious
description of himself as a prick going up and down
elicits a Rabelaisian response from the Second Lord
which unites high satire with low vulgarity. He tells
Cloten that he is (1) prick and fool (*fowl*); (2) all-
phallus but without balls as well (a bragging bully but
also a coward); (3) a penis with *cap on* (that is, with
foreskin, uncircumcised); (4) lord of the dungpile, like
a cock, with his head covered too (keeping his *cap on*,
a sign of superiority, while everyone else has to doff
theirs as a mark of respect to his rank); (5) a strange
bird, with and without testicles (perhaps a sneer that
Cloten is bisexual, or at least of uncertain gender: at
this time, fools and simpletons were taken to be sexually incapable, so the Second Lord is probably
suggesting that Cloten is an impotent freak, an idiot
and eunuch).

22–3 *and you crow cock with your comb on*: And you (or 'if
you', if *an* was intended) crow 'cock-a-doodle-doo'
with your cockerel's crest on you – that is, if you curse
and blaspheme (swearing 'by Cock', a corruption of
'by God'), thus showing that you are a true fool as
much as if you had a jester's cox*comb* (cap and bells)
on your head. It is possible that the Second Lord is

again referring to Cloten's cowardice and arrogance (*crow cock* may mean 'admit defeat', or 'crow over your rival').

24 *Sayest thou*: Cloten either overhears part of the Second Lord's aside, 22–3, and asks him 'what did you say?', or the lines are spoken to his face, deliberately and provocatively, leaving him, in his stupidity, to wonder whether he has been insulted (or if he knows he has, what he is to do about it).

25 *not fit*: Not appropriate.

25–6 *undertake*: Deal with, take on (in a fight).

26 *companion*: Base fellow (a term of contempt); presumably the Second Lord pretends that in 22 he had said *companion* rather than *cock and capon* and *comb on*, and that Cloten must have misheard him.

27–8 *commit offence to*: Do battle with.

29 *Ay . . . your lordship only*: Yes indeed, it is right for your lordship alone (a foolish knave) to behave like this (the Second Lord takes *commit offence to* to mean 'do wrong, be a nuisance to'; only someone as ill-bred and ungentlemanly as Cloten would strike or insult a social inferior).

30 *so I say*: That's what I'm saying (Cloten wrongly takes 29 to be advice and approval; he thinks that he alone, as the Queen's son, is entitled to browbeat people of lesser rank).

31 *stranger*: Foreigner (Jachimo).

33 *on't*: About it.

34 *strange fellow*: Odd freak (the Second Lord may also mean 'a former equal of ours (*fellow*), who is unacquainted (*strange*) with the proper conduct for a prince'; the Court is so *strange* to Cloten that even his page knows about the arrival of a foreign aristocrat before he does, 39–40).

41–2 *no derogation in't*: No discredit in it (nothing in it which would be damaging to my social position).

43 *You cannot derogate*: (1) Nothing you could do would hurt your social standing (your rank as prince makes you invulnerable), *but also* (2) it would be impossible

for you to be more degenerate (*derogate*) than you are
already are (Cloten probably takes the Second Lord to
mean (1) in 44).

45–6 *You are a fool . . . do not derogate*: Everyone knows that
you are a fool, so your actions (*issues* which proceed
from you), being foolish, cannot be worse than you are
(the Second Lord is quibbling on 'you have had the
title of fool bestowed on you, so your offspring (*issues*)
are as foolish, by right of lineage, as you').

48 *I'll win tonight*: By playing dice (see II.3.1–2 and note).

49 *attend*: (1) Follow *or* (2) wait on.

52 *Bears all down with her brain*: (1) Manages *or* (2) overturns (subverts the proper order of) everything, through
her intelligence and cunning.

53 *for his heart*: To save his life.

57 *coining*: Fabricating (with the suggestion of making
plans and passing them off as Cymbeline's, like a forger
stamping the King's image on false coins).
a wooer: Cloten.

58 *expulsion*: Exile (from Britain).

60 *he'd make*: He (Cloten) would bring about.

62 *stand*: Remain unbowed, survive (the attacks on your
walls and *temple*).

II.2

The setting is Imogen's royal bedchamber, just before
midnight (2). Once again Shakespeare drew on the
Decameron and *Frederick of Jennen* for this scene; see
Sources.

0 *Imogen is in bed . . . Helen*: At the Globe Imogen's bed
was probably positioned against the back wall of the
stage, pushed out through the doors to the tiring-house,
with bed-curtains all around it; the curtains could then
be pulled back, on three sides, to reveal Imogen.
Jachimo's trunk was either carried on, or winched up
through a stage trapdoor. At 50, when he is getting
back into the trunk, he says *hell is here* – a reference,
whatever else it means, to the 'hell' or space beneath
the Jacobean stage, down into which the actor playing
Jachimo could have exited, through a false bottom in

the trunk placed over the trapdoor (for other meanings of *hell* see the note to 50). When the scene begins
the Princess may be in bed already (reading a book,
3–4); when she says *To bed* (4), it may be an order to
Helen, or she may be telling herself to go to sleep.

1 *Who's there*: Helen's entry either interrupts Imogen's
  reading, possibly startling her, or wakes her from
  drowsiness.

2 *hour*: Pronounced as two syllables (as with *hours* in 3).

3 *weak*: Tired.

4 *leaf*: Of the book.

  left: Stopped (reading).

8–10 *To your protection . . . beseech ye*: Imogen prays that the
  gods protect her while she sleeps from visitations by
  malevolent fairies and *tempers of the night* – by which
  she means nightmares, or perhaps *incubi*, male demons
  who were believed to copulate with women.

11 *The crickets sing*: The hush in the chamber is so complete
  that the slightest noise – the chirp of crickets – can be
  heard.

11–12 *man's o'er-laboured sense . . . by rest*: Human senses,
  worn out with excessive work, are being restored in
  (the deepest) repose (in other words, everyone is
  sleeping so soundly that nothing will wake them).

12–13 *Our Tarquin . . . rushes*: Tarquin, one of we Romans,
  in the same way trod silently on the rushes; see the
  Introduction, pp. xlii–xlv.

14 *Cytherea*: One of the names of Venus. Jachimo exclaims
  that Imogen is as beautiful as the goddess of love herself.

15 *How bravely thou becom'st thy bed*: How marvellously
  you match your bed.

15–16 *fresh lily . . . sheets*: What a fresh (unplucked) lily you
  are, with skin more beautifully pale than your white
  sheets (the lily was an emblem of chastity).

17–18 *But kiss . . . they do't*: Merely kiss her, take just one
  kiss; her lips, rubies of unrivalled value, how exquisitely
  they kiss, or close on each other (her lips are like
  precious jewels that, one above the other, make a perfect
  symmetry and an enticing shape).

21 *canopied*: Covered.

22 *windows*: Eyelids, literally 'shutters', which close in *lights*, and which are *white* with sky-blue tracery, *azure-laced* (a poetic figure for Imogen's closed white eyelids, with their tiny blue veins).

23 *tinct*: Colour.

24 *note the chamber*: Note down everything about the room (in a notebook).

26 *arras*: Wall-hanging, tapestry (described at II.4.68–72: see note).
    figures: Probably the sculptures or figures above the fireplace (see II.4.80–85 and notes).

27 *contents o'th'story*: (1) Contents of the room (andirons in the fireplace etc.: see II.4.88–91) *or* (2) details of the narrative represented on the *arras* of Cleopatra's arrival at Cydnus, or the one above the fireplace (Diana bathing).

28–30 *some natural notes . . . mine inventory*: (If only I could find) a few birthmarks hidden about her body to *enrich* my list, because these would *testify* far more to my intimacy with her than notes on ten thousand less valuable articles of furniture (*meaner movables*).

31 *ape*: Mimic, imitator.
    dull: Heavy.

32 *be her sense . . . a monument*: Let her be as insensible as a (recumbent alabaster) effigy on a tomb.

34 *Gordian knot*: The intricate knot tied by Gordius of Phrygia that no one could untie. An oracle declared that whoever undid it would conquer Asia; Alexander the Great simply cut the knot with his sword and fulfilled the prophecy. Jachimo means that Imogen's bracelet was as *slippery*, as easy to slip off, as *the Gordian knot was hard* to untie, but he is also thinking of an unfaithful (*slippery*) woman, sexual conquest and Imogen's virgin knot.

36 *as the conscience does within*: (As strongly) as Posthumus' internal conviction (that she has been unfaithful).

37 *madding*: Maddening.

38 *cinque-spotted*: Having five spots (Jachimo is correct:

there are five *drops* in the *bottom* or corolla of a *cowslip*;
cinque was probably pronounced 'sank').

39–40 *voucher . . . law could make*: A stronger proof (more
convincing piece of evidence) than would be expected
even in law (with perhaps a reference to the wager with
Posthumus, drawn up by *lawful counsel*, I.4.161).

44 *late*: Lately.

45 *tale of Tereus*: A story in Ovid's *Metamorphoses*, Book
6. After the Thracian king Tereus raped his sister-in-
law, Philomela, and cut out her tongue, his wife,
Procne, and Philomela took revenge by murdering his
son and serving up the body in a dish for Tereus to
eat. Tereus was changed to a hoopoe, Procne to a
swallow and Philomela to a nightingale.

46 *Philomel gave up*: Philomela was forced to yield (to
Tereus).

47 *spring of it*: Its spring-lock.

48 *dragons*: The chariot of the night was said to be drawn
by dragons (on account of their wakefulness); Jachimo
urges them to run more swiftly to let the dawn arrive.
Throughout these lines, and this scene more generally,
there are allusions to the final scene of Marlowe's *Doctor
Faustus* (*c.* 1590).

48–9 *that dawning . . . bare the raven's eye*: So that (the light
of dawn) may waken the raven (*bare* or open its eyes:
the raven was believed to sleep facing east so as to be
woken by the first rays of the sun).

49 *I lodge in fear*: I am in a state of terror (at my moral
predicament *or* at being discovered).

50 *this*: This is.
   hell is here: (Although Imogen is a *heavenly angel*) (1)
I have made this room hellish, defiled it *or* (2) I am
tempted by devilish thoughts about her *or* (3) she is a
woman too, with a *hell* (vagina).

50 *Clock strikes*: A clock offstage sounds (1) three times,
for three o'clock *or* (2) four times, with the fourth
stroke (for four o'clock, when the Lady is to wake
Imogen) as Jachimo closes the lid of the trunk.

51 *Exit . . . with the bed*: F has merely *Exit*. In perform-

ances at the Globe the trunk must have been carried
offstage, or lowered through a trapdoor, and the bed
drawn back into the tiring-house (perhaps with the bed-
curtains closed).

II.3

The scene is outside Imogen's private rooms and
bedchamber, at dawn, only a short time after Jachimo
has got back in the trunk. Cloten continues to struggle,
hopelessly, to understand what others are saying to him
and to be alive to insults from them (he is suspicious
about the Second Lord's asides and quibbles in I.2 and
II.1, and he even takes his mother up sharply, and
wrongly (50), for suggesting that he is *senseless*). Once
again Cloten has to be instructed in all things: how he
should win Imogen by bringing music to her in the
mornings, and how he should pretend to be *inspired*
(47), or impassioned with love in his suit to the Princess.
At 87 and 96–7 he tries to be the lover, swearing his
love and refusing to give over, but so sloppily that
Imogen teaches him another lesson, this time about self-
restraint in speech and manners (91–102). But although
Cloten is dim, he does know how the world goes. The
language of the song itself may be of the golden sun-
god, marigolds and *golden eyes*, but the gold which
matters to Cloten, and which he hopes the song may
help him to, is the stuff he can bet with, and use for
bribes (7–9 and 67–70).

2 *the most coldest . . . turned up ace*: The calmest man ever
to come up with an *ace* in a throw of the dice (the ace
was the lowest number on the dice). There is probably
a pun on *ace* and 'ass': that is, even a roll of the dice
shows up Cloten as an ass (fool).

3 *cold*: Gloomy, dispirited.

5 *most hot and furious*: Cloten takes these as compliments (the simple opposites of being gloomy and
dejected, when he loses) in the face of what the First
Lord means, that winning makes him over-excited and
wild.

7 *courage*: Good heart, high spirits (but Cloten's mind is

also on sex, as in 13–14: *put into . . . courage* could mean
'arouse sexually').

12 *o'mornings*: In the mornings (F has *a'mornings*, perhaps
an indication of Cloten's unschooled, vulgar speech).
penetrate: (1) Touch her heart *or* (2) stimulate her sexually (so that she is more responsive to his love suit);
Cloten makes the word into a lewd quibble.

13–14 *tune . . . tongue too*: Tune up (your instruments); if you
can affect her feelings by (1) plucking the strings on
your lute *or* (2) covering the stops on your recorder,
well and good; we'll try to work on her with singing
as well (there are crude allusions to masturbation and
cunnilingus in *tune*, *penetrate*, *fingering* and *try with
tongue*).

16 *good-conceited thing*: Well-devised piece (a musical
prelude to be played before the song, perhaps by an
off-stage consort of viols and recorders).

17 *air*: Solo song.

19–25 *Hark, hark . . . Arise, arise*: These lyrics are an aubade.
For a seventeenth-century setting of the song, see Music
and Songs.

20–22 *Phoebus 'gins . . . flowers that lies*: The sun god, Phoebus
Apollo, begins to mount up into the sky, and his horses
begin to drink from the waters (the dew) which lie on
(or in) the cupped (*chaliced*) petals of *flowers* (in classical mythology, the sun represented as a god who
drove a chariot and horses across the heavens every
day: at V.5.189–91 Jachimo refers to Phoebus' chariot
as bejewelled).

23 *winking Mary-buds*: Marigolds with petals closed.
ope their golden eyes: Open their bright yellow petals.

26 *consider*: (1) Reward, pay you for *or* (2) appreciate (at
18, Cloten says that Imogen should *consider*, which may
mean 'let her appreciate what I'm doing for her' as well
as 'take this music and song to her heart').

27 *vice*: Flaw (that is, Imogen must be tone-deaf or
unresponsive to music); Cloten may intend a pun on
vice for voice (F has *voyce*).

28–9 *which horse hairs . . . never amend*: Which neither

bow-strings and fiddle-strings, nor the voice of an
unpaved (without stones, that is testicles, so 'castrated')
eunuch as well, can ever put right. In 1611 the song
would have been performed by a boy with an unbroken
voice, or by a counter-tenor, rather than by a real
eunuch, or castrato.

33 *fatherly*: In a fatherly fashion (approvingly).

35 *Attend you here*: Are you waiting here at.

37 *she vouchsafes no notice*: She does not deign to pay me
any attention.

38 *minion*: Darling.

40 *wear the print . . . out*: Wear out the impression he has
made in her memory (F has *on't* for *out*).

41 *most bound*: Under the greatest obligation.

42-3 *vantages that . . . Prefer*: Opportunities which may
recommend.

43-5 *Frame yourself . . . season*: Shape your conduct to
making well-managed and decorous approaches (to
Imogen), and make these harmonize (be in keeping)
with the times that are most appropriate. Perhaps the
Queen is hinting to Cloten that, whatever he has been
told to the contrary (11-12), waking Imogen up at the
crack of dawn with music and love-songs may not be
the best way to her heart.

48 *that you in all*: As if in everything you.

49 *command*: That is, her command.
   dismission: Rejection.

50 *therein you are senseless*: You are unconscious (on
purpose), deliberately insensible to any command of
hers which means that you accept her rejection of you
(Cloten misunderstands his mother and takes *senseless*
to mean devoid of sense or stupid).

51 *So like you*: If it please you.

55 *the honour of his sender*: That is, the high rank and
distinction of the Emperor Augustus, who has sent him.

56 *towards himself*: To Lucius personally.
   his goodness forespent on us: In view of his past goodness towards (1) us (the Britons) *or* (2) me (if Cymbeline
is using the royal plural pronoun: 'Lucius has shown

me personal kindness and favour in the past').

57 *notice*: Attention.

62 *By your leave, ho*: This is a term of courtesy, the equivalent of the modern 'excuse me', which Cloten uses as
he knocks on the door and calls for attention.

63 *women are about her*: Maids and ladies-in-waiting are
hurrying to dress her.

64 *line one of their hands*: Bribe one of them (put money
in her hands).

65–7 *makes Diana's rangers . . . o'th'stealer*: Makes Diana's
gamekeepers behave falsely (betray themselves) and
surrender the very deer they should protect to the bow-
shot (or gun-sights) of the poacher who has bribed
them, and who has taken up his *stand*, or concealed
shooting-position. Diana, the virgin goddess of
hunting, was accompanied by female attendants who
vowed to preserve her chastity and their own; Cloten
refers to them lewdly as bawds who can be corrupted
to *yield up their deer* (their 'dear' or precious Diana) to
the *stand* of the *stealer* (crude puns on *stand*, which can
mean 'an erect penis', and a 'staler' (*stealer*), which is
something that passes 'stale' or urine).

68 *true*: Honest.

71–2 *lawyer to me . . . the case myself*: The polite meaning is
'(make her) my advocate (to persuade Imogen to accept
me), for I don't yet know how best to conduct my *case* or
suit to her'; the lewd meaning is '(make her) lower (*lawyer*)
to me, go down for me, for I'm not yet standing under
(Imogen's) *case* (that is, sexually erect in her vagina)'.

74–5 *A gentleman . . . gentlewoman's son*: Important revelations about the social origins of Cloten and his mother;
see the note to I.1.5–6.

74 *No more*: Nothing more (than a mere gentleman)?

75–7 *That's more . . . justly boast of*: That's more than some
(people at court), whose tailors charge just as much as
yours do (for expensive and lavish clothes), can justly
claim (because (1) they are even less well born than
you, *a gentlewoman's son*, or (2) they are the sons of
*un*gentlewomen – that is, whores *or* (3) they are

bastards, sons of women whom gentlemen haven't married). F does not mark an aside here, nor at 79, so it is possible that the Lady insults Cloten to his face.

77 *What's your lordship's pleasure*: The Lady asks Cloten 'what does your lordship want?', but he understands (or deliberately misconstrues) *pleasure* to mean 'sexual pleasure', and replies *Your lady's person* (to see Imogen in person, but also to have her body).

78 *ready*: (1) Dressed *or* (2) prepared (which is the meaning the Lady chooses, in an aside, or perhaps as an explicit rebuff to Cloten: yes, the Princess is prepared to *keep her chamber* (that is, to stay in her private room), but also, to preserve her private parts from the likes of you).

80 *Sell me your good report*: Cloten means 'let me pay you to speak well of me with the Princess', but the Lady pretends to be shocked that he is asking her to sell him her *good name*, or her reputation for chastity (that he wants to pay for sex with her); she asks whether she should report of Cloten what she thinks is *good* (tell the truth about him, which would hardly be the same as giving him a good report).

84 *lay out*: Expend.

88 *If you but said so . . . with me*: If you merely said 'I love you' (rather than swore it), it would make as deep an impression with me (that is, none at all).

89 *still*: Constantly, for ever.

92 *Faith*: In truth.

93 *unfold equal discourtesy*: Display (1) discourtesy equal *or* (2) as much discourtesy (as I have shown you in the past).

94 *One of your great knowing*: Someone as knowledgeable, with as much experience as you (said ironically, since Cloten is an ignoramus).

95 *Should learn . . . forbearance*: Should learn self-restraint, having had it shown to you (Imogen means 'even though you have pestered me, I've refrained from being impolite to you; why don't you learn the same self-control?', perhaps with a glance at his sexual grossness, 'can't you be at all abstemious?'). Cloten evidently takes *forbearance* to mean 'withdrawal' – he

thinks Imogen means only 'learn to leave me alone'.

97 *Fools cure not mad folks*: F has *are*, but 96–7 are more
pointed if this is emended to *cure*. Cloten has said that
it would be wrong to leave Imogen in her *madness*, to
which she replies, '(there's no need to stay with me)
fools (like you) can't restore mad people to sanity (your
folly only aggravates their condition)'. As it stands in
F, Imogen means 'I may be a fool to refuse you, but it
doesn't follow that I'm mad'.

98 *As I am mad, I do*: (1) In the same way that I am insane
(according to you), I do *or* (2) because I am beside
myself with anger (at your pestering), I do (forget my
manners, 100, and call you a fool).

101 *put me*: Compel me.

102 *being so verbal*: (1) By your being so talkative (Cloten's
senseless chatter has made her speak impolitely to him,
against her will and manners) *or* (2) by making me say
so much more than a lady ought to (she would have
preferred to remain silent in the face of his unwanted
attentions) *or* (3) by driving me to speak in such plain
terms to you.
   for all: Once and for all.

103–4 *pronounce . . . truth of it*: Declare, by the absolute truth
in it (my heart).

105–6 *am so . . . I hate you*: I am so near to lacking (Christian)
charity (1) as to be forced to accuse myself of hating
you *or* (2) that, to accuse myself for feeling it, I hate
you.

108–9 *For . . . contract you pretend*: As for the marriage contract
you claim to have made (as a pretext for refusing me).

109 *that base wretch*: Posthumus.

110–11 *fostered with . . . scraps o'th'court*: Brought up on a diet
of nothing but cold leftovers from court meals.

112 *allowed in meaner parties*: Permitted for people of much
lower rank and less importance (than you).

113–15 *to knit . . . in self-figured knot*: To tie their souls in a
marriage-knot of their own choosing (*self-figured*,
formed by themselves) because (1) the outcome of
marriage between such *meaner parties* has nothing more

depending on it than rearing brats in beggary *or* (2) the retinue (*dependency*) which attends *meaner parties* is (or will be) no more than brats and poverty. In the parenthetical *On whom . . . beggary* Cloten is probably referring to Posthumus, as he does in 108.

116–20 *you are curbed . . . not so eminent*: You are restrained from that freedom (of choosing the husband you want) because of the *consequence* to (importance of *or* succession to) the crown – as the heir apparent you mustn't pollute (*foil*) the precious reputation (*note*) of the monarchy by marrying a lowly-born wretch (Posthumus), a good-for-nothing (*hilding*) fit only to wear the *livery* (of a lackey), or the clothes of a squire, or those of a pantry-servant (*pantler*) – no, not even as exalted in social rank as that (he's beneath even the most menial of servants).

120 *Profane*: Foul-mouthed, disrespectful.

123 *groom*: Servant.

123–7 *thou wert dignified . . . so well*: Enough honour would have been bestowed on you – to the point where you were envied for being so fortunate – that if the respective qualities (*virtues*) of the two of you were the basis of comparison, and he (Posthumus) were to be made a king, and you (Cloten) were given the title and office of (*styled*) assistant hangman in his kingdom, even then you would be hated for being preferred so generously (above your merits).

127 *south fog*: South wind (thought to be damp and unwholesome).

129 *of*: By.

130 *clipped*: Embraced, fitted around.

131 *respect*: Regard.
   all the hairs above thee: All the hairs on your head.

132 *How now*: An exclamation, prompted by (1) her irritation at Cloten *or* (2) her sudden realization that the bracelet is not on her arm (137–8).

134 *hie thee presently*: Go instantly.

135–6 *sprited with a fool . . . angered worse*: Haunted by a fool (as by a sprite or tormenting ghost), made fearful (at the thought that the bracelet is missing), and made angrier (by the combination of this annoyance and apprehension).

137-8 *a jewel . . . left mine arm*: A piece of jewellery (the bracelet) which has disappeared from my arm too easily and adventitiously (perhaps with the suggestion that she has not taken enough care of it).

138 *'Shrew me*: Beshrew me, damn me (a mild imprecation).

140 *king's*: King.

144 *aught but he*: Anyone but him.

147 *If you will make't an action, call witness to't*: If you want to make my saying it (the phrase *his meanest garment*) the grounds for a lawsuit (an action for slander), call witnesses (and I'll repeat it in front of them).

149 *She's my good lady*: She's my good mother and friend (Imogen says this ironically).

149-50 *and will conceive . . . the worst of me*: And she will, I trust, think nothing but the worst of me (continue to put the worst construction on everything I do).

151 *th'worst of discontent*: The worst vexation possible.

II.4

The setting is Philario's house in Rome. This is a single scene in F but modern editions often divide it into two, after 152 when Philario and Jachimo exit. Posthumus leaves three lines earlier, but re-enters immediately after they have gone. Editors mark his return as a separate scene because the stage is cleared briefly. The present edition follows F on the grounds that by not dividing the scene, the pace and continuity of action are more truly maintained, as well as the psychological tension in Posthumus (his sudden return shows his loss of self-control, and purposeless chasing about – is he trying to keep away from Philario and Jachimo, or does he come back looking for them?).

The tribute Britain owes Rome, introduced at 10–15, begins the entwining of the love plot with the story of war and invasion. The Britons have been conned into paying for a conquest the Romans never made (dealt with in the next scene, III.1), and similarly Posthumus will pay Jachimo, a Roman lord, for a phoney conquest over Imogen, the British princess.

Much of Posthumus' misogyny in the final part of the scene is traditional. Renaissance writers declared that men would be happier if they could procreate without women, and there were many satires on the fickleness and perfidy of the female sex. Just as predictable was the anxiety that women undermined male authority. All women are unfaithful, so all men must be illegitimate. If Posthumus' real father was not Sicilius, but an unknown counterfeiter, Posthumus too must be a fake.

The speech is more unusual because of Posthumus' vivid memory of Imogen's pleading with him to be patient when he wanted sex, resisting him although this was *a lawful pleasure* (they were married, not just engaged: note to I.1.96). Imogen did this with *A pudency so rosy the sweet view on't | Might well have warmed old Saturn* (163–4). Saturn was the god of cold melancholy, old age and impotence, a repressive father who had been overthrown by his son Jupiter, yet even Saturn would have been warmed by Imogen's *pudency*. One reading of this is that the god, a grandfather, would have been moved in his heart by the blushing bashfulness in her face; a less innocent reading is that even his frozen body would have become aroused at the sight of the red hue around her virginal genitalia (*rosy* is a colour but also the unplucked rose). This hint of voyeurism on an old father's part is a reminder that Posthumus too, as he remembers them together, is aroused by the sight of sex withheld because of another repressive father, Cymbeline.

This leads Posthumus to the problem of synecdoche. The man who has control of the part should have control of the whole, thus Imogen was wholly Cymbeline's child for so long as her virginal part was intact. In I.4 Jachimo bet Posthumus that he could possess Imogen's *dearest bodily part*, and in the present scene he brings him proof in parts (the birthmark, details of the little phallic statues of Cupid, and the bracelet, its circular shape an image of her private part), saying that he has enjoyed her whole body. Posthumus is so maddened by this that he can think of nothing but her *part*, to the exclusion of all else. The whole order of what is real is temporarily dissolved in his mind and replaced by a phantasmagoric (and ludicrous) image of Jachimo turned into a boar. The spellings in F are important indicators (167–9):

> Perchance he spoke not, but
> Like a full Acorn'd Boare, a Iarmen on,
> Cry'de oh, and mounted.

This image functions, in miniature, like a gruesome Ovidian metamorphosis, where bodies are transformed to reveal an awful moral truth. Jachimo is eloquent and civil, while the wild pig, his opposite, is speechless and nature in the raw, but in Posthumus' mind these two are no longer separated but fused. The boar is there – a *German one* stuffed with mast, grunting as it mounts – but so too is the boorish man, with his civility stripped away, his acorn nuts (testicles) full and his 'germen on' (penis erect), crying out 'O!' when he sees the shape of the woman's vulva.

What Posthumus imagines is a strange subversion of the story of Diana. In classical mythology the virgin goddess Diana was the patron of the hunt, of women in labour and of chastity. It was she who chased and slew the boar in the forests, with a courage that frightened men away. Here Posthumus inverts the relationship between hunter and hunted: the boar turns on the virgin lady, Imogen, and she surrenders her hymeneal part to him without a struggle (see 169–71 and note).

The first crazed half of Posthumus' speech ends when he says *the woman's part* (172 and 174), and nearly says what he would like to do to it. The images are replaced immediately with a torrent of angry but conventional women-hating vocabulary. He finally talks himself into a blather, in which the *part* becomes an abstraction, a summation of all vices, all of which are female.

2 *win*: Win back the favour of.

bold: Confident.

3 *means*: Overtures, approaches.

5 *Quake*: Shiver.

6 *feared hopes*: Hopes imbued with fear.

7 *gratify*: Repay.

they: That is, the hopes for better times.

10 *this*: This time.

11 *of*: From.

12 *do's commission throughly*: Carry out his mandate from Augustus with care and completeness (*throughly* means 'thoroughly').

13–14 *He'll grant . . . Or look upon*: Cymbeline will pay the tribute; he will either send the arrears (*arrearages*), or he will have to face (*Or* here may mean 'ere', that is, 'rather than').

14–15 *whose remembrance . . . their grief*: The memory of whose conduct in war is still fresh in the grief the Britons feel (at the suffering and deaths inflicted on them: Posthumus' own brothers had died in the Roman *wars o'th'time*, I.1.35).

16 *Statist*: Statesman.

17 *prove*: Come to.

19 *not-fearing*: Fearless.

20 *any penny tribute*: One single penny of tribute (if a compound was intended, *penny-tribute* may mean tax or impost).

21 *more ordered*: Better organized.

23 *frowning at*: (1) Consternation at *or* (2) of his grim, war-like expression.

24 *mingled*: Neither F's *wing-led* nor F2's *mingled* has satisfied editors, who are divided in regarding the former as an error or sophistication, and the latter as uninspired and un-Shakespearian. The notion of a new British military discipline soaring on wings of courage is not impossible, given the literal and metaphorical references to

Jupiter's eagle (V.4.63 and IV.2.348–50); but the
compound *wing-led* is awkward and perhaps out of place
in the easier idiom of this early part of the scene.

25–6 *their approvers . . . world*: (Make known) to those who
put them to the test that they are men (1) whose reputation is going up in the world *or* (2) who have improved
themselves beyond, and now surpass, other nations.
The Britons' *lack of skill* at the time of Julius Caesar's
invasion (20–22) is referred to by Holinshed, and so
too is Britain's dependency on Rome for training its
young men for war and peace (Holinshed gives this as
one of the reasons why Cymbeline was unwilling to
break with the Romans).

27–8 *swiftest harts . . . your sails*: Horses as quick as the swiftest
deer have conveyed you by land, and favourable winds
have filled your sails from every compass point (*corners*
may be the four corners of the map). Posthumus'
vocabulary is faintly, albeit conventionally, amorous:
the quickest hearts (*harts*) have carried Jachimo, the
winds *kissed* his sails; there is a marked difference
between this language, almost that of the Petrarchan
love-sonnet, and the coarseness in 33–5.

30 *I hope . . . answer*: I anticipate it was the short answer
you received (from Imogen).

33 *therewithal the best*: More than that, the most virtuous
(Posthumus interrupts Jachimo to correct his suggestion in 32 that Imogen is merely *one of the fairest*, or a
very beautiful woman).

33–5 *let her beauty . . . false with them*: Posthumus means that
unless Imogen *is* the most virtuous lady, her physical
beauty should be accounted no better than that of a
prostitute looking out from her *casement*, or window,
presenting herself for sale to the corrupt hearts of
clients with whom she will be faithless.

37 *PHILARIO*: F has *Post*, rejected here, as in most modern
editions, as a mistake made by the scribe or the printer.
Philario asks the question about Caius Lucius (37–8)
while Posthumus quickly scans Imogen's letter, or parts
of it, looking for signs that there is anything amiss.

40–41   *Sparkles ... wearing*: Posthumus associates the lustre
         of Imogen's honour with the diamond ring she gave
         him and which he has wagered: 'does it (she) still shine
         as resplendently as it (she) was accustomed to?' he asks,
         and then, with irony, 'or is it (she) not too unbrilliant
         and unshowy to be worn by your good self?' The word
         dull may also have a hint of sexual unresponsiveness
         about it (Posthumus is sure that Imogen could never
         be turned on by a flashy dresser like Jachimo).

41   *have*: Some editors emend this to 'had', but the alter-
         ation makes Jachimo show his hand too quickly; as in
         I.4, he is here playing with Posthumus, tormenting
         him, keeping him guessing through an uncertainty in
         the tenses (*have* I lost? *will* I make another journey, for
         a *second night?*, 42–4).

42   *should have lost*: Jachimo means he would gladly have
         paid the price.

44   *such sweet shortness*: The night passed so quickly because
         of their sweet sexual pleasure together.

47–8   *Make not ... your sport*: Don't make a joke of the wager
         you have lost (also with the nuance, don't pretend you
         played the game with her, when you lost it from the
         start; *sport* could mean 'amorous play').

50   *keep covenant*: Abide by our agreement.

51   *knowledge*: Carnal knowledge, sexual intercourse (as at
         79).

52   *were to question*: Would be obliged to dispute (as in a
         duel).

56   *both your wills*: Jachimo puns on *wills*: Posthumus
         desired that Imogen's honour be tested; and she desired
         Jachimo sexually (so he says).

57   *my hand*: A handshake (given after losing a bet, to show
         that there is no ill-feeling).

59–61   *gains ... find them*: That is, the *foul opinion* gains one
         of us the other's sword, or else let both our swords be
         found *masterless* (that is, because we, their owners, have
         killed each other in the duel); the word *loses*, although
         not strictly necessary to the meaning, makes for
         symmetry with *leaves*.

61 *circumstances*: Particulars, evidence.

65 *give me leave to spare*: Allow me to omit the oath.

68 *watching*: Staying awake for (but also with a suggestion
of voyeurism, that is, it was a sight worth looking at;
this anticipates Posthumus' recollection of a moment
of intense sexual intimacy with Imogen).

68–72 *it was hanged . . . or pride*: The tapestry hanging on the
wall is worked in silk and silver thread, and pictures
Cleopatra's first meeting on the river *Cydnus* (at Tarsus
in Asia Minor) with *her Roman*, Mark Antony (there is
a hint from Jachimo that Imogen received him as *her*
Roman). The river is shown flooding its banks, either
because the waters are displaced by so many boats
crowded on it, or because of its *pride* at being the
meeting-place for these famous lovers at a crucial
moment in world history (this is another of Jachimo's
conceits, a pathetic fallacy which attributes human
consciousness to a natural object). Shakespeare had
already described this encounter in Enobarbus' speech
in *Antony and Cleopatra*, II.2.191–223. In that version,
however, Cleopatra was supposed actually to be
present, a woman larger than life and beyond anything
art could do to represent her (instead of silk fabric and
silver thread, her barge was made of real gold, the oars
were real silver, and the ship's tackle was real silk).

73 *bravely*: Finely.

73–6 *it did strive . . . life on't was –*: It was doubtful which
was the greater, the quality of the workmanship in the
tapestry, or the value of the materials from which it
was made. I was amazed that it could be so superbly
and precisely fashioned, since the true life in it was –
(Posthumus interrupts at this point, according to F's
punctuation. If 76 is emended to *Such the true life on't
was*, the meaning is 'so true was the life in it').
Shakespeare, and perhaps Jachimo, has in mind a saying
well known in the Renaissance, from Ovid's
Metamorphoses, 2.5: 'Their workmanship was even more
wonderful than their material' (tr. Innes, p. 258).

75 *rarely*: Exquisitely.

79 *justify*: Prove.

80–82 *The chimney . . . Dian bathing*: The fireplace is situated
in the south of the bedchamber, and the sculpture (*or*
carving) set above the fireplace has as its subject the
goddess Diana, as she bathes.

82–5 *Never saw I . . . breath left out*: I never saw figures in
a work of art so likely to speak for themselves; the
cutter (sculptor or carver) was like Nature in creative
power (*another Nature*), although unable to give his
figures speech; he excelled her, except for the living
movement and breath she endows her creatures
with.

86 *relation*: Report.

87 *roof*: Ceiling.

88 *fretted*: Elaborately carved, adorned.
   andirons: Firedogs, ornamental supports to the grate in
   the fireplace.

89–91 *winking Cupids . . . brands*: Two small silver statues of
Cupid, with eyes closed, each figure standing on one
foot and propping himself, in exact symmetry with the
other (*nicely*), against his wedding torch. (The eyes of
the little boys are closed because, by tradition, Cupid,
god of love, was blind; the figures are much smaller
than the torches, which are upright, so that the Cupids
lean their weight against them, with one leg set slightly
across the other.)

91 *This is her honour*: This is what you mean by winning
her honour (Posthumus exclaims, ironically and with
confidence) – giving a detailed account of her bedroom
ceiling and a couple of statues in the fireplace! (Posthumus may also be suggesting that all these beautiful
works of art only add further to Imogen's *honour*, or
her distinction as a princess.)

93 *your remembrance*: (The exactness of) your recollection.

95–6 *Then . . . air this jewel*: Well then, if you can remain
unflushed (that is, cool and collected) at (1) what I have
told you so far *or* (2) anything I tell you, give me but
leave to show this jewel (*air* the bracelet) in the open for
a while.

  97 *'tis up*: It's put away (in his pocket or up his sleeve).
97–8 *married . . . your diamond. I'll keep them*: It must go
      with that diamond ring of yours. (Unlike you and your
      lady, who have lost them so easily) I shall hang on to
      them both (the bracelet and the ring).
      Jove: By Jupiter (an exclamation).
 102 *outsell*: Exceed in value.
 105 *She writers . . . doth she*: Jachimo takes a small risk here,
      trusting that in her letter Imogen will have said nothing
      about his attempt to seduce her, and will probably have
      said very little about him at all, to ensure that her
      husband is in no way made suspicious or jealous of
      their meeting.
 107 *basilisk*: Fabulous monster, a reptile which was said to
      kill its victims with a single glance (Posthumus seems
      to be saying that it kills him to look at the basilisk-like
      ring).
 108 *Let there be no*: Let no one believe that there is.
 109 *semblance*: Exterior show.
111–12 *no more bondage . . . which is nothing*: (Let women's
      vows) be of no more binding force on those with whom
      they are made (that is, with men) than the extent to
      which women themselves feel constrained by their
      own virtue – which is, not at all. Posthumus also means
      that Imogen's virtues are no more than sexual desire
      (*nothing* could mean the vagina).
 115 *probable*: Provable.
 116 *one*: One of.
      corrupted: Bribed into betraying Imogen.
 118 *Back*: Give me back.
 120 *evident*: Indubitable, conclusive.
 125 *All sworn*: They have all sworn an oath of loyalty to
      Imogen (in Shakespeare's day, it was customary for
      servants in noble households to take such an oath when
      they began their duties).
 127 *cognizance*: Literally, the badge worn by servants to
      distinguish them as retainers in a particular noble
      household; Posthumus is contrasting the loyalty of
      Imogen's servants (125), and their *cognizance*, with her

own faithlessness, and the visible sign of her *incontinency* (that is, *this* (128), the bracelet).

129 *thy hire*: Your payment (the diamond ring, which is
Jachimo's reward for being Imogen's lover, as well as
for winning the wager with Posthumus).

132 *Of one persuaded well of*: About someone whom we are
persuaded to think well of. It may be that Posthumus
interrupts Philario and that the text should read 'well
of –', which would mean '(believed) by one convinced
of –', followed by an unsaid phrase, something like
'her virtue' or 'her honour'.

133 *colted*: Possessed sexually, mounted as if she were a
mare (it may be important that the word could also
mean 'tricked').

134 *satisfying*: Confirmation (but in 133–4 Jachimo probably also means 'if you're asking for more information
about her and my sexual satisfaction').

137 *present*: Immediate.

139 *stain*: Blotch, birthmark.

140 *stain*: Corruption, disgrace.

142–3 *never count . . . a million*: That is, don't bother to count
for me the number of *turns*, or times you did it – as
far as I'm concerned, her coupling with you just once
is the same as if she had done it a million times (with
turns, Posthumus is also thinking of them turning over
in bed together).

145 *thee . . . thou*: Posthumus' anger and hysteria are indicated by this change from the polite pronoun *you* (with
which he has addressed Jachimo until now) to *thee* and
thou, pronouns usually reserved for social inferiors,
and for moments of intense feeling.

147 *limb-meal*: Limb from limb.

150 *government*: Self-control.

151–2 *pervert . . . against himself*: Stop him from inflicting on
himself the anger he feels against Imogen at this instant
(that is, prevent him from harming himself, or even
committing suicide while he is in this rage).

152 *Enter Posthumus*: This sudden re-entry is discussed in
the headnote above.

153 *be*: Exist, be born.

154 *half-workers*: That is, joint partners in procreation.

157 *stamped*: Minted (used figuratively for 'conceived').

    coiner with his tools: Counterfeiter (with a pun on *tools* or genitalia). It is worth noting that in his 1605 *Remains* (which Shakespeare had certainly read) Camden the historian described Cymbeline as the first British king to have his image on coins.

159 *Dian*: Diana, the goddess of chastity.

160 *the nonpareil*: The lady without an equal (for her chasteness).

162 *forbearance*: Abstention (from sexual intercourse).

163–4 *A pudency . . . warmed old Saturn*: See the headnote above.

166 *yellow*: Referring to Jachimo's (1) suntanned or liverish complexion *or* (2) jealous or envious nature *or* (3) social status (as a gilded aristocrat, where *yellow* means 'golden'). Alliteration may have been intended: 'yellow yackimo', or perhaps even 'giallo jackimo' (since Posthumus could be sneering at Jachimo's way of speaking, or accent, and '*giallo*' is the Italian for *yellow*).

166–7 *in an hour . . . at first*: He'd have had her in an hour, wouldn't he? or less – maybe straightaway?

167 *Perchance*: Perhaps.

167–9 *he spoke not . . . and mounted*: See the headnote above.

169–71 *found no opposition . . . from encounter guard*: (Jachimo) encountered no other resistance than *what* he had expected would block his way (*or* that he was looking for, and which ought to oppose him), and which she should protect from *encounter*, or love bouts. It becomes clear in 172 that the *what* in 170 is the *woman's part*, which in this case is Imogen's hymenal membrane: this was the only obstruction she offered to Jachimo, and which he was looking for (because he believed she was a virgin). It is possible that at 140, when Posthumus speaks of a *stain*, *as big as hell*, he is thinking of a physical as well as a moral blemish (that is, blood from her loss of virginity: see *Othello*, V.1.36). It seems likely

that Imogen is a *wedded lady* (I.6.2) who has not
consummated her marriage.

172 *woman's part*: Literally, vagina; but 'fault' or 'respon-
sibility' at 174.
   motion: Impulse.

173 *vice*: Sinful act (but in the context of the *woman's part*,
the word *vice* probably also means 'the genitalia and
closed thighs').

176 *rank*: Lascivious.

177 *change of prides*: (1) Varying extravagancies *or* (2) one
form of excess changed for another *or* (3) all the forms
that the sin of pride can assume.

178 *Nice longing*: (1) Wanton desires *or* (2) over-fastidious
wishes.

179 *All faults . . . hers*: Editors have emended 179–81 in
several ways (see An Account of the Text, p. 140), but
the reading in F, followed here with a relineation, is
intelligible as it stands: all faults which *name . . . knows*
(which have been given a name) – no, more, even faults
that have no name and which hell alone knows – why,
they are all hers (woman's).

183–6 *I'll write . . . better*: Posthumus first says that he will
write satirical attacks against women, then that it would
be *greater skill*, or more cunning, if one truly hated
women, to pray the gods to let them have *their will*,
that is, their own way, but also whatever they want
sexually. This will *plague them better* than *devils* from
hell, because (1) their sinfulness will be punished by
their souls being damned *or* (2) their unhindered
promiscuity will cause them to catch sexual diseases.

185 *greater skill*: Much smarter, wiser.

III.I

With this scene, set in the British palace, the action
shifts from the private concerns of the wager story to
the larger public world. Britain in *Cymbeline* is a prov-
incial monarchy on the northern edge of Augustus
Caesar's superstate, the Roman Empire. As Lucius
coolly observes, when demanding the unpaid tribute,
Caesar has more kings as servants than Cymbeline has

domestic officers. In Act V, when the Britons win an
unexpected victory over the Romans, it is a freak and
temporary success. Even in defeat and facing summary
execution, Lucius gives the Britons an unnerving
reminder of what they are up against. If the gods have
decided that he and his men must die, he says, then

> let it come. Sufficeth
> A Roman with a Roman's heart can suffer:
> Augustus lives to think on't. (V.5.80–82)

This is laconic, stoic and assured about the direction
of history under the deified emperor: the Romans will
never give up.

The rights and wrongs of the Roman conquest of
Britain are set out in different ways by the Queen,
Cloten and Cymbeline. The Queen emphasizes the bad
luck the Britons had, Cloten declares that only might
is right and Cymbeline reminds Lucius that before the
Romans came Britain was a sovereign nation with its
own laws. Jacobean audiences would have expected to
hear how courageous their ancestors were, and how
they detested the Roman yoke (there were grumblings
throughout the reign of King James about the 'Norman
Yoke', the rule that foreign kings had imposed on free-
born Saxons and their laws).

o *in state*: With royal pomp, appropriate for a state occasion.

   at one door, and at another: The Britons and the Romans
enter as separate parties from the two sides of the double
doors of the tiring-house at the back of the stage.

1–2 *Augustus Caesar . . . Julius Caesar*: Augustus was the
name assumed by Octavius after he became the first
emperor of Rome. Julius Caesar was Octavius' great-
uncle, but when Octavius' father was murdered Caesar
adopted him as his son. Some of these relationships are
mirrored in the British court: *Cassibelan* was Cymbeline's uncle (his great-uncle according to Holinshed),
and Cymbeline had adopted Cloten as *his* son, but also

rejected another child, Posthumus, whom earlier he had starred for favour (see note to I.1.42).

2 *remembrance*: Memory.

5 *conquered it*: The Britons have a different account of things; see 22–33 and notes to 23–4 and 30–31.

6–7 *Famous . . . deserving it*: Famous because of Caesar's praise of him not a jot less than for the deeds which deserved the praise (that is, Cassibelan's fame was as much due to Caesar's praise as the *feats* he performed).

7–9 *for him . . . thousand pounds*: (Cassibelan) agreed, on behalf of himself and the kings who would succeed him in Britain (in other words, in perpetuity), to pay Rome an annual tax of three thousand pounds (in (1) sterling *or* (2) weight in gold or silver).

8 *succession*: Successors.

10 *untendered*: Unpaid.

to kill the marvel: To bring to an abrupt end the aston-ishment (which non-payment has caused the Romans).

11–14 *There be many . . . noses*: There will be many more Caesars (emperors) before Rome produces another one like Julius. Britain is a world to itself, separated from everywhere else, and we Britons will pay nothing to Rome for the right to be ourselves (in Cloten's idiom, Romans have *crooked noses* (37); why should we pay them tribute simply for *wearing our own noses*, that is, having ones which are a different shape?). The notion of Britain as a world by itself came from Virgil, *Eclogues*, 1:67.

14–16 *That opportunity . . . have again*: That opportunity which the Romans took at the time to extract payment from us, we can take back to ourselves.

18 *natural bravery of your isle*: The defiant posture which Nature has given your island of Britain (that is, even its physical character stands ready to resist invasion).

19 *Neptune's park*: In classical mythology Neptune was the god who ruled the sea; the island of Britain is here imagined as his park, a tract of land reserved (*palèd*) for a ruler's pleasure.

ribbèd and palèd in: Enclosed (as if within a rib-cage,

or within the side-timbers of a ship's hulk) and fenced
in. F has *ribb'd and pal'd*, and editors have tried to
repair the irregularity of the metre, often by treating
the endings as syllabic.

20 *oaks*: This is sometimes emended to 'rocks', but the
image in F is clear: Britain is protected by an impenetrable forest of *unscalable* oak trees, ribbed around and
over the island (19), which can be neither climbed over
nor gone through.

23–4 *made not here his brag . . . 'came and saw and overcame'*:
The Queen is right. Julius Caesar is reported to have
written this, not of Britain, but of a conquest in Asia
Minor. According to Plutarch, Caesar 'fought a great
battle with King Pharnaces', and to 'advertise one of
his friends of the suddenness of this victory, he only
wrote three words unto Anitius at Rome: *Veni, vidi,
vici*: to wit, "I came, I saw, I overcame"' (*Shakespeare's
Plutarch*, ed. T. J. B. Spencer (1964), p. 71); this is a
parallel to what Jachimo claims he did with Imogen in
Britain, and what Posthumus thinks happened.

27 *Poor ignorant baubles*: Mere toys, wretched and inex-
perienced (in British waters).

30–31 *was once at point . . . sword*: Was once just about – O
capricious, giddy fortune – to wrest Caesar's sword
from him (F has *giglet Fortune*, which perhaps means
'you faithless lady, Fortune'); *giglot* is a word for a
whore.

32 *Lud's Town*: Ancient Britain's capital city, enlarged and
improved by King Lud, Cymbeline's grandfather (for
Lud, see note to I.1.28–40); the Jacobeans believed that
this city was the foundation of London.

37 *crooked noses*: The ancient Romans were famed for their
long, angular noses (see note to 11–14).
to owe . . . none: Not one of them possesses as strong
and unbending arms as Julius Caesar did (*owe* means
'own' and *straight* means 'strong, forceful').

39 *grip*: Take hold of, clutch (a weapon); F has *gripe* (to
seize).

43 *sir*: Addressed to (1) Cymbeline *or* (2) Lucius.

46 *injurious*: Insulting (in the wrong they have done Britain by imposing the tax).

49 *all colour here*: Without any pretence of right (there may be a pun on *colour* and *collar*: the Romans put a *yoke* or a collar *upon's* that is, 'upon us Britons').

53 *Mulmutius*: The first king of Britain, according to Holinshed.

54 *use*: Application and exercise, by custom.

55 *whose repair and franchise*: The restoration and unfettered operation of which laws (that is, without Roman interference in their working).

62–3 *that hath more kings ... domestic officers*: Who has more kings as his servants than you have petty functionaries (in your royal household).

64 *confusion*: Destruction.

66–7 *defied ... for myself*: Having done my public duty to declare war on you, I can now, as a private individual, thank you (for the reception you have honoured me with).

67 *Caius*: Cymbeline perhaps uses Lucius' first name to respond to the ambassador's expression of private feeling.

69–71 *of him I gathered honour ... at utterance*: I gained honour by my service with Augustus, which I'm obliged to defend to the death (*keep at utterance*), since he is now seeking to take this honour back from me (that is, dishonouring me by insisting on payment of the tribute).

71 *perfect*: Fully aware.

72 *Pannonians and Dalmatians*: These were peoples who in Roman times inhabited what are now Hungary and the Balkans.

74 *not to read ... Britons cold*: Not to be instructed by (or to follow) would show the Britons to be lacking in spirit.

75 *Let proof speak*: Let us leave it to (1) the outcome *or* (2) the experience of the coming war to confirm or refute what you are saying.

79 *adventure*: Attempt.

80 *shall fare the better for you*: Will feed much better

because of your corpses lying slain on the battlefield.

81 *So*: So be it.

sir: Addressed to (1) Cymbeline *or* (2) Cloten.

82 *pleasure*: That is, what Augustus wants and intends.

83 *the remain*: That remains (to be said).

III.2

The setting is Cymbeline's palace. For Imogen, as for her brothers in the next scene, things are just about to change. Her delight at Posthumus' letter is genuine and irrepressible, but she is still a schoolgirl court prodigy, who speaks in over-elaborate comparisons and whoops of book-learning (the *horse with wings*, 47, is Pegasus, not just a swift horse). At the end of the scene, when she tells Pisanio to fetch her some real lower-class travelling clothes, so that she can do some proper riding, we see the first signs of her changing from the little court lady she has been until now (see the Introduction, pp. xxxiii–xxxv). This change of clothes will be the first of her self-transformations on a journey that leads her far from where she started. The murderous threat from Posthumus (1–22 and 40–46) precipitates the changes in her, but she herself has to see them through.

1 *you*: This pronoun indicates how angry Pisanio is with Posthumus (he reverts to the more intimate or more dutiful use of *thy* in 4).

3 *strange*: Foreign.

infection: Pronounced as four syllables, 'in-feck-shi-on'.

4 *false*: Lying, deceiving.

5 *poisonous-tongued as handed*: That is, as poisonous in their slander as in their poisoning of people by a sleight of hand (in Shakespeare's day Italians were thought to be notorious defamers as well as dexterous poisoners).

7 *truth*: Fidelity (to Posthumus, by refusing to be divorced from him).

undergoes: Endures.

9 *take in some virtue*: (1) Overcome a great deal of goodness (in other people, but she still has more) *or* (2) overwhelm some kinds of sexual and moral virtue (but not

hers) *or* (3) draw heavily on the resources of courage
in anyone (let alone a young girl).

10–11 *Thy mind . . . fortunes*: Your mind, in comparison with
hers, is now as inferior as your prospects and status
(*fortunes*) were (compared with hers, as the heir
apparent), when she married you (that is, she is now
as far above you in moral character as in social rank).
F has *her* in 10, which would mean 'your mind compared
to Imogen herself'.

12 *Upon*: (1) Because of *or* (2) on top of, in addition to.

13 *command*: (1) Service *or* (2) authority.
Her blood: (1) (That I should shed) her blood? *or* (2)
kill someone of royal birth?

15 *serviceable*: Diligent in service (with the suggestion of
'usable to any end').

15–17 *How look I . . . comes to*: What is there in my expression or appearance that makes me seem so inhuman
that I could do something as dreadful as this crime or
fact (of murdering Imogen) would amount to?

17 *Do't*: Do it (the murder).

18 *by her own command*: By the orders she herself will give
you.

20 *Black as . . . on thee*: As black (evil) as the ink which
is written on you.
Senseless bauble: (You) insentient, worthless thing.

21 *fedary for this act*: Accomplice in this crime. For *fedary*,
F has *Foedarie* or a feudal tenant, a meaning probably
not intended here. If the F spelling was a mistake, it
was either because the word was miscopied, or set incor-
rectly by the compositor, or because Shakespeare associated it, wrongly, with the Latin word *foedus* meaning
'accomplice'.

21–2 *look'st . . . virgin-like*: That is, because the colour of
the paper is white, and the letter is sealed up with a
knot of red wax and not yet opened (perhaps a reminder
that Imogen is still a virgin: see II.4.169–71 and note).

22 *without*: Outside.

23 *I am ignorant . . . commanded*: I must pretend to know
nothing of what I have been ordered to do.

26 *Who, thy lord . . . Leonatus*: Imogen is evidently
surprised that Posthumus has written to Pisanio, but
not to her (perhaps she is correcting Pisanio, half questioningly, half in play, 'who, *thy* lord? No, that is *my*
lord?').

27 *astronomer*: Astrologer.

28 *characters*: Handwriting (Imogen plays delicately on
another meaning of *characters*, that is, the astrological
symbols of the planets, from which the future might
be foretold, or laid *open*, 29).

30 *relish*: Have a taste.

31 *yet not*: Yet not content.

33–4 *Some griefs . . . physic love*: Some griefs make us
healthier, and being apart (from one's lover) is one of
them because it invigorates love, makes it stronger;
med'cinable means 'able to heal'.

34–5 *of his content . . . in that*: (In his letter) let him tell me
that everything about Rome pleases him, except for
that (our being separated).

35–9 *Good wax . . . Cupid's tables*: Renaissance letters and
documents were sealed with a globule of bees' wax;
the seals on legal documents were the sign of the bond
or contract which had been entered into. In 35–6 Imogen
asks permission of the seal (by *thy leave*), as she breaks
it open to unfold Posthumus' letter, and she blesses the
bees which made the wax *locks* that keep the secrets
(the *counsel*) written in such letters. The meaning in
36–9 is: lovers and men who have violated their
contracts do not share the same faith (they *pray not
alike*) about these wax seals: the wax causes *forfeiters*
to be thrown into prison (because it sealed the bond
they have broken), but it embraces and shuts in (clasps)
the notes of *Cupid*, the young god of love (that is, it
seals love-letters). Imogen's comparisons between
lovers and men who have broken their agreements, and
who will go to jail for it, anticipate what is to happen
to Posthumus in V.5.

39 *tables*: Writing tablets, notebooks.

41 *as you, O*: F has *as you: (oh*, so perhaps Posthumus is

being cunning (*as you*, followed by a slight pause, can
mean, momentarily, '(as cruel) as you are' as well as
'but that you (would renew me)').

43   *Cambria*: Wales.
Milford Haven: A port on the south coast of Wales, in
Pembrokeshire, which was associated with the acces-
sion of the Tudor monarchs (see *Cymbeline and the
Court of King James*).

45–6 *your increasing in love, Leonatus*: F has *Loue. Leonatus*,
which is unsettlingly ambiguous, with at least three
meanings: (1) (Posthumus wishes) your increasing in
love (but he has no confidence that it will happen) *or*
(2) (Posthumus remains loyal to) your increasing in
love with him (but no longer loyal, if the love is not
increasing) *or* (3) yours, always increasing in love for
you, Leonatus (that is, a loving farewell). As with *as
you* in 41, perhaps Posthumus intends these nuances
both to tell and not to tell Imogen that he has found
her out.

49   *one of mean affairs*: Someone with (1) merely ordinary,
everyday matters *or* (2) of humble standing and
concerns.

53   *bate*: Modify (qualify what she has just said).

54   *fainter kind*: Less extreme (*or* less passionate) way.

55–7 *For mine's beyond . . . the sense*: Because my longing (to
see Posthumus) exceeds the uttermost limit; speak and
tell me quickly (*or* in words profuse and crammed
together), since love's (1) confidant *or* (2) adviser should
stop up the passages of hearing in a lover's ears
(blocking out everything but words of love), to the
point where the hearer's senses are overwhelmed.

56   *bores of hearing*: Cavities of the ears.

58   *by th'way*: On our way (as we ride there).

60   *T'inherit*: (1) To possess *or* (2) to have bestowed on it.
haven: Harbour, port (but Imogen is also thinking of
a sanctuary, a place of refuge and safety for Posthumus,
who is an exile; there is a pun too on *haven* and 'heaven',
Milford as a heavenly place).

64   *Why should excuse . . . begot*: Why devise an excuse

even before we have planned the act (leaving the court) which will make the excuse necessary?

67 *'Twixt hour and hour*: (How many scores of miles can we ride) in an hour? Pisanio tells her that twenty miles a day is more than enough for her (*score . . . ride* is the reading in F2, but F has *store . . . rid* which could mean 'what quantity of miles can we dispose of').

68 *Madam's*: Madam, is.

69 *to's*: To his.

70–72 *riding wagers . . . behalf*: Races, with bets laid on the outcome, where horses have galloped faster than the sands running in an hourglass. An hourglass was used *i'th'clock's behalf*, to serve in place of a clock, and the horse would race against the sands in the glass (rather than against another horse), with the aim of covering a set distance before the sands had run out. Imogen's mind is on the speed at which horses can travel, but the wager and the hourglass suggest other things to the audience: a bet has been laid on her honour and time is running out for her.

72 *fool'ry*: Childish (a silly distraction from the urgent business in hand).

74 *presently*: Immediately.

75–6 *no costlier . . . franklin's housewife*: No more expensive-looking than would be suitable for the wife of a *franklin* (a small landowner). Imogen plans to leave court disguised as her lady-in-waiting (who is to say she is sick and going home to her father, 73–4); *housewife* is pronounced 'huzzif'.

76 *you're best consider*: You had better reflect on this more, give it more thought.

77–9 *I see before me . . . look through*: I see (1) what is immediately before me *or* (2) the way to Milford clearly ahead of me. I cannot see what is to this side of me, nor to that, nor what *ensues* ((1) is behind *or* (2) will be the eventual outcome); these are all shrouded in a fog which I cannot see through.

III.3

The setting is among the mountains in south Wales, near Milford Haven. On the Jacobean stage the tiring-house, which served as Cymbeline's palace in III.1, now became Belarius' cave in the side of a rock. By 1610 images of a palace and a mountain rock were clichés for civilized and uncivilized life (around this date Inigo Jones put the images together in the masque *Oberon*, where a rock opens to reveal a splendid palace within, suggesting that there is courtliness and grace inside even a savage, flinty exterior).

The scene tells us what Belarius has been teaching the brothers – the court corrupts and exploits (21–6, 60–64) and the wilderness keeps them pure – but it also shows, in their responses, how undreamy, unreflective and hard their lives are. Belarius stole the boys from their nursery to pay Cymbeline back, but he has obviously fallen in love with them, and has been holding them back, in his version of an idyll, to prevent them leaving him (see the discussion in the Introduction, p. xxxvi, for how close the moment of change is, and how Belarius half knows it).

1 *A goodly day, not to keep house*: (It's) a fine day, not one for staying indoors.

1–2 *with such . . . low as ours*: With people who are as lowly as us.

2 *Stoop*: F has *sleep*, perhaps a contraction for 'asleep'.
    gate: That is, the entrance to the cave, through which Belarius and the brothers enter (onstage, presumably the open doorway of the tiring-house).

3 *Instructs you*: Because the *gate* (the lintel of the cave) makes the brothers bow their heads as they come out, as if in prayer, or as a mark of respect – a religious ceremony to match their sister's in court.

5 *giants*: People with enormous power (wearing *impious turbans* because in Renaissance romances giants were often associated with Saracens, or unholy infidels).
    jet: Strut.

6–7 *without . . . morrow*: Without (saying) good morning.

8–9 *We house i'th'rock . . . prouder livers do*: We only dwell

in a mountain cave, yet we don't behave as badly
towards you (heaven) as people who live more grandly
than us. There is perhaps a pun on *livers*, since the liver
was thought of as the seat of passion and intemperance.

11 *flats*: Level ground, the plain beneath the mountains.

12 *like a crow*: (1) As small as a crow *or* (2) as a crow
would, flying above, looking down.

13 *it is place . . . sets off*: It is one's position (literally, on
the mountain, or figuratively, in the social hierarchy)
which diminishes and displays to advantage whatever
is looked at (distant objects or social inferiors).

14 *revolve*: Meditate on, turn over in your minds.

15 *tricks in*: (1) Stratagems of *or* (2) character of.

16–17 *This service . . . being so allowed*: (1) Duty in this world
of princes and wars (15) is not enough by itself, even
when done properly; the reward you receive depends
on the service being generally acknowledged (because
opinion is as important as merit) *or* (2) this way of
serving (heaven) – doing it as we do, in our mountain
life – is not like being in service: our duty being like
this, it is *allowed* (we approve of it, enjoy it).

17 *To apprehend thus*: To see things this way.

19 *comfort*: Benefit, consolation.

20 *sharded*: (1) With shards or cases for its wings *or* (2)
living in shard (at this time, a dialect word for cow
dung). In 20–21 Shakespeare (or Belarius) alludes to
Aesop's fable of the beetle and the eagle, with its moral,
not to despise the weak.

hold: Stronghold *or* place of refuge.

21–2 *this life . . . a check*: This life (of ours in the mountains) is nobler than (1) doing service at court only to
receive a *check* or rebuke for one's efforts *or* (2) waiting
for advancement, only to be checked (prevented from
going higher).

23 *Richer than . . . a babe*: More rewarding than doing
nothing for a child (who is in one's care). Editors often
emend *babe* (see An Account of the Text, p. 141), but
it is appropriate to the theme in *Cymbeline* of care for

children: the King took the *babe* Posthumus to his *protection* (I.1.40–41), and Belarius has reared the princes for twenty years. By contrast, some Jacobean courtiers had become notorious for exploiting the wards of court they had in their charge, and for whom they had done very little (wards were young children whose parents had died and whose estates could be milked for the benefit of their guardians).

25 *Such gain . . . makes him fine*: (1) Such (behaviour) wins approval from him who makes himself fine (that is, acting like this makes other fine fellows think well of you) *or* (2) such (rewards at court) are the top (*the cap*) of what a man receives who makes himself grand *or* (3) such (people at court) receive salutes from, or have respect shown to them by *him* (their tailor) who dresses them elegantly *or* (4) such gain is the best reward for *him* (a tailor) who makes them (people at court) look good. (Readings (3) and (4) require the alteration in 25 of F's *makes him* to *makes 'em*.)

26 *Yet keeps his book uncrossed*: Yet such behaviour *or* rewards *or* people at court *or* gain ensure(s) that his account *book* (his own *or* the tailor's) remains *uncrossed* (that is, his debts are not struck through as a sign of having been paid).
No life to ours: (1) This court life is nothing compared with ours *or* (2) there is no life which can compare with ours.

27 *proof*: Experience.

29 *What air's from home*: What other places are like (the *air* of foreign countries).
Haply: Perhaps.

33 *travelling abed*: Travelling to other places (1) in our dreams, when asleep in bed *or* (2) in our day-dreams (perhaps with a pun on 'travelling' and *travailing* (the spelling in F) or labouring).

34 *or a debtor*: That is, their life is like a debtor, because it has not paid them what they deserve (the word *or* is sometimes emended, needlessly, to 'for').

35 *stride a limit*: Step over the boundary (at this date,

prisoners for debt were not confined in the prison itself
but had to keep within its prescribed *limit*, or liberties).

38 *pinching*: Bitterly cold.

40 *beastly*: Like mere beasts.

subtle as the fox: (Only) as cunning as the fox (which
sneaks up on its *prey*).

41 *Like warlike*: (1) As valorous *or* (2) as aggressive and
greedy.

42 *what flies*: Animals which flee from man (not dangerous
ones or warriors).

43–4 *We make a choir . . . bondage freely*: We pretend that
our confinement is a place for making hymns to heaven
(*a choir*), like a bird does in a cage, and we sing about
the restraints on us with as much freedom as we like
(for we have no other).

46 *knowingly*: From personal experience.

art: Artfulness, guile.

47 *keep*: Stay there.

50 *pain*: Task, endeavour.

51 *which*: This is presumably the *pain* at 50 (also the subject
of *deserve*, 54, and *curtsy*, 55).

54 *Doth ill deserve*: Receives a poor (or an evil) reward.

57–8 *my report . . . of note*: At one time my reputation was
unrivalled (1) in comparison with men of the highest
estimate *or* (2) in the opinion of the most reputable
men *or* (3) and the account of me was unblemished.

63 *hangings*: Fruit (hanging down from the tree).

64 *weather*: Bad weather, storms.

70 *demesnes*: Lands, estates.

71 *at honest freedom*: Honourable and free within myself.

73 *fore-end of my time*: Earlier part of my life.

76 *minister*: Be servants.

77 *attends*: Is present (poison waits on, and is waiting for
those who dine at court).

82 *meanly*: Humbly.

85 *prince it*: Behave like princes.

86 *trick*: Capacity.

89 *three-foot stool*: Stool with three legs (a humble piece
of furniture).

92 *on's*: On his.

94 *nerves*: Sinews.

96 *as like a figure*: (1) As graphically (as his brother does) *or* (2) playing his part (stage-role) equally well.

98 *conceiving*: Understanding *or* interpretation (of what Belarius has said).

the game is roused: The animals being hunted have emerged from cover (signalled on the Jacobean stage, although not marked with a stage direction in F, by blasts from a hunting horn, perhaps accompanied by distant shouts from the brothers, who are by now supposed to have reached the top of the mountains).

100 *whereon*: For which reason.

103 *reft'st*: Deprived (the word is pronounced *refts*, the spelling in F).

105 *her*: Euriphile's.

107 *The game is up*: The horn would have been sounded again at this point (*up* means the same as *roused* at 98). Whether or not he is fully aware of it, Belarius is also saying that the *game* of outlaw which he has been playing *is up*; he forewarns the audience that the hard idyll he and the brothers have lived is almost at an end (see the Introduction, pp. xxxv–xxxvi).

III.4

The setting is Wales, on the way to Milford Haven. This scene is full of shocks, for Imogen first, and then for the audience. Until this moment Imogen's sense of her self has rested on four things: Posthumus' love for her, her reputation for chastity, the position she has as heir-apparent and her sexual identity. She has to surrender all of these in this scene. Even Britain, the special world by itself, turns into something that is not secured and can float away (135–8). In his 1590s comedies Shakespeare's heroines, when they had to pretend to be boys, at least had some of the fun of cross-dressing and trying on new stuff from a male costume box. For Imogen, becoming a boy is not much fun at all (164–6), and the audience shouldn't expect it to be: what they are watching is the painful break-up of her pubescent character.

Some critics have been hard on Imogen for almost succumbing to self-pity, and even playing the victim (the *lamb entreats the butcher*, 95). But she has this to shed, together with some of her highfalutin rhetoric (Shaw missed the point entirely when he criticized Shakespeare for making Imogen speak the overwrought lines about *false Aeneas*, 56–62; these show what she still has to free herself from).

1 *came from horse*: Dismounted.

2–3 *Ne'er longed . . . I have now*: My mother never longed to see me for the first time (that is, felt as strong birth-pangs, wanted to give birth to me) with as much longing as I have now (to see Posthumus).

6–10 *One but painted . . . my staider senses*: Someone in a painting who had the expression you have on your face would be thought a creature distressed beyond the point where he could explain himself (that is, he had lost his wits). Assume a less terrifying look (*haviour*), before the madness in your manner overwhelms my senses (which for the moment are less disturbed, or *staider* than yours).

7 *perplexed*: Distressed.

8–9 *Put thyself . . . less fear*: Behave in a less frightening way.

9 *wildness*: Terror, panic.

11 *tender'st thou*: Are you offering.

12 *summer*: Pleasant.

14 *hand*: Handwriting.

15–16 *drug-damned Italy . . . hard point*: Italy, damnable (*or* detestable) for its use of poisons, has overcome him with guile, and he is in a tight spot.

17 *take off some extremity*: Take the edge off the extreme painfulness, lessen the shock (of what is written in the letter).

18 *even mortal to me*: Enough to kill me.

23 *my grief*: The injury done to me (but also 'my anguish').

29 *pander . . . dishonour*: Pimp who's helping her to gratify her lust and dishonour herself.

30 *What*: Why.

33 *Outvenoms . . . Nile*: Is more poisonous than all the snakes in the River Nile.

34 *posting*: Hastening, speeding.
    doth belie: Fills with lies.

35 *states*: People of the highest rank.

37 *What cheer*: Are you all right, how do you feel?

39 *in watch*: Awake.

40 *'twixt clock and clock*: From one hour to the next.
    charge: (1) Should weigh down, lie heavy on *or* (2) should compel (in either case, *sleep charge nature* means 'if I fall asleep, because my tired body demands it').

41 *a fearful dream of him*: A dream apprehensive about his safety.

42 *to's*: To his.

44 *Thy conscience witness*: (1) (Posthumus) let your inward conviction about me testify (how faithful I am) *or* (2) (Posthumus) let your conscience tell the truth (that it is you not me who has been false) *or* (3) (Pisanio) on your conscience, bear witness (to my fidelity). F has *witnesse: Iachimo*, so it is conceivable that what was intended was *witness, Jachimo*, in which case Imogen is saying 'on your conscience, Jachimo, bear witness (that I resisted you)'.

45 *incontinency*: Infidelity.

47 *favour's*: Appearance is.
    jay: Promiscuous woman, whore. In Italian, as Shakespeare probably knew, '*puta*', the word for a jay (bird), also means a promiscuous woman.

48 *Whose mother was her painting*: Whose looks come from powder and paint (from cosmetics rather than natural beauty inherited from a mother).

49 *stale*: No longer attractive to him (yesterday's meal).

50–51 *for I am richer . . . with me*: Because I am too costly to be set aside, I must be torn up. Rip me to shreds! In Shakespeare's day, clothes that had gone out of fashion were either hung up on the *walls*, or were cut up and reused. Posthumus wants to get rid of her, Imogen says, but because she is a princess she is too grand a possession to be put away and forgotten about; he has decided to have her murdered, torn to pieces, with the pretence that she has been unfaithful to him.

52–3 *All good . . . thy revolt*: Everything which appears to be good from the outside, by your inconstancy (that is, by your discarding your vows to me).

53 *revolt*: Betrayal.

54 *not born where't grows*: That is, transplanted (a goodness feigned or put on *for villainy*, rather than natural and rooted in its true place).

55 *a bait*: As a bait.

56 *honest*: (1) Honourable *or* (2) genuine.
     heard like: Heard (to speak and profess love) like.
     false Aeneas: Aeneas was false because he told Dido, Queen of Carthage, that he loved her, and yet he deserted her for a new life in Italy (an action which Imogen believes Posthumus is repeating).

57 *Sinon's weeping*: Sinon's feigned tears and lies persuaded the Trojans to draw the Wooden Horse into Troy (which let in the Greeks and brought the destruction of the city).

58–9 *Did scandal . . . true wretchedness*: Brought into disrepute many tears which were truly holy (unlike Sinon's irreligious ones), and removed pity from people's hearts even for instances of the most genuine wretchedness (because Sinon had been so convincing when he pretended to be distraught).

60 *Wilt lay . . . proper men*: (Your behaviour) will taint all honourable men, cause them to be regarded as corrupt (*leaven*, or sour dough, is imagined as an evil ferment which ruins even good reputations).

61 *Goodly and gallant*: Handsome looks and chivalrous behaviour.

62 *fail*: Failure, fault.

64 *A little witness*: Testify somewhat to.

69 *riches of it*: Wealth in my heart.

71 *But now*: Just now, for the moment.

74 *self-slaughter*: Suicide.

76 *cravens*: Makes a coward of.

77 *Something's afore't*: Imogen reaches into her tunic to
pull out the letters which Posthumus has sent her and
which she has placed over her heart (see note to 82).

Soft, soft, we'll no: Wait, wait (an exclamation, shortened from 'go soft'), I mustn't have any.

78 *Obedient as the scabbard*: (1) Imogen herself *or* (2) her
heart is as ready to receive Pisanio's sword as the scabbard itself is (since the *defence* or obstruction of the
letters has been removed, 77).

79 *The scriptures*: Posthumus' letters (Imogen calls them
scriptures because she had believed that, like sacred
writings, they were absolutely true and divinely
inspired. Because his disloyalty has exposed them as
perversions of the truth, they are *heresy* which has
abused her *faith* in him, 80–81).

82 *stomachers*: A stomacher was a piece of ornamental
clothing which covered a woman's breasts, worn under
the lacing of the bodice; the letters have been covering
her breast and heart in the same way (Imogen also
means that until now they have given her the stomach
or courage to endure his absence).

85 *worse case of woe*: This is presumably because the *traitor*
is guilty, or because treason is such a wicked crime.

86 *set up*: Instigate.

88–9 *put into contempt . . . princely fellows*: Disdain the offers
of marriage from princes of my own rank (Posthumus,
a commoner, was very much her social inferior).

89–91 *shalt hereafter . . . rareness*: Some day you will learn that
(1) my choice of you for my husband *or* (2) my disobedience to my father and rejection of other suitors
(87–9) was not something ordinary, but came from special
qualities in me (that is, love, virtue, determination).

92–4 *when thou shalt be disedged . . . by me*: When you have
taken the edge off your appetite, and surfeited on her
whom now you are gorging yourself on, how much
you will remember me, and be tormented (*panged*)
then by the memories.

94 *Prithee, dispatch*: Please, kill me at once (get it over with).

100 *I'll wake . . . first*: I'll sooner stay awake till my eyes

drop out (than kill you).

101 *abused*: Misused.

105 *whereunto*: To which.

106–8 *Why hast thou . . . deer before thee*: Why have you gone
so far – even to the point where you have taken up a
position to shoot from, with your bow ready, and with
the *deer* marked for death (*Th'elected*) in front of you
– only to unbend your bow again? (in other words,
why have you gone to all these preparations to lure me
to my death, only to stop just before you kill me?).

110 *considered of a course*: Worked out a plan.

113 *false struck*: Wounded with slander.

113–14 *take . . . to bottom that*: Receive no deeper wound, not
even from the *tent* (the probe of surgical lint used to
cleanse a wound to its depth), which could *bottom that*
(penetrate further into me).

115 *back*: Go back (to the court).

117 *if I were . . . honest*: If I could prove as skilful as I am
honourable.

119 *abused*: Deceived.

120 *singular*: Unrivalled.

122 *courtesan*: Prostitute.

124 *it*: Your death.

127 *Where bide*: Where might I live?

131 *noble*: Imogen is referring to Cloten, with heavy irony
(*churlish* is added here to supply an obvious deficiency
of one or two words in 131 in F).

136 *not but*: Only.

136–7 *I'th'world's volume . . . not in't*: That is, part of the
world, yet separate from it. Britain is likened to (1) a
page in (or torn out of) the *volume* or book of the
world *or* (2) a drop in the *world's volume* or ocean (a
comparison which would complement the image of the
island as *a swan's nest* floating in *a great pool*, 138).

138–9 *Prithee think . . . out of Britain*: Consider this (Imogen
tells herself), there are people who live beyond the
shores of Britain (it isn't the only place in the world).

141 *Milford Haven*: Lucius sets out for Milford at III.5.17
(to take charge of the Roman army, something Pisanio

doesn't know; see note to 149).

142–6 *if you could wear . . . full of view*: If you could assume
an identity which is as *dark* or impenetrable to others
as your destiny is to you, and simply disguise your sex
– something impossible to reveal at present without
danger to yourself – you'd be following *a course* of
action which was *pretty*, or becoming for you, and *full
of view*, that is, (1) which allowed you to examine these
matters fully with your own eyes (by being in Rome)
or (2) which offered you a good prospect of events
turning out to your advantage (it is possible that *pretty
and full of view* means 'quite full of view' (a hendia-
dys), that is, a course of action reasonably promising
in its prospects).

143 *Dark*: (1) Concealed *or* (2) dismal.

146 *haply*: Perhaps (F has the spelling, as so often, *happily*,
which would also be appropriate here).

149 *render him*: Give an account of what he is doing.
Pisanio's plan (146–50) is that Imogen, disguised as a
boy, should present herself to Lucius, in the hope that
when he returns to Rome, she will go with him, and
arrive somewhere close to where Posthumus is living,
or at least close enough to hear exactly and frequently
what he is doing, even if she is unable to see him herself.
(The latter part of this scheme is very like the course
of action the heroine Julia takes in *The Two Gentlemen
of Verona*, from which she learns that her lover is indeed
pursuing someone else, although without success.)
Pisanio mistakenly thinks Lucius is going home, when
in fact he is about to assume command of the Roman
army being shipped to Milford for the campaign against
Britain.

151–2 *Though peril . . . I would adventure*: I would certainly
risk (what you have suggested), but only as far as it
might place my reputation for chaste conduct (*modesty*)
in danger, not to the point where I could actually lose
my chastity (Imogen means that she would risk everything but the loss of her virginity: *death on't* means
destruction of it).

152 *point*: Nub of the matter.

154–8 *Command into obedience . . . saucy*: Change your custom
of giving orders to that of obeying them; change your
shy fearfulness and fastidiousness – the *handmaids*
which all women use to adorn themselves and for their
own ends, or rather (to speak more truly), the qualities which are the essence of delicate womanhood
herself – into a boyish, pert courage; be ready to gibe
and to answer back straightaway, be impudent.

158 *quarrelous*: Quarrelsome.

160 *the harder heart*: Pisanio says this (1) about Posthumus
(how much harder his heart must be than Imogen's,
that he could behave so cruelly towards her) *or* (2) about
himself (I shall have to harden my heart in order to
help Imogen transform her delicate beauty) *or* (3) about
Imogen (she will have to make her heart tougher, like
a man's, so as to match her male disguise).

161–4 *to the greedy touch . . . Juno angry*: Imogen must expose
her cheek to the sun (here figured as Titan, one of the
ancient gods, who greedily touches and kisses everything alike (*common-kissing*) with his rays), and forget
her elaborate and dainty dresses, which, when she wore
them, made great Juno angry (the Queen of the gods
was notorious for being jealous of beautiful women).
In other words, Imogen will no longer be able to protect
her complexion from the sun with a lady's mask (worn
over the face by some upper-class women in Shakespeare's day), nor wear her finely wrought dresses. At
this date, only lower-class people had tanned skin: see
note to IV.4.29.

165 *end*: Purpose, what you have in mind.

167 *Forethinking*: Anticipating.
fit: Prepared.

168 *cloak-bag*: Large bag for carrying clothes.
doublet: A man's jacket, which was worn above *hose*
(breeches).

168–9 *all . . . to them*: And everything to go with them
(presumably a man's outdoor clothes, cloak, boots,
worn over *doublet* and *hose*).

169 *in their serving*: With their help.

171 *From youth of such a season*: From what you know of
how young men of your own age conduct themselves.
'fore: Before.

172 *desire his service*: Ask him to employ you as his servant.

172–5 *tell him . . . embrace you*: Tell him what your accom-
plishments are – one of which, if he has an ear for
music, he will realize the moment he hears your voice
– and doubtless he will welcome you gladly as his
servant (Imogen's voice is so sweet and tuneful that
Lucius will know that she must be able to sing well).

176 *holy*: Virtuous.

176–8 *Your means abroad . . . nor supplyment*: As for (1) the
money you will need abroad *or* (2) your expenses in
travelling abroad you have me, and I am rich enough,
and I shall never fail you, neither at the outset nor in
keeping you supplied.

179 *diet me with*: Provide me with, allow me to have.

180–81 *we'll even . . . time will give us*: (1) We'll keep pace with
all (use to our advantage everything) that time, in its
goodness, will present us with *or* (2) we'll smooth out,
make even everything which good time gives us (make
the best of it all) *or* (3) we'll even (do) everything that
time, at its own pace (that is, in good time), will give
us (take every chance we get).

182 *soldier to . . . abide it*: Brave enough for, and will endure
it.

184 *short*: Hurried.

186 *Your carriage from*: (1) Carrying you off, stealing you
away from *or* (2) being the means by which you left.

188 *precious*: Neither Imogen nor Pisanio is aware that the
Queen has been making poisons (at this point, like
Cymbeline, they think that her drugs are life-saving).

189 *stomach-qualmed at*: Feel sick travelling by.

190 *distemper*: Sickness.
some shade: Some secluded place (where Imogen can
change into man's clothes, *fit* or dress herself for
manhood).

III.5

The setting is Cymbeline's palace. Service and duty are key themes in this scene: the duty of nations to conduct themselves properly, even in war, the duty of a daughter, and the duty of a servant (Pisanio may disobey Posthumus' order to kill Imogen, but he is still true to him, and doesn't betray him). Cloten shows what he thinks duty is in 107–18 and 147 (where he wants Pisanio to be as slavishly obedient and silent as an Ottoman houseboy). Maintaining necessary ceremonies is dealt with too (7–17), which points forward to the end of the play, where the planned slaughter of the Romans would indeed have been barbaric (V.5.69–73). The dangers of not observing ceremony are shown in Cloten's knocking Pisanio about (80–101) and in his vengeful fantasy of raping and degrading Imogen and insulting Posthumus' dead body (133–9).

5 *ourself*: Me (Cymbeline uses the royal first person plural pronoun here, and for most of the scene).

6 *sovereignty*: (1) Royal dignity *or* (2) (concern for) Britain's right to govern itself.

7 *So, sir*: Very well, sir (probably a polite way of declining to respond to what Cymbeline has said).

8 *conduct*: Escort, guard.

9 *you*: Addressed to (1) Cymbeline *or* (2) the Queen (Lucius may be wishing her joy both as a queen and as a woman).

10 *office*: Duty.

11 *The due . . . omit*: Cymbeline tells his lords not to neglect the smallest part of the ceremony and civility which Lucius is entitled to, in his own right, as an individual, and as Rome's ambassador (even though he is now Britain's enemy).

12 *Your hand*: Lucius offers to shake hands with Cloten in farewell, but perhaps also as a polite gesture to put right any ill feeling between them in their earlier exchanges (see III.1.76–80).

14 *the event*: The war, and its outcome.

17 *the Severn*: The River Severn, here the natural frontier

between England and Wales (the river rises in Wales
and flows south through the western counties of England
into the Bristol Channel). Lucius will have an escort
until he crosses the Severn into Wales, a country which
is still part of Cymbeline's territory, but which, because
of its terrain, is beyond immediate control and a hiding-
place for outlaws (among them, Belarius and the princes).

20 *in it*: That is, in refusing to pay the tribute and choosing
to go to war.

22 *It fits . . . ripely*: It is high time therefore (that).

24 *he*: Augustus (as also in 25–6).

25 *drawn to head*: Gathered together (to make an army).

26 *not sleepy business*: Not a matter we can afford to be
sluggish in.

28–9 *Our expectation . . . made us forward*: My expectation
that matters would turn out like this made me get things
ready in advance.

31–2 *nor to us . . . the day*: Imogen has not presented herself
to her father (1) to show the obedience to him which
he has stipulated she should do each day (see the note
to 49) or (2) as part of the customary obligation which
the heir apparent owes to the monarch.

32 *She looks us like*: To me she looks like.

35 *too slight in sufferance*: Too easy-going in tolerating
(such behaviour from her).

36–7 *most retired . . . her life been*: That is, she has withdrawn
from society.

39 *Forbear*: Refrain from making.

40 *tender of*: Sensitive to.

42 *answered*: Accounted for, justified.

44 *th'loud'st of noise*: The loudest noise.

46–7 *She prayed me . . . her infirmity*: She asked me to excuse
her for staying shut up (*close*, in her private rooms),
where she was confined because sick.

49 *bound to proffer*: Obliged to offer you. From 31–2 and
48–9 it seems that Cymbeline has ordered Imogen to
appear before him every day, since she disobeyed him
by marrying Posthumus, and that he has put the Queen
in charge of her (her *jailer*, I.1.73). Imogen has made

an excuse for not presenting herself (46–9), but the
Queen has not passed it on (50–51) because she is hoping
for the worst (that Imogen's sickness will be fatal, or
that she will kill herself because she is so miserable, or
that she will flee to Posthumus, 60–62).

50 *great court*: Important state affairs (with Lucius).

51 *to blame in memory*: At fault in forgetting (to tell you);
F has *too blame*, so perhaps 'shamefully forgetful'.

52 *that which I fear*: (1) That Imogen is dead (through sickness or suicide) *or* (2) that she has gone to Posthumus.

55 *Go, look after*: Go on, look for (the King). The Queen
probably addresses this to Cloten, perhaps impatiently
because she has already told him at 53 to *follow* after
Cymbeline. Cloten leaves, but his mention of Pisanio
at 54 makes the Queen think about him too: she begins
some threat or angry curse against Pisanio (56), only
to break off as she remembers the drug she has passed
on to him and its likely effects (57; see I.5.60–66 and
78–9).

56 *stand'st so for Posthumus*: Support Posthumus so un-
swervingly.

58 *Proceed by*: Results from.

61 *winged with*: On the wings of, lifted up with (perhaps
the Queen is being droll about Imogen, sneering at her
as a passionate lovebird, fluttering to Posthumus).

63 *end*: Purpose.

65 *the British crown*: If Imogen is dead or in exile for ever,
Cymbeline will have no natural heir, and the Queen is
sure she can persuade him to make Cloten the next in
line to the British throne.

66 *How now*: What has happened.

67 *cheer*: Comfort.

69 *forestall . . . the coming day*: Prevent him from living
to see tomorrow. The Queen hopes that this will be
Cymbeline's last night (an old man, his anger and
ranting (67–8) may be enough to kill him from a fit or
heart attack). Some editors take 68–9 to be an aside,
believing the Queen would never reveal her true feelings so openly, not even to her son.

71 *that*: Because.

    courtly parts: Personal qualities befitting a court.

72 *Than lady, ladies, woman*: Than any lady, than all ladies, than all womankind.

74 *Outsells them all*: Exceeds them all in value.

75–7 *Disdaining me . . . and in that point*: (The fact) that she disdains me and bestows her favour on the low-born Posthumus is such a disgrace to her judgement that everything in her which is otherwise excellent is made lifeless (*choked*) by it, and for that reason (disdaining me, favouring Posthumus).

80 *packing*: Plotting (but the word could also mean 'running away').

    sirrah: A term used to address social inferiors (also at 106).

81 *precious pander*: Arrant bawd (Cloten thinks Pisanio is a paid go-between for Imogen and Posthumus).

83 *Thou art . . . fiends*: That is, I shall kill you and send your soul to hell at once.

85 *Close villain*: Secretive scoundrel (Cloten is preoccupied with social rank, so the word *villain* will carry with it nuances of 'servant' or 'lackey' as it does here and at 108).

89 *dram*: Very small amount.

91 *Come nearer*: Get to the point (but Cloten may also have grabbed hold of Pisanio and be drawing him physically *nearer*).

92 *No farther halting . . . home*: No more hesitation: answer me fully, tell me everything you know about.

95 *Discover*: Reveal.

99–100 *This paper . . . her flight*: This letter contains the full story of what I know about her flight from court. Presumably this is the same letter which Posthumus had written to Imogen to lure her to her death at Milford Haven (III.2.40–46): she threw it away, together with other letters, at III.4.77–82, but Pisanio picked it up and brought it back to court with him. Cloten now reads it and plans to kill Posthumus at the supposed rendezvous. (Pisanio tells what happened here at

V.5.278–81.) The dramatic function of the letter is like that of the Queen's drug, which circulates among the characters (as poison to some, but balm to others).

101 *Or this or perish*: I must either give him this (letter) or he will kill me.

103 *prove his travel . . . danger*: Put him to the effort of travelling (to Milford Haven, to no purpose), but not place her in danger (in *travel* there is a pun on 'travail' or labour).

107–8 *if thou . . . a villain*: Cloten uses *villain* in two ways: (1) if you wish to stop being a mere servant (Posthumus' serving-man) *and* (2) if you decide not to behave like a scoundrel (towards me).

108–9 *undergo those employments*: Perform those tasks.

110 *industry*: Assiduity.

112–13 *neither want my means . . . preferment*: Lack neither my financial support to help you out (*relief* means 'assistance'), nor my recommendation for your advancement at court.

121 *late*: Former (since Cloten takes himself to be Pisanio's new master).

122 *suit*: Suit of clothes (doublet and hose).

127 *Milford Haven*: The rendezvous mentioned in the letter (see the note to 99–100).

127–8 *I forgot to ask . . . remember't anon*: The question Cloten has forgotten is presumably the one he asks at 143, how long is it since Imogen went to Milford Haven?

130 *She said upon a time*: Cloten recalls the remark at II.3.129–32.

132–3 *than my noble . . . person*: Cloten means 'than myself, both as someone of high rank, and in my own person', but once more he unknowingly describes himself as a fool (*natural* could mean 'half-witted').

137 *insultment*: Scornful triumph (one root of the word, appropriate to the dreadful fantasy just described, may have been the Latin verb *insultare*, meaning 'to leap (over)').

140 *knock her back*: Force her back (home) with blows, beat her.

140 *foot*: Kick.

141 *rejoicingly*: With great joy, taking pleasure in her contempt of me.

147 *a voluntary . . . design*: Willingly silent about my plan. A *mute* was (1) an actor in a play who had no speaking part *or* (2) a slave in a Turkish harem, who was either dumb from birth or whose tongue had been cut out to make sure he couldn't give away any secrets (Cloten wants tyrannical control over Pisanio, but he also wants him to betray Posthumus from choice, not by compulsion, to be *a voluntary mute*).

147–8 *Be but duteous . . . tender itself*: Only be dutiful (in your service to me) and substantial advancement will present itself (the *true* kind which I can give you, but which Posthumus cannot). Editors sometimes emend F's punctuation to 'Be but duteous and true, preferment'.

151 *my loss*: My loss (of honour, of reputation for loyalty).

153 *him*: Posthumus (Pisanio still regards him as *most true* to Imogen, despite his plan to murder her, because he has been misled by some villain, III.4.118–21).

154–5 *Flow . . . on her*: That is, may heaven pour down blessings on her.

155–6 *This fool's speed . . . meed*: May this fool's haste be thwarted with slowness, and may his only rewards be the efforts he puts in (sentiments expressed in the contemporary proverbs 'a fool's haste is no speed' and 'he has his labour for his pains').

III.6

The setting is Belarius' cave. The emphasis on hunger and near-starvation throughout the scene is Shakespeare's way of showing how close the brothers and sister are to pure animal instinct (the word *browse* at 38 was mostly used of horses and cattle feeding). This removes all traces of inhibition when they meet, allowing them their sudden instinctive mutual attraction. The mix of brother and sister in Imogen excites the princes and wakes in them the possibilities the future may hold (Guiderius thinks of marriage, Arviragus of a long overdue reunion within the family, 66–71). Imogen's response to them at

first, because Posthumus had betrayed her, is to choose
to give up being a woman altogether, so long as she can
merge with them, in their maleness (79–86).

2 *tired myself*: Worn myself out. There may also be a
pun on 'tired' or 'attired' (F has *tyr'd*), that is, dressed
myself: perhaps Imogen reminds the audience who she
is – yes it's me, even though I'm dressed as a boy – or
she remarks on something quite exceptional for her, as
a princess, I have dressed *myself* (that is, without help
from my maids).

4 *helps*: Cures.

6 *within a ken*: In sight.

7 *Foundations fly the wretched*: (1) To the poor folk who
are journeying towards them, fixed places seem to move
further and further into the distance *or* (2) places set
up to succour the poor and the sick (almshouses, hospi-
tals) flee from the very people they were intended for
(they evade their responsibilities to relieve them). The
link between (2) and (1) is Milford Haven: its name
declares that it is one of the *foundations* (a haven), but
Imogen has been unable to get there, even though she
has been travelling towards it for days and days. It is
possible that the qualifying clause in 7–8 indicates that
Imogen, who is hungry and exhausted, is not entirely
sure what she is saying: is *Foundations fly the wretched*
a rational remark, or a wise paradox, or is it delirious
and silly (fixed places can move)? Perhaps she is quick
to define it as a proverbial saying so as to reassure
herself that she has not lost her wits.

10–11 *knowing 'tis . . . trial*: Knowing that either they will be
punished for it or that they have failed the *trial* or test
of their truthfulness.

12–13 *To lapse . . . sorer than*: To lie (*or* to fall into sin) in
prosperity is worse than.

16–17 *but even before . . . sink for food*: Only a moment ago I
was about to collapse for lack of food.

18 *hold*: Stronghold *or* lair.

19–20 *yet famine . . . o'erthrow nature*: Yet starvation, before
it completely overwhelms the body's life-force.

20 *clean*: Completely.

21 *hardness*: Hardship, difficulty.

22 *hardiness*: Courage.

23 *civil*: Civilized.

24 *Take or lend*: (1) Either take what money I have, in payment for food, or give it to me freely (let me beg it from you: see 45–8) *or* (2) either take my life or give me food (if F's *or* is emended to 'ere' (before), perhaps 'take what I have before you give me anything').

25 *Best*: I were best to.

27 *Such a foe*: (Grant me) that sort of foe.

28 *woodman*: Huntsman.

30 *match*: Agreement (see III.3.74–6).

31–2 *The sweat of industry ... works to*: The energy of hard work would dry up and die but for the purpose it has, to obtain a reward (no one would work hard unless he had a goal).

33 *what's homely*: What is plain (food) taste.

34 *snore upon the flint*: Sleep on stony ground (Imogen's condition for the two previous nights).
   resty: Restless *or* sluggish with too much rest.

36 *keep'st thyself*: That is, their house (the cave) has no one to look after it (it is empty and has no housekeeper).
   throughly weary: Completely worn out.

38 *browse*: nibble, eat lightly (at this time a word normally used of animals feeding on leaves and twigs).

41 *fairy*: Enchantment, illusion. Here this probably doesn't mean a creature from fairyland. Belarius can hardly mean that Imogen would be taken for a fairy creature, but for the fact that she is eating their *victuals* (40): on the contrary, it was thought that the fairies not only ate human food, but depended on human beings to feed them. Moreover, fairies were real beings, although they had come from another world, whereas Imogen looks beautifully unreal, and it is only by her eating that Belarius realizes she is not an illusion; once again, as her name suggests, she is an imagine or imogen (see the Introduction, pp. xliii ff., and An Account of the Text, p. 131).

What's the matter . . .: What are you speaking about?

46 *Good truth*: In truth.

48 *i'th'floor*: (1) On the floor *or* (2) in the rushes covering the floor.

   meat: Food.

49 *board*: Table.

50 *parted*: Departed.

52–4 *All gold . . . worship dirty gods*: May all gold and silver rather (1) be thrown back into the earth where they came from *or* (2) be turned back into the dirt which they are, since these metals are valued as nothing more than dirt, except by people who worship disgusting idols (Arviragus may be thinking of Mammon, the grimy god of riches and avarice, who was said to live in a cave).

56 *made it*: Done it (committed the fault).

58 *Fidele*: The name means 'one who is faithful' (see IV.2.379–81).

59 *He embarked*: He is already on board ship and waiting to sail.

61 *in*: Into.

62 *churls*: Peasants *or* churlish lowlifes.

63 *rude*: Rough, wild.

64 *cheer*: Entertainment, food and hospitality.

65 *thanks*: Receive our thanks.

67 *I should woo . . . in honesty*: I would woo boldly (1) but to be your bridegroom in honourable wedlock *or* (2) but prove a fit companion for you in honesty (that is, my wooing would be strenuous but I would remain as virtuous and chaste as you are) *or* (3) before I'd fail to be your servant in an honourable love-suit.

68 *I bid . . . buy*: I am bidding for you on terms I would actually offer if you were a woman and this were a real bargain between us (in other words, I mean what I say – if you were a woman, I'd seek your hand in earnest). One proposed emendation 'Ay, bid' for F's *I bid* is tempting since it maintains the flow in the speech.

68–9 *I'll make't . . . my brother*: I'll console myself that he is a man by loving him as if he were my brother.

70–71 *such a welcome . . . is yours*: The welcome I'd give him, as my brother, after we had been apart for a long time, that's the welcome you (Fidele) have from me.

72 *sprightly*: Cheerful.

72–3 *'Mongst friends? . . . brothers*: Imogen repeats Arviragus' last words questioningly, then (1) she accepts the offered friendship, 'yes, if we are indeed brothers' *or* (2) she means 'I am among friends for as long as we are brothers and you take me for a man (but your feelings might be different if you knew I was a woman)'.

74–6 *then had my prize . . . Posthumus*: Then I would be of less importance and so more equal to you, Posthumus (if these were her long-lost brothers, Imogen would no longer be the heir apparent, and her value as a *prize* (a ship captured for its cargo) would be reduced: the weight of her cargo, or *ballasting*, would become more equal to that of Posthumus).

76 *He wrings*: (1) He writhes (Imogen's demeanour suggests *distress* and unhappiness) *or* (2) he wrings his hands.

77 *free't*: Remove it.

79–84 *Great men . . . these twain*: Powerful and distinguished men, were they to live in a court *no bigger than this cave*, without servants to wait on them, possessing the *virtue* which only *their own consciences* can confirm that they have (*sealed them*), and renouncing that worthless tribute (the *nothing-gift* of adoration), which the fickle mass (*differing multitudes*) bestows on them – such great men could not surpass these two young men. It is possible that *laying by* means 'setting aside, disregarding'.

86 *Since Leonatus' false*: (1) Since Leonatus is false *or* (2) because of Leonatus' lies.

87 *go dress our hunt*: Go and prepare and cook the game we have caught.

88 *Discourse is heavy, fasting*: Conversation is wearisome on an empty stomach.

89 *mannerly demand thee of*: Ask you, with due civility, about.

91 *The night to th'owl . . . less welcome*: That is, you are more welcome to us than the night is to the owl and the morning is to the lark.

III.7

This tiny scene, located in Rome, tells the audience that
the legions setting out for Britain will be made up of
gentry (the usual lower-rank troops are tied up in the
east and the legions in Gallia are not at full strength),
and that Lucius is to be their commander. Shakespeare
follows some of the sources in this, but he is also
concerned to show that the Britons fought and defeated
the highest grade of Romans. The scene also provides
an interval of time for Cloten to ride to Milford Haven
and appear in the next scene, IV.1.

  0 *Senators and Tribunes*: In Ancient Rome senators were
from the patrician upper class and tribunes were the
representatives of the common people.

  1 *writ*: Command.

  2 *common men*: Plebeians, common soldiers.

  3 *Pannonians and Dalmatians*: See note to III.1.72.

  5 *Full weak*: Not at all able.

  6 *fall'n-off*: Revolted.

9–10 *commends . . . commission*: Entrusts his full authority
(F has *commands*, so perhaps 'orders his complete
authority (be given to you)').

 14 *supplyant*: Supplementary *or* ready to supply troops.

 15 *Will tie you to*: Will give you (1) exact instructions as
to *or* (2) precise limits to.

IV.1

The scene is in Wales, not far from Belarius' cave. This
is the first moment the audience sees Cloten dressed in
Posthumus' clothes, so there is a small shock, either
because he is so like him, or because he is nothing like
him at all. There are important parallels in the ways
the men intend to punish Imogen for choosing, as they
see it, to be with another man (Posthumus thinks she
prefers Jachimo, Cloten knows she prefers Posthumus).
See the Introduction, p. lx, for a discussion of Cloten
as Posthumus' double, and the possibility that in 1611
a single actor played both roles.

  1 *they should meet*: (Imogen and Posthumus) are to meet.

  2 *fit*: Fittingly, well.

3-4 *Why should his mistress . . . not be fit too*: Why shouldn't
     Posthumus' mistress (Imogen) – who was *made* by him
     (given life by Cymbeline) that *made* (gave work and
     status to) the tailor of this suit – also be *fit* or suitable
     for me (Cloten also means 'why shouldn't her body fit
     me as well as his clothes do')? The clause *made by him
     that made the tailor* may refer to God rather than
     Cymbeline, in which case Cloten is saying that Imogen
     is no more special than any other human being (since
     God has made us all).

4-6 *The rather . . . by fits*: All the more so – though I do
     beg pardon for using such an indecent word – because
     it's said that a woman's *fitness* (her sexual desire) comes
     by *fits* ('by fits and starts', spasmodically, with an intri-
     cate pun on 'fittings with a tailor', that is, when she has
     her dresses made she is aroused by her tailor).

6   *Therein . . . play the workman*: (1) In this respect
     (catching Imogen when she is in one of her 'fitnesses',
     or feeling randy), I shall have to do my job with her
     (have sex with her) *or* (2) in this suit of Posthumus', I
     shall have to pretend to be the lower-class serving man
     he is *or* (3) dressed as fittingly as this, I really must play
     the part of the tailor (who does fittings for ladies).

7   *glass*: Looking-glass, mirror.

8   *I mean*: F's punctuation (*chamber: I mean*) points to a
     vulgarism (the equivalent of 'what I mean to say is'),
     but some editors have taken *I mean* to qualify the previous
     sentence ('to confer, in his own chamber, I mean.'). It is
     conceivable that once again Cloten says, 'I, mean!'
     (speaking in snatches, as Belarius says of him at IV.2.105),
     and recalling Imogen's disparagement of him in compar-
     ison with Posthumus: see II.3.120-32 and III.5.130-33).

10-13 *not beneath him . . . in single oppositions*: Not beneath
     him in wealth, beyond him (1) in opportunities for
     advancement *or* (2) in present reputation in the world,
     above him in birth (born into a higher social rank than
     him), just as experienced in military service and other
     duties, and more notable than him for prowess in duels
     (one-to-one combat).

13 *imperceiverant*: Imperceptive, undiscerning (it is possible that F's *imperseverant* is correct, and means 'exceedingly obdurate', or that Shakespeare intended Cloten to make a stupid blunder).

14 *mortality*: Human life.

16 *be off . . . enforced*: Be cut off, your lady raped.

17–18 *spurn her home*: (I shall) kick her back home (*also*, treat her with contempt).

20–21 *having power of . . . my commendations*: Having control over (Cymbeline's) peevishness (*testiness*), (she) will turn everything I have done (murder, rape) into a matter for which I deserve praise.

21 *sore purpose*: (1) Grievous purpose (to kill Posthumus) *or* (2) cause of suffering (with a lewd quibble on 'sore' as 'wound', a crude word for the vagina: Cloten's *sword* (penis) will wound her *sore*).

Fortune: May fortune.

22–3 *This is the very description*: This place corresponds exactly with the description.

23 *the fellow*: Pisanio.

IV.2

This scene, outside Belarius' cave, has four phases: 1–61, Fidele–Imogen grows sick, takes the drug and goes into the cave, and the brothers praise him–her (see the Introduction, pp. lxii–lxv); at 62–169, Guiderius fights with Cloten, cuts off his head offstage, shows it to Belarius and then exits to throw the head in the stream; at 169–290, Fidele, apparently dead, is brought out of the cave by Arviragus and the brothers lay him beside the decapitated Cloten and speak the dirge over them; at 291–403, Imogen wakes to find a body beside her which she misidentifies as her husband's (discussed in the Introduction, pp. lv–lvii), she grieves over the body until the entry of Lucius, who takes her as his page, and has the body buried.

Shakespeare knew that the many shifts of mood in this sequence would fascinate and enthral an audience, and that the puzzles in the story would too. Why don't Belarius and the princes bury the bodies at once? Are

they lying in state perhaps? Is the beheading supposed
to be an appropriate penalty for treason (as it was for
high-born Elizabethan traitors), or is it an indication
of some atavistic pagan instinct? Deeper puzzles are
shown to us too, as with, for instance, Guiderius'
beheading of Cloten. This, as no one inside the play
knows, is a hidden revenge story: Guiderius kills a man
dressed as his brother-in-law for wanting to violate the
sister he, Guiderius, didn't know he had.

One of the deepest concerns in the scene is with the
death of the body and whether there is peace for it after
death. The dirge tells us that there is, but there are
signs, in the references to ghosts and to fairy haunt-
ings, that the spirit may still be vulnerable. Is this, we
ask, because pagans, living before Christ, could know
nothing better? Questions like this are normally
reserved for tragedy (Hamlet asks whether death is a
sleep filled with nightmares), and it is one of Shakespeare's achievements in *Cymbeline* that he has made
them look entirely in place in a comic romance.

3–5 *So man . . . is both alike*: Imogen means 'all men should
indeed be brothers, as we are, yet in the world beyond
this cave, even though they all come from the same
earth or *clay*, and at death will return to the same *dust*,
men are separated and differentiated from one another
by rank and social position (*dignity*)' (the commonplace that God formed man of the dust of the ground
comes from Genesis 2:7). It has been claimed that
Imogen is here reproving Arviragus for his presumption – insisting that he keep his distance – but this is
hardly likely, given what she says throughout the scene
about the snobbish lies she has heard, that *all's savage
but at court* (33).

8 *so citizen a wanton*: Such a city-bred, spoilt child (namby-
pamby).

10–11 *Stick to your journal course . . . breach of all*: Keep to
your daily way (of life); a break in the pattern of one's
behaviour brings confusion to everything.

12 *amend*: Cure.

Society: Companionship, company.

14 *reason of*: Talk about.

  trust me here: Trust me (1) to look after the cave *or* (2) in this matter.

15–16 *let me die . . . so poorly*: Let me be put to death (if I should rob myself) for stealing something so worthless (Imogen means that she possesses nothing and that her life is not worth much if she should steal away, or die).

16–18 *I love thee . . . my father*: (1) I love you – there, I have said so. How great is my love? As great as the love I have for my father *or* (2) I love you – I have declared my love to be as great in quantity and substance as my love for my father.

19–20 *yoke me | In*: Link myself with.

22 *Love's . . . reason*: 'Love is without reason' was a contemporary proverb.

22–3 *The bier at door . . . shall die*: If the *bier* (the stand to support a coffin) were waiting at the *door* (to remove a corpse), and the question were put to me, 'which of these two would you rather have taken from you by death?'

24 *strain*: (1) Inherited disposition *or* (2) lineage, social descent *or* (3) sentiment.

25 *breed*: Inheritance *or* species.

27 *meal and bran*: Flour and husks.

28–9 *who this . . . loved before me*: (1) It is miraculous that this boy, whoever he is, should be loved more than me *or* (2) the identity of this boy, whom they love more than me, is a mystery.

31 *sport*: Success in your hunting (also, pleasure in the chase).

  You health . . . sir: Arviragus says '(I wish) you health' to Imogen, and then 'I am ready when you are, sir' to Belarius.

35–6 *Th'imperious seas . . . sweet fish*: Poor tributary rivers breed fish just as sweet to the taste as those from the lordly, overbearing oceans, but they do it without spawning sea-monsters as well (the literal meaning of *imperious* is 'imperial').

38 *stir him*: (1) Move him (to tell his story) *or* (2) rouse him from his melancholy.

39 *gentle*: Well-born (from a family of gentry or gentlemen).

40 *Dishonestly . . . honest*: Treated dishonourably by others, yet honourable himself.

42 *To th'field*: To the chase (let's begin the hunt).

43 *for this time*: For the time being.

46 *bound*: Indebted (in his response, *shalt be ever*, Belarius means 'we will always be *bound* together, there will always be a bond of affection between us').

47 *appears he hath had*: Shakespeare has conflated the construction 'it appears he hath had' with 'he appears to have had'.

49–51 *He cut our roots . . . he her dieter*: F mistakenly assigns these lines to Arviragus.

49 *neat*: Dainty.

   characters: (1) Letters of the alphabet *or* (2) emblems and designs.

50 *as*: As if.

51 *her dieter*: The person who looks after her diet. Imogen cossets the brothers with her singing and by cutting their food into shapes to please them, as if they were children. She makes their soups (1) with as much care as if she were tending the goddess Juno in her sickness *or* (2) as though she were responsible for tempting Juno, known for her tetchiness, to follow a diet for her health.

53 *that*: What.

57 *them*: That is, the smile and the sigh in 52–4; see the Introduction, pp. lxii–lxiv.

58 *spurs*: The large lateral roots of a tree.

58–60 *Grow patience . . . vine*: (1) May *patience* grow, and as the *vine* flourishes, let *grief*, the evil *elder*-tree, untwist and disentangle its dying roots *or* (2) let *patience* grow, and let *grief*, the evil *elder*-tree, no longer entwine its destructive root with that of the life-giving vine (*patience*). At this date, grief was thought to be literally destructive, or *perishing*, because it dried up the

blood in the body: perhaps patience is figured as the
vine because its fruit could be made into wine, a life-
giving restorative. The *elder* is described as *stinking*
because of its evil-smelling leaves, but also because it
was, by tradition, the tree on which Judas hanged
himself after he betrayed Christ (with whom the vine
is often associated in biblical metaphor).

61 *great morning*: Broad daylight.

62 *runagates*: Runaways (Imogen and Posthumus).
    That villain: Pisanio.

64 *partly*: Slightly.

67 *held*: Regarded.
    Hence: Let us get away from here.

69 *companies*: Companions of his, retainers.

70 *Let me alone with him*: Leave me to deal with him.

71 *villain mountaineers*: (1) Rascally *or* (2) ill-born savages
    from the mountains.

72 *slave*: Low-born servant (a term of abuse, thrown back
    at Cloten in 74).

72–4 *A thing . . . without a knock*: I have never done anything
    more slavish than now in replying to a slave like you
    without giving you a beating (*answering A slave* may
    mean 'in responding to being called a "slave"').

81 *Know'st me not by my clothes*: Don't you recognize my
    rank from how I'm dressed? (perhaps Cloten forgets
    at first that he is wearing Posthumus' clothes; even so,
    these would be sufficiently grand to show that he is
    from the court).

83 *precious varlet*: Arrant scoundrel.

84 *My tailor*: The emphasis is on *My* (these low-grade
    clothes were made by Posthumus' tailor, not mine).

86 *injurious*: Insulting.

89 *Cloten . . . be thy name*: (1) Even if your name is 'Cloten,
    thou double villain' (that is *Cloten, thou villain* doubled) *or*
    (2) granted that your name is 'Cloten', you villain twice over.

90 *Toad or Adder, Spider*: All venomous creatures (*Spider*
    may be a term of abuse: were your name Toad or
    Adder, you mere spider).

91 *move*: Agitate, bother.

92 *mere confusion*: Utter discomfiture.

93 *not seeming*: Since you don't seem to be.

94 *afeard*: Afraid.

95 *Those . . . the wise*: I have respect for those whom I am in awe of – people who are wise.

96 *Die the death*: Well, take death at my hands (the phrase was also used when a man was condemned to death by law, so Cloten may mean that he is entitled to enforce the death sentence, which was imposed on outlaws and exiles: cf. I.1.165–6).

97 *proper*: Own.

99 *Lud's Town*: See the note to III.1.32. There may be an allusion here to 'Lud's gate', or Ludgate, the precinct in London which contained the Blackfriars Theatre that Shakespeare's company, the King's Men, began to use around 1610, and where some of the first performances of *Cymbeline* may have been played; see The Play in Performance, p. lxxxi.

100 *Yield, rustic mountaineer*: Give in, you boorish mountain savage.

101 *No company's abroad*: Are there no other people about?

103 *I cannot tell*: I am not sure if it *was* him (by 107, after he has recalled Cloten's features and way of speaking, Belarius is certain).

104–5 *time . . . then he wore*: The passing of time hasn't altered in the slightest the essential features of his face.

105 *snatches in his voice*: Halting or hesitating in his speech (perhaps stammering).

106 *burst of speaking*: Rapid, uncontrolled speaking.
     absolute: Certain.

107 *very Cloten*: Cloten himself.

108–9 *I wish my brother . . . so fell*: I hope that my brother will acquit himself well against Cloten since you say he is so fierce.

109–12 *Being scarce . . . cease of fear*: Belarius insists that Cloten is a menace, even to Guiderius, because he is so stupid as to be insensible of fear: 'even as a boy, when Cloten was scarcely *made up* – I mean, just reached in manhood – he had no awareness of threatening terrors; for defect in judgement is often what extinguishes fear'.

114 *Not Hercules*: Not even Hercules (the hero famous for carrying out seemingly impossible tasks).

118 *perfect*: Well aware.

121 *take us in*: Capture us.

125 *that*: What.

126-7 *be tender . . . let*: Be (so) sensitive as to permit (since we're outlaws, why should we care what the law says about killing him).

129-30 *What company . . . abroad*: What companions of his have you found around here?

131 *safe*: Sound.

132-3 *Though his humour . . . but mutation*: Even though his disposition (chief characteristic) was one of changefulness (alteration in mood).

137 *may be*: May have been.

138 *Cave*: Live in caves.

139 *make some stronger head*: Band together into a stronger force.

140 *it is like him*: It would be his way of behaving (making sudden oaths to do this or that).
    break: Burst.

141 *fetch us in*: Capture us, bring us in.

142-3 *To come alone . . . suffering*: That he would have come by himself – he wouldn't have ventured it and the court wouldn't have permitted it.

144 *tail*: Retinue of attendants (see 132).

145 *ord'nance*: Whatever is ordained.

146 *foresay*: Determine, will.

149 *Did make my way long forth*: Made my journey out from the cave seem long (the thought of *Fidele's sickness* was weighing on his mind).

154 *reck*: Care.

157 *alone pursued me*: Pursued me alone.

159-61 *I would revenges . . . answer*: I wish that the forces seeking revenge – mustered to as large a host as three men like us might take on – would search high and low for us (*seek us through*), and make us answer them in battle (this is what happens, although not as Arviragus expected, when they confront the fleeing Britons and the Romans: see V.2 and V.3.1–50).

165 *hasty*: Rash.

167–8 *To gain his colour . . . blood*: To restore the colour to his cheeks I'd spill the blood of (kill) a parishful of men like Cloten. Shakespeare may have intended *Clotens* to mean 'Cloten's' or 'Clotens' (that is, many Clotens).

170 *thyself thou blazon'st*: You proclaim yourself.

172 *zephyrs*: Mild breezes.

173 *Not wagging his*: Not moving or disturbing its (the *violet*'s).

174 *enchafed*: Roused to anger.
     rud'st: Roughest.

177 *instinct*: The stress is on the second syllable.
     frame: Fashion, direct.

178 *royalty*: Royal character and conduct.

179 *Civility not seen from other*: Civilized behaviour not seen in or imitated from other people (as the brothers would have acquired it at court).

180 *wildly*: Without cultivation.

184 *clotpoll*: Dolt, blockhead (with a play on Cloten's name).

186 *ingenious*: Skilfully constructed (F has *ingenuous*, at this date often confused with 'ingenious'). Belarius' instrument is probably an automaton (see Music and Songs), since Arviragus is said to have given it *motion*, 188. The idea that the instrument is a mechanical marvel helps to divert the audience from asking too closely how *Solemn music*, 186, could be heard in these remote mountains.

192 *answer solemn accidents*: Correspond to solemn events.

193–4 *Triumphs for nothing . . . boys*: Exultation (*or* festivity) for no good reason, and lamentations over trifling matters – this is gaiety for fools (*or* children *or* apes) and melancholy felt by ungrown boys (presumably Guiderius is indignant because he thinks that Arviragus has sounded a solemn requiem for the dead Cloten, an arrogant nonentity who deserves none of these rites).

198 *on*: Of.

200 *my leaping time*: This is the mark of being sixteen

(*leaping* means 'jumping about energetically', but also 'copulating', hence the time when a boy reaches manhood); *a crutch* is the symbol of sixty or old age (Arviragus himself is about twenty-two: see I.1.59–62).

203 *when thou grew'st thyself*: When you were still growing (before you were plucked, and died).

203–6 *O melancholy . . . harbour in*: Melancholy is addressed, metaphorically, as a sea with uncharted depths, with its ship or *crare* – a person weighed down with melancholy – moving slowly on its surface: 'O melancholy, who could cast a lead so deep as to sound your waters, find your muddy seabed, and establish on which coast your vessel, heavily laden, might best find harbour?' Belarius means that no one can tell a person suffering from melancholy how to unburden himself of the feeling, because he is moving alone in an unfathomable experience. In 205, F's *care* (meaning 'charge' or 'burden') has been emended here to *crare* (a small trading ship).

207 *but I*: But all I know is (Jove knows what man Fidele might have become, had he lived: Belarius only knows that he died of *melancholy*, a *rare* or wonderful boy).

209 *Stark*: Rigid in death.

210–11 *as some fly . . . laughed at*: As if some fly had merely tickled him while he was sleeping, not as if (as is really the case) he had been stung by *death's dart*, at which he was quietly laughing (this probably alludes to 1 Corinthians 15:55, 'O death where is thy sting?', the consolation that Christ has conquered death).

213 *thus leagued*: Folded like this.

214 *clouted brogues*: Heavy outdoor shoes, studded with hobnails (*or* patched).

214–15 *whose rudeness . . . too loud*: The clumsy coarseness (of the shoes) made my footsteps resound, echo back too loudly (they might have woken the sleeping Fidele).

217 *fairies*: Probably fairy creatures rather than illusions in this case (see note to III.6.41).

222 *azured harebell*: Sky-blue wild hyacinth.

223–4 *eglantine . . . not thy breath*: Sweet-brier (wild rose),

the fragrance of which – it is no reproach to the flower
to say it – was not sweeter than your breath.

224 *ruddock*: Robin redbreast.

228–9 *and furred moss ... thy corpse*: And besides, he will bring
furred moss, when there are no flowers, to protect your
corpse from the winter with this covering (according
to contemporary folklore, the robin would cover with
moss a body which had not been buried).

230 *wench-like*: Womanish, effeminate.

232–3 *And not protract ... due debt*: And not delay payment,
because of our wonder and veneration, of the debt that
is now due (that is, we should not put off any longer
the duty we have to bury him, delayed while we feel
wonder at his beauty and person).

233 *shall's*: Shall us (we).

235–6 *now our voices ... mannish crack*: Now our voices have
broken (this presumably means that when Euriphile
died, the brothers were still boys and their voices had
not yet broken).

237 *As once our mother*: As we did once for our mother (F
has *to our*, so perhaps 'as once we sang to our mother');
once means (1) at her funeral *or* (2) in days past, when
she was alive.

238 *Save that ... Fidele*: Except that the song is for Fidele
rather than Euriphile (editors have suggested that it is
their names which are to be substituted, within the song,
'Fidele' for 'Euriphile', but this is unlikely since these
are metrically different, and in the song as we have it
in F there are no personal names at all).

240 *word*: Recite.

242 *fanes*: Temples.

243 *med'cine the less*: Cure lesser (griefs).

246 *paid*: Punished.
    mean and mighty: People of humble rank as well as
    powerful ones.

247 *reverence*: Proper regard for subordination towards
social superiors.

248 *That angel of the world*: The power which maintains
order in the world (it is an *angel* because it came from

heaven to show men how, through due respect, they
could imitate the divine hierarchy).

250 *as being*: Because he was.

251 *as*: Because he was *or* in a manner fitting for.

252 *Thersites' body . . . Ajax'*: Thersites, a Greek warrior
in the Trojan war, was deformed and vituperative, and
of a much lower rank than the hero Ajax, but he was
the strongest and bravest of the Greeks, second only
to Achilles.

254 *say*: Speak.
the whilst: In the meantime.

255 *to th'east*: This is the opposite of the practice in Christian
burials (presumably because the play is set in pagan
Britain).

257 *remove him*: Move him (lay his body in the opposite
direction).

261 *Home art gone*: You have gone back home (to heaven)
and *ta'en* the *wages* for your toil in this world (*thy worldly
task*, 260).

262-3 *Golden lads . . . come to dust*: Death is the leveller, who
takes *Golden lads and girls* as inexorably as he takes
working folk. In Warwickshire dialect dandelions were
called *chimney-sweepers* when they went to seed
(because their grey heads, once golden, resembled a
chimney-sweeper's brooms). The image is of death as
the blowing of a common flower.

263 *As*: The same as.

265 *stroke*: Blow or lash (that is the *tyrant's* power over you,
even to cut off your head); but also cruel, deceptive
petting of you (as with the *tyrant* Queen, who can *tickle
where she wounds*, I.1.84-5).

267 *the reed is as the oak*: These were traditional opposites
– the reed was all-yielding and the oak all-strong –
which had other associations too (woodwind music
from reeds, a garland of oak leaves as the prize of
victors in war); the differences between them no longer
matter to Fidele, now that he is dead.

268 *sceptre, learning, physic*: Princely power, scholarship,
medical knowledge.

269 *this*: This path (to death).

271 *thunder-stone*: Thunder-bolt (often thought to be a stone).

275 *Consign to thee*: (1) Co-sign the same contract with you (meet the same fate, die as you do) *or* (2) sign where you have (adding their names to yours on the register of death).

276 *exorciser*: Person who can raise spirits from the dead.

277 *charm*: Put a magic spell on.

278 *Ghost unlaid forbear thee*: May any ghost which has not been laid to rest leave you in peace.

280 *consummation*: Fulfilment, end.

285 *Upon their faces*: Not literally on their faces, since Cloten is headless. Belarius says (1) (put the flowers) on the front of their bodies *or* (2) turn their bodies over, lay them face down. With the emendation 'upon th'earth's face', 285–6 means 'you were like flowers on the earth's face, but now in death you are withered' (see An Account of the Text, p. 141).

286–7 *even so . . . herblets shall*: These small herbs will wither in the same way.

287 *strew*: Perhaps pronounced 'strow', to rhyme with 'so' in 286.

288 *upon our knees*: (We will pray) on our knees.

289 *that gave them first*: Like flowers, the earth gave them their first life (they are made of its clay: see note to 3–5).

293 *'Ods pittikins*: This is the diminutive (perhaps little-girlish) form of the profanity 'God's pity' (for 'God have mercy').

294 *gone*: Walked.
     Faith: In faith, truly.

295 *But soft, no bedfellow*: But wait, there shouldn't be anyone sleeping beside me (even half-awake, Imogen knows that she was alone when she fell asleep; she also has it in mind that she mustn't go to bed with anyone but her husband Posthumus).

297 *the care on't*: (Is like) the grief of it (the world).

298 *For so*: For in the same way (that is, while I was dreaming).

299 *honest*: Innocent, decent.

   'tis not so: The cave and its inhabitants were only part
   of a dream; Imogen hopes that the sight of this *bloody
   man* will prove to be equally imaginary (throughout
   297–305 she presumably looks away from the body).

300 *bolt*: Arrow.

301 *fumes*: Bodily vapours (which were thought to rise to
   the brain and cause dreams and imaginings).

   very eyes: Eyes themselves.

305 *As a wren's eye . . . part of it*: (1) As a wren's eye (tiny
   in size) *or* (2) as (a drop of moisture in) a wren's eye,
   you almighty revered gods, grant me a part of it.

307 *Without me as within*: (The same) outside me, as it is
   within.

309 *of's*: Of his.

310–11 *His foot Mercurial . . . Jovial face*: Imogen means 'this
   is Posthumus' *foot*, swift like that of the god Mercury;
   this is his *thigh*, powerful like that of Mars, the god of
   war; these are his *brawns* (muscles), strong like those
   of the hero Hercules; but his face, regal and divine like
   that of Jove'.

313 *All curses . . . Hecuba gave the Greeks*: All the curses
   which Queen Hecuba, maddened by her grief, wished
   on the Greek warriors (as they sacked Troy and
   murdered her husband, King Priam).

314 *mine to boot*: Mine too (my curses added to Hecuba's).

   darted: Hurled (as if they were darts or javelins).

315 *Conspired*: Having conspired.

   irregulous: Lawless, unruly.

316 *cut off my lord*: Killed my husband (also, cut off his
   head).

319 *this most bravest*: This, the most (1) excellent *or* (2) handsome *or* (3) valiant, invincible (emphasizing that Cloten
   and Pisanio could never have killed Posthumus in a fair
   fight).

320 *main-top*: The top part of a ship's mainmast.

324 *lucre*: Greed for money.

325 *laid this woe*: Inflicted this misery (but also, laid out this
   dreadful decapitated corpse).

325 *'tis pregnant, pregnant*: (1) It is obvious, utterly clear
(that Cloten and Pisanio have murdered Posthumus)
or (2) it (their plan to murder us both) is ripe, it has
come to fruition (they have lured Posthumus to his
death, and beheaded him, and they believe they have
poisoned me).

327 *cordial to me*: Would revive my spirits.

328 *home*: Fully.

330 *Give colour to my pale cheek*: Imogen falls on the corpse
and either (1) she embraces it and is covered with blood
from the severed neck *or* (2) she dips her hands into
the blood and smears it on her face, perhaps as a sign
that in her despair and delirium she has broken with
normal behaviour and gone half-mad. In either case,
bloodying her face is related to what Arviragus says at
167–9.

331 *horrider*: More ghastly, more frightening.

332 *Which chance*: Who may happen.

333 *To them*: (1) In addition to them (the speech begins
mid-conversation with the Captain listing the troops
that have arrived in Britain from *Gallia*) or (2) attack
the Britons with. It has been suggested that *To them*
was misplaced in F from the previous stage direction
(thus, *and a Soothsayer to them*).

334 *After your will*: According to your instructions.
attending: Waiting for.

336 *what from*: (1) What forces are coming from *or* (2) what
news is there from.

337 *confiners*: Native inhabitants (troops from Italy itself,
rather than from other parts of the Roman Empire).

340 *conduct*: Command.

341 *Siena's brother*: The brother of the Duke (or Prince)
of Siena (the title was Shakespeare's invention or ignorance: Siena was a republic at this date).

342 *benefit o'th'wind*: Favourable wind.
forwardness: Promptness.

345 *this war's purpose*: Concerning this war.

347 *fast*: Fasted.
intelligence: Communication, message.

349 *spongy*: Damp, humid.

350 *portends*: Signifies.

351 *abuse*: Make unreliable, pervert.

352-3 *Dream . . . false*: May you dream *often* like this (of Roman victories), and *never* mistakenly.

353 *Soft, ho*: But wait.

trunk: Cloten's decapitated body (without its *top* or head).

354 *speaks*: Proclaims.

sometime: Once.

356 *Or*: Either.

357 *nature doth abhor*: A living creature hates.

358 *defunct*: Deceased.

362 *demanded*: Asked about.

364 *did*: (1) Fashioned him, portrayed him (Nature painted his *picture*, but someone has defaced it by cutting off his head) *or* (2) behaved in this matter (Nature took away his life but she did not mutilate his body — someone else did that).

365 *What's thy interest*: What have you to do with (perhaps, in 365–6, 'what have you lost in this ship*wreck*?').

372 *occident*: West.

cry out for service: Call out for masters to employ me as their servant.

374 *'Lack*: Alack (alas).

375 *complaining*: Lamentations, mourning.

377 *Richard du Champ*: French for 'Richard Field', the name of a contemporary of Shakespeare's from Stratford, a printer who printed Shakespeare's poems in the 1590s.

379 *Say you*: Pardon? what did you say?

380 *approve*: Prove.

386 *prefer*: Recommend.

387 *an't*: If it.

389 *poor pickaxes*: Imogen means her fingers.

390 *wild wood-leaves and weeds*: Leaves and weeds growing wild in the wood ('wild-wood leaves and weeds', a feasible alternative, would mean 'leaves and weeds growing in the uncultivated, unfrequented forest').

391 *century of*: Hundred.

392 *Such as I can*: Those that I know.

394 *So please you entertain me*: If you choose to employ me.

399 *pikes and partisans*: Weapons used by soldiers in Shakespeare's day (a pike was a type of lance, a partisan was a combination of spear and battle-axe).

400 *arm him*: Take the body up in your arms, carry him.
     preferred: Commended.

402 *As soldiers can*: According to the rites that soldiers are entitled to.

403 *falls*: Downfalls.

IV.3

The scene is Cymbeline's palace. The King, unnerved by the Queen's sudden madness and the disappearance of Imogen, dithers, then recovers when he is reassured that everything is in place and ready for the war. One question raised by this scene is why the Queen loses her wits so easily. Cloten has gone missing, it is true, but only a few days earlier. Perhaps this is an indication of her fragility and motherly obsessiveness, but it is also possible that Shakespeare intended the Queen to know at once, at some level, what had happened to Cloten in Wales (that Guiderius was sending his head (*clotpoll*) downstream in *embassy* to her, IV.2.184–5).

1 *Again*: Go to her again.

2 *with*: Caused by.

3 *of*: As a result of.

4 *touch*: Wound.

6 *Upon a desperate bed*: Desperately ill.

7 *fearful wars point at me*: A terrible war is on its way towards me.

8 *present*: Present moment.
   past: Beyond.

9 *comfort*: Recovery.

11 *enforce*: Extract.

14 *I nothing know*: I know nothing at all about.

16 *Hold*: Consider.

18 *I dare be bound*: I am absolutely sure.

19 *his subjection*: The duty he owes you as a subject.

20 *wants no diligence*: Is no lack of effort.

21 *will*: He will.

troublesome: Disturbed, full of troubles.

22–3 *We'll slip you . . . yet depend*: I'll let you go free for a while, but my suspicion (*jealousy*) about you remains – literally, is still hanging (in the balance).

25 *a supply*: Reinforcements.

26 *gentlemen*: Gentry (cf. III.7.6–7).

27 *Now for*: Would that I now had.

28 *amazed with matter*: Confused by the pressure of these matters.

29–30 *Your preparation . . . ready*: The forces you have drawn together are enough, at the least, to confront the enemy numbers you have just heard about. If more of them do come, you're prepared for them too.

31 *The want is but*: The only thing lacking is for you.

34 *annoy*: Harm.

35 *chances*: Events.

36 *I heard no letter*: I've heard nothing at all (comparable to 'I haven't heard a syllable') *or* (2) I've had no news.

40 *is betid*: Has happened.

43 *present wars shall find*: Wars which are upon us will reveal.

44 *to the note o'th' King*: To the point where the King himself takes notice (of my loyalty).

IV.4

The scene is the cave in Wales. Belarius makes his final, faintly desperate attempt to keep the boys from becoming the warrior princes nature intended them to be. 'There is no chance of you ever having the manners and dignity *your cradle promised* (28)', he tells them, and almost gives away the thought uppermost in his mind: how he stole them from their nursery.

1 *noise*: Sounds (of preparations for battle).

2 *lock it*: Shut it away.

4 *This way*: If we do so.

5 *Must . . . slay us*: Must either kill us because we are Britons.

6–7 *revolts . . . their use*: Rebels, while they have use for us.

8 *secure us*: Make ourselves safe.

10–11 *not mustered . . . the bands*: Not entered on the muster-
roll of troops.

11 *render*: Account.

12 *extort from's*: Extract from us.

13 *whose answer*: The requital (punishment) for which.

14 *Drawn on*: Brought about.
doubt: Fear, uncertainty.

16 *satisfying us*: Convincing us, making us satisfied (with
your advice).

18 *quartered fires*: Camp-fires (from their quarters in the
field).

19 *so cloyed importantly*: So fully occupied (clogged) with
matters of importance.

20 *upon our note*: In taking notice of us.

22 *Of*: By.

23 *not wore*: Hadn't worn out, erased.

24 *remembrance*: Recollection.

26 *Who find . . . breeding*: Who, because you have been in
exile with me, have experienced the lack of proper
education (a courtly one).

27 *certainty*: (1) Result *or* (2) certain continuance.

27–8 *aye hopeless . . . your cradle promised*: Forever without
hope of having the manners (*or* prestige) your rank at
birth promised.

29 *But to be still*: (You are destined) to be forever but.
tanlings: Young creatures tanned by the summer sun
(in Shakespeare's day, tanned skin was a mark of social
inferiority, a sign of outdoor physical work).

30 *shrinking*: Wincing or shivering with cold.

33–4 *thereto so o'ergrown . . . questioned*: Besides (you are) so
(1) overgrown with hair and a beard (see V.3.17) *or* (2)
grown out of the Britons' memory (replaced in their
thoughts, by time or by the preparations for war), that
no questions can be raised (about your identity).

35 *What thing is't*: What a (disgraceful) thing it is.

37 *hot*: Lecherous.

39–40 *rowel . . . iron*: Spurs (perhaps of two kinds, one with
a *rowel* or wheel, the other, part of the armour worn
on the heel).

45 *I'll take the better care*: I shall be the better protected.
46 *hazard therefore due*: The risk I run, in disobeying you, and not receiving your blessing.
50 *cracked one*: Broken down old life.
    Have with you: I'll go with you.
51 *country*: Country's.
53–4 *their blood . . . fly out*: Their noble spirit despises everything until it may break forth.

V.1

The setting is Wales, between the British and Roman lines. Posthumus' regret and remorse in this scene would have surprised Jacobean audiences. In all versions of the wager plot before *Cymbeline* the husband's behaviour goes uncriticized and unpunished. He is the 'blameless hero', entitled to have his wife murdered for her supposed adultery, indeed to be commended for avenging the dishonour he believes she has done him. (Real Jacobean husbands, although they didn't have the same licence to murder, were constrained by fewer rules in marriage and sexual conduct than their wives were.)

Audiences in 1611, judging Posthumus by these standards, wouldn't have thought him more reprehensible than his predecessors. Shakespeare completely overturns this convention. He makes Posthumus determined to die for his wife's sake, and to wish that the gods had spared her and taken him, because he is a greater sinner than she is. Most notably, Posthumus regrets what he has done, even though he remains convinced that she has been unfaithful: his repentance precedes her vindication. Not all modern critics have accepted that Posthumus' change of heart is complete, or even appropriate. One view is that he is still cynical about women, as he was in II.4 (murder unfaithful ones, and how many wives would survive?), while another criticizes him for not being scrupulous enough, and for not sticking to the moral code of the play: since he still believes Imogen is guilty, his attitude towards her should remain unchanged.

Shakespeare intended this speech as the climax of an attack, not so much on Posthumus, as on the notion that he is the perfect, blameless gentleman. The idea of his perfection begins with the hyperbolic account of him in the first scene of the play, and it is confirmed, so it seems, by the Princess choosing him as her husband, despite his inferior social rank. These estimates of him are undermined, however, by his hysterical behaviour and distrust of Imogen in Rome, and by the gross parody of him in his rival, Cloten (a parody that emphasizes the similarity of his own failings and dereliction). In the present scene, Posthumus acknowledges his faults, and implicitly accepts that he has been overvalued (32–3). His new attitude towards Imogen *wrying but a little* (5) is a revaluation of himself: he is a human being with limitations in a world where there are no phoenix-like unspotted gentlemen, nor immaculate wives, and where no one is blameless.

1 *bloody cloth*: Some garment of Imogen's (a scarf or handkerchief, sent by Pisanio as a *bloody sign* to convince Posthumus that he had murdered her: III.4.124).

2 *coloured*: Dyed.

   You married ones: Lines 2–5 are often taken to be addressed to the audience, but they may be an apostrophe, or a general reflection, rather than a conscious remark to onlookers and husbands in the theatre (who are fellow victims).

5 *wrying*: Going astray, deviating from virtue (or faithfulness).

6 *does not*: Does not perform.

7 *No bond but to do*: There is no obligation to obey any orders but.

9 *put on this*: (1) Instigate this (Imogen's murder) *or* (2) take upon myself, be encumbered with such a fault *or* (3) be dressed like this (as an Italian gentleman, who has come to fight against Britain).

10–11 *repent . . . Me*: Repent (that she was unfaithful to me), and struck me down (taken my life).

12–13 *that's love . . . fall no more*: That's (an expression of your) love for them, to ensure that they never fall from virtue (sin) again.

13–15 *you some permit . . . doers' thrift*: You (gods) allow some wrong*doers* to follow up (*second*) one sin with another, each worse than its predecessor, and make them *dread it* (fear further degeneration) – from which consciousness of their evil they may draw profit (by their salvation, when they repent). The phrase *each elder worse* may mean 'each sin they commit is less than its predecessor' (some people are permitted to carry on doing wrong, but to a diminishing extent – the *elder* sins are *worse*), so that they are gradually made aware of their sin as it lessens. Posthumus is either thinking of Imogen as one of the sinners (because of her supposed adultery), or of himself (because he had ordered her murder).

16 *Imogen is your own*: (1) You have taken Imogen back to you (in heaven) *or* (2) Imogen is your chosen one (and I have no right to question your care for her).

19 *my lady's kingdom*: Britain.

23 *weeds*: Clothes.
   suit: Dress.

24 *Briton peasant*: British underling, common working-man (the *peasant* was almost the lowest social rank in Jacobean England, not much above a beggar or an outlaw). There is no stage direction in F, and it is conceivable that Posthumus changes his clothes offstage at the end of the scene, but more likely that here and at V.3.73 he changes onstage to ensure that the audience recognize him (especially after IV.1, where Cloten had been seen wearing his clothes).

25 *the part I come with*: (1) The side (the Romans) I have come with *or* (2) the identity (jealous wife-murderer) I had earlier *or* (3) one role I have acted in this play so far (that is, the degenerate Cloten: see Introduction, p. lx).

26–7 *even for whom . . . death*: On whose account, every breath I take is a living death to me.

28 *Pitied*: Neither pitied.

29 *Myself I'll dedicate*: I shall devote myself (to being at the forefront, the *face* of danger in the battle).

30 *my habits show*: (1) My (poor) clothes indicate *or* (2) my conduct so far would suggest.

31 *Leonati*: Posthumus' dead family (see the note to I.1.28–40).

32 *guise o'th'world*: (1) General custom *or* (2) worldly ways *or* (3) how things look in the world.
   I will begin: (1) I shall start behaving in *or* (2) I shall set the trend for.

33 *The fashion ... within*: The new (and unconventional) manner, of having more inner substance to me than outer show (Posthumus is also referring to his change of clothes at 22–4: he will dress in a different way, less bothered about fashionable attire – as a *peasant* (24), perhaps wearing fewer clothes altogether – and more concerned with the man inside it).

V.2

The setting is the battlefield. This and the next scene are complementary, with the action first shown in V.2 (allowing the fight between Jachimo and Posthumus to be zoomed in on), and then described by Posthumus in V.3. Some critics suspect this is a duplication that Shakespeare or the actors would have removed in performance – by cancelling one of the scenes, or merging them – but the reason for the two scenes may be simpler, that this is part of Shakespeare's response to the restrictions placed on drama and the theatre by sixteenth-century neoclassical critics. The rule in neoclassical drama was that actions (suicides or deaths or battles) should be kept offstage and only described onstage, after the event, by a messenger. Here in *Cymbeline*, by contrast, Shakespeare gives theatre audiences both the showing and the telling of action (see the Introduction, pp. xxi–xxv and li–lii for the contexts of his debate with neoclassical writers and their rules and conventions).

It has been suggested that in V.2 Shakespeare was reviving an old-fashioned, more stagey way of showing a battle in the theatre, possibly because this was appropriate to the setting in Ancient Britain, or as a preparation for the wildly improbable defeat Belarius and the brothers inflict on the Romans. In modern productions the action is often played in slow motion, even in a semi-trance, as if the battle were a ritual or a dance, the steps of which are choreographed so that the Britons must win.

0 *at one door . . . at another*: The Roman and British armies enter separately from the two sides of the double doors of the tiring-house at the back of the stage (there is a similar entry at the beginning of III.1).

Alarums: Trumpet blasts or battle cries.

1 *heaviness*: Dejection.

bosom: Heart.

2 *Takes off*: Destroys.

belied: Slandered.

4–5 *or could this carl . . . Nature's*: Otherwise could this churl (low-born fellow), a natural born drudge.

6 *profession*: Calling (as a soldier).

7 *titles but of scorn*: Nothing but contemptible titles.

8 *go before*: Surpass.

9 *odds*: Probability.

10 *excursions*: Sounds of men attacking.

12 *guarded*: Safe (protected by them).

13 *seconds the Britons*: Comes to the aid of Belarius and the brothers.

16 *hoodwinked*: Blindfolded (since war seems to be striking out indiscriminately in every direction).

supplies: Reinforcements.

17 *strangely*: Astonishingly.

17–18 *or betimes . . . reinforce*: Let's either obtain reinforcements (1) quickly *or* (2) before it's too late.

V.3

The scene is the battlefield, or close to it. Shakespeare borrowed the story of three men holding out against an army from an episode he found in Holinshed. His reasons for handling the episode the way he does — some of them concerned with dramaturgy and the public theatre – are discussed in the Introduction, pp. xlix–liii.

1 *made the stand*: Resisted (the Romans).

2 *fliers*: Britons who had fled earlier.

4 *But that the heavens fought*: If it had not been for the fact that the gods themselves fought (on the side of the Britons).

5 *Of his wings destitute*: Deprived of both flanks or side formations of his army.

6 *but*: Nothing but.

7 *strait*: Narrow.
   full-hearted: Full of courage and confidence.

8 *Lolling the tongue*: With their tongues hanging out (like wild animals).

9 *tools*: Weapons.

10 *mortally*: Fatally.
    touched: Wounded.

11 *that the strait pass was dammed*: So that the narrow passage was stopped up.

12 *hurt behind*: With fatal wounds on their backs (received as they were fleeing).

13 *To die with length'ned shame*: With their shame (at being cowards) prolonged for the rest of their lives.

14 *battle*: Battlefield.
    ditched . . . turf: Dug out beneath ground level (like a trench), its walls built up with earth on either side.

15 *ancient*: (1) Noble *or* (2) old.

16–17 *who deserved . . . came to*: Who (1) deserved (of his country) the nurturing it had given him through the long life his white beard showed he had lived *or* (2) justified living as long a life as his long white beard showed he had lived *or* (3) showed that he had profited by the long life of soldiering and hardship his white beard testified to *or* (4) deserved to be cherished (by his country) for as many years into the future as his white beard showed he had already lived.

18 *this for's*: This deed for his.

19 *striplings*: Young men.

19–20 *lads . . . base*: Mere boys, who at their tender years seemed more ready to play *country base* (a children's game, also known as 'prisoners' base', played especially by boys, in which two opposing sides chased and tried to capture players in the other team).

21–2 *With faces fit . . . shame*: With pale complexions which deserve masks (of the kind worn by women) to protect them from sunburn and the wind – rather, I should say, more delicate in complexion than ladies, who use their masks to preserve their looks, or for the sake of modesty (*or* to conceal themselves when they are behaving shamelessly); Arviragus, in other words, has the beauty but none of the vanity, bashfulness and deceitful coyness of women.

23 *Made good the passage*: Secured the position they had taken up in the lane.

24 *harts*: The Britons are behaving like timid deer, not men (the spelling in F, *hearts*, indicates a pun).

25 *To darkness . . . backwards*: The souls of men who die fleeing in retreat (1) pass into hell without the slightest delay *or* (2) vanish into dark oblivion, forgotten at once.

25–8 *Stand . . . frown*: Stand your ground, or we will behave like the Romans and inflict on you, as if you were hunted animals, that death which you are trying to avoid in such a cowardly (*beastly*) fashion – a death which you may avert simply by turning to face the enemy with a look of defiance (*frown*).

28–34 *These three . . . pale looks*: These three men, as confident as and performing as much as three thousand – for three active men are the entire force (from front *file* to rear) when *all the rest do nothing* – with this cry '*stand, stand*', with the advantage of (*Accommodated by*) their position in the lane, and working their spell on (*charming*) the Britons even more by their noble deeds than with their words – deeds which could have transformed a *distaff* into a *lance* (inspired even a housewife to be as courageous as a soldier) – these three men put colour back into the Britons' *pale*, fearful cheeks (that is, filled them with blood, often described as golden, hence *gilded pale looks*).

34 *distaff*: Pole for spinning yarn.

35–9 *Part shame . . . hunters*: Shame revived some (of the
Britons), courage others, so that some, who had turned
cowards merely from following the *example* of others
– O cowardice, *sin in war*, accursed in those who first
set this example – began to assume the (warlike) expression on the faces of these three heroes, and to bare
their teeth like *lions* at bay against the hunters' spears.

40 *stop i' th' chaser*: Sudden check to the pursuing force (the
Roman charge on the fleeing Britons was halted
abruptly, pulled up short like a galloping horse).

a retire; anon: A retreat (by the Romans); straight away.

41–3 *forthwith they fly . . . victors made*: At once the Romans
fled like *chickens* back up the lane which (but moments
before) they had charged down like swooping *eagles*;
as beaten *cowards* they retraced the steps they had taken
before as *victors*.

44–5 *Like fragments . . . need*: Like bits of food on a prolonged
sea voyage (fallen back on as a last resort), they became
what sustained *life* in time of *need*.

47–8 *Some slain before . . . ten chased by one*: Some killed
earlier, some dying, some of their fellow troops tram-
pled down in the first onslaughts (by the Romans), *ten*
of them *chased by one* (Roman).

49 *twenty*: Twenty Romans.

50 *or ere*: Sooner than.

51 *mortal bugs o' th' field*: Deadly terrors of the battlefield.

strange chance: Extraordinary thing to happen.

53–5 *Nay do not wonder . . . work any*: Don't be astonished
at this miraculous deed: you were born to *wonder* at
stories of heroism, rather than do any heroic thing
yourself.

55–6 *Will you rhyme . . . one*: Do you want to make up
rhymes about it (the exploit), and give out (*vent*) that
it was something absurd? Here is a rhyme for you.

57 *twice a boy*: In his second childhood.

58 *bane*: Ruin.

60 *stand*: Withstand.

61 *made*: Born, naturally inclined.

63 *put me into rhyme*: Got me speaking in rhymes now.

64 *Still going . . . O noble misery*: Are you still running
away? Can this be a nobleman? What a miserable
specimen of nobility he is (*or* what a doleful condition
for one who is called 'noble'); *This is* was perhaps
pronounced as 'This'.

66 *honours*: Titles.

67 *took heel to do't*: Took to their heels to do it (save their
lives).

68 *too*: Anyway.

  in mine own woe charmed: My wretchedness protecting
me (causing me to live a charmed life).

71-2 *fresh cups . . . words*: Ways of being killed at court,
through poison (*fresh cups* means 'refreshing drinks'
into which poison can be poured), assassination, and
being lured by flattery and murdered.

72 *more ministers*: Other servants *or* more instruments
(means).

74-5 *For being . . . a Briton*: Since he (death) is on the side
of the Britons (in killing the Romans), I mustn't be a
Briton any more.

76 *part*: (1) Role *or* (2) attire (as an Italian gentleman) *or*
(3) side (for the Romans).

77 *veriest hind*: The lowliest peasant, menial.

78 *Once touch my shoulder*: With the slightest gesture, take
me captive.

79 *Roman*: Romans.

  answer: (1) Retaliation *or* (2) recompense.

  be: Will be.

81 *On either side . . . my breath*: On one side or the other
I come to give up my life.

86 *in a silly habit*: Dressed in humble clothes.

87 *affront*: Attack.

88 *Stand*: Stand still there.

90-91 *if seconds . . . answered him*: If (1) supporters had
followed his example *or* (2) reinforcements had backed
him up.

92 *A leg of Rome shall not*: That is, nothing of them will
get back to Rome (the images of a dismembered *leg*

and *crows* pecking at corpses in 93 evoke the battlefield
after the fighting).

93 *brags*: Brags about.

94 *As if he were of note*: As if (1) he had done something
noteworthy (in this battle) *or* (2) he is someone
important.

V.4

The setting is probably an open place (which would
explain the joke in 2) not far from the battlefield, near
Cymbeline's camp. In F, most of the entry directions,
from *Enter Cymbeline* to *delivers him over to a Jailer*, are
located at the end of V.3, and V.4 begins with *Enter
Posthumus and Jailer*. This means that the action may
in fact be continuous between these scenes, with
Posthumus and the Jailer(s) remaining onstage after
Cymbeline exits with the Britons and their Roman
captives (according to this view, V.4 wasn't Shakespeare's, but a scene mistakenly created by a scribe or
a compositor). Running V.3 and V.4 together does make
a long scene (over 250 lines), however, with a great deal
in it, which is followed by an even longer scene (almost
500 lines), with still more in it. Would Shakespeare have
expected audiences to pay full attention throughout the
whole action with only one change of scene?

The lineation of the verses in 30–62 (called 'fourteeners' because of the number of syllables in the line)
is misleading in F. The compositor set them as full lines
wherever he had sufficient space (about a third of the
total), but he divided them, after the fourth foot, where
they were too long to fit across the column. This means
that in F most of the speeches are printed as stanzas,
and modern editions follow this arrangement, to the
extent of dividing full lines so that they fit into the
stanzas too. This relineation obscures what Shakespeare
intended, that at first the speeches of the Leonati should
look like lines in a Senecan English tragedy of the 1580s,
appropriate in manner and rhythm for ancient spirits
(see Introduction, p. lxx). In the present edition, 30–62
are set in a smaller type to accommodate the long lines.

Posthumus' dream and the Jupiter masque inside it (29–92) are discussed in the Introduction, pp. lxviii–lxxi. Shakespeare constructs a frame around the dream with Posthumus' soliloquies and his exchanges with the lugubrious Jailer. The vision of the afterlife in the dream is strange but it is supposed to be comforting: Jupiter does care for us, and most of the time the dead do sleep in rest. The Jailer's version of death is down to earth and darkly comic – there is no more getting drunk nor having to pay bar bills – but men won't die willingly, not even if they're stoic Romans. The scene concludes with a brief apocalyptic moment, and the hint of a different kind of comfort, which some critics say is the Christian consolation. If we were all one, the Jailer declares, then there would be no more hangmen, no more gibbets and no more thunder-masters and punishment.

1–2 *You shall not . . . stomach*: Printed as four lines in F; since the Jailer and the Messenger (who is perhaps the Second Jailer) speak in prose later in the scene, it is possible that this is what they are speaking here.

1 *be stol'n*: Steal away, escape *or* be stolen away (rescued by other Romans); the word is monosyllabic (*stolne* in F), but not necessarily for metrical reasons (it may represent lower-class speech or dialect).

2 *graze . . . pasture*: This is the Jailer's joke: Posthumus is manacled at the wrists and legs (8–9), with *locks* on him, hobbled like a horse left to *graze* in an open field. *stomach*: Appetite (for grazing).

7 *sure*: Infallible.

9 *You*: If you *or* may you (a petition).

10–11 *penitent . . . for ever*: Means of repentance which will release my conscience (from its burden of guilt), then I shall be *free for ever* (in death).

11 *Is't enough I am sorry*: Posthumus considers in turn the three parts of repentance which might relieve his conscience, or, in Christian terms, bring him absolution for the sin of ordering Imogen's death: first, sorrow (11); second, penance (13–14); third and the *main part*

(16), satisfaction or atonement (in 15–17 and 22 he asks the gods to take his life in expiation of the crime).

12–13   *So children . . . of mercy*: Children are able to appease human fathers in this way (that is, by being sorry), and the gods (divine fathers) have more mercy in them than mortals do; Posthumus may also mean that the gods, in their mercy, will grant him the death he desires and deserves, rather than leave him to linger in fetters, weighed down with guilt.

13   *Must I*: If I have to.

14–15   *in gyves . . . constrained*: In shackles which I wear willingly (to do my penance) rather than because they were forced on me.

15–17   *To satisfy . . . my all*: To atone – if atonement is the most important *part* of clearing (giving *freedom* to) my conscience – take no sterner payment from me than my life (*stricter* in 17 is a kind of grim understatement).

21   *their abatement*: That is, the amount that they are allowed to keep after their *vile* creditors (18) have taken a portion.
   that's not my desire: I have no wish to *thrive again* by only paying in part for my crime (that is, I don't want to carry on living).

23   *dear*: Valuable *or* beloved.

24–6   *'Tween man . . . being yours*: Men don't weigh every coin they pass between them to test whether its face value (its *stamp*) matches the real value of the metal it contains; they accept coins (*pieces*), even if they are worth less than the face value (though *light*), because of the royal image stamped on them (*for the figure's sake*). You gods ought to accept my life (in payment, 18–23) all the more readily because I am yours (I bear your image, and it was you who made me, or pressed life into me, *coined* me, 23).

27   *take this audit*: Accept this account.

28   *cancel these cold bonds*: This has literal and metaphoric meanings: free me from the cold shackles on my wrists; loosen the dead (*cold*) ties which are still holding me in this life; and release me from the obligations (*bonds*)

which I am making void (*cold*) by my repentance.

29 *Solemn music . . . lies sleeping*: The music was probably
provided by a consort of viols; the ghosts enter in pairs,
the parents and then their sons, each pair introduced
by music, and they form a circle around Posthumus,
over which Jupiter is to descend and hover.

30 *thunder-master*: The god Jupiter, who was thought to
have thunder and lightning at his command; one of his
sons was *Mars*, the god of war, and his wife was *Juno*.
mortal flies: Frail human beings whom the gods can
squash like flies.

31–2 *that . . . revenges*: Who scolds (*Rates*) you and takes
revenge for your *adulteries* (Jupiter had many affairs
with mortal women, whom Juno punished in various
ways).

34 *attending Nature's law*: Waiting for the completion of
the natural process (his full nine months in the womb).

35 *orphans' father*: An attribute of the Christian God
('father of the fatherless', Psalm 68:5).

36 *earth-vexing smart*: Suffering which afflicts the earthly
life (of men).

37 *Lucina*: The goddess of childbirth (whose name and
attributes were sometimes associated with Juno).
throes: Pains of childbirth.

38 *ripped*: Born by caesarian section.
'mongst his foes: Into a world of enemies.

40 *stuff*: Substance (cf. I.1.23).

42 *was mature . . . man*: (Posthumus) was grown to mat-
urity.

43–4 *fruitful object . . . Imogen*: (What man) could Imogen
ever see who was as ripe as him.

44 *deem his dignity*: Judge his worth.

46 *Leonati seat*: The ancestral home of the Leonati, that
is, Britain.

48 *you suffer*: You (Jupiter) allow.
slight: Worthless, contemptible (perhaps also a reference to Jachimo's physical size).

49 *taint*: Infect.

50 *geck*: Dupe.

51 *For this . . . we came*: Because of this injustice we have
   come from a more peaceful place (the Elysian Fields,
   67–8).

53 *Tenantius*: Cymbeline's father, King of Britain (see note
   to I.1.28–40).

54 *Like hardiment*: Similar deeds of valour.

55 *adjourned*: Delayed.

56 *graces*: Rewards and recognition.
   dolours: Sorrows, suffering.

57 *crystal*: Transparent.
   ope: Open.
   look: F has *looke, looke* (probably a printer's mistake).

58 *race*: Family (but perhaps 'Britons').

61 *synod of the rest*: Assembly of the other gods.

62 *Jupiter descends in thunder and lightning, sitting upon an
   eagle*: In Jacobean performances Jupiter was perhaps
   lowered by suspension gear through the ceiling of the
   cover over the stage to a position where he could hover,
   on the eagle's back, immediately above the heads of
   the ghosts (who think the eagle is about to seize them
   with its talons, see 86 and note).

63 *region low*: Elysium (see 67–8).

65 *bolt*: Thunderbolt.

66 *Sky-planted*: Placed in the heavens.

67 *shadows*: Ghosts of the dead who (because they are the
   favourites of the gods) are chosen to rest forever in the
   demi-paradise called Elysium.

69 *mortal accidents*: Events in the world of the living.

71 *Whom . . . I cross*: Another attribute of the Christian
   God: 'whom the Lord loveth, he chasteneth' (Hebrews
   12:6).

72 *delighted*: (The more) delighted in, relished.

74 *His comforts . . . are spent*: The comforts (I have planned
   for him) are on course; he has been tested to good effect
   (*or* his trials are very nearly over).

75 *Our Jovial star*: Posthumus was born when the planet
   Jupiter, which the god describes as his *star*, was in the
   ascendant; this mark of good fortune, signalled by
   Jupiter's astrological predominance, has an intriguing

parallel in Galileo's *Siderius Nuncius* (discussed in the
Introduction, pp. lxii–lxiii). When Galileo dedicated
the book to Cosimo de Medici, and called the planet's
four new moons the Medici stars, he praised Cosimo
for being born when Jupiter was in the ascendant. *Jovial*
is presumably something of a joke (it means 'Jove's'
but also 'merry, good-humoured').

79 *tablet*: Scroll or leaves on which the prophecy is written
(called a *book* at 103).

79–80 *wherein . . . confine*: In which *tablet* is set out in a small
space the limitless (*or* ample) good fortune it has pleased
me (to grant him).

86 *Stooped, as to foot us*: Swooped down as though about
to seize us in its talons (terms used in falconry).

86–7 *His ascension . . . blest fields*: Jupiter descends in anger,
his *breath* as *sulphurous* as the smell of the thunderbolt,
but as he ascends he gives off an odour more fragrant
than even the *sweet*-smelling *fields* of Elysium (a sign
which in pagan religious ceremonies indicated that
suppliants had been granted their prayer).

88 *Prunes*: Preens, trims its feathers with its beak.
claws: Scratches its beak with its claws.

90 *marble pavement closes*: Perhaps an allusion to the
closing of the trapdoor in the underside of the stage
cover through which Jupiter has ascended (the heavens
have a marble ceiling, see the Introduction, p. lxii).

92 *vanish*: Exit rapidly.

95 *O scorn*: What a bitter joke.

97 *depend*: Hang.

99 *I swerve*: I'm mistaken, on the wrong track.

103 *fairies*: (1) Apparitions, illusions *or* (2) mischievous
sprites from fairyland.
book: The *tablet* in its binding.
rare: Marvellous.

104 *fangled*: Dressy, showy *or* taken with finery and frip-
peries.

105–6 *thy effects . . . be*: May what you deliver turn out to be.

107 *promise*: What they promise.

108–13 *Whenas a lion's whelp . . . peace and plenty*: Shakespeare probably took the idea of the prophecy and some of its text from Holinshed; see the note to V.5.435–40.

109 *Whenas*: When.

112 *stock*: Trunk (of the *stately cedar*, 110); the word also means 'family line'.

114–17 *'Tis still a dream . . . untie*: Posthumus says that the prophecy is unintelligible, either because it is so deep that the rational mind cannot understand it, or because it's like the meaningless chatter of madmen, or because it is *both*, a combination of profundity and nonsense.

115 *Tongue, and brain not*: Speak, but do not understand themselves *or* have no conscious purpose as they say the words.

116 *Or senseless*: Either irrational.

117 *sense cannot untie*: Makes it too mysterious to understand it rationally.

118 *is like it*: That is, impossible to understand, and without meaning, but perhaps signifying something more than the power of reason can grasp.

  which I'll keep: Which (1) (life) I'll carry on with (not die) *or* (2) (*tablet*) I'll keep (not throw away).

119 *If but for sympathy*: If only because of the resemblance, the harmony between them.

122 *Hanging*: In response to Posthumus's culinary jokes (about being *Over-roasted* and *ready*), the Jailer quibbles on hanging, as execution, and hanging up bacon or game after it has been *well cooked*, 123).

124 *repast*: Meal, quibbling on 'entertainment' for the *spectators* at a hanging.

125 *the dish pays the shot*: An excellent meal is worth paying for (justifies its cost in a tavern).

  shot: Bill, reckoning.

126 *heavy reckoning*: Costly settling of the bill (the quibbles in 126–39 are elaborated from a contemporary proverb, 'death pays all debts').

129–30 *want of meat*: Lack of food.

131 *you are paid too much*: That is, the liquor has paid you back, punished you by leaving you drunk.

132–3 *heavier for being too light*: Duller, more stupid, because delirious with drink (light-headed).

133–4 *drawn of heaviness*: Emptied of coins.

134 *contradiction*: Paradox (an old and familiar one, summed
up in the contemporary proverb, 'a light purse makes
a heavy heart').

quit: Set free (with a play on 'acquitted').

134–5 *the charity . . . in a trice*: The mercy and generosity of
a cheap piece of rope (with which a man is hanged);
it instantly settles accounts for thousands of men,
paying off their debts (or perhaps 'thousands of pounds
that are owed').

136 *no true debitor-and-creditor but it*: No other account-
book is as reliable.

137 *discharge*: Payment, settlement.

138 *counters*: Tokens used for calculations.

acquittance: Receipt (with a quibble on a man being set
free, legally acquitted, even though executed).

141 *were to*: Who was destined *or* scheduled (that is, whose
execution was arranged for an appointed time).

143 *officer*: Executioner.

look you: Consider.

which way: That is, to heaven or hell or some other
place.

146 *Your death . . . head*: In your version of death, his eyes
are still in their sockets (the Jailer means 'so you'll be
able to see what will happen to you after death').

147 *so pictured*: Represented like this (death was normally
shown as a death's head or skull).

147–8 *some . . . know*: That is, priests or churchmen.

148–50 *take upon yourself . . . peril*: Either you are presuming to
know about the afterlife (which is something no one can
be sure of), or you are disregarding the day of judgement (*after-enquiry*), and risking your own damnation.

150 *speed in*: Fare at.

151 *on*: Of it (F has *one*, so perhaps 'anyone' was intended).

153 *wink*: Shut their eyes (152–4 elaborate on the proverb
'there's none so blind as he who will not see').

155 *infinite mock*: Extraordinary and ridiculous paradox.

157 *winking*: Closing a man's eyes (for ever).

161 *made free*: That is, by being put to death.

162 *I'll be hanged then*: A curse, but also part of the world
turned upside down throughout the Jailer's speeches,
where condemned men are to be set free and their
captors hanged.

163–4 *no bolts for the dead*: The dead can't be fettered with
bolts like men (with perhaps an unconscious pun, since
the ghosts are kept in their place by the thunder*bolt*
thrown by Jupiter).

166 *prone*: Eager (to die).

168 *for all he be*: Even though he is.

168–9 *them, too, that die*: The Romans as well, who die (the
Jailer debunks the traditional courage and stoical
unflinchingness of Romans in the face of death: some
of them are just as afraid of dying as any one, and as
I would be if I were a Roman).

171 *there were desolation*: (1) That would be nothing but a world
or (2) would the world were depopulated, cleared of.

172 *my present profit*: What pays my wages now.

173 *preferment*: Promotion; that is, he would hope to do
better in a world which had no need of jailers and
gibbets.

V.5

The setting is Cymbeline's camp. Modern critics have
praised Shakespeare's skill in managing the recognitions and unravelling of plots in this scene, particularly
the order in which the characters learn about one
another (this is my lost daughter, or my dead wife, or
the sister we didn't know we had, and so forth).
Shakespeare's aim in the scene was to create pleasure
for the audience at the neatness with which matters
could be resolved, and a sense of wonder, among the
characters, that there was coherence within the confusion of events (for the importance of wonder in
Shakespeare's theatre see The Play in Performance, pp.
lxxix–lxxx).

The temptation to interpret this coherence as a
divine plan, and to make everything fit, is also addressed
in the scene. The Soothsayer, presented with Jupiter's

riddling message, comes up with a set of glosses that
makes Cymbeline say *this hath some seeming* (meaning
either 'hmm, well perhaps' or 'yes, that's surely right').
We are bound to have doubts about the Soothsayer,
though, since he is happy to reinterpret his own dream
as soon as events change (first he says the dream is a
promise of a Roman victory then that it is a sign of
Jupiter's blessing on a Romano-British peace pact). For
Shakespeare's contemporaries prophecies in the real
world, when they bore on state matters, could be
dangerous to the established order, and might need to
be banned. The prophecy in *Cymbeline*, brought into
the play very late (much later than where the prophecies appear in *Pericles* and *The Winter's Tale*), looks
suspiciously like Jupiter's attempt to claim a divine
order to things that have already been settled by human
choice and effort (see the Introduction, pp. lxxi).

The interplay between choice and necessity is one
of the oldest elements in Western drama, and in this
final scene in *Cymbeline* Shakespeare is deeply interested in it. How much of what happens to us depends
on chance, how much on a predetermined unfolding
of events, how much on the choices we make? When
Imogen sees Jachimo among the Roman prisoners she
recognizes him at once. She stares at him, *perplexed*
(108), because she has spotted – at who knows what
distance – the ring he is wearing, because it is the one
she gave to Posthumus. From this, all the untying of
knots in the story begins. Was this something Jupiter
intended, or was it just good luck and good eyesight,
or was it that she was still waiting, against all hope, for
some sign that she and her husband, although he might
be dead, might one day meet again?

2 *Woe is my heart*: I grieve.
3 *richly*: Nobly *or* with such great success.
4 *gilded arms*: (1) Burnished or plated body-armour *or*
(2) heraldic coats of arms, decorated with gilt (marks
of lineage and social position among the gentry and
aristocrats).

4 *naked*: Unprotected by armour.

5 *Stepped before targes of proof*: (1) The *poor soldier* (Posthumus) presented his *naked breast* to the enemy, alongside or ahead of shields (*targes*) of proven strength wielded by the Britons *or* (2) he set his *naked breast* in opposition to the enemy's tried and tested shields. *Stepped before* may be figurative (meaning 'surpassed'), and *targes* (a monosyllable) a synecdoche for 'soldiers', so perhaps 'he excelled troops of the best calibre'.

7 *Our grace*: My (royal) favour.

9 *precious*: Valuable.

10 *poor looks*: (1) A poor showing (in the battle), achieving nothing beyond what his dismal appearance promised *or* (2) a fearful or sorrowful expression (looking sorry for himself).

11 *searched*: Sought.

13 *heir of his reward*: I must keep the reward he would have had from me (for his valour).

14 *liver, heart, and brain*: In Shakespeare's day these represented the full range of mental faculties (of, respectively, appetite, feeling and intellect): Belarius and the brothers are the very life of Britain.

15 *grant*: Acknowledge.

17 *are*: Were.

19 *honest*: Honourable.

20 *knights o'th'battle*: Knights created on the battlefield in recognition of extraordinary valour were held to be of special distinction. Cymbeline makes Belarius and the brothers part of his personal entourage (*companions to his person*), and proposes to bestow on them high offices and titles to match their new rank (*dignities becoming your estates*).

23 *business*: Serious concern.

24 *like Romans*: As despondent and apprehensive as the defeated Romans.

28 *consider*: Reflect (on this).

31 *madly dying, like her life*: Her death was mad, as was her life.

32 *Which*: (1) Who (the Queen) *or* (2) which (her life).

35 *trip me if I err*: Correct me if I misreport her confession (perhaps with a suggestion that Cornelius is taking a risk in relating what the Queen disclosed: 'her ladies can catch me out, expose me, if I make a mistake').

36 *finished*: (1) Died *or* (2) finished her confession.

38 *Affected*: (1) Loved *or* (2) aspired to, desired.

40 *your person*: You as a person.

41 *but*: Except that.
    she spoke it dying: According to contemporary proverbs, a person who was dying would always speak the truth (hence Cymbeline must believe what the Queen said).

42 *opening*: Revealing.

43 *bore in hand*: Pretended, professed.

44 *such integrity*: Such freedom from falseness and so thoroughly.

45 *scorpion*: Proverbial in Shakespeare's day for its venomous sting (Imogen was poisonous, or deadly to the Queen's *sight*).

46 *her flight prevented it*: Her flight (from court) (1) anticipated it *or* (2) did away with the need for it (to poison her).

47 *Ta'en off*: Destroyed, removed.
    delicate: (1) Ingenious *or* (2) delightful, charming (said ironically).

48 *read*: Understand.

50 *mortal mineral*: Deadly poison (its effects in 51–2 suggest arsenic).

51–2 *Should by the minute . . . waste you*: Should minute by minute feed on your life and, taking its time over it, kill you little by little.

53 *By watching, weeping, tendance*: By watching over you (perhaps also 'sitting up at night to take care of you'), weeping at your sickness, devoting attention to you.

54 *show*: Display, pretence (of love).
    in time: Sometimes emended to 'in fine' meaning 'in the end, at last'.

55 *fitted you*: (1) Shaped you to her ends (turned you into an enfeebled invalid) *or* (2) done away with you, disposed of you (perhaps even 'tortured you, caused

you to have fits').

55–6 *to work . . . crown*: To contrive matters so that Cloten
was entitled, as your adopted heir, to succeed you as
king.

58 *opened, in despite*: Revealed in defiance.

59 *purposes*: Schemes.

64 *Mine ears that heard*: (Nor were) my ears (at fault) that
listened to.

65 *seeming*: (Feigned) appearance.
It had been vicious: It would have been wrong (reprehensible of me).

68 *And prove . . . thy feeling*: And (1) (you may have to)
experience the effect of my foolishness in your
sufferings *or* (2) (you will) show up (my folly) by your
perceptiveness (you saw what she was like, I didn't).

70 *razed out*: Erased, blotted out.

72 *good souls*: The souls of Britons killed in the battle.

74 *your estate*: (1) The state (of your souls) *or* (2) your
situation.

75 *chance*: (Uncertain) fortune.

76 *by accident*: By chance (the Romans would have won,
Lucius says, but for the chance arrival of the Britons
who turned the battle against them).

78 *with the sword*: With (being put to death by) the sword.

80 *called*: Accepted as.

81 *a Roman's heart*: See headnote to III.1.

82 *think on't*: Reflect on it (the defeat, the proposed
massacre of Roman prisoners and the execution of a
general, which Lucius implies Augustus will seek
revenge for).

83 *my peculiar care*: My concern for myself (which is negli-
gible).

84 *my boy*: My page (Fidele, or Imogen).

85 *Never master*: No master ever.

87 *tender over his occasions*: (1) Sensitive to his (master's)
needs *or* (2) attentive (to his master) over and above
what service might be expected of him.

88 *feat*: (1) Adroit in speech *or* (2) dexterous and graceful
in manner.

virtue: Merit, virtuous conduct.

89 *make bold*: Presume to suggest (or believe).

92 *And*: Even if you.

surely seen him: (1) Undoubtedly seen him before *or* (2) certainly considered him (perhaps in response to what Lucius says in 84–92).

93 *favour*: Face.

94 *Thou hast looked . . . my grace*: Your expression and appearance have won you a place in my favour.

95–6 *I know not why . . . say, 'Live, boy'*: I have no idea what induces me to say 'live, boy' and spare you (but say it I do).

96 *Ne'er thank thy master*: (1) You don't owe your Roman master any thanks for this (it is not his plea which has saved you) *or* (2) you owe me, your new master, no extra thanks for this (since I have already adopted you as *mine own*).

98 *Fitting my bounty and thy state*: If what you request is appropriate for me, as a king, to grant it, and for your position, as a servant, to ask it.

99–100 *though thou . . . noblest ta'en*: Even if you asked me to spare the life of one of the Roman prisoners, (even) the most noble of them captured in this battle (that is, Cymbeline would spare even Lucius's life, if this boy asked for it).

103 *a thing*: Imogen has caught sight of the ring which she gave to Posthumus (see I.1.112), and which is now on Jachimo's finger.

105 *shuffle for*: Look after.

106 *Briefly*: Quickly.

107 *truth*: Fidelity.

108 *perplexed*: Distressed.

wouldst thou: Do you want.

113–14 *born your vassal . . . nearer*: (Who) born your subject (and so a Briton) am somewhat closer to you in ties of loyalty than this Roman is (Imogen is punning on *vassal* and 'vessel': she is the weaker vessel, Cymbeline's daughter, and so closer to him in blood than anyone, except his male heirs, her long-lost brothers).

117 *lend*: Give you.

120–22 *One sand another . . . was Fidele*: One grain of sand is
no more like another than this boy (now before us) is
like (1) Fidele, that *sweet lad* who died *rosy*, in his bloom
or (2) that *sweet, rosy*-cheeked *lad* called Fidele, who
died (Arviragus means that the two boys are utterly
alike).

124 *forbear*: Be patient.

126 *But we see him dead*: (1) But what we see must be his
ghost *or* (2) unless we see him dead *or* (3) but we see
him who is dead *or* (4) but we saw him dead (*see* could
be a past tense at this date).

135 *render*: State.

139–40 *Thou'lt torture me . . . torture thee*: You wish to torture
me for leaving unspoken that which, by being spoken,
would torture you (but perhaps Jachimo also means,
in phrasing which is characteristically involved and half-
menacing, '(in time) you will torture me to make me
unsay that which, once spoken, would be a torture to
you'). There are reminders in this of how Iago responds
to the prospect of torture, at the end of *Othello*.

141 *constrained*: Forced.

141–2 *that* | *Which*: What it.

148 *and*: And whom.

149 *give me leave*: Pardon me.

151 *while nature will*: For as long as nature allows (that is,
for the rest of your natural life, not cut short by being
executed here).

156 *viands*: Food.

157 *heaved to head*: Lifted to my mouth.

160 *rar'st*: Very best.
sadly: Soberly, in a serious mood.

161–3 *Hearing us praise . . . could speak*: (Posthumus) heard
us praise our Italian girlfriends for a beauty in them
which made the inflated boast of the most eloquent
man seem dull and sterile by comparison (that is, their
beauty outdid the hyperboles of the smoothest talker).
It is possible that Jachimo means that it was their praise
of the ladies' beauty that excelled such big talk (if *that*
in 162 refers to *praise* rather than to *beauty*).

163–5 *for feature . . . brief Nature*: (We praised our ladies) for
the *feature* or proportion of their bodies, which made
the images of both *Venus* and *Minerva* (her body and
limbs *straight-pight*, straight-pitched, drawn erect) –
immortal forms expressed in art, beyond what short-
lived (*or* hasty) *Nature* could do – seem deformed by
comparison. The shapeliness of their ladies surpasses
even the perfectly formed bodies of Venus, goddess of
love, and Minerva, the goddess of wisdom and the arts.
Jachimo doesn't make it clear whether these forms are
abstract ones, ideals of immortal symmetry, or those
given physical shape by artists in statues and images
(in a *shrine*). *Postures beyond brief Nature* may refer to
the ladies themselves rather than the goddesses, in
which case it is their mortal perfection that excels
Nature's transient creations.

165–6 *for condition | A shop*: (We praised our ladies) for char-
acter, a storehouse.

167 *hook*: Fishhook (of *fairness* or beauty, with which,
according to Jachimo, a woman angles to get a husband;
wiving means 'seeking to get married').

168 *I stand on fire*: I am burning with impatience.

169 *matter*: Point.

172 *lover*: Mistress, beloved.
hint: Opportunity.

176 *then a mind put in't*: Then he (Posthumus) added an
account of her mind to his *picture* (his description of
her appearance).

177 *Were cracked of kitchen-trulls*: Were uttered boastingly
(*cracked*) about common sluts, drudges that work in
kitchens (compared with Imogen our beautiful ladies
were no better than coarse, promiscuous serving-
women).

178 *Proved us unspeaking sots*: Showed us up as inarticulate
dunces (because we had failed to be as eloquent about
our ladies as he was about Imogen).

180 *as Dian had hot dreams*: As if, in comparison with
Imogen, Diana (goddess of chastity) had lustful
dreams.

181 *she alone were cold*: Imogen were the only chaste female (among immortals as well as mortal women).

182 *Made scruple of*: Expressed doubts about.

184 *honoured finger*: Posthumus' finger was *honoured* because it had on it the token of Imogen's love, the ring.

184-5 *to attain . . . of's bed*: To obtain, through amorous advances, Posthumus' place (as her husband) in her bed.

186 *hers and mine*: Her and my.

188 *I did truly find her*: (1) I found her to be truly honourable *or* (2) I found in fact that she was.

189-90 *would so had it been . . . Phoebus' wheel*: Would have done so had it been a precious jewel (*carbuncle*) from the *wheel* of (the sun god) *Phoebus'* chariot.

191 *all the worth of's car*: Worth as much as his (*Phoebus'*) whole chariot.

194 *Of*: By.

195 *'Twixt amorous and villainous*: Between (1) her pure, unassailable love for her husband and my vile, lustful designs on her *or* (2) her passion for him, within their marriage, and the disloyal passion I had hoped she would succumb to with me.

195-6 *Being thus quenched . . . longing*: Her response having extinguished my hope (of seducing her), but not my desire (1) for her body *or* (2) to win the wager with her husband.

197 *your duller Britain*: It was a Renaissance commonplace that, because of the effect of their colder climates, the countries of northern Europe produced men whose minds were slower and more plodding than those born in the hot south: in 196-7, Jachimo means that the dullards in Britain simply couldn't keep up with his quick *Italian brain* or wits.

198 *for my vantage*: To my (1) gain *or* (2) opportunity.

199 *practice*: Trickery, stratagem.

200 *simular*: Specious (but plausible).

202 *renown*: Good name.

203 *averring notes*: Presenting, in confirmation, details.

207-8 *her bond of chastity . . . forfeit*: That her contract to be faithful to him was utterly broken, and that I had been

paid the forfeit (sexual intercourse) for her breach of
contract (the legal metaphors convey another meaning,
that Posthumus was led to believe that Jachimo had
broken Imogen's hymen; see note to II.4.169–71).

211 *Egregious*: Shocking.

211–12 *anything . . . due*: (As well as fool, murderer, thief, I
deserve to be called) any name *that's due* (to all villains
past, present and future).

213 *cord*: Rope (to hang himself).

214 *justicer*: Judge.

215 *ingenious*: Skilful at devising (tortures).

216 *amend*: Improve the reputation of, make seem less vile
(the worst hatefulness is less when it is compared with
mine).

219 *a lesser villain*: Pisanio (who murdered her for him, so
Posthumus believes; he was a *sacrilegious thief* when he
broke into the sacred *temple*, Imogen, and stole her
life).

220–21 *The temple . . . and she herself*: Imogen was the place
where *virtue* (fidelity and sexual continence) might be
worshipped, and also the goddess (*or* embodiment) of
virtue herself (in other words, her chastity was both
human and divine).

223 *bay me*: Howl at me, hound me to death.

225 *Be villainy less than 'twas*: (1) Let every other villainy
be thought less heinous (in comparison with mine) *or*
(2) let the word *villainy* mean less than it used to
(because of what I have done).

227 *hear, hear*: Listen to me, do listen (F has *heare, heare*,
but it is possible that what was intended was 'here, I
am here').

228 *Shall's*: Shall us (we).

    play: (1) Stage-play *or* (2) game, bit of fun.

229 *There lie thy part*: Play your role in the play (*or* game)
lying there.

232 *Does the world go round*: Contemporary sayings attributed the illusion of the world going round to giddi-
ness or the effects of drink, but perhaps there was
another topical meaning: because of Galileo's *Siderius*

Nuncius, which implied that the world was not the fixed centre of the universe but in movement around the sun (see the Introduction, p. lxxii).

233 *staggers*: Dizziness, delirious agitation (normally used of sick animals).

235 *mortal*: Deadly, fatal.

238 *tune of Imogen*: Sound of Imogen's voice.

240 *stones of sulphur*: Thunderbolts.

242 *precious*: Beneficial.

245 *approve*: Prove.

246 *confection*: Drug.

247 *for cordial*: As a medicine, restorative.

249 *importuned*: Pestered (the word is accented on the second syllable).

250 *temper*: Mix, refine (to increase in strength).

250–51 *still pretending . . . knowledge*: Always alleging (but falsely, and as a pretext) that she wished to complete her understanding.

252 *vile*: Base, unimportant (in the hierarchy of beings).

257 *offices of nature*: The body's operations.

259 *Most like . . . dead*: (1) Most probably I did, because I was like someone who was dead (Imogen is not sure whether she swallowed the drug, only that she became utterly insensible) *or* (2) most definitely I did, because for a while I was dead (the effects of the drug were the ones Cornelius describes – total cessation of life).

260 *is sure Fidele*: Is Fidele himself (the phrase means 'is Fidele for certain' if punctuated as *is, sure, Fidele*).

262–3 *Think . . . again*: This is the reading in F, which may be glossed: '(As we embrace) imagine yourself to be standing on the edge of a mountain precipice – throwing me from you then would be fatal once and for all.' Imogen urges Posthumus, half accusingly, half in play, to hold on to her this time and keep it in mind that love is poised in a delicate, even precarious balance: if he discards her again, it will kill her. He responds to her image of poised love with a metaphor of fruit suspended on the branch of a tree (263–4), perhaps lifting her from the ground as he speaks: they will never separate again, until he (as the tree) dies. Some editors emend *upon a rock* to 'upon a lock', meaning '(held) in an arm grip' (a term from wrestling), but this changes Imogen's hold over Posthumus into something much more assured ('you can't get away from me this time').

264 *my flesh*: My flesh and blood, my daughter (Cymbeline says this in contrast to what Posthumus calls Imogen in 263, *my soul*; perhaps he is also reminding the couple that until he blesses their marriage, his daughter is still *his* flesh – not yet one flesh, man and wife, with Posthumus).

265 *mak'st thou . . . in this act*: Are you treating me like a fool *in this act* (leaving me out, treating me as if I were a *dullard*, a foolish old man in an old comedy, in this final act of your play)?

267 *I blame ye not*: You can hardly be criticized for it (it's no surprise).

268 *motive*: Cause, reason.

269 *Prove holy water*: Cymbeline's tears are falling on her as he gives her his blessing: may the water too, he says, *prove* to be blessed, become *holy water*, transformed from human signs of joy and reconciliation into divine ones.

270 *mother*: Stepmother (the Queen).

271 *she was naught . . . was*: She was wicked (*or* nothing), and it was because of her.

272 *strangely*: (1) Oddly *or* (2) as strangers, unknown to one another.

275 *missing*: Absence.

277 *discovered*: Revealed.

278 *accident*: Chance.

279 *feignèd letter*: This is the letter in which Posthumus pretended that he was waiting for Imogen at Milford Haven (see III.2.40–46, and III.5.99–100 and note).

280 *directed him*: Led him (Cloten).

283 *enforced from me*: Took from me by force.
posts: Rushes.

287 *forfend*: Forbid.

289 *Pluck a hard sentence*: Draw down a death sentence on you (the image is perhaps of fruit plucked from a tree,

which is *hard* or bitter to the taste: see 307–8).

290 *Deny't again*: Speak again, unsay what you have said.

292 *incivil*: Unmannerly.

295 *off's*: Off his.

297 *sorrow*: Sorry.

299 *Thou'rt dead*: You must die for it.

303 *As well . . . thyself*: Of as good lineage and birth as you yourself.

304–5 *More of thee . . . scar for*: (He) has deserved more from you than a whole troop of men like Cloten ever deserved because of wounds they received in your wars (perhaps with the nuance that cowards like Cloten risk so little in battle that they haven't got a scratch on them).

307–8 *undo the worth . . . wrath*: (1) Undo the high estimate *or* (2) destroy the merit (you have won for yourself in battle), for which you have not been rewarded, by experiencing my fury.

309 *spake too far*: Exaggerated.

310 *thou*: Addressed to (1) Belarius (for his presumption) *or* (2) Arviragus (he too will die because of Belarius's rashness).

311–12 *But I will prove . . . him*: (1) Yet I shall show that *or* (2) if I don't prove that two of us (*on's*) are of as good birth as I have declared him (Guiderius) to be.

313 *unfold . . . speech*: Give expression to a story which is dangerous to me.

315 *our good his*: What good fortune we have is his too (Guiderius addresses this (1) to Arviragus *or* (2) to Cymbeline, in defiance).

Have . . . by leave: Well then, let me begin. With respect.

319 *Assumed this age*: (1) Reached this age *or* (2) become so aged in appearance.

321 *hot*: (1) Passionate *or* (2) impetuous, hasty.

323 *let it be confiscate all*: Let all of it (my payment for nursing your sons) be forfeit; in *confiscate* the accent falls on the second syllable.

325 *saucy*: Impudent.

326 *prefer*: Promote in rank (by revealing that his 'sons'

are princes rather than commoners).

331 *blood*: Offspring.

334–6 *Your pleasure . . . I did*: My whole offence, and the punishment it incurred, and everything about my (alleged) treason, had their beginning in your royal whim (your *pleasure*): beyond what I *suffered*, because of your capriciousness, I did no harm (in other words, I had done nothing wrong, but I was punished because it pleased you to think that I had).

337 *For such . . . are*: A chiasmus, meaning 'because they are indeed princes, and gentle ones too' (Belarius insists that the brothers' upbringing in Wales has neither obscured their rank nor impaired their character).

338 *arts*: Accomplishment, skills.

339 *put into*: Teach.

340 *As*: That which (in 338–40 Belarius says that his own birth and education at court had made him – as even Cymbeline would concede – entirely suitable as a tutor and mentor for the princes).

342 *moved her to't*: Incited her to do it (to abduct the brothers).

344–5 *Beaten for loyalty . . . treason*: The fact that I was beaten, when I had been loyal, impelled me to treason.

345–7 *Their dear loss . . . stealing them*: The more keenly you felt their great loss, the better it fitted my purpose in stealing them (I achieved what I wanted, your suffering).

352 *To inlay heaven with stars*: (Worthy) to be commemorated for ever by being set, as stars, in the face of heaven (Belarius means that the brothers are as wonderful as the ancient heroes whom the gods loved and made into stars, to adorn heaven, when they died).

353 *service*: Service in battle.

353–4 *more . . . than this*: More improbable than this story (Cymbeline means that the *service* they have performed in battle – which he knows is true – seems even more incredible than the extraordinary story Belarius has told him; on this basis, these young men may indeed be his sons).

355   *wish*: Wish for.

356   *Be pleased awhile*: Please give me your attention for a
      moment.

360–61   *lapped . . . curious mantle*: Wrapped in a cloak of the
         most intricate and exquisite design.

362   *his queen mother*: His mother, the Queen (Cymbeline's
      first wife).

      more probation: Further proof.

364   *sanguine*: Blood-red.

366   *natural stamp*: Birthmark.

367   *end in the donation*: Purpose in giving it.

368   *To be his evidence*: (That this birthmark) should serve
      as proof of who he is.

369–70   *Ne'er mother . . . more*: No *mother* ever *rejoiced* more at
         the delivery (birth) of her child.

371   *strange . . . orbs*: Extraordinary, abrupt movement out
      of your spheres (the princes are likened to the planets,
      which, according to Ptolemaic astronomy, moved
      within fixed, concentric spheres and reigned or exerted
      influence over human affairs).

373   *lost . . . kingdom*: Lost the right to rule the kingdom of
      Britain (because Guiderius and Arviragus have replaced
      Imogen as the immediate heirs to the British throne).

376   *But*: Anything other than *or* nothing more than.

381   *dram*: Dose.

382   *fierce abridgement*: (1) Drastically abridged account *or*
      (2) wild narrative.

383–4   *circumstantial branches . . . rich in*: Distinct and detailed
         parts which ought to be distinguished fully from one
         another (Cymbeline has heard only a much-abridged
         version of a story which has several episodes, each
         with details that deserve separate and elaborate treat-
         ment).

388   *your three motives to*: What motives you *three* (Belarius,
      Guiderius and Arviragus) had for joining.

390   *by-dependences*: Side issues (literally, growing out of,
      hanging down from the *circumstantial branches*, 383).

391   *From chance to chance*: From event to event.

      But nor: But neither.

392 *inter'gatories*: Questions (Cymbeline uses a legal term for formal questioning answered under oath: F has *Interrogatories*, emended here to the syncopated form).

393 *anchors upon*: (1) Fixes his attention on *or* (2) links himself to (but also perhaps 'places her hope in', as in the Latin motto *'anchora spei'*, the Christian's anchor of hope).

395 *her master*: (1) Cymbeline *or* (2) Lucius (her former master, as in 403).

396–7 *the counterchange . . . severally in all*: The exchange (of joyful looks) passes between all of us together, and between each of us individually.

398 *smoke the temple . . . sacrifices*: Fill the temple with the smoke of our burnt offerings to the gods.

399 *hold*: Consider, but also, hold you close to me.

400 *relieve me*: Help me (in my distress).

401 *gracious season*: (1) Joyful occasion *or* (2) time blessed by heaven.

403 *taste our comfort*: Share in our happiness.

405 *forlorn*: (1) Lost, untraced (after the battle) *or* (2) wretched-looking.

406 *becomed*: Fitted, suited.
    graced: Adorned.

408 *company*: Accompany, serve alongside.

409 *beseeming*: Appearance.
    a fitment: (1) A device, preparation *or* (2) suitable, appropriate.

412 *finish*: Die.

413 *sinks my knee*: Makes my knee bend to the ground.

415 *so often owe*: Owe (you) so many times over.

420 *doomed*: Judged.

421 *freeness*: Generosity.

422 *holp*: Helped.

424 *Joyed*: Overjoyed.

427 *upon his eagle backed*: Mounted on the back of his eagle.

428 *spritely shows*: Spectral visions.

430 *This label*: The tablet (see V.4.79 and note).

430–32 *whose containing . . . of it*: The contents of which (the tablet) are so remote from *sense*, and difficult to understand, that I can infer nothing from them (*so from sense* means (1) so lacking in meaning *or* (2) so beyond my capacity to grasp their meaning).

433 *construction*: Interpretation (of the prophecy).

Philharmonus: The name means 'lover of harmony', appropriate for a soothsayer who explains how the many reconciliations (between Britain and Rome, Imogen and Posthumus, and so forth) restore harmony in the world and the heavens.

435–40 *Whenas a lion's whelp ... peace and plenty*: The prophecy is repeated *verbatim* from V.4.108–13. Shakespeare probably derived Philharmonus' interpretation, 441–56, from medieval accounts of the deathbed vision of the king and saint Edward the Confessor, in which, among other things, there was a tree which was taken to mean 'the realm of England'.

442 *fit and apt construction*: Proper and natural (unforced) construing.

443 '*Leo-natus*': Latin for 'lion-born'.

import: (1) Express *or* (2) portend.

445 '*mollis aer*': Latin for 'tender air'. The derivation of the other Latin word *mulier* (woman or wife) from *mollis aer* was a mistake of medieval origin (the correct etymology is *mulier* from 'mollis', or 'soft'). It is noticeable that Philharmonus does not interpret *a piece of tender air* (436) to mean '(Cymbeline's) young female heir', an obvious pun in English which occurs elsewhere in the play. Perhaps he is merely being tactful, since Cymbeline's two male heirs have just been recognized, but his interpretation does emphasize the change of Imogen's status from a daughter to a wife.

446 *divine*: Interpret (divinely inspired).

448 *Answering the letter*: Corresponding exactly to the literal meaning (of the words in the prophecy, *himself unknown, without seeking find, and be embraced* (435–6), which Philharmonus applies literally – to Imogen embracing Posthumus – rather than decoding them further as an obscure part of the riddle).

449 *clipped*: Embraced.

450 *seeming*: Plausibility.

452 *Personates*: Represents.

452–3 *point . . . forth*: Signify your two sons.

460 *wonted tribute*: The tax we are accustomed to pay (if Shakespeare meant *wanted*, the phrase means 'unpaid tribute').

462 *Whom*: On whom.

   her and hers: Herself and her son Cloten.

464–5 *The fingers . . . harmony*: The gods themselves (1) pluck the strings of their instruments *or* (2) put their instruments into tune, correct them *or* (3) turn their divine spheres to create the *harmony* (*or* harmonious music; see next note, meaning 4). Presumably some contrast is intended between the *heavy hand* of divine justice, which strikes down the Queen and Cloten (462–3), and the heavenly *fingers*, which create harmony through their gentle touches.

465 *peace*: (1) Cessation of war *or* (2) tranquillity, calm *or* (3) piece of music (a pun) *or* (4) silence. According to Renaissance (Ptolemaic) cosmology, the crystalline spheres around the earth made divine music as they turned, but human ears couldn't hear this sound. Philharmonus claims that the gods are so pleased with this British and Roman *peace* that they have allowed him to hear the *harmony*, playing high above the *peace*, or silence, that normally cuts humans off from the heavens (some critics have connected this notion of peace to the *peace* promised by Christ).

   The vision: Philharmonus first describes this at IV.2.346–52 (interpreting it there as a prefiguring of victory for the Romans).

466–7 *the stroke | Of*: The onset (of fighting) in.

468 *full accomplished*: Fulfilled completely.

470 *Lessened herself*: Grew smaller as she flew into the distance.

472–3 *unite . . . favour with*: (1) Join in friendship with *or* (2) make his (imperial) benevolence one with that of.

474 *Which*: Who.

474 *Laud we*: (1) Let us *or* (2) let me give praise to.

475 *crooked smokes*: Curling smoke (from sacrifices on their altars).

476 *Publish we this peace*: (1) Let this my peace *or* (2) let this peace of ours (the Britons) be made known.

477 *Set we forward*: Let us march on.

479 *Lud's Town*: Britain's capital (the armies are to march back together from Wales, and through the city, as allies).

481 *seal*: Confirm.

482 *Set on there*: Begin marching.

The National: three theatres and so much more…

www.nationaltheatre.org.uk

In its three theatres on London's South Bank, the National presents an eclectic mix of new plays and classics, with seven or eight shows in repertory at any one time.

And there's more. Step inside and enjoy free exhibitions, backstage tours, talks and readings, a great theatre bookshop and plenty of places to eat and drink.

Sign-up as an e-member at www.nationaltheatre.org.uk/join and we'll keep you up-to-date with everything that's going on.

NT NATIONAL THEATRE
SOUTH BANK
LONDON SE1 9PX

PENGUIN SHAKESPEARE

TIMON OF ATHENS
WILLIAM SHAKESPEARE

WWW.PENGUINSHAKESPEARE.COM

After squandering his wealth with prodigal generosity, a rich Athenian gentleman finds himself deep in debt. Unshaken by the prospect of bankruptcy, he is certain that the friends he has helped so often will come to his aid. But when they learn his wealth is gone, he quickly finds that their promises fall away to nothing in this tragic exploration of power, greed, and loyalty betrayed.

This book includes a general introduction to Shakespeare's life and the Elizabethan theatre, a separate introduction to *Timon of Athens*, a chronology of his works, suggestions for further reading, an essay discussing performance options on both stage and screen, and a commentary.

Edited by G. R. Hibbard

With an introduction by Nicholas Walton

General Editor: Stanley Wells

PENGUIN SHAKESPEARE

THE WINTER'S TALE
WILLIAM SHAKESPEARE

WWW.PENGUINSHAKESPEARE.COM

The jealous King of Sicily becomes convinced that his wife is carrying the child of his best friend. Imprisoned and put on trial, the Queen collapses when the King refuses to accept the divine confirmation of her innocence. The child is abandoned to die on the coast of Bohemia. But when she is found and raised by a shepherd, it seems redemption may be possible.

This book includes a general introduction to Shakespeare's life and the Elizabethan theatre, a separate introduction to *The Winter's Tale*, a chronology of his works, suggestions for further reading, an essay discussing performance options on both stage and screen by Paul Edmondson, and a commentary.

Edited by Ernest Schanzer

With an introduction by Russ McDonald

General Editor: Stanley Wells

Penguin Shakespeare

MEASURE FOR MEASURE
WILLIAM SHAKESPEARE

WWW.PENGUINSHAKESPEARE.COM

In the Duke's absence from Vienna, his strict deputy Angelo revives an ancient law forbidding sex outside marriage. The young Claudio, whose fiancée is pregnant, is condemned to death by the law. His sister Isabella, soon to become a nun, pleads with Lord Angelo for her brother's life. But her purity so excites Angelo that he offers her a monstrous bargain – he will save Claudio if Isabella will visit him that night.

This book includes a general introduction to Shakespeare's life and the Elizabethan theatre, a separate introduction to *Measure for Measure*, a chronology of his works, suggestions for further reading, an essay discussing performance options on both stage and screen by Nicholas Arnold, and a commentary.

Edited by J. M. Nosworthy

With an introduction by Julia Briggs

General Editor: Stanley Wells

Read more in Penguin

PENGUIN SHAKESPEARE